ROCKY MOUNTAIN NATIONAL PARK

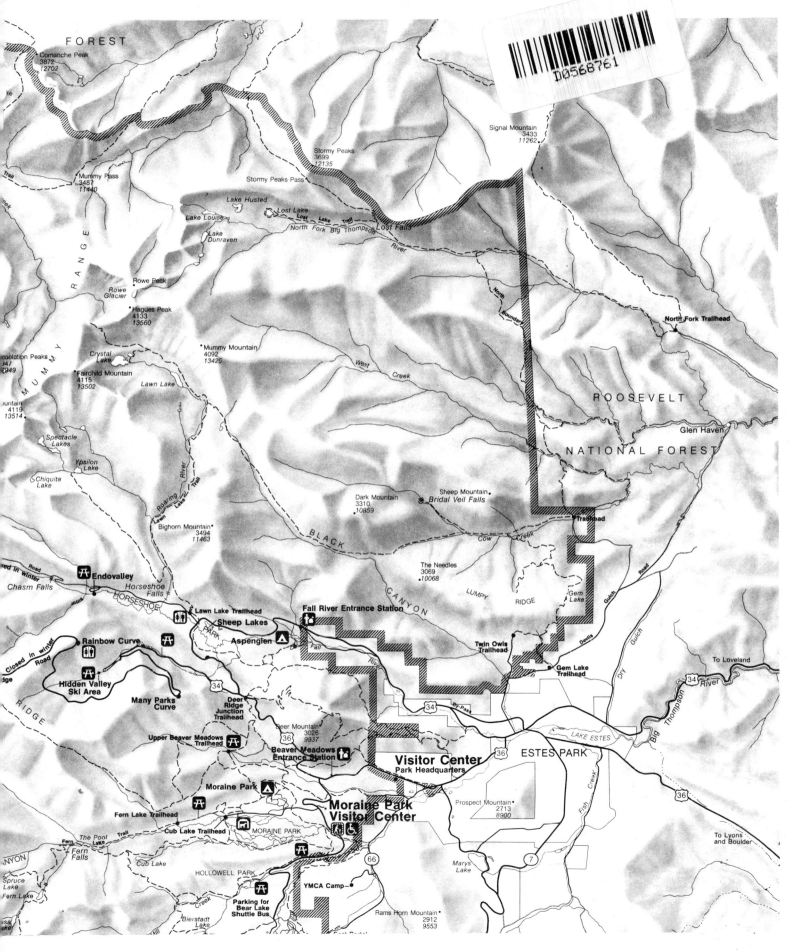

ROCKY MOUNTAIN NATIONAL PARK

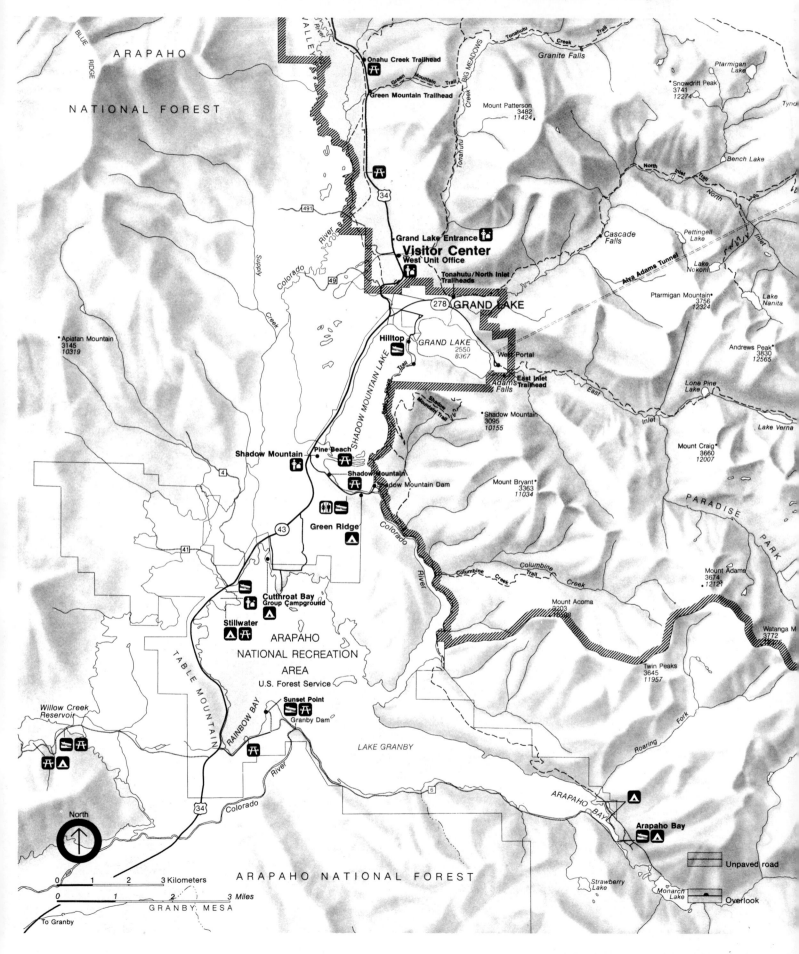

ROCKY MOUNTAIN NATIONAL PARK

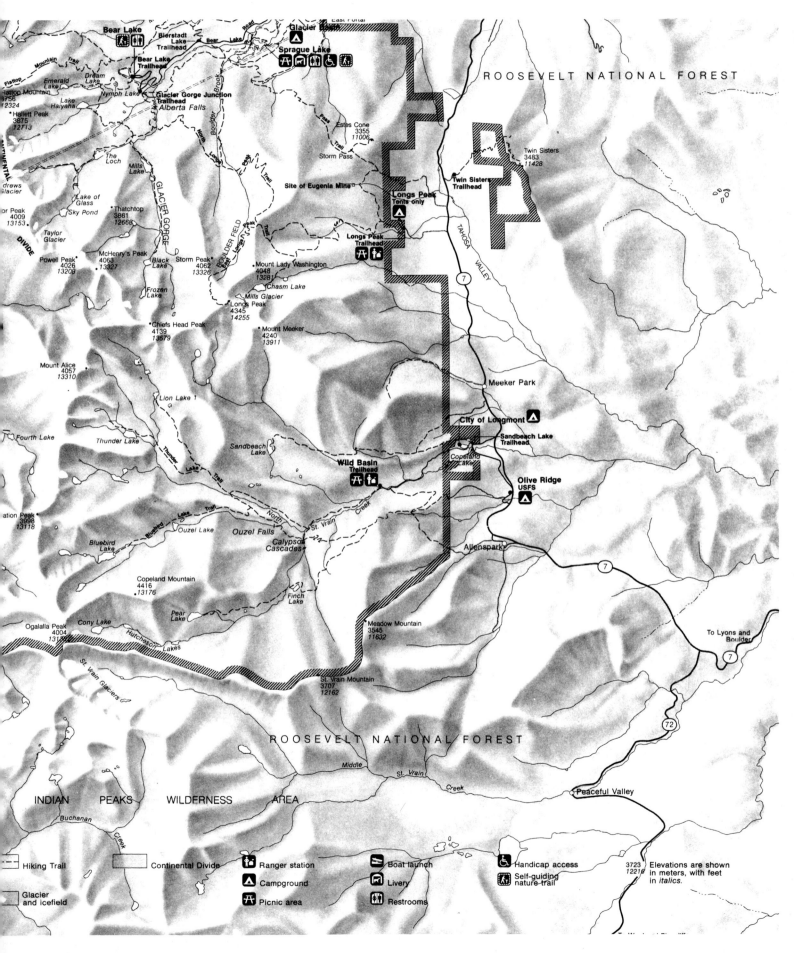

ROOSEVELT NATIONAL FOREST

Bear Lake
Bierstadt Lake Trailhead
Bear Lake Trailhead

Glacier Basin
Sprague Lake

East Portal

Flattop Mountain Trail

Emerald Lake
Dream Lake
Flattop Mountain
3756
12324
Nymph Lake
Lake Haiyaha
Hallett Peak
3875
12713

Glacier Gorge Junction Trailhead
Alberta Falls

Estes Cone
3355
11006

Storm Pass

Twin Sisters
3483
11428

Site of Eugenia Mine

Twin Sisters Trailhead

The Loch
Mills Lake

drews Glacier

Lake of Glass
Sky Pond

or Peak
4009
13153

Taylor Glacier

Thatchtop
3861
12668

GLACIER GORGE

BOULDER FIELD

East Longs Peak Trail

Longs Peak
Tents only

Longs Peak Trailhead

TAHOSA VALLEY

7

DIVIDE

Powell Peak
4026
13208

McHenry's Peak
4063
13327

Black Lake

Storm Peak
4062
13326

Mount Lady Washington
4048
13281

Chasm Lake

Frozen Lake

Mills Glacier

Chiefs Head Peak
4139
13579

Longs Peak
4345
14255

Mount Meeker
4240
13911

Mount Alice
4057
13310

Lion Lake 1

Meeker Park

City of Longmont

Sandbeach Lake Trailhead

Fourth Lake

Thunder Lake

Sandbeach Lake

Wild Basin Trailhead

Copeland Lake

Olive Ridge
USFS

Thunder Lake Trail

Bluebird Lake Trail

ation Peak
3998
13118

Bluebird Lake

Ouzel Lake

Ouzel Falls

Calypso Cascades

North St. Vrain Creek

Allenspark

7

Copeland Mountain
4416
13176

Finch Lake

Pear Lake

Ogalalla Peak
4004
1317

Cony Lake

Hutcheson Lakes

Meadow Mountain
3545
11632

To Lyons and Boulder

7

St. Vrain Glaciers

St. Vrain Mountain
3707
12162

72

ROOSEVELT NATIONAL FOREST

Middle
St. Vrain Creek

Peaceful Valley

INDIAN PEAKS WILDERNESS AREA

Buchanan

Creek

3723
12218
Elevations are shown in meters, with feet in *italics*.

Hiking Trail

Continental Divide

Ranger station

Campground

Picnic area

Boat launch

Livery

Restrooms

Handicap access

Self-guiding nature trail

Glacier and icefield

ROCKY MOUNTAIN SPLENDOR

A MILE BY MILE GUIDE®
for
ROCKY MOUNTAIN NATIONAL PARK

by

Doris B. Osterwald

Doris B. Osterwald

author of

CINDERS & SMOKE
A Mile by Mile Guide® for the
Durango to Silverton Narrow Gauge Trip

and

TICKET TO TOLTEC
A mile by mile guide® for the
Cumbres and Toltec Scenic Railroad

Western Guideways, Ltd.

P.O. Box 15532 · Lakewood. Colorado 80215

International Standard Book Number 0-931788-89-7

Color separations by
LithoColor
Denver, Colorado

Linotronic typsetting by
National Teleprinting, Inc.
Denver, Colorado

Printed by
Golden Bell Press
Denver, Colorado

This book is dedicated
to
my father, Carl Beck
(1881-1971)

and to
Dr. Margaret F. Boos
(1892-1978)

Carl Beck, landscape artist and owner of Beck Art Shop in Denver,
helped me discover and develop a love of the mountains and also gave
me a lasting concept of beauty through his paintings of the
Colorado Rockies. When I was a child we spent many memorable days
hiking and fishing in Rocky Mountain National Park.

Margaret F. Boos, my first geology professor who knew and loved
Rocky Mountain National Park, served as one of the first
Park Naturalists in 1926 and 1927. Her vivid explanations of
geologic processes gave me a more complete understanding of
nature and a clearer appreciation of the true meanings of
mountain scenery.

And

a special dedication to my husband Frank W. Osterwald, February 11, 1922 -
August 27, 1989. Without his daily love, work and encouragement, this book never
could have been completed. Even though Frank's death came days before the book
was completed, Rocky Mountain Splendor had been shaped and completed
with his continuous nurturing.

ACKNOWLEDGMENTS

Without the love, constant support and encouragement of each member of my family, this book would never have been completed. My husband, Frank, aided in the research, fieldwork, and editing and then took on the new and challenging job of mastering typesetting and layout of the texts and maps on a Macintosh® SE computer using Aldus Pagemaker® and Freehand® software. The final guide maps are entirely the results of his efforts. He also mapped many of the glacial moraines using National Park Service air photos. Without the help of number three son, Carl, and his friend David Lovering, both electrical engineers with much computer experience, we would never have attempted this major change in book publishing. Thanks fellows for all your support.

Other members of the family who were intimately involved include Becky Osterwald, editor/publisher of the Eastern Colorado Plainsman, who field checked road logs, edited texts and did much photographic work. She also kept propping me up when I became discouraged with the magnitude of the project. All drawings are the work of Carl's wife, Yvonne, who also helped with the layout and prepared all the panoramas. Ed Osterwald and his wife, Candy Wood, also field checked road logs several times and in addition, came from New York to help layout and edit the book. Thanks also to Ray and April Osterwald for their continuing support; April also did the final proofreading most capably. Teenage grandsons, Ren and Martin Osterwald, helped with field checks of the Trail Ridge guides.

My hearfelt thanks to Helen Huckenpahler for her constant help, friendship, encouragement and excellent editing. The idea for a guide to Rocky Mountain National Park belongs to Bettie Willard and her contributions are gratefully acknowledged. I found that writing a highway guide is much different from a railroad guide and many trials, errors and false starts were made before the present format was developed. Friends and associates who graciously field checked the guides include Helen and Lee Huckenpahler, Polly and Peter Stanley, Pat and the late Charlie Chilvers, Sandy Chapman, Dee and Scott Webber, Fran and Jane Stetson, Becky Foster, Joan Bartelt, Jean Goldberg and Sandy Cooper.

The staff at the Rocky Mountain National Park office in Estes Park were most helpful. Retired Ranger-Naturalist, Ferril Atkins, edited several early versions of the manuscript. He spent many summers researching the history of the Park and surrounding area, and his excellent reports in the Park library were an invaluable resource. Glen Kaye, recently Chief Park Naturalist, also reviewed early versions and offered many suggestions for improvments. Michael Smithson spent many hours helping locate photographs and supervised the printing of black and white photographs. Special thanks also to Chief Park Naturalist Jim Mack, Naturalist Skip Betts and Public Information Clerk Christy Metz who reviewed the final version, and to Jean Meunchrath and Judy Rosen who helped locate some needed photographs.

I am most grateful to Enda and Bob Kiley of Estes Park who provided photographs and much information about Enda's father, Enos Mills. Mel Busch, director of the Estes Park Historical Society, provided several old photographs and helped identify several vintage photographs. Wallace Hansen, Glen Scott, Gerry Richmond and Paul Carrara of the U.S. Geological Survey freely shared their knowledge of the geology of the Park and of the Colorado Front Range. Patience Cairns Kemp of Grand Lake provided photographs and information on early western slope road construction. As always, Augie D. Mastrogiuseppi, photo curator of the Western History Department of the Denver Public Library, knew where to find special old photographs. I feel very fortunate to have met Chase Swift of Estes Park, Colorado whose outstanding wildlife photographs are valuable additions to the book. Thanks also to John B. Bennetti, Jr. whose skillful mountain flying made possible a memorable trip to take aerial views of the Park. Unless otherwise credited, all the photos are my own. The cover photograph was taken on the Bear Lake Road in September 1985. The back cover photograph was taken on Trail Ridge Road after an early fall snowstorm. I would also like to acknowledge the help and encouragement of Robert W. Becker, John E. Reilly, Ellen Hansen and Susen Schmitt. Charles A. Davis, M. D. gave some needed information on tick-borne diseases and Thomas M. Golbert, M. D. explained problems of high-altitude sickness; my thanks to both.

And finally, to each of the staff of Golden Bell Press, a big thank you for another job well done. Larry Bell, Bob Metzger, Dave Anderson, Joe Simpson George Permann and Lee Darrigrand offered much help and encouragement in solving the inevitable layout and production problems.

[**Note**: The captions for Clark's nutcracker and gray jay on p. 35 and for alumroot and waxflower on p. 155 were inadvertently switched.]

CONTENTS

ROUTES TO THE PARK

Three routes lead to the Park from Colorado's eastern plains. From Greeley and Loveland, US 34 ascends into the mountains through the spectacular Big Thompson Canyon. From Denver, both US 36 and Colo. 7 via Lyons lead to Estes Park at the eastern boundary of the National Park. From Grand Lake and Kremmling on the western slope, US 34 leads northward into the Park.

INTRODUCTION

Early-day campers in the Estes Park area, probably near Black Canyon. (NPS collection)

"It is a rare realm in which to rest and romp and take hope again during vacation's carefree days."

——Enos A. Mills, <u>RockyMountain National Park</u>, Memorial Edition, 1932.

WELCOME TO ROCKY MOUNTAIN NATIONAL PARK, also affectionately called "The Park" or "Rocky." If this is your first visit to northern Colorado's scenic wonderland, expect many glimpses of splendor as you drive its roads and hike its trails. If you are a Coloradoan and visit often, this MILE by MILE GUIDE® offers new insights into the history, nature, wildlife, geology and ever-changing beauty of these snow-decked mountain peaks, tumbling mountain streams and flower-filled meadows.

If you wonder what kinds of trees, flowers and shrubs grow along the roadways; what mammals and birds live in the forests; what sort of rocks stand as sentinels above the valleys; why huge piles of loose rock, rubble and debris are scattered around; or wonder about the history of this magnificent area, this book was written for you.

The 414-square mile Park spans the Continental Divide in the Colorado Front Range of the Rocky Mountains. It includes 104 named peaks whose summits are over 10,000 feet and 59 peaks that are over 12,000 feet in elevation. The highest point, world-famous Longs Peak, towers 14,255 feet high. The lowest elevation is about 7800 feet, where the Big Thompson River leaves the Park.

The Front Range, rising above the western edge of the Great Plains of Colorado, has been a landmark since early man first came to what is now the State of Colorado. The highest peaks have always been guiding beacons for travelers. Longs Peak and its slightly lower neighbor, Mt. Meeker, elevation 13,911 feet, were known to the Plains Indians as "The Two Ears" because they could be seen from long distances on the Plains. French fur traders in the 1700s picked up the Indian name and called them *"Les Deux Oreilles."*

Longs Peak was named for explorer Major Stephen Long who led a U.S. Army Expedition into what became Colorado in 1820. They entered near present-day Julesburg and followed the South Platte River upstream toward the southwest. Edwin James, one of the scientists of the expedition, made a notable trip into the mountains through the South Platte canyon and also led a small party up Pikes Peak. Mt. Meeker was named for Nathan C. Meeker who helped establish the Union Colony of Greeley in 1870.

One of the earliest adventurers to record his trips in Rocky Mountain National Park was Rufus Sage, who came twice during 1843. In Sage's day, it was called the "Longs Peak area." By 1860, when Joel Estes began ranching in the secluded mountain-rimmed park later named for him, many traders, trappers, prospectors and even early tourists had wandered into this bountiful wilderness.

The idea for National Parks originated in the United States. After a visit to Yellowstone in 1870,

members of the Washburn–Langford–Doane expedition were impressed by its natural wonders. While sitting around a campfire in Montana discussing what they had seen, the possibility of reserving it for the enjoyment of future generations was born. They successfully encouraged Congress to fund a more formal exploration the following year, led by Dr. F. V. Hayden. Reports of Hayden's Survey, including many photographs by the pioneer western photographer, William H. Jackson, led to an unanimous Act of Congress in 1872 establishing the National Park. Another Act in 1916 organized the National Park service:

> "....to conserve the scenery and the natural and historic objects and the wildlife therein and to provide for the enjoyment of the same in such manner and by such means as will leave them unimpaired for the enjoyment of future generations."

This paradoxical charge to preserve the scenery and wildlife and at the same time provide facilities so that people can enjoy the National Parks has been difficult, to say the least.

Rocky Mountain National Park was established in 1915, largely through the efforts of naturalist Enos Mills, who lived in the Estes Park area. Mills, an internationally-known nature guide, conservationist, writer, lecturer and photographer, worked for about six years to convince Congress to set aside land in the Longs Peak region as the nation's tenth National Park. He recognized that the majestic mountain scenery, the wildlife and wilderness were national treasures that should be preserved for all to enjoy.

Part of this national treasure is the geology. Rocks in Rocky Mountain National Park are very old, hard, tough and durable metamorphic gneisses and schists that have been around in one form or another about 1.8 billion years. Slightly younger igneous granites are about 1.7 billion years old. A few "young" rocks blown from volcanos were deposited on the older crystalline rocks between 28 and 26 million years ago. The rocks and their evolution through the vastness of geologic time are summarized in the Geology chapter, p. 223.

In addition to fascinating geology and spectacular scenery, the Park is endowed with abundant wildlife. In 1906, residents of Estes Park formed the Estes Park Protective and Improvement Association to build a fish hatchery, construct new roads and to actively protect the deer, elk, bighorn sheep and wildflowers. Today's visitors, who find these now abundant animals peacefully grazing on grassy hillsides, should be grateful to those far-sighted citizens for their efforts.

One word you will encounter many times during your visit is "park." It has many different meanings and connotations in Colorado. To most people, the word refers to an urban area with walks, drives, playgrounds, trees and flowers, or to scenic areas set aside as state or National Parks. But in the Colorado Rocky Mountains, the word also describes open, grassy areas surrounded by tree-covered mountains. Such open areas were called *"parques"* by early French fur traders and trappers. Similar areas in Wyoming are called "holes" or "basins."

North Park, Middle Park and South Park are large well-known geographic features in Colorado. Other small "parks" within Rocky Mountain National Park are Moraine Park, Tuxedo Park, Willow Park, Horseshoe Park, Hondius Park, Hollowell Park and Paradise Park. Confusing? It should be, especially when proper names are added. Thus the large Estes Park valley was named for the Joel Estes family. Meeker Park, Allenspark, Hondius and Hollowell Parks also were named for individuals.

The MILE by MILE GUIDES® in this book are detailed self-guided tours for exploring Rocky Mountain National Park by automobile. These guides cover about 60 miles of paved roads and 17 miles of gravel roads in and near the Park. In addition, information on the length and difficulty of many of the 355 miles of hiking trails is briefly summarized, including parts of the ancient Ute Trail, a route used for thousands of years by American Indians and their ancestors.

The DEER RIDGE ROAD is a delightful way to become acquainted with the eastern edge of Rocky Mountain National Park. The 8-mile drive starts at the National Park Headquarters and Visitor Center near Beaver Meadows Entrance and circles Deer Mountain to the Fall River Entrance. This scenic drive offers a sneak preview of distant, high mountain scenery, grass-covered slopes and some of the plants and animals living in the montane forests.

TRAIL RIDGE ROAD is the most spectacular drive in the National Park. It is the highest, continuous, paved automobile road in the United States (12,183 ft.). Eleven miles of highway are above **treeline**[1] along an open, windswept treeless ridge with magnificent vistas in all directions. This exciting and exhilarating drive passes through three **life zones**[2] before reaching Fall River Pass. The road normally is open between Memorial Day and early October. Along the way are beautiful alpine life zone wildflower gardens of tiny ground-hugging plants specially adapted to survive in the harsh climate that is similar to that above the Arctic Circle.

The western part of Trail Ridge Road descends to the North Fork of the Colorado River which in turn flows through the Kawuneeche Valley. Rival Indian tribes fought one another in this valley, mountain men

trapped beaver and prospectors grubbed for a gold or silver strike long before the first ranches and resorts were started. Many hiking trails lead from the valley to remote areas of the Park.

If you travel from east to west, follow the TRAIL RIDGE ROAD WESTBOUND guide which is divided into two sections: Part 1 describes the 17.2 miles between Deer Ridge Junction and Fall River Pass. Part 2 covers the 20.6 miles from Fall River Pass to the Kawuneeche Visitor Center near Grand Lake.

Likewise, visitors traveling from west to east should follow the TRAIL RIDGE ROAD EASTBOUND guides. Part 1 starts at the Kawuneeche Visitor Center and continues to Fall River Pass. Part 2 continues eastward from Fall River Pass to Deer Ridge Junction.

Information for each segment of the four guides is arranged for convenient viewing and stopping. The guides are also keyed to parking areas on the right side of the highway wherever possible.

The BEAR LAKE ROAD, 18 miles round trip, is open all year and offers much more than a short drive to a secluded mountain lake. Every curve of the road reveals magnificent mountain vistas. Ice-cold mountain streams tumble through ancient glacial moraines, beautiful forests carpet the hills and sharp, jagged peaks tower above Glacier Gorge. Bear Lake, at the end of the road, is set in a rock basin chiseled out by ice and dammed by a moraine. Also included is a short road guide starting near the Moraine Park Museum and leading to Cub Lake and Fern Lake Trailheads.

Another very special drive is the 12-mile, unpaved, one-way (up-only) OLD FALL RIVER ROAD. It follows the route of the first trans-mountain automobile road built in northern Colorado. Return to Estes Park or continue to Grand Lake via Trail Ridge Road. Highlights include the opportunity to stand in potholes carved by the Fall River Glacier and to drive through beautiful montane and subalpine forests before reaching the alpine tundra near Fall River Pass.

From Estes Park, Colo. Highway 7, the PEAK to PEAK HIGHWAY, leads 15 miles southward along the eastern edge of the National Park to Allenspark. Longs Peak and Mt. Meeker are revealed in unforgetable vistas as the road winds through the Tahosa Valley. Deposits from the oldest known glaciers in the Front Range are exposed at several sites along the way. The highway passes Enos Mills' former home. Notes on the short drive to Wild Basin and to the Longs Peak Trailheads are included.

An overview of Estes Park and its long, colorful history unfolds on the DEVILS GULCH ROAD to Glen Haven. From this small resort community, trails lead westward along the North Fork of the Big Thompson River into the Mummy Range. The trip suggested in

---

[1] Terms in **bold-face type** are defined in the Glossary, page 256.

[2] Life Zones are communities of plants and animals that live together at particular climates and altitudes.

the guide passes the U.S .Bureau of Reclamation Power Plant, the Estes Park Area Historical Musem and Lake Estes. The round trip is 17 miles.

Points of interest around GRAND LAKE include historical sites and a 2.5-mile drive to the west portal of the 13.1-mile Alva B. Adams tunnel which carries water under the Continental Divide. Grand Lake, Shadow Mountain Lake, Lake Granby and the Granby Pumping Station are parts of the extensive Colorado-Big Thompson Trans–Mountain Water Diversion Project. The Pumping Station is open to visitors during the summer months.

Many unique experiences await visitors to Rocky Mountain National Park. Take time to listen to the roar of a rushing mountain stream or the chatter of a chickadee. Watch billowy, ever-changing clouds drift across the Continental Divide. Sniff the bark of a ponderosa pine and touch the tips of fir and spruce needles. Watch for bighorn sheep in Horseshoe Park. Examine the debris in an ancient glacial moraine. Search for beautiful blue Colorado columbines blooming among aspen groves and explore the fascinating alpine world above treeline. Enjoy the magnificence, grandeur and splendor of this exquisite Park.

Great care has been taken to point out safety hazards and safe driving tips.

All driving instructions and precautions are in bold italic type.

DO NOT TRY TO DRIVE AND READ AT THE SAME TIME.

Drive carefully.   Remember you are in the mountains. **Think safety.**

USING THE MILE BY MILE GUIDES®

The ten detailed guides are self-guided tours for exploring the Park by automobile. Each guide, with accompanying maps, locates scenic viewpoints and gives information about the plants, wildlife, geology and history at each stop or point of interest. The guides give hints for taking photographs and also give some information on the length and difficulty of trails leading from parking areas. If you plan to hike, do carry the appropriate U.S. Geological Survey topographic maps that are available at the Visitors Centers and in the Moraine Park Museum.

Reading the guides in advance will make it easier to select stops of particular interest. Don't feel you must read everything at each stop or point of interest; pick and choose the items of most interest to you—and maybe make another trip to see features you missed.

If one of the parking areas shown on the maps is full, similar features may be seen at the next parking area. DO NOT CROSS DOUBLE-YELLOW LINES to reach parking areas; stop in the ones on your side of the road. Pull completely off the road when stopping or parking.

Because there are no mileposts in the Park, the Guides are keyed to mileages on your odometer. These mileages are listed in narrow left-hand columns as shown below:

4
MILE
10.2
Mileage to next point of interest:
(0.5)

SUGGESTED STOP.

Cumulative mileage from start of log.

[These mileages should agree with odometers of all vehicles to within plus or minus 0.2 miles.]

When a geograpic feature is first mentioned, it is in CAPITAL LETTERS.

See page 260 for other useful information.

SYMBOLS ON GUIDE MAPS

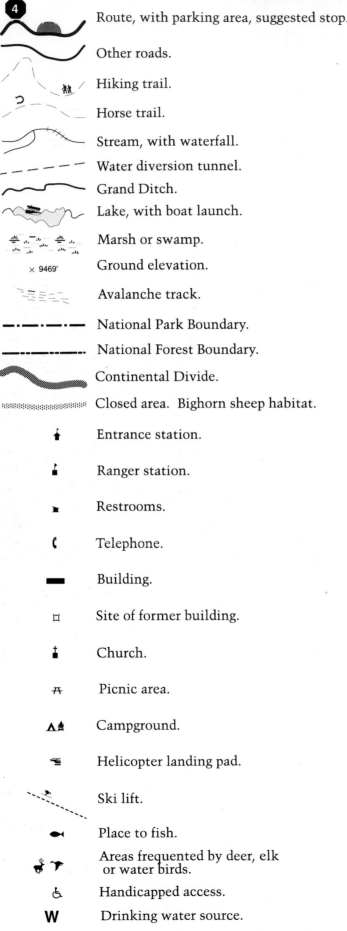

Route, with parking area, suggested stop.

Other roads.

Hiking trail.

Horse trail.

Stream, with waterfall.

Water diversion tunnel.

Grand Ditch.

Lake, with boat launch.

Marsh or swamp.

× 9469' Ground elevation.

Avalanche track.

National Park Boundary.

National Forest Boundary.

Continental Divide.

Closed area. Bighorn sheep habitat.

Entrance station.

Ranger station.

Restrooms.

Telephone.

Building.

Site of former building.

Church.

Picnic area.

Campground.

Helicopter landing pad.

Ski lift.

Place to fish.

Areas frequented by deer, elk or water birds.

Handicapped access.

W Drinking water source.

al Modern stream alluvium, landslides, talus and Holocene glacial outwash.

  rock glacier Holocene rock glacier.

Active rock slide.

GLACIAL FEATURES

l p Late Pinedale.

m p—r Middle Pinedale recessional moraine.

m p Middle Pinedale.

e p Early Pinedale.

l bl Late Bull Lake.

e bl Early Bull Lake.

bl u Bull Lake undivided.

p bl Pre-Bull Lake.

r m Roche moutonnèe.

TERTIARY ROCKS

T t Troublesome Formation.

T v Volcanic ash-flow tuff.

PRECAMBRIAN ROCKS

Precambrian undivided.

Granite, pegmatite.

Gneiss, schist.

"Iron Dike" or other diabase dikes.

Shear zone.

Fault.

Approximately located fault.

Inferred or concealed fault.

DEER RIDGE ROAD

This drive starts at the Park Headquarters and Visitor Center 3 miles west of downtown Estes Park on U.S. 36.

Approaching Rocky Mountain National Park from the east near Beaver Point.

"On approaching the Park by the east entrance, through the long-famed Estes Park region, even the dullest traveler is thrilled with the first glimpse and those who frequently behold it find the scene as welcome as a favorite old song."

—Enos A. Mills, <u>Your National Parks</u>, 1917

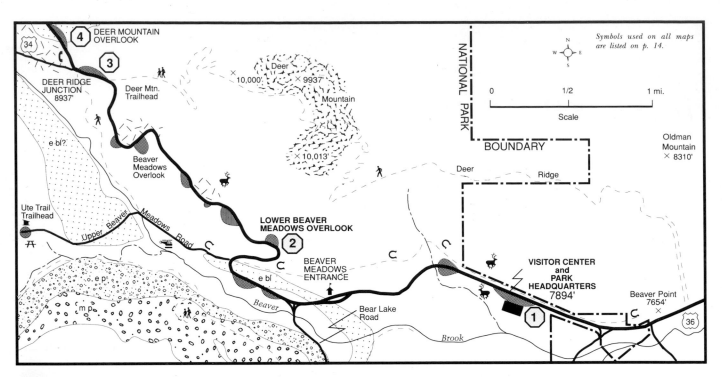

VISITOR CENTER.
El. 7840 ft.
—RESTROOMS, TELEPHONE.

THINGS TO DO:
—A 20-minute Park orientation film is shown in the auditorium.
—Check schedules for evening programs.
—Park activity schedules available.
—Camping and hiking permits issued.
—Books, maps and film for sale.

SCENERY:
—From the south side of the Visitor Center, or from the west end of the parking area, the high mountains standing on the southern skyline are, from left to right, MT. MEEKER (p. 199), LONGS PEAK and MT. LADY WASHINGTON, the slightly lower triangular-shaped peak.
—To the northwest is DEER MTN., el. 10,013 ft.

PLANTS:
—Signs along the parking area sidewalk identify typical shrubs and trees of the **montane life zone**[1] (6,000 to 9,000 ft. elevation). **Life zones** are plant and animal communities classified by those dominant species which thrive in a particular combination of climate and elevation.
—A mature ponderosa pine *(Pinus ponderosa)* forest surrounds the Visitor Center and extends westward toward Deer Ridge Junction.

—Many montane zone wildflowers bloom on the open, grassy, south-facing slopes of Deer Mtn. from May into July.

WILDLIFE:
—Deer often browse on shrubs surrounding the Visitor Center.

HISTORY:
—The Visitor Center, completed in 1967, was designed by Taliesen West Associates, the architectural firm founded by Frank Lloyd Wright.

Set your odometer at 0.0 or write down your mileage at the west end of the parking area. Suggested stops are numbered on the map and in the text.

DO NOT CROSS DOUBLE YELLOW LINES TO ENTER PARKING AREAS.

---

[1]Terms in **bold-face** type are defined in the Glossary, page 256.

1

MILE

0.0

Mileage to next point of interest

(1.2)

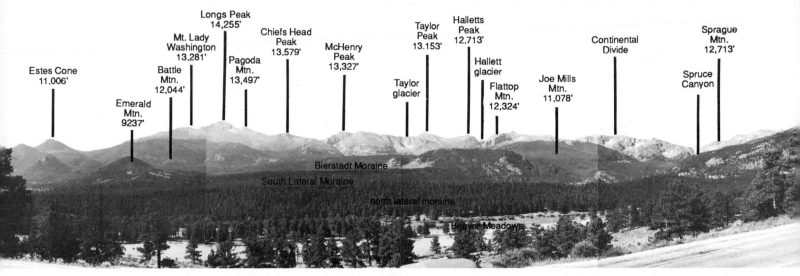

Estes Cone 11,006'
Emerald Mtn. 9237'
Battle Mtn. 12,044'
Mt. Lady Washington 13,281'
Longs Peak 14,255'
Pagoda Mtn. 13,497'
Chiefs Head Peak 13,579'
McHenry Peak 13,327'
Taylor glacier
Taylor Peak 13,153'
Halletts Peak 12,713'
Hallett glacier
Flattop Mtn. 12,324'
Joe Mills Mtn. 11,078'
Continental Divide
Spruce Canyon
Sprague Mtn. 12,713'

Bierstadt Moraine
South Lateral Moraine
north lateral moraine
Beaver Meadows

Panorama from Lower Beaver Meadows Overlook.

MILE 1.2

Mileage to next point of interest:

(0.2)

BEAVER MEADOWS ENTRANCE STATION.

El. 8200 ft. Stop to pay entrance fees.

SCENERY:
—The panoramas along the southern skyline of Longs Peak and the Continental Divide are spectacular at any time of the year. The Notch on the left side of Longs Peak and the triangular summit of Mt. Lady Washington are still visible.

HISTORY:
—This entrance station, built in 1960, replaced an old one along the Big Thompson River.

GEOLOGY:
—The low, gently-rounded tree-covered hill on the right opposite the Bear Lake Road junction, west of the Entrance Station, is all that is left of an Early Bull Lake-age moraine (see map).

MILE 1.4

(0.5)

BEAR LAKE ROAD JUNCTION on left.

The MILE by MILE GUIDE® for this spectacular drive starts on p. 125.

MILE 1.9

(0.6)

UPPER BEAVER MEADOWS ROAD

on the left leads west 1.3 miles to:
—Small picnic area. RESTROOMS.
—Trailhead for modern UTE TRAIL, which climbs 3000 ft. in 6.0 mi. to the Old Ute Trail Crossing on Trail Ridge Road.
—Fenced plots used to study effects of overgrazing by deer and elk on native vegetation.

2

MILE 2.5

Mileage to next point of interest:

(1.0)

LOWER BEAVER MEADOWS OVERLOOK.

El. 8540 ft. Parking area on right.

SCENERY:
—Panorama above identifies landscape features.
—Longs Peak and Continental Divide to south.

PHOTO HINTS:
—Early morning or late afternoon light ideal for photos to the south.

PLANTS:
—Ponderosa pines, with some aspens, Douglas firs and limber pines.
—Many wildflowers on open, south-facing slopes during early summer.
—A large patch of sagebrush (*Artemesia tridentata*) grows along a curve just east of Beaver Meadows Overlook.

WILDLIFE:
—Home of dark brown, black or gray Abert's squirrels. Easy to recognize because of their long, bushy tails and ear tufts.
—Mule deer and elk sometimes browse in the valley.
—Other animals in abundance include Colorado chipmunks, Nuttall's cottontails and porcupines.

GEOLOGY:
—Panorama above shows the north **lateral moraine** deposited by the Thompson Glacier.
—Rocks along the road are weathered **Precambrian gneisses, schists** and some **granite**. Symbols for the rock types are on p. 14.

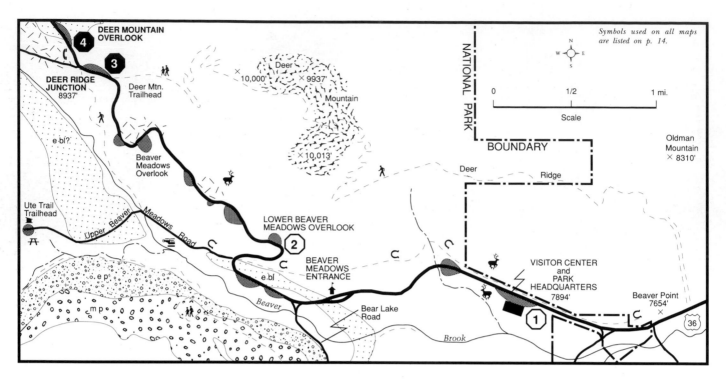

Symbols used on all maps are listed on p. 14.

MILE
3.5

Mileage to next point of interest:

(0.8)

BEAVER MEADOWS OVERLOOK
on left.

DO NOT CROSS DOUBLE YELLOW LINE.
—This is a lovely stop for an eastbound return trip.
—Features are similar to STOP 2.

GEOLOGY:
—Large sign explains origins of mountains, moraines and meadows.
—Two large outcrops are **granite**.
—Several **potholes** are just below the parking area.
—Look for the tree roots growing from cracks in the rocks.
—More views of north lateral moraine.

3 DEER RIDGE JUNCTION.
El. 8937 ft. Parking area on right before junction.

MILE
4.3

Mileage to next point of interest:

(0.2)

Junction US 36 and US 34. Turn right to continue this guide. Go straight ahead to follow US 34, TRAIL RIDGE ROAD. The MILE by MILE GUIDE® for this drive starts on p. 27.

An EMERGENCY TELEPHONE, in a dark green box, is on a post on the hillside northwest of the junction.

SCENERY:
—To the south are vistas of Longs Peak and of the peaks along the Continental Divide.
—To the north are the first glimpses of the MUMMY RANGE.

THINGS TO DO:
—Trail for DEER MTN., el. 10,013 ft., starts here and climbs 1000 ft. in about 3 mi. Open much of the year.
—From Deer Mtn. summit are vistas of Horseshoe Park, Fall River, Big Thompson River, Estes Park, Longs Peak and the Continental Divide.

HISTORY:
—In 1917 this land, homesteaded by E. O. Schubert, was leased to Orville W. Bechtel who built a small stand to sell postcards and lemonade.
—By 1959 the business, named DEER RIDGE CHALETS, included a gift shop, restaurant, service station, cabins, viewing tower, small railroad and livery stable (photo p.19).
—By 1960, because of traffic congestion, all buildings were removed and the area revegetated.

DEER MOUNTAIN OVERLOOK.
El. 8920 ft. Parking area on right.

4

MILE
4.5

Mileage to next point of interest:

(0.7)

SCENERY:
—Mt. Ypsilon is straight ahead; to its right is Fairchild Mtn. The lower tree-covered, rounded mountain is Bighorn and the bare slope above it is Mummy Ridge. To the right of Bighorn is the rounded hump of Dark Mtn. and McGregor Mtn.
—Deer Mtn. is to the east.

Deer Ridge Chalets in the 1940s. (NPS)

View northeastward into Little Horseshoe Park in 1935, two years after a CCC camp and a Ranger Station were built. McGregor Mountain is on the right skyline. The low rounded hill behind the tents is an Early Pinedale moriane. Note the growth of the trees since 1935. *(NPS)*

—LUMPY RIDGE., a number of rounded granite outcrops are northeast, and north of Fall River. The name came from the Arapaho Indian name which meant "little lumps."
—LITTLE HORSESHOE PARK is the small, secluded meadow below the parking area.

PLANTS:
—Trees on the north-facing slope of Deer Mtn. are mainly Douglas firs *(Pseudotsuga menziesii)* that prefer more moist, cool growing conditions than the ponderosa pines on the south-facing slope near STOP 2.
—Fewer ground plants grow in such dense coniferous forests because less sunlight reaches the forest floor.

WILDLIFE:
—Chickaree squirrels, also called spruce, tree, pine, or red squirrels, live in Douglas fir forests. Their ears are only slightly tufted.

GEOLOGY:
—**Precambrian metamorphic** rocks cap the summit of Deer Mtn.
—This stop is on the drainage divide between Beaver Brook to the south and Fall River to the north.

HISTORY:
—The land in Little Horseshoe Park was once owned by rancher and innkeeper, Willard H. Ashton, who built HORSESHOE INN (p. 21), and a cabin at

LAWN LAKE for use of his guests.
—Ashton's daughter, Ruth Ashton Nelson, grew up in the Park. She became a botanist and wrote two books about the plants of Rocky Mountain National Park.
—A Civilian Conservation Corps (CCC) camp was here from 1933 to 1942.

BETWEEN STOP 4 and STOP 6 WATCH FOR:

PLANTS:
—Douglas fir trees on both sides of road were killed by spruce budworms which feed on the tips of green fir or spruce needles.
—The National Park Service does not use pesticides or other methods to interfere with this natural and self-limiting process of thinning.

GEOLOGY:
—Beyond STOP 4, at mile 4.8, the road passes through an Early Pinedale-age **lateral moraine**. The guide maps show the outlines of this moraine and also of thin patches of Early Bull Lake–age glacial debris.
—Hidden Valley Creek seeps through the porous glacial debris to reach Fall River.
—Ample underground water in the debris nurtures a dense forest that includes clumps of aspens, willows, alders, birches and long-leafed poplars interspersed with lodgepoles, Douglas firs and blue spruces (the Colorado state tree).

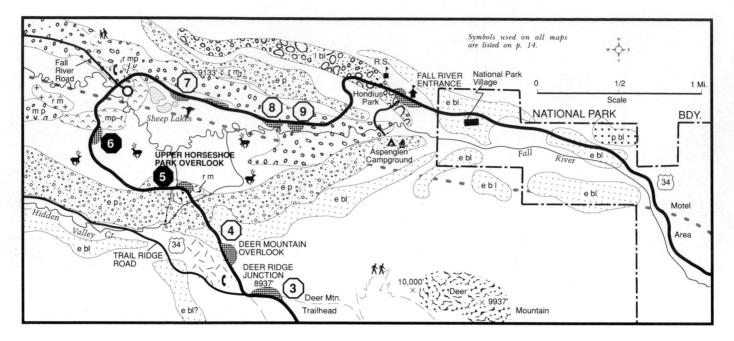

Symbols used on all maps are listed on p. 14.

Symbols used on all maps are listed on p. 14.

5 UPPER HORSESHOE PARK OVERLOOK.

MILE 5.2

Mileage to next point of interest:

(0.7)

El. 8720 ft. Parking area on right.

SCENERY:
—Panorama on p. 21 identifies landscape features.
—To the northwest, the scar on the side of Fall River valley is a new **alluvial fan** deposited almost instantly on July 15, 1982 when Lawn Lake dam, located high in the Mummy Range, failed. (See p. 25 and p. 150 for more on this disaster).
—Horseshoe Park is the flat valley below the overlook. Fall River meanders back and forth across a rich meadow **wetland.**
—Sheep Lakes are near the north side of Horseshoe Park.
—More views to the east and northeast of Lumpy Ridge.
—On the mountainside to the southwest are the lower switchbacks of Trail Ridge Road and Rainbow Curve.

THINGS TO DO:
—Golden-mantled ground squirrels, least and Colorado chipmunks may greet your arrival. <u>DO NOT FEED THE WILDLIFE</u>. It is against Park regulations because it causes over-population of animals that are unable to adapt to wild conditions.
—Great place to birdwatch. Clarke's nutcrackers, Stellar's jays, gray jays, ravens, magpies, chickadees and juncos are often seen at this point.
—Identify the different species of conifers surrounding the parking area with the key on p. 253.

PHOTO HINTS:
—Good animal and bird photos are possible, if you wait for the right moment.

PLANTS:
—Waxflower shrubs (*Jamesia americana*) grow in cracks in the rocks.
—Many **lichens** cover exposed rock surfaces.

GEOLOGY:
—Parking area is built on **Precambrian metamorphic gneisses** and **schists** that were polished but not completely ground away by the powerful glaciers that flowed down Fall River Canyon and into Horseshoe Park.
—Horseshoe Park was the site of an ancient lake dammed by a **terminal** moraine at the eastern end of the valley. The lake was drained about 14,000 years ago and by about 10,000 to 11,000 thousand years ago its floor was covered by thick vegetation.

Mt. Chapin 12,454' Mt. Chiquita 13,069' Alluvial fan Mt. Ypsilon 13,514' Fairchild Mtn. 13,502' north lateral moraine Sheep Lakes Bighorn Mtn. 11,463' Horseshoe Park Fall River

Upper Horseshoe Park Panorama.

6 MILE

5.9

Mileage to next point of interest:

(0.2)

UPPER END OF HORSESHOE PARK.
El. 8520 ft. Large parking area on right.

THINGS TO DO:
—Listen to bull elk bugle during mating season in September and October.
—Visitors who wish to hear elk bugling should first check with Park Rangers or Naturalists and **must follow all regulations.**

PHOTO HINTS:
—Use a telephoto lens to photograph bighorn sheep, deer and elk that are often seen here. <u>DO NOT APP-ROACH   THE ANIMALS</u>.

SCENERY:
—BIGHORN MTN., el. 11,463 ft., to the north, is home to a herd of bighorn sheep, the Colorado state mammal and the symbol of Rocky Mountain National Park.
—Peaks in the Mummy Range to the northwest from left to right are Mt. Chapin, Mt. Chiquita, Mt. Ypsilon and Fairchild Mtn.

PLANTS:
—Moist areas west of the parking area are prime habitat for blue Rocky Mountain iris *(Iris missouriensis)* that bloom during June.
—Some Indian tribes poisoned arrowheads by dipping them in a concoction of iris roots and animal bile.
—During June and July, the meadows, open woods and hillsides are dotted with bright yellow golden banners *(Thermopsis divaricarpa).* Wild game animals and livestock rarely eat these plants because of their unpleasant taste.

WILDLIFE:
—Bighorn sheep visit Horseshoe Park to graze and search for salt in the soil.
—Deer, elk and bighorn sheep winter throughout Horseshoe Park.

HISTORY:
—HORSESHOE INN was across the road opposite the parking area until the early 1920s.
—Private inns and hotels within the Park boundaries gradually were purchased and removed by the National Park Service because there are ample accomodations outside the Park.
—The Park Service's policy is to return the Park as closely as possible to its original appearance.

MILE 6.1

CROSS FALL RIVER.
A new bridge was built after the 1982 Lawn Lake flood.

MILE 6.2

Mileage to next point of interest:

(0.4)

ENTRANCE TO ENDOVALLEY PICNIC GROUNDS and OLD FALL RIVER ROAD on left.
El. 8515.
—Lawn Lake Trailhead is 0.1 mi. west of this junction. RESTROOMS. EMERGENCY TELEPHONE.
—Endovalley Picnic grounds are 1.8 mi. west along Fall River. RESTROOMS.
—The MILE by MILE GUIDE® for the unpaved, one-way, <u>up-only</u> Old Fall River Road adventure starts on p. 147.
—Formal dedication ceremonies for Rocky Mountain National Park were held on the hillside northwest of this junction on Sept. 4, 1915.

Aberts squirrel.
(Chase Swift©)

Chickaree (pine) squirrel.
(NPS)

Mature bull elk, still losing the velvet from their antlers, sparring at the start of the fall mating season.
(Chase Swift©)

Mature bighorn ram.
(Chase Swift©)

Five-point buck mule dee
(Chase Swift

Rocky mountain iris.

Blue columbine, Colorado's State Flower.

Oblique aerial view of Horseshoe Park eastward, showing the scarred Roaring River valley and the alluvial fan from the Lawn Lake dam failure. Deer Mtn. (in the shadow) and Estes Park are in the back-ground. Terminal moraine dammed the ancient Fall River to form a lake in Horseshoe Park. The old lake was gradually filled with sediment that washed into the valley. Finally the lake washed out the morainal dam. Since then, Fall River has changed its course many times as it meanders back and forth across the valley.

This photo, taken before 1920, shows the old Horseshoe Inn on the left with Mt. Ypsilon on the skyline. Compare this photo with the appearance of Horseshoe Park today. (NPS)

During the summer of 1889, these visitors enjoyed the scenery from Sheep Lakes. The grass around the lake was much shorter than it is today. Perhaps either a dry weather cycle or overgrazing by livestock kept the grass from growing taller. The original road across the **kame** is on the left, beyond the lake. (NPS collection)

People came by auto, horse, wagon, or on foot to take part in the formal dedication of Rocky Mountain National Park, September 4, 1915. The Park was proposed by Herbert N. Wheeler, first superintendent of the Colorado National Forest. In 1908 he suggested to the Estes Park Improvement Association that a game refuge be established to attract visitors to Estes Park. From that suggestion, the idea of Rocky Mountain National Park evolved. View is southwestward from the hill above the junction of the Fall River and Deer Ridge roads. (Fred Clatworthy photo, NPS collection)

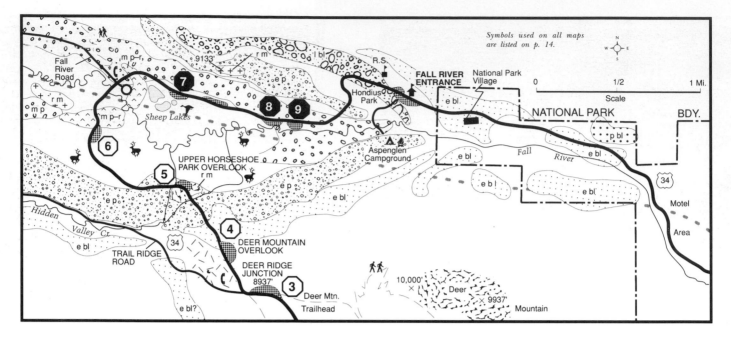

Symbols used on all maps are listed on p. 14.

Symbols used on all maps are listed on p. 14.

⬡7 SHEEP LAKES OVERLOOK.

MILE 6.6

Mileage to next point of interest: **(0.5)**

El. 8508 ft. Large parking area on right.

THINGS TO DO:
—Sheep Lakes are a short distance down the hill to the right.
—This is another place to see bighorn sheep, deer and elk browsing in the meadow, as well as to watch ducks on the lakes.
—The information booth may be staffed by a naturalist to answer questions and lead hikes.

GEOLOGY:
—Sheep Lakes are **kettle lakes** that formed about 35,000 years ago as the Middle Pinedale-age glacier melted, leaving behind large blocks of stagnant ice.
—These blocks of ice were buried by glacial debris from the retreating glacier. As the buried ice slowly melted, water collected in basin or bowl-shaped surface depressions called **kettles**.
—The lakes have no surface drainage and sometimes dry up completely during droughts.
—The low, irregular, rounded, grass-covered hill west of Sheep Lakes is a **kame** of Middle Pinedale age. Kames form when meltwater streams deposit poorly sorted, but layered sand and gravel within a melting glacier.
—Kames and kettle lakes are uncommon in glaciated mountains, but are very common where the land formerly was covered by **continental glaciers**.

WARNING—DO NOT STOP BET-WEEN MILE 6.6 AND 6.7.
—Bighorn sheep cross back and forth from the hillside on the north to the meadow. <u>DO NOT DISTURB THESE ANIMALS</u>.

⬡8 EASTERN END OF HORSESHOE PARK.

MILE 7.1

Mileage to next point of interest: **(0.2)**

El. 8495 ft. Parking area on right.

An alternate parking area is 0.2 mi. farther east.

SCENERY:
—The view westward of the ice-carved, flattened U-shaped, Fall River Canyon is superb.
—To the south and from left to right, Mt. Meeker, Longs Peak and the pointed summit of Mt. Lady Washington rise above the tree-covered slope of Deer Ridge.
—Switchbacks of Trail Ridge Road are visible on the tree-covered southwestern hillside.
—The northwestern side of Deer Mtn. is to the southeast.

PLANTS:
—Willows line the banks of Fall River.
—Many Montane grasses and wildflowers bloom, particularly in June and July.
—Most of the trees in the forest on the north side of the road are ponderosa pines, with a few Douglas firs.
—Shrubs include chokecherries, Rocky Mountain thimbleberries and wax currants.

Site of Cascade Dam in 1985. The abutment of the dam was in the light-colored glacial debris in the left center of the photo.

Debris on the damaged bridge leading to the Aspenglen Campground after Lawn Lake flood, August 1982.

HISTORY:
—Many large, extinct mammals may have grazed on plants covering the floor of this valley about 11,000 to 10,000 years ago. Perhaps prehistoric hunters pursued them, using long stone lance points called "Clovis Points".

9 MILE 7.3

Mileage to next point of interest:

(0.1)

CASCADE DAM SITE.

SCENERY:
—To the east, is the best place to see the site of Cascade Dam, destroyed in July 1982 when rushing flood-water from Lawn Lake over-topped and destroyed it by eroding the abutments.
—Built in 1908, the dam supplied water to a hydro-electric power plant downstream and drinking water to Estes Park

HISTORY:
—The dam and power plant were financed by Freelan O. Stanley, inventor of the Stanley Steamer automobile and one of Estes Park's most famous summer residents (p. 208).
—In 1987 the National Park Service agreed to permit the City of Estes Park to rebuild the dam for drinking water and hydroelectric power providing that the river's flow is kept at a natural level during the winters. Construction began in the spring of 1988.

MILE 7.4

CASCADE COTTAGES (private property) and the site of CASCADE LAKE are on the right.

Mileage to next point of interest:

(0.7)

BETWEEN CASCADE COTTAGES and the WESTERN END of HONDIUS PARK WATCH FOR:

GEOLOGY:
—The road crosses several low, curved ridges that were left as **recessional moraines** when Early Pinedale-age glaciers briefly halted their retreats between 75,000 and 60,000 years ago and again when Middle Pinedale-age glaciers retreated between 50,000 and 35,000 years ago.
—Roadcuts expose loose boulders, cobbles, sand and soil in these moraines.

MILE 8.1

EASTERN END of HONDIUS PARK.
Parking area on right.

Mileage to next point of interest:

(0.1)

SCENERY:
—The north-facing slope of Deer Mtn. is to the south-southeast.

PLANTS:
—Most of the trees on both sides of this small meadow are ponderosa pines with interspersed aspens, Douglas firs, Engelmann spruces and lodgepole pines.
—The trees thrive here because the glacial moraines contain much underground water.

GEOLOGY:
—The hillside north of the road is a Late Bull Lake-age moraine deposited here between 145,000 and 130,000 years ago.
—The soil in Bull Lake-age moraines is rusty to light-brown color and the

Stephen Gillette, at Lawn Lake Trailhead, heard the roaring water and the crash of tumbling rocks. He called Park headquarters at 6:22 AM; the headquarters staff in turn alerted the town of Estes Park. By 8:45 AM the floodwater reached Elkhorn Avenue, as shown in this photograph.

One camper, still in his sleeping bag, was swept away just below Lawn Lake dam. After Cascade dam failed, a second pulse of water roared down Fall River, killing two more campers who had returned to retrieve their belongings at Aspenglen Campground. Property damage in Estes Park was more than $26 million, while damage in the Park to roads, bridges, trails and Aspenglen Campground amounted to about $5 million.

(Estes Park Trail Gazette photo)

boulders are so weathered and cracked that very few glacial scratches or striations are left on them.

HISTORY:
—This small park was named for Pieter Hondius who homesteaded it many years ago.

MILE 8.2

Mileage to next point of interest: **(0.1)**

ASPENGLEN CAMPGROUND ENTRANCE on right.

THINGS TO DO:
—Camp ground has both drive-in and walk-in campsites.
—The 1982 flood destroyed the access road into the campground; much evidence of this disaster still remains along the roads.

MILE 8.3 (0.3)

FALL RIVER ENTRANCE STATION.
El. 8242 ft.
—BIGHORN RANGER STATION, built in 1934, is on the hill west of the entrance station.
—Perhaps you will have time to make this drive again, going in the opposite direction.
—Parking areas for travel in the opposite direction are shown on the guide maps.

MILE 8.6

NATIONAL PARK VILLAGE and NATIONAL PARK RESORT CAMPGROUND.

THINGS TO DO:
—National Park Village has a large restaurant, gift shops, and a service station. Other facilities include a laundromat, livery stable, free observation tower, and a miniature railroad that winds through a small petting zoo. Look for the swallows nesting on the porch.
—The campground is on the hillside across the highway from the stores.

GEOLOGY:
—The stores and campground are built on an Early Bull Lake-age lateral moraine deposited between 192,000 and 156,000 years ago.
—Farther east a few patches of even older Pre-Bull-age Lake debris have been identified.
—Pre-Bull Lake glaciers were the largest and the ones that first carved Fall River Valley into a flattened U-shape. These glaciers traveled the farthest because the climate was colder and wetter. Little evidence remains today of those very ancient rivers of ice.

HISTORY:
—These businesses were located at Deer Ridge Junction until 1960.

To return to Estes Park from Fall River entrance,
follow US 34 BY-PASS five miles eastward,
or follow US 34 along Fall River to downtown Estes Park.

TRAIL RIDGE ROAD WESTBOUND

Part 1 — Deer Ridge Junction To Fall River Pass

Longs Peak from Trail Ridge Road after the first fall snowstorm.

"Few experiences can put so much life into one's life as to climb a mountain summit and from among the snows and clouds look down upon the beautiful world below."

——Enos A. Mills, <u>Rocky Mountain National Park</u>, Memorial Edition, 1932.

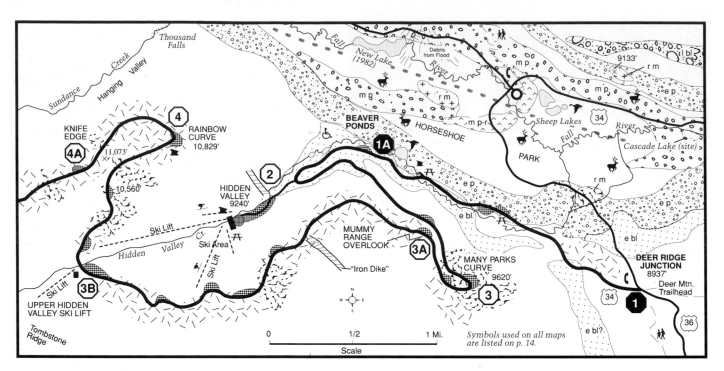

Symbols used on all maps
are listed on p. 14.

DEER RIDGE JUNCTION.
El. 8937 ft.

Follow US 34 west. This is also STOP 1 on the National Park Service Trail Ridge Road Guide pamphlet. Numbered Arrowhead–shaped signs beside the road identify these major stops.

Additional points–of–interest and stops in this guide are marked on the maps with number–letter combinations, ie. STOP 1A. All parking areas are shown on the maps.

Set your odometer at 0.0 or write down your mileage at this junction. There are NO service stations between Estes Park and Grand Lake.

An EMERGENCY TELEPHONE is on the hillside northwest of the junction, in a dark green box on a post.

SCENERY:
—To the south are Longs Peak and the Continental Divide.
—Estes Cone is the lower, cone-shaped peak to the left of Longs Peak.

THINGS TO DO:
—Trail to DEER MTN., el. 10,013 ft. starts here.
—Trail climbs 1000 ft. in about 2.8 mi. (p. 18).

1

MILE

0.0

Mileage
to next
point of
Interest:

(1.0)

PLANTS:
—This drive starts near the upper limit of the **montane life zone**[1] (6000-9000 ft. elevation).

HISTORY:
—This junction was the site of DEER RIDGE CHALETS until 1960 (photo, p. 19).
—Construction of Trail Ridge Road started here in the fall of 1929 and the road was opened for travel to Fall River Pass, July 16, 1932.
—This spectacular drive, the highest continuous paved highway in the U.S., has gentle grades with wide, sweeping curves and magnificent vistas in all directions.
—Paving was completed in 1938. Completion cost was less than $2 million.
—The road is on the National Register of Historic Places.

BETWEEN STOP 1 and STOP 1A WATCH FOR:

GEOLOGY:
—Outcrops of weathered **granite** on right before road descends into HIDDEN VALLEY and crosses HIDDEN VALLEY CREEK.

[1]Terms in **bold-face** type are defined in the Glossary, p. 256.

Beaver pond and lodge in Hidden Valley, about 1938.
(NPS)

Beaver. (NPS)

MILE **1.0**	**EASTERN END OF HIDDEN VALLEY.**

MILE
1.0

Mileage to next point of Interest:

(0.5)

MILE
1.5
(0.5)

1A

MILE
2.0

Mileage to next point of interest:

(0.5)

EASTERN END OF HIDDEN VALLEY.
El. 8940 ft.
Parking areas on both sides of the road.
—Picnic table.

DO NOT CROSS DOUBLE— YELLOW LINE.

WILDLIFE:
—Beavers lived in the meadow on left until the 1950s when they moved upstream to find new sources of food and building materials.

GEOLOGY:
—Parking areas are built on an Early Pinedale-age **lateral moraine** left by the Fall River Glacier between 75,000 and 60,000 years ago (see map).

PICNIC   AREA on right.
—RESTROOMS.
—No fishing permitted here.

BEAVER PONDS.
El. 9160 ft. Parking area on right.

THINGS TO DO:
—A boardwalk, suitable for people using wheelchairs, winds around several beaver ponds and dams.
—Dusk and daybreak are the best times to see these animals as they are primarily nocturnal.
—Fishing for greenback cutthroat trout is permitted on a catch-and-return basis only between August 1 and December 31. <u>Colorado fishing license is required.</u>

PLANTS:
—Grass along water's edge is Canadian reed-grass *(Calamagrostis canadensis).*
—Yellow golden banners, lavender locoweeds and red Indian paintbrushes bloom throughout the valley in June and July.
—Indian paintbrushes *(Castilleja linariaefolia),* named for Spanish botanist Domingo Castillejo, have very small flower blossoms. The red color is in the upper bracts or leaves of the plant.

WILDLIFE:
—Greenback cutthroat trout, once near extinction, were succesfully re-introduced into Hidden Valley.
—This is one of the best places in the Park to see beavers.
—Several species of ducks frequent the ponds.

HISTORY:
—The boardwalk, completed in 1984, was built with public donations.

BETWEEN STOP 1A and STOP 2:

—Road passes more ponds with beaver lodges along Hidden Valley Creek.
—Fishing is permitted on a catch-and-return basis only.

GEOLOGY:
—The tree-covered hill on the right beyond Hidden Valley Creek is an Early Pinedale-age **lateral moraine** which blocked the creek from its former course into Horseshoe Park (photo, p. 36-37).

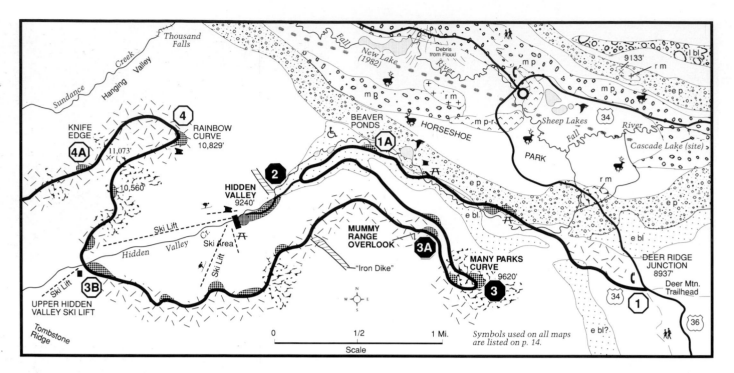

⬣ 2

MILE

2.5

Mileage to next point of Interest:

(1.4)

ENTRANCE TO HIDDEN VALLEY PICNIC and SKI AREA.

El. 9240 ft. on right.
—RESTROOMS in ski lodge.

THINGS TO DO:
—Picnic area.
—Downhill ski area is operated by the Estes Valley Recreation and Park District in season.
—Ranger Station in ski lodge.
—Headquarters for Rocky Mountain Nature Association seminars.
—First snow plow used on Trail Ridge Road is displayed.

PLANTS:
—Ski lodge is at the lower limit of the **subalpine life zone** (9000 ft. to treeline).
—Aspen groves, subalpine spruces and firs grow in lush forests on mountain sides above the ski lodge where winter snows reach 3 to 5 ft. deep while steep upper slopes receive 10 to 15 ft.
—Lavender to whitish Rocky Mountain locoweeds, pink wild roses, white pussytoes and yarrows bloom around parking area during July and August.

GEOLOGY:
—A low, rounded ridge of rusty-brown, very fine-grained, iron-rich, igneous **diabase** (photo p. 31) extends up the hill just above and across Hidden Valley Creek, 0.2 mi. west of the entrance to Hidden Valley Ski area.
—Termed the "Iron Dike" by early Front Range miners because in some places the iron-rich **diabase dike** contains valuable metallic minerals.
—The **intrusive igneous dike** was injected as a liquid into **faults** in solid granite about 1.05 billion years ago.
—This is one of a series of similar northwest-trending **dikes** in the Park, but none contain economically valuable **minerals**.

HISTORY:
—Before 1900, Abner Sprague (p. 129, 130, 204) ran a sawmill near the present ski lift.
—From 1907 to the 1930s, Dan Griffith operated another sawmill here.
—On October 31, 1915 a pile of sawdust ignited and started a forest fire which burned much of Hidden Valley. Aspen and lodgepole pine forests that subsequently sprouted in the burned area outline the fire limits.
—The ski area started in 1935 when a group of Estes Park residents built rope tows. The present lodge and ski lifts were built in 1955.

BETWEEN STOP 2 and STOP 3:

The highway climbs about 400 ft., winding through lodgepole pine and aspen forests. The aspens are glorious in the fall when their leaves turn color.

Former cabin near the Hidden Valley sawmill. (NPS)

Dan Griffith, owner of the Hidden Valley sawmill in 1907, is third from the left in the back row.   (NPS)

The elusive "Iron Dike", an igneous diabase, crops out across Hidden Valley Creek from the northwest side of the parking area at STOP 2. This rock is more resistant to weathering than the rocks that surround it so it stands out as a dark-colored, low, rounded ridge extending up the slope.
(F. W. Osterwald)

View eastward during paving of Trail Ridge Road through Hidden Valley in October 1933.
(NPS)

Ice skating was popular at the Hidden Valley ski area during the 1950s.   (NPS)

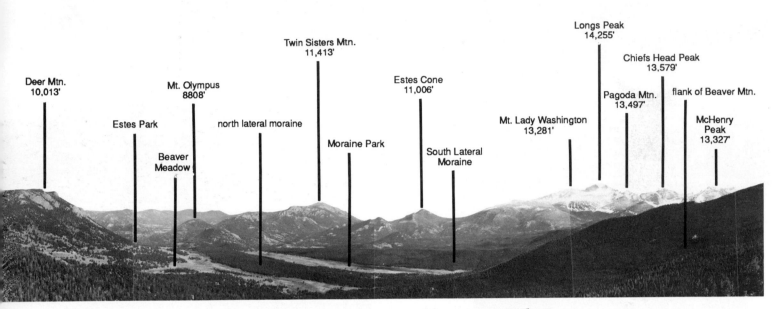

Deer Mtn.
10,013'

Estes Park

Mt. Olympus
8808'

Beaver
Meadow

north lateral moraine

Twin Sisters Mtn.
11,413'

Moraine Park

Estes Cone
11,006'

South Lateral
Moraine

Mt. Lady Washington
13,281'

Longs Peak
14,255'

Chiefs Head Peak
13,579'

Pagoda Mtn.
13,497'

flank of Beaver Mtn.

McHenry
Peak
13,327'

Panoramic view southwestward from Many Parks Curve.

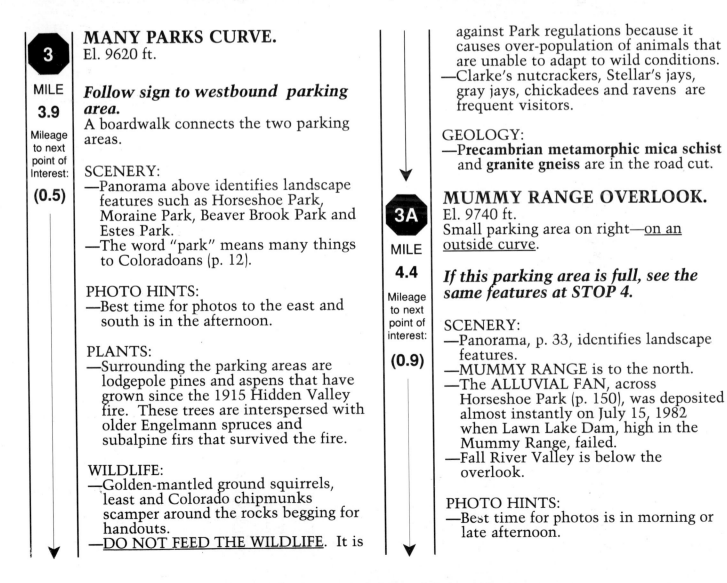

MANY PARKS CURVE.
El. 9620 ft.

3

MILE

3.9

Mileage
to next
point of
Interest:

(0.5)

Follow sign to westbound parking area.
A boardwalk connects the two parking areas.

SCENERY:
—Panorama above identifies landscape features such as Horseshoe Park, Moraine Park, Beaver Brook Park and Estes Park.
—The word "park" means many things to Coloradoans (p. 12).

PHOTO HINTS:
—Best time for photos to the east and south is in the afternoon.

PLANTS:
—Surrounding the parking areas are lodgepole pines and aspens that have grown since the 1915 Hidden Valley fire. These trees are interspersed with older Engelmann spruces and subalpine firs that survived the fire.

WILDLIFE:
—Golden-mantled ground squirrels, least and Colorado chipmunks scamper around the rocks begging for handouts.
—<u>DO NOT FEED THE WILDLIFE</u>. It is against Park regulations because it causes over-population of animals that are unable to adapt to wild conditions.
—Clarke's nutcrackers, Stellar's jays, gray jays, chickadees and ravens are frequent visitors.

GEOLOGY:
—**Precambrian metamorphic mica schist** and **granite gneiss** are in the road cut.

MUMMY RANGE OVERLOOK.

3A

MILE

4.4

Mileage
to next
point of
interest:

(0.9)

El. 9740 ft.
Small parking area on right—<u>on an outside curve</u>.

If this parking area is full, see the same features at STOP 4.

SCENERY:
—Panorama, p. 33, identifies landscape features.
—MUMMY RANGE is to the north.
—The ALLUVIAL FAN, across Horseshoe Park (p. 150), was deposited almost instantly on July 15, 1982 when Lawn Lake Dam, high in the Mummy Range, failed.
—Fall River Valley is below the overlook.

PHOTO HINTS:
—Best time for photos is in morning or late afternoon.

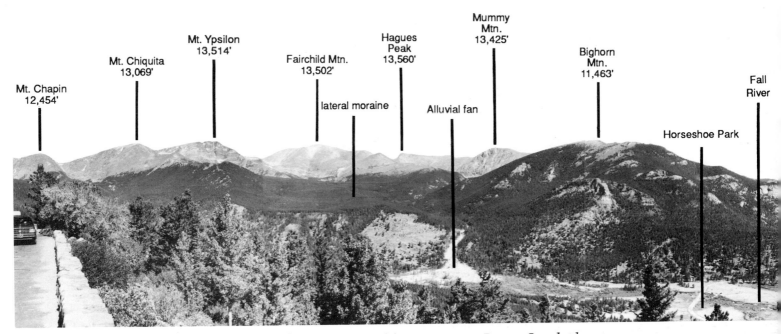

Panoramic view northward from Mummy Range Overlook.

HISTORY:

—MUMMY RANGE was named by either the Earl of Dunraven (p. 200) or by mountaineer William Hallett because the skyline supposedly looks like an Egyptian mummy lying on its back.

—MT. CHAPIN was named for Frederick Hastings Chapin, a mountain climber from Hartford, Conn. who first visited Estes Park in 1886 and climbed the peak the following year.

—MT. CHIQUITA probably was named by Enos Mills.

—YPSILON MTN. was named for the huge "Y" outlined by the cracks in its southeast face. Mrs. F. H. Chapin probably named the peak in 1887.

—FAIRCHILD MTN. was named for Lucius Fairchild. He served as governor of Wisconsin and as foreign minister to Spain. Fairchild was a veteran of the Civil War and Commander-in-Chief of the Grand Army of the Republic, who visited Colorado in 1886. This is one of the few landmarks in the Park named for a political figure.

—MUMMY MTN. presumably resembles the head of an Egyptian mummy.

BETWEEN MUMMY RANGE OVERLOOK and UPPER HIDDEN VALLEY SKI LIFT:
Several parking areas are on the right (shown on map).

MILE

5.3

Mileage to next point of interest:

(1.6)

PLANTS:

—From the parking areas there are many chances to see the virgin, unburned, **subalpine zone** spruce-fir forest and the plants that grow on its shady floors.

—Limber pines grow on rocky, wind-swept ridge crests. Tops of many of these trees are flat, rather than spire-shaped (see key, p. 253).

OUTCROP OF THE "IRON DIKE" is on the left. There is no stopping place.

GEOLOGY:

—The dark, rusty-brown very fine-grained **diabase** fills a **fault** or crack in the surrounding granite.

—This is another segment of the elusive "Iron Dike" seen at Stop 2.

—This outcrop is best seen on the eastbound trip.

BEYOND THE "IRON DIKE" WATCH FOR:

PLANTS:

—Redberried elder shrubs grow along the roadsides. They have large clusters of small white flowers in June and July. By late August they bear many small, dark red berries that are a favorite food for deer, elk, bears and birds.

—So many small conifers have sprouted along the roadsides since the 1950's that they look like a miniature forest below the older, taller trees.

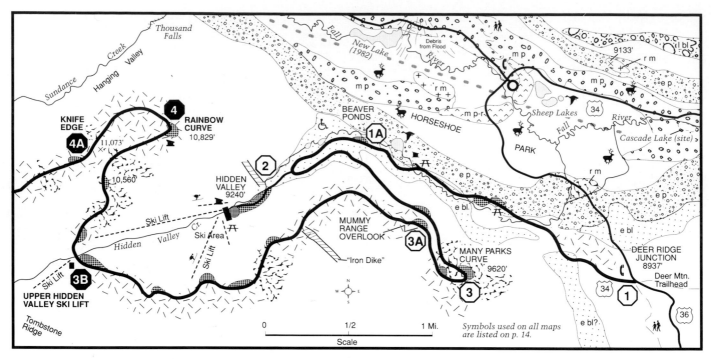

3B

MILE

6.9

Mileage to next point of interest:

(0.6)

UPPER HIDDEN VALLEY SKI LIFT.
El. 10,470 ft.
Parking areas on right on both sides of Hidden Valley Creek, which flows past the ski lift.

SCENERY:
—More chances to enjoy the huge, old, **subalpine** spruce-fir trees in the unburned parts of the forest.
—To the east are glimpses of Hidden Valley and Fall River Valley beyond.
—To the southwest is TOMBSTONE RIDGE, above **treeline.**

PLANTS:
—During June and July, water from melting snow cascades down the steep hillsides.
—Many **subalpine** plants thrive in this moist area. Along rock retaining walls are white brookcresses, yellow heart-leaf arnicas and blue larkspurs. Also growing are tall clumps of greenleaf chiming bells *(Mertensia ciliata),* called "blue medicine" by Cheyenne Indians who used it to treat smallpox and measles.
—The slopes are being revegetated.

WILDLIFE:
—Chickaree (gray) squirrels are common.
—Residents of the spruce-fir forests include snowshoe hares, jack rabbits, a few bobcats, coyotes, long-tailed weasels, woodrats ("packrats") and elusive martens and ermines.

HISTORY:
—The Estes Valley Recreation and Park District operates this lift during the ski season.

TWO MILES ABOVE SEA LEVEL.
El. 10,560 ft.
Parking area on right.

—Only a few aspens grow above this elevation.

GEOLOGY:
—Boards, rocks and logs were placed along the left roadbank to stabilize remnants of Early Bull Lake-age glacial debris.

MILE

7.5

Mileage to next point of interesst:

(0.6)

Greenleaf chiming bells.

Aerial view westward of Trail Ridge Road clearly shows the area burned during the 1915 Hidden Valley fire. Elevation of treeline is lower above the Hidden Valley ski lift because cold air flows down the valley. Classic ribbon forests grow on Tombstone Ridge at treeline. Forest Canyon separates Tombstone Ridge from the peaks of the Continental Divide on the skyline. (NPS)

Gray jay.   *Clarke's nutcracker.*   *Steller's jay.*

(Three photos, Chase Swift©)

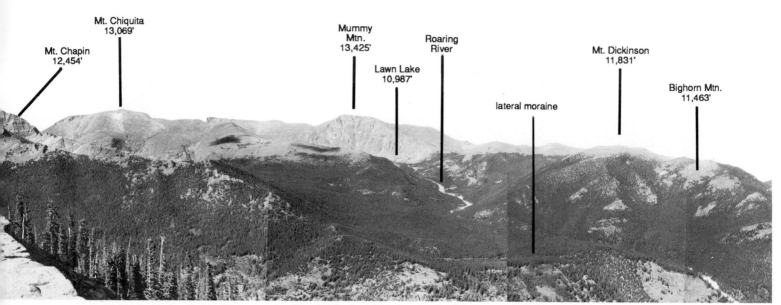

Mt. Chapin
12,454'

Mt. Chiquita
13,069'

Mummy
Mtn.
13,425'

Roaring
River

Lawn Lake
10,987'

lateral moraine

Mt. Dickinson
11,831'

Bighorn Mtn.
11,463'

Panoramic view eastward from Rainbow Curve.

RAINBOW CURVE.
El. 10,829 ft.

4

MILE

8.1

Mileage
to next
point of
interest:

(0.8)

Large parking area on right—on an
outside curve.
—Solar-powered RESTROOMS.

SCENERY:
—Panorama above identifies landscape
features.
—Summer showers often produce
rainbows in the eastern sky.
—Deer Mtn. is the flat-topped mountain
behind Hidden Valley.
—Objects on the Great Plains about 100
mi. away can be seen on clear days.
—To the northeast, the Lawn Lake
Flood scar is seen from a different
perspective than the viewpoints lower
on the mountain. Lawn Lake is just
above the trees at the top of the rock
debris.
—Directly below this overlook is
Hidden Valley and the south **lateral
moraine** that blocked the flow of
Hidden Valley Creek into Fall River
valley (labeled on panorama).

PHOTO HINTS:
—Best time for photos is morning and
late afternoon.

PLANTS:
—Below the overlook are more vistas of
the **subalpine** spruce-fir forest.

WILDLIFE:
—Least and Colorado chipmunks,
golden-mantled ground squirrels,
Clarke's nutcrackers, gray jays and
some Stellar's jays vie for your
attention and pose for photos.
—PLEASE, DO NOT FEED THE
WILDLIFE.

GEOLOGY:
—**Granite** in the roadcut is about 1.45
billion years old.
—Prominent **joints** (cracks) make this
rock easy to quarry. Rock retaining
walls along the road were built with
blocks from this cut and from a quarry
west of Toll Memorial (p. 44).

WEST OF RAINBOW CURVE WATCH FOR:

SCENERY:
—Mt. Chapin in the Mummy Range to
the north.
—SUNDANCE CIRQUE, a small cirque
at the head of Sundance Creek, photo,
p. 39.

PLANTS:
—Raspberry bushes and the Colorado
state flower, the blue columbine,
bloom along left edge of the road
during early July.

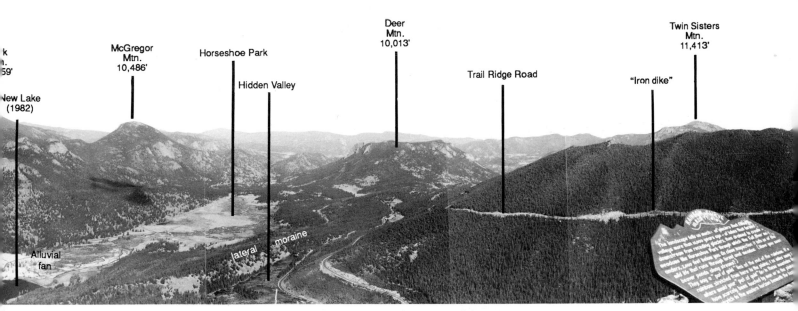

Panoramic view eastward from Rainbow Curve.

4A

MILE
8.9

Mileage
to next
point of
interest:

(1.2)

KNIFE-EDGE.
El. 11,073 ft.

Small parking area on right, just west of
the sharp, narrow divide between
Hidden Valley and Sundance Creeks.

*If this parking area is full, two more
small ones are on the right between
the KNIFE-EDGE and the OLD UTE
TRAIL CROSSING.*

SCENERY:
—Fire destroyed much of a very old
spruce-fir forest sometime before
1860.
—Ahead to the west are the first views
of **treeline** that averages about 11,400
ft. elevation at this latitude where
only **krummholz** forests of low,
crooked and gnarled spruces and firs
survive.
—These twisted, wind-whipped trees
mark the **forest-tundra transition zone**
where tall **subalpine** spruce-fir forests
are unable to grow.

PHOTO HINTS:
—Photos of gnarled, twisted, dead trees
can be dramatic, especially at sunrise,
sunset or during storms.

PLANTS:
—Isolated patches of an old spruce-fir
forest remain on both sides of the
ridge. This forest was burned in a pre-
1860 fire.
—Before the fire, the dense forest stood
straight and tall. Today, however,
Engelmann spruces, subalpine firs and
limber pines grow very slowly at this
elevation and are twisted and bent by
fierce winds. They grow best in the
shelter of rocks and fallen timber.
—The fire may have changed the local
climate because when trees are killed
or removed, wind and solar radiation
on the ground increase, thus
decreasing snow cover and soil
moisture.
—Alternatively, the change in the forest
may also be the result of cold weather
and climate during the second
advance of the **Arapaho Peak
Glaciation** which reached its
maximum between 1850 and 1870.
—Low, compact clumps of subalpine
willows (*Salix*) grow along the
roadsides. They are regularly pruned
by savage winds carrying ice and soil
particles.
—Purple fringes (*Phacelia sericea*)
bloom along the edge of the road in
July. They bloom earlier at lower
elevations and literally climb the
mountain as summer progresses.

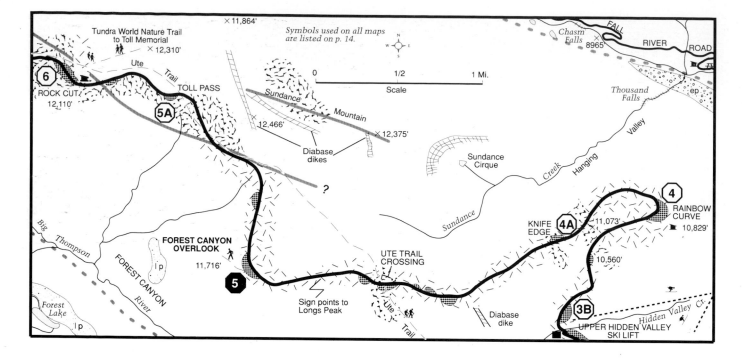

Symbols used on all maps are listed on p. 14.

MILE
10.1

Mileage
to next
point of
interest:

(0.5)

OLD UTE TRAIL CROSSING:
El. 11,440 ft.
Small parking area on left. This is a stop for the eastbound drive.

DO NOT CROSS DOUBLE-YELLOW LINE.

THINGS TO DO:
—A good hiking trail descends 3000 ft. in about 6.0 mi. to Upper Beaver Meadows. The trail leads along Tombstone Ridge to Timberline Pass and around Beaver Mtn. to the lower trailhead. Only one section is rough.

PLANTS:
—On the right are several dead **tree islands** that were alive as recently as the late 1970s.

HISTORY:
—Cairns, (piles of rocks used as markers) were built to guide early settlers, prospectors and tourists on horseback. Most have been removed and in some places the present trail diverges from the older one because it was rebuilt during the 1920s.
—Trail Ridge Road generally follows a route used for thousands of years by American Indians and their ancestors to cross the Front Range. These early visitors came to hunt deer, elk, bighorn sheep, bison and possibly, at an earlier time, for mammoths.

—Prehistoric people built a rock game-drive wall on a flat area along Tombstone Ridge, so that animals could be channeled into a small enclosure and easily killed.
—Three small rock-faced cabins stood against the hillside north of the highway from 1931 until the mid-1970s. One was used as a garage and two for emergency shelter for road-clearing crews and for Park Service research personnel doing high-altitude studies.

MILE
10.6

Mileage
to next
point of
interest:

(0.4)

SIGN POINTS TO LONGS PEAK.
El. 14,255 ft., 11 miles away as the crow flies.

On the slope above the road are several windblown spruce-fir **tree islands** at **treeline.**

Entering the **alpine life zone.** For the next 9 mi. the road is above **treeline,** which averages about 11,400 ft. at this latitude.

"Iron Dike" on south face of Mt. Chapin.

Sundance cirque.

Least chipmunk.

Golden-mantled ground squirrel.

(Becky Osterwald)

Purple fringe.

Shooting star.

Little red elephant.

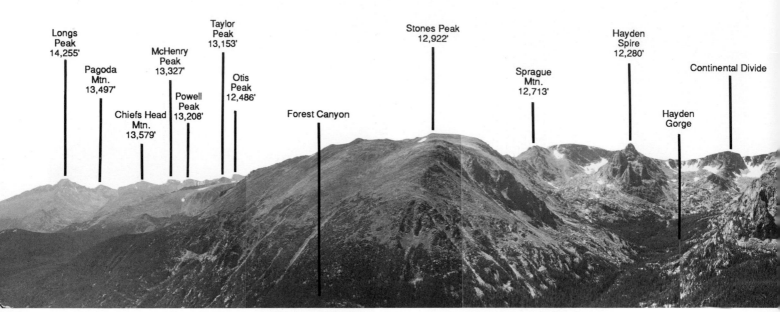

Longs Peak 14,255'
Pagoda Mtn. 13,497'
McHenry Peak 13,327'
Chiefs Head Mtn. 13,579'
Powell Peak 13,208'
Taylor Peak 13,153'
Otis Peak 12,486'
Forest Canyon
Stones Peak 12,922'
Sprague Mtn. 12,713'
Hayden Spire 12,280'
Continental Divide
Hayden Gorge

Panoramic view southward from Forest Canyon Overlook.

5

MILE

11.0

Mileage to next point of interest:

(1.3)

FOREST CANYON OVERLOOK.
El. 11,716 ft.

Use caution when turning left at entrance to large parking area.

REVIEW PRECAUTIONS CONCERNING ELECTRICAL STORMS, p. 262.

REMEMBER—THE AIR CONTAINS LESS OXYGEN AT HIGH ALTITUDES SO WALK SLOWLY AND CAREFULLY.

SCENERY:
—Panorama above identifies landscape features.
—Peaks of the Continental Divide on the southwestern skyline include STONES PEAK and TERRA TOMAH.
—Below the divide are HAYDEN GORGE, HAYDEN SPIRE and the GORGE LAKES.
—First views of the NEVER SUMMER MTNS. to the west.
—SUNDANCE MTN. is to the north.
—FOREST CANYON, below the overlook, was filled with thousands of feet of ice during each of the three major glaciations.
—This is one of best places to see how glaciers carved and sculpted the landscape.
—First chance to see how the land on the rolling, upland surface of Trail

Ridge has been reshaped by repeated cycles of freezing and thawing.

THINGS TO DO:
—Walk to the overlook to see awesome FOREST CANYON.
—PLEASE STAY ON THE PATH.
—Be careful not to drop any trash. Even a tissue dropped carelessly on a tundra plant will kill it.
—Signs explain glacial history and identify peaks.
—During the short summer this is a great place to see many alpine wildflowers.

PHOTO HINTS:
—Many photo possibilities at any time of the day, but lack of shadows at noonday may make the pictures appear flat.
—Even on cloudy and stormy days, dramatic photos are possible. Don't put your camera away.

PLANTS:
—This harsh, windswept, tree–less land is called **tundra**, a Lapp word that describes the vast tree–less areas of Arctic and Alpine regions.
—Because this area is swept by strong winds, little snow remains on the ground during winter.
—Plants that survive such a forbidding climate are low-growing mats or cushions; some have deep tap roots.
—These plant communities are small, complex and delicate.

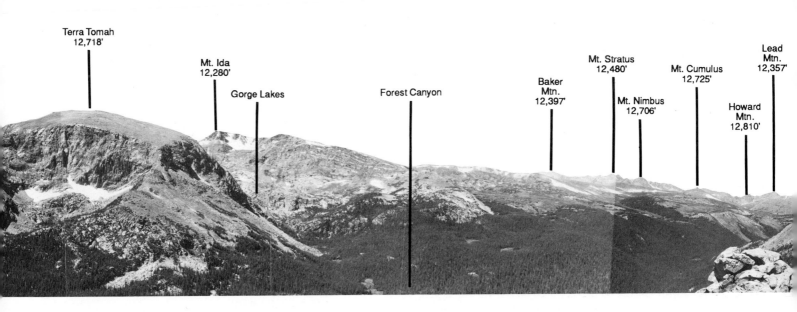

Terra Tomah
12,718'

Mt. Ida
12,280'

Gorge Lakes

Forest Canyon

Baker
Mtn.
12,397'

Mt. Stratus
12,480'

Mt. Nimbus
12,706'

Mt. Cumulus
12,725'

Howard
Mtn.
12,810'

Lead
Mtn.
12,357'

—Cushions of pink moss campions, three species of alpine clovers, white sandworts, alpine phlox and blue phlox, blue greenleaf chiming bells, sky pilots, white bistorts and yellow alpine avens are a few of the more than 100 species of sturdy wildflowers that bloom from late June until August.

—A test plot near the parking area was fenced in 1958 to study the recovery rate of tundra vegetation that was abused by visitors after this overlook was built in 1957. Hundreds of years may pass before the plants fully recover.

WILDLIFE:
—Pocket gophers burrow beneath the ground in search of food, mainly roots of plants. Signs of these animals are piles of loose, disturbed soil meandering through clumps of alpine plants along both sides of the path (photo p. 42).
—Yellow-bellied marmots.
—Pikas.
—Long-tailed and montane voles.
—Deer and elk sometimes are seen on distant hillsides.

GEOLOGY:
—Forest Canyon was filled with about 2000 feet of ice during Bull Lake Glaciation and probably with more ice during Pre-Bull Lake time. Later glaciations were less extensive because the climate was warmer.

—Examples of **cirques, horns, tarns, morainal lakes and U-shaped valleys** carved by the ancient Forest Canyon Glacier and its tributary glaciers are visible across the canyon in the peaks and valleys along the Continental Divide.
—Banded and layered **metamorphic** rocks are exposed on glaciated walls across the canyon.
—Forest Canyon follows an ancient **fault zone** (see map) that first moved about 1.4 billion years ago.
—Blocky **granite** boulders surround the parking area.

PERIGLACIAL FEATURES:
(Processes and topographic features formed near glaciers and former glaciers.)
—With repeated cycles of freezing and thawing, rocks near the surface are broken and thrust up out of the ground. The jumbled mantle of rocks and soil surrounding the parking area formed is this way. The processes are termed **frost heaving** or **up-freezing**.
—The ground <u>below</u> the layer exposed to freezing and thawing remained perennially frozen and is termed **permafrost**.
—Much of the **tundra** on Trail Ridge was underlain by permafrost during the Great Ice Ages. Permafrost still remains at a few places in the Front Range tundra.

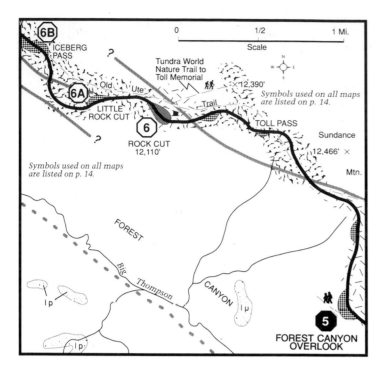

These rounded, meandering piles of soil around the larger rocks at Forest Canyon Overlook are filled burrows pushed up by northern pocket gophers. Gophers kill many tundra plants by eating the roots from their underground burrows.
(F. W. Osterwald)

—When thin, near-surface layers of rock and soil thaw during spring and summer, the soil particles become mixed with meltwater and flow downslope to form small ridges termed **solifluction terraces**.
—Many terraces cross the slopes of Sundance Mtn. to the north and at other places westward from this stop. Large ones are easy to find, especially in late summer, because plants on the terraces stay green.

HISTORY:
—STONES PEAK was named for G. M. Stone, a geology professor at Colorado College in Colorado Springs from 1881-1888. In the summer of 1886, while climbing with F. H. Chapin and William Hallett, he confirmed that actual flowing glaciers were in the Park.
—TERRA TOMAH MTN. was named by a group of Colorado Mountain Club members who were climbing in the Gorge Lakes area in 1914 and they came upon an unnamed lake. One member, an alum of Pomona College in California, sang out a portion of the school's yell, *"He ne terratoma"* and the climbers decided to give the small lake that name. But the Colorado Geographic Board misread the members' handwriting and assigned the name to the mountain. The words were from a

Cohuila Indian chant. The lake was later named Doughnut.
—In 1911, Abner Sprague (p. 130, 204) named HAYDEN SPIRE and JULIAN MTN. for Al and Julian Hayden while the three friends were on a fishing trip. The Hayden brothers then named the peak south of Hayden Spire, SPRAGUE MTN.
—MT. IDA appeared on the 1915 USGS map, but the source of the name is unknown.

MILE **12.3**

Mileage to next point of interest:

(0.3)

TOLL PASS.
El. 11,920 ft.
Parking area on left. This is a fine stop for the eastbound trip.

—During winter, snow drifts 30 to 40 ft. deep pile up on this small divide.
—An active **solifluction terrace** is left of the road.
—An active **nivation depression** (p. 47) is beside the road on the right.

MILE **12.6**

(0.5)

PARKING AREA on left.
This parking area is closed in mid-summer to protect tundra vegetation from hikers after a large snowbank on the hillside above the road melts.

Pika.

Yellow-bellied marmot.

(Both photos, Chase Swift©)

Aerial view southwestward in September 1986, showing the gently sloping surface of Terra Toma Mtn. on the left. Arrowhead and Inkwell Lakes are in the cirques. The Vasquez Mtns. near Berthoud Pass are on the distant skyline.   (F. W. Osterwald and J. B. Bennetti, Jr.)

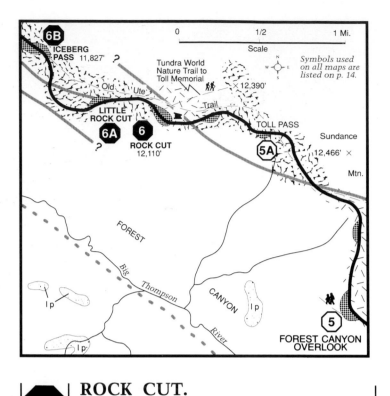

"After standing on the summit of an eternal peak and feeling the inspiring influence of its pictured and silent story, one will return to duty and live amid life's changing scenes more kindly and cheerfully than before."

——Enos A. Mills, <u>Rocky Mountain National Park</u>, Memorial Edition, 1932

6
MILE
13.1

Mileage to next point of interest:

(0.4)

ROCK CUT.
El. 12,110 ft.

Large parking area on both sides of the road.
—Solar-powered RESTROOMS.

SCENERY:
—Panoramas on p. 46-47 identify landscape features.
—More vistas of glaciated mountains along the Continental Divide to the southwest.
—Never Summer Mtns. to the west.
—TUNDRA CURVES and LAVA CLIFFS, near the highest point on Trail Ridge Road, are to the northwest.

THINGS TO DO:
—TUNDRA WORLD NATURE TRAIL starts at northwest end of parking area. The asphalt pathway climbs 200 ft. in 0.5 mi. to the TOLL MEMORIAL PEAK FINDER. The steepest part of the trail is near the parking area where it crosses the Old Ute Trail.
—The peak finder, at the top of the larger crag, honors Roger Toll, the third Superintendent of "Rocky", who served from 1921 to 1929. He vigorously promoted and helped design Trail Ridge Road.
—Signs along the trail identify and explain unique features of the tundra.
—Loose rocks on the ground along the trail are sorted into distinctive geometric forms and shapes, making

what is termed **patterned ground**, (photos p. 113 and 247). Many examples are close to the trail. **Precambrian granite** crops out along the trail, but the crags are **Precambrian metamorphic gneisses** and **schists** with several irregular dikes and pods of light-colored **igneous pegmatites.**
—Views from the crags are spectacular in all directions.
—Watch for pikas, marmots and the usual variety of birds.

PHOTO HINTS:
—Dramatic photos of many subjects are possible any time of the day.
—Telephoto lenses help bring the mountains closer.
—Macro lenses are useful for close-up photos of the tiny wildflowers.
—If you take close-ups, step on rocks— <u>NOT</u> on the plants.

PLANTS:
—Alpine wildflowers abound.
—The largest and most striking plant on the tundra is the bright yellow sunflower, old-man-of-the-mountain (*Hymenoxys grandiflora*). "Compass flower" might be another good name because the blossoms always face the rising sun.
—A fenced plot along the right side of the parking area is used to study the rate of recovery of tundra plants from countless footsteps. No new clumps

View eastward through Rock Cut during construction of Trail Ridge Road. This was the only place where blasting was needed. Logs were placed below the grade to keep any loose rocks from rolling down the slope. The lattice-work of poles shown on the right, was placed around the outcrop to protect rock surfaces and lichens during the blasting. *(NPS)*

Entering Rock Cut from the east. The tall poles along the road are placed every fall to guide snow-clearing crews next spring. The rocks are gneiss and schist.

of elk sedges *(Kobresia myosuroides)* have started to grow since the plot was fenced in 1959.

WILDLIFE:
—White-tailed ptarmigans live year-round on the tundra, especially in this area. Their summer plumage blends so well with the lichen-covered rocks, they are hard to find. Winter plumage is white.
—Brown-capped rosy finches, horned larks, water pipits and white-crowned sparrows nest on the tundra.
—American kestrals (sparrowhawks), prairie falcons, gray jays, Clarke's nutcrackers, western red-tailed hawks and ravens are frequent summer visitors.
—Pikas and yellow-bellied marmots are often seen along the parking area.
—Nine species of butterflies live on the tundra throughout their life cycles. Meade's sulfur and the gray variety of Phoebus parnassian have "solar collectors" on their wings and survive by converting solar radiation into heat.
—Foxes, coyotes, martens, mountain lions, deer, elk, and bighorn sheep are summer visitors to the tundra.

GEOLOGY:
—Outcrops are **schist** and **gneiss**. Some small **pegmatite dikes** cut through the **metamorphic** rock outcrops along the road.

PERIGLACIAL FEATURES:
—Above the rail fence and along the Tundra World Nature Trail, are spectacular examples of **rock circles, polygons, nets, garlands** and **stripes**. These distinctive arrangments of rocks and soil are called **patterned ground**.
—Illustrations of these interesting but strange features are on p. 113, 247 and 248.

HISTORY:
—Trail Ridge Road was carefully designed not to scar the landscape and to blend with nature.
—Minimum damage to the landscape by the equipment and crews is evident by how well the roadbed blends into the natural sites.
—Construction equipment included 5 gasoline-powered shovels, 3 roadgraders, 20 trucks and 8 horses. The contractor, W. A. Colt and Sons of Las Animas, Colorado, hired 6 foremen, 8 shovel operators, 5 cooks, 3 blacksmiths, 2 mechanics and 150 laborers to handle all construction.

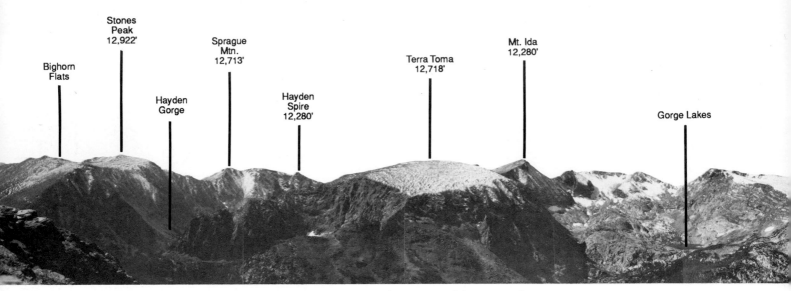

Bighorn
Flats

Stones
Peak
12,922'

Hayden
Gorge

Sprague
Mtn.
12,713'

Hayden
Spire
12,280'

Terra Toma
12,718'

Mt. Ida
12,280'

Gorge Lakes

Panoramic view southwestward from Rock Cut.

Oblique aerial view northwestward showing Trail Ridge Road, September 1986. The two parallel lines on the tundra surface are faults. Lava Cliffs are in the left center of the picture. The Old Fall River Road approaching Fall River Pass is in the right center. On the center skyline are the summits of the Snowy Range, Medicine Bow Peak and Centennial Ridge in Wyoming. The Never Summer Mtns. are on the left skyline. (F. W. Osterwald and J. B. Bennetti, Jr.).

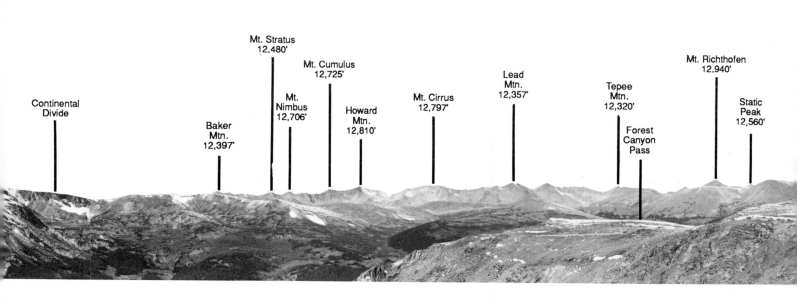

Continental Divide

Baker Mtn. 12,397'

Mt. Stratus 12,480'

Mt. Nimbus 12,706'

Mt. Cumulus 12,725'

Howard Mtn. 12,810'

Mt. Cirrus 12,797'

Lead Mtn. 12,357'

Tepee Mtn. 12,320'

Forest Canyon Pass

Mt. Richthofen 12,940'

Static Peak 12,560'

6A
MILE

13.6

Mileage to next point of interest:

(0.7)

LITTLE ROCK CUT.
El. 12,000 ft.
Parking area on the right along rail fence.

THINGS TO DO:
—During the early summer, a boardwalk leads to a large snowbank.
—After the snow melts, the boardwalk is removed to protect an active **nivation depression** (photos p. 110).
—Nivation depressions form where deep snowbanks accumulate. As the snow melts, soil-water mixtures flow from under the drifts like syrup or honey, leaving residues of rocks near the margins of the snow. Gradually the nivation depression is enlarged. If this process is carried far enough, a **cirque** may result.
—***Do not walk in the moist, boggy depression after the snow melts.***

SCENERY:
—Never Summer Mtns. are to the west.
—An opportunity to see more **periglacial features**.

PLANTS:
—Distinctive communities of alpine wildflowers grow where thick snowbanks 20 to 40 ft. thick cover the ground all winter.
—As the snowbanks melt, sedges and yellow snow buttercups bloom on the wet, boggy surfaces followed by tiny

yellow sibbaldias and snowlovers.
—By late July and August, white-flowered black-headed daisies bloom. The "black" heads are actually dark purple hairs on the undersides of the blossoms.

GEOLOGY:
—Outcrops of **schist** and **gneiss** break into angular, slab-like pieces as the ground freezes and thaws because of their layered structure. This contrasts with the way **granite** breaks into rough blocks.

6B
MILE

15.2

Mileage to next point of interest:

(0.5)

ICEBERG PASS.
El. 11,827 ft.
Large parking areas on each side of the road.

DO NOT CROSS DOUBLE-YELLOW LINE.

This divide, between Lava Cliffs to the northwest and the ridge of Rock Cut to the east, is blown free of snow most of the winter.

SCENERY:
—Tundra Curves and Lava Cliffs are to the northwest.
—Peaks of the Continental Divide are to the south and southeast.
—Never Summer Mtns. are to the west.
—MARMOT POINT, the rounded hill below the Mummy Range, and the Old Fall River Road are to the north.

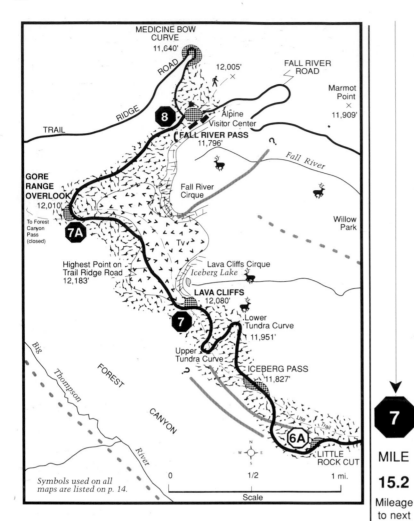

MEDICINE BOW
CURVE
11,640'

12,005' ×

FALL RIVER
ROAD

Marmot
Point
× 11,909'

8

Alpine
Visitor Center

FALL RIVER PASS
11,796'

Fall River

**GORE
RANGE
OVERLOOK**
12,010'

To Forest
Canyon
Pass
(closed)

7A

Fall River
Cirque

Willow
Park

Highest Point on
Trail Ridge Road
12,183'

Lava Cliffs Cirque
Iceberg Lake

LAVA CLIFFS
12,080'

7

Lower
Tundra Curve
11,951'

Upper
Tundra Curve

ICEBERG PASS
11,827'

Big Thompson

FOREST

CANYON

River

6A

Ute Trail

LITTLE
ROCK CUT

*Symbols used on all
maps are listed on p. 14.*

0   1/2   1 mi.

Scale

temperatures. These processes are still active in polar regions where the ground remains frozen because sunlight strikes the ground at very low angles in Arctic regions. The sun warms the ground surface much less than it does in Colorado where both temperatures and sun angles are much greater.

BEYOND ICEBERG PASS:

The road climbs 250 ft. on the beautiful, wide, sweeping TUNDRA CURVES. The scenery is breath-taking in all directions.

GEOLOGY:
—This area is an old **erosion surface** with deeper, and better drained soil than elsewhere on Trail Ridge.
—Plant cover also is much thicker and there are fewer loose, jumbled rocks on the surface than at previous stops.

LAVA CLIFFS.
El. 12,080 ft.

Large parking area on right at overlook.

SCENERY:
—First chance to look <u>down</u> into a glacial **cirque**.
—A small pond, called Iceberg Lake, is in the bottom of a rock basin quarried by former glaciers. The lake has become smaller in recent years, probably because ice within the glacial dam melted.
—Marmot Point, Old Fall River Road, Mount Chapin and the Mummy Range are to the north.
—To the west, the Never Summer Mtns. are much closer than they were at earlier stops.

PHOTO HINTS:
—Morning is the best time for photos into the cirque.

WILDLIFE:
—Brown-capped rosy finches, horned larks, swallows and ravens nest in the cracks and crevices of Lava Cliffs.
—Elk and deer frequent the valley below the overlook.

7

MILE

15.2

Mileage
to next
point of
interest:

(0.5)

—The rocky crags at the summit of Sundance Mtn. are to the east.

THINGS TO DO:
—A wide variety of wildflowers bloom from late June to August.
—<u>PLEASE</u> step on rocks if you walk away from the parking area to photograph the wildflowers and scenic beauty.
—See more changes in the landscape from cycles of freezing and thawing.

GEOLOGY:
PERIGLACIAL FEATURES:
—An active **solifluction terrace** (p. 49) with ponds is over the brow of the hill to the north where deep snow drifts pile up in winter.
—**Frost boils, hummocks, ponds** and **turf-banked terraces** (p. 247) are down the hill on both sides of the road.
—Processes that formed these periglacial features during the Ice Ages are now mostly dormant nearly everywhere on Trail Ridge because of less precipitation and warmer

Moss campion.

Alpine sandwort.

Alpine forget-me-not.

Alpine or fairy primrose.

Characteristic ground-hugging tundra flowers.

GEOLOGY:
—The vertical cliffs around the cirque are volcanic **welded ash-flow tuffs**.
—About 28 to 26 million years ago, a volcano in the Never Summer Mtns., about 8 mi. to the northwest, spewed red-hot glowing clouds of gas, rock fragments and ash which filled a broad, shallow valley in an old upland surface. The old surface also extended to Milner Pass and La Poudre Pass.
—After cooling, the explosive volcanic material compacted into the welded ash-flow tuffs seen here and in roadcuts to the west.
—Later, water and glacial ice eroded away most of the ash-flow tuffs, leaving only small patches today (map and photo, p. 107).

BEYOND LAVA CLIFFS WATCH FOR:

GEOLOGY:
—Rusty-red rocks in the roadcut 0.1 mi. west of Lava Cliffs were created when the hot volcanics settled on ancient **Precambrian schists**. Heat from the volcanics baked and altered iron-bearing minerals in the schist to **hematite**, a red iron-oxide mineral.
—There are no stopping places to see these features unless one walks from the Lava Cliffs parking area (photos p. 108).

PERIGLACIAL FEATURES:
—On the open, rounded slopes above Lava Cliffs are more examples of freeze-thaw processes at work. These are best seen on the eastbound drive.

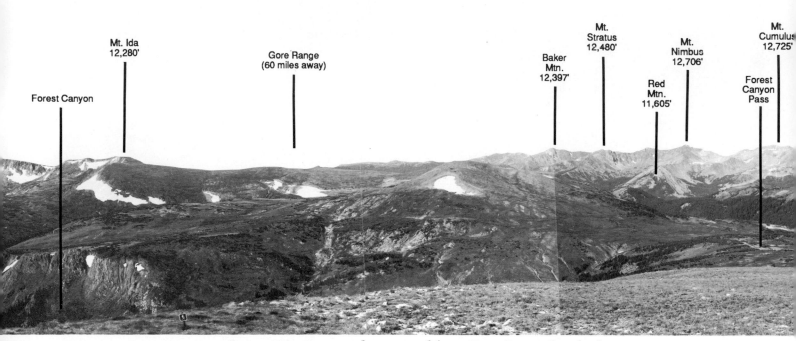

Forest Canyon

Mt. Ida
12,280'

Gore Range
(60 miles away)

Baker
Mtn.
12,397'

Mt.
Stratus
12,480'

Red
Mtn.
11,605'

Mt.
Nimbus
12,706'

Forest
Canyon
Pass

Mt.
Cumulus
12,725'

Panoramic view southwestward from Gore Range Overlook.

MILE

15.7

(0.5)

HIGHEST POINT ON TRAIL RIDGE ROAD.
El. 12,183 ft.
__No place to stop__.

7A

GORE RANGE OVERLOOK.
El. 12,010 ft.

MILE

16.2

Mileage
to next
point of
interest:

(1.0)

BE CAREFUL WHEN TURNING LEFT INTO the PARKING AREA.

This overlook gets the full force of strong westerly winds that sweep across the Never Summer Mts. and assault the western end of Trail Ridge.

Summertime gusts of 79 mph have been measured. The temperature is also cooler than at lower elevations because air cools from 3 to 5 degrees for every 1000 ft. increase in altitude.

SCENERY:
—Panorama above identifies landscape features.
—GORE RANGE is 60 mi. to the southwest.
—Peaks of Continental Divide.
—Forest Canyon Pass is below the overlook.
—Never Summer Mtns .are to the west.
—MEDICINE BOW MTNS. in Wyoming are to the north.

HISTORY:
—The old Ute Trail descended past here to the Kawuneeche Valley and the Colorado River but is closed from this point to Forest Canyon Pass for revegetation.
—Parts of the old trail used by miners, traders, hunters and early tourists on horseback are now closed to hiking because some of the steep slopes are severely eroded.
—The Gore Range was named for Scottish baronet Sir St. George Gore. In 1854 he led a notorious three-year hunting expedition from Ft. Laramie, Wyoming, southwestward into North and Middle Parks (Colorado). He tried to cross Gore Pass but was stopped by a band of Gros Ventre Indians, so the expedition returned to Wyoming.
—Gore's entourage included his fancy yellow-wheeled carriage, 21 two-wheeled, Red River carts, 4 Conestoga wagons, 2 large freight wagons, a fur-lined commode and a portable bathtub.

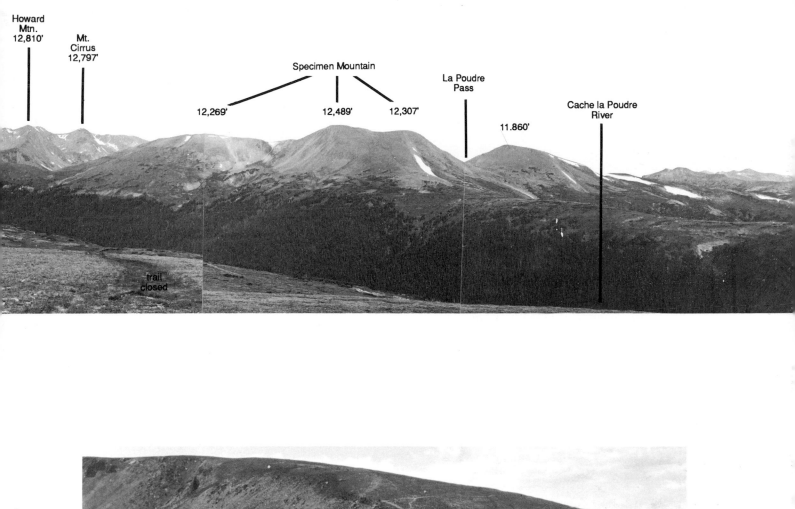

Howard
Mtn.
12,810'

Mt.
Cirrus
12,797'

Specimen Mountain

12,269'   12,489'   12,307'

La Poudre
Pass

Cache la Poudre
River

11.860'

trail
closed

Fall River Pass has been a popular stopping place since the first road (the Old fall River Road) was built. This picture probably was taken about 1930.   *(NPS)*

Lava Cliffs and Lava Cliffs cirque .

Both pictures were taken June 16, 1978 following a severe winter with many heavy snowstorms.

Visitor Center at Fall River Pass.

8

MILE

17.2

ALPINE VISITOR CENTER and TRAIL RIDGE STORE at FALL RIVER PASS.

El. 11,796 ft.
Entrance on right.
—RESTROOMS.

SCENERY:
—Don't miss the views into Fall River Cirque and Fall River Canyon to the east from the overlook between the two buildings.
—Mt. Chapin and the Mummy Range are to the east and northeast.
—From the lower end of the parking area are views toward SPECIMEN MTN., MILNER PASS and the Never Summer Mtns.
—Medicine Bow Mtns. are on the northern skyline.

THINGS TO TO:
—VISITOR CENTER has a small museum devoted to the **alpine tundra**.
—Naturalists are on duty to answer questions.
—Books and maps for sale.

—TRAIL RIDGE STORE has a lunch counter, and a fine collection of authentic Indian souvenirs, as well as books, film, gifts and general souvenirs.
—Near Trail Ridge Store, a steep 0.4 mi. trail climbs about 200 ft. to a scenic overlook. Visitors are rewarded with magnificent mountain vistas in all directions. Fall River Cirque is to the south, the Mummy Range is to the north and northwest and Medicine Bow Mtns. in Wyoming are to the north.
—Along the trail are several white masses of **pegmatite** with large **crystals** of **albite**, **microcline**, **quartz** and **mica**.

HISTORY:
—Fall River Pass is on one of six ancient trans-mountain Indian trails in the Park. Many other trails crossed the Front Range outside Park boundaries.
—Since 1920 when the Old Fall River Road was completed from Estes Park to Fall River Pass and on to Grand Lake, this has been a favorite stop for travelers.

***To return to Estes Park,
follow the Trail Ridge Eastbound, Part 2 Guide, p. 103.
To reach Grand Lake,
follow the Trail Ridge Westbound, Part 2 Guide, p. 53.***

TRAIL RIDGE ROAD WESTBOUND

Part 2.—Fall River Pass to Kawuneeche Visitor Center.

Panoramic view westward of Specimen Mountain and the Never Summer Mountains from the Alpine Visitor Center at Fall River Pass, July 1987.

"The high rugged peaks are set with lovely spaces, primeval forest, scattered groves and eternal snowfields: the mountain slopes and intervening valleys are splendidly adorned with spruce, great pines and restless aspens."

——Enos A. Mills, <u>Rocky Mountain National Park</u>, Memorial Edition,1932

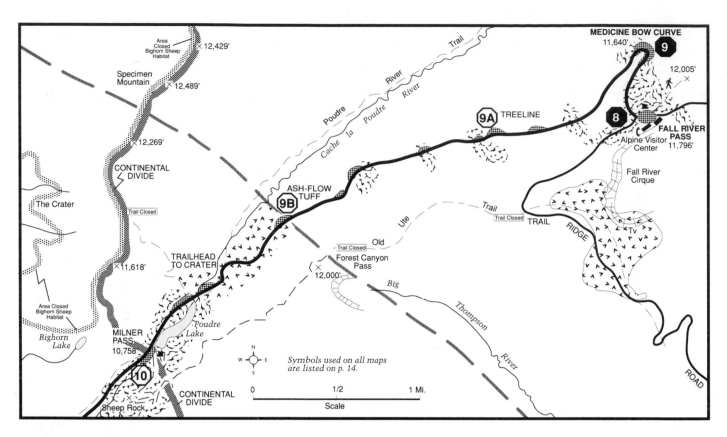

8

MILE

0.0

Mileage to next point of interest:

(0.4)

ALPINE VISITOR CENTER and TRAIL RIDGE STORE at FALL RIVER PASS.
El. 11,796 ft.

Set your odometer at 0.0 or write down your mileage at the parking area exit and follow U.S. 34 west toward Grand Lake.

The road descends 3,400 ft. in elevation between here and Grand Lake.

SCENERY:
—At the parking area exit, SPECIMEN MTN. and the NEVER SUMMER MTNS. are directly ahead on the skyline (panorama p.53).

HISTORY:
—The first road between Fall River Pass and the floor of the KAWUNEECHE VALLEY was surveyed in 1912 by Frank L. Huntington, Grand County Surveyor (map, p. 63). Construction started in 1913 and by 1918 had reached MILNER PASS. In 1920, the road reached Fall River Pass.
—When Trail Ridge Road was completed in 1932, the route from Fall River Pass to Milner Pass was redesigned. Traces

of that first road are still visible on the **tundra**[1] slopes below the exit from the Visitor Center parking area, and on the slope above STOP 9.

HISTORY:
—The road descends into CACHE LA POUDRE RIVER VALLEY, which was so named because in November, 1836 some French trappers buried ("cached") their supplies including a supply of gun powder somewhere along the river. The next spring they returned and dug up their "cache of powder" and supplies.
—The Stewart Toll Road between Grand Lake and Ft. Collins was started in 1880. It crossed La Poudre Pass and went down Cache la Poudre River valley. This primitive wagon road was rebuilt as far as Squeaky Bob's Place in the Kawuneeche Valley (p. 73) in the early 1900s.

---

[1]Terms in bold-face type are defined in the Glossary, p. 256.

View northward of the original dirt road between Milner Pass and Fall River Pass, probably in 1920 or 1921.

Aerial view west-northwestward cross the Cache la Poudre Valley showing Specimen Mountain, the Never Summer Mountains on the middle skyline and North Park in the distance. The Medicine Bow Mountains are beyond North Park.   *(U.S. Forest Service)*

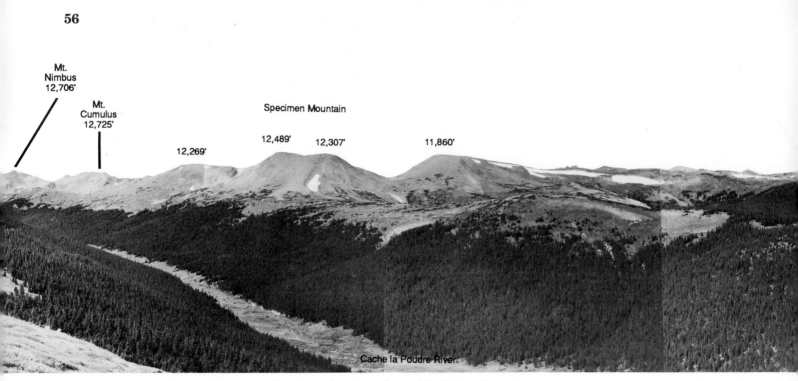

Mt. Nimbus 12,706'
Mt. Cumulus 12,725'
Specimen Mountain
12,489'
12,307'
12,269'
11,860'
Cache la Poudre River

Panoramic view from Medicine Bow Curve.

MEDICINE BOW CURVE.

9

MILE
0.4

Mileage to next point of interest:

(1.2)

EL. 11.640. Parking area on right at a switchback.

SCENERY:
—Panorama above identifies landscape features.
—Cache la Poudre River valley is below the parking area.
—Never Summer Mtns. are west and southwest of the overlook.
—Specimen Mtn., with its three rounded summits, is directly west across the valley.
—MEDICINE BOW PEAK (62 miles away), CENTENNIAL RIDGE AND THE LARAMIE BASIN in Wyoming to are to the north.
—The rocky crags at Fall River Pass Overlook are on the eastern skyline.
—Mummy Range is to the east and northeast.

PHOTO HINTS:
—Best time for photos to the west is in the morning.

PLANTS:
—A dramatic view of the irregular **treeeline** along the southeastern side of the Cache la Poudre Valley is beyond this stop. This is the **forest-tundra transition life zone of krummholz** (crooked wood) forests.

Because species of both zones overlap, a great variety of plants grows here.
—Tundra plants include mountain dryads *(Dryas octopetala)*, a creeping dwarf shrub with cream-colored 8-petaled flowers, whose plume-like seeds wave in the wind during August.
—Yellow alpine avens, western yellow paintbrushes and white bistorts also are abundant.

WILDLIFE:
—Herds of elk or deer may be browsing in the open meadows above **treeline** on the opposite slope to the west.

GEOLOGY:
—During both Bull Lake and Pinedale Glaciations, ice was so thick in the Colorado River glacier that it overflowed northeastward across Milner Pass to carve the broad, flattend U-shaped Cache la Poudre River valley below.

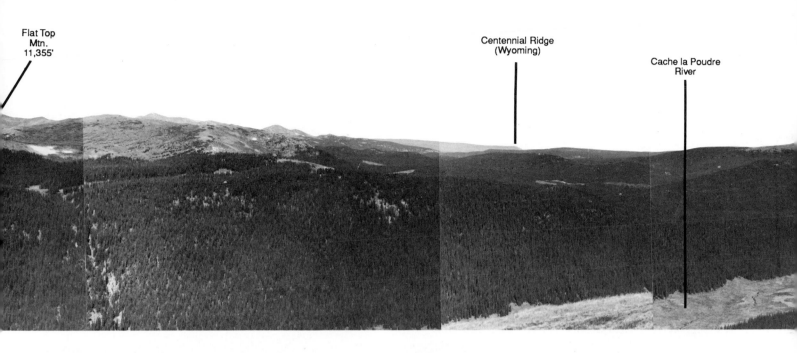

Flat Top
Mtn.
11,355'

Centennial Ridge
(Wyoming)

Cache la Poudre
River

Globe flower.

Marsh marigold.

Rose crown.

Kings crown.

Common subalpine wildflowers that grow in moist areas.

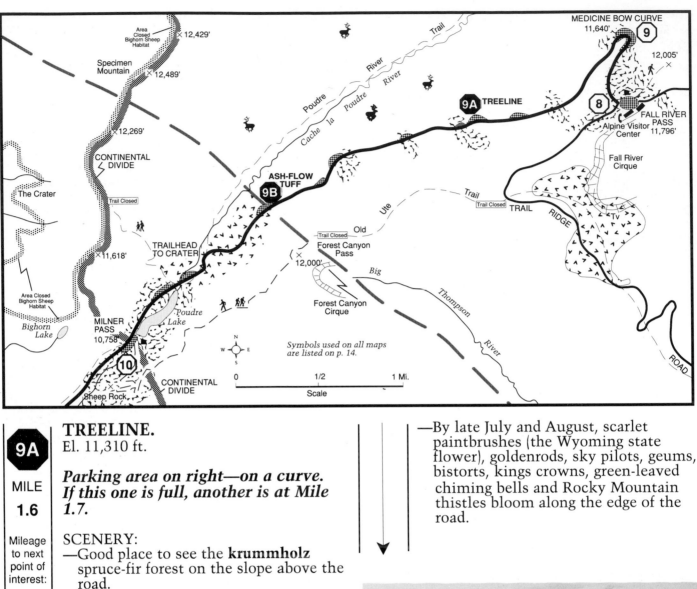

9A MILE **1.6**

Mileage to next point of interest: **(1.5)**

TREELINE.
El. 11,310 ft.

Parking area on right—on a curve. If this one is full, another is at Mile 1.7.

SCENERY:
—Good place to see the **krummholz** spruce-fir forest on the slope above the road.

PLANTS:
—Elevation of **treeline** varies according to wind direction and speed, snow depth, angle of slope, and the angle at which sunlight strikes the ground.
—Spruces and firs, which grow straight and tall at lower elevations, are gnarled and twisted by fierce winds, as they battle to survive in the severe Alpine climate by growing closely together in "islands" of dwarfed trees.
—Precipitation on the western side of the Continental Divide is about 6 in. more than on the eastern slope and more water is available for plants. Wildflowers grow profusely on these subalpine slopes.
—When the snow melts in June and early July, white marsh marigolds and cream-colored globeflowers bloom first, followed by yellow alpine avens and paintbrushes.

—By late July and August, scarlet paintbrushes (the Wyoming state flower), goldenrods, sky pilots, geums, bistorts, kings crowns, green-leaved chiming bells and Rocky Mountain thistles bloom along the edge of the road.

View southwestward from Medicine Bow Curve, STOP 9 showing the Never Summer Mtns. on the skyline, Cache la Poudre River valley, and the irregular treeline on the west-facing slope.

9B

MILE

3.1

Mileage to next point of interest:

(0.7)

ASH-FLOW TUFF OUTCROPS.
El. 10,920 ft.
Small parking area on right.

GEOLOGY:
—Light gray to cream-colored **welded ash-flow tuffs** crop out in roadcuts opposite the parking area.
—They were deposited 28 to 26 million years ago when a violently explosive volcano in the Never Summer Mtns. spewed unsorted, fine-grained, hot, gaseous, nearly molten rock debris, filling an old, shallow valley with fine-grained rock.
—These rocks partially buried some older volcanic rocks in the lower part of Specimen Mtn. (directly west) and in the Never Summer Mtns. The older volcanics are 55 to 54 million years old.

PLANTS:
—This stop is in the **subalpine life zone** which extends from about 9000 ft. to **treeline**.
—Dominant trees are Engelmann spruces and subalpine firs. Use key on p. 253 to identify the trees along the parking area.
—Ground cover in spruce-fir forests includes tiny blueberry shrubs. Many birds and mammals (including humans) enjoy the sweet berries. They are a favorite of the few black bears that live in the Park.

WILDLIFE:
—The climate in **subalpine** spruce-fir forests is cool and moist because the winter snows are deep and melt slowly. The short growing season limits the amount of food produced.
—This in turn limits the number of animals and birds that live in these forests.
—Chickaree (red) squirrels scold and chatter if you enter their territory. They collect pine cones into large piles, called **middens.**
—Deer mice, least chipmunks, southern red-backed voles and pine martens live here and frequently raid the squirrels' middens.
—Deer and elk feed in forest openings.
—Birds include blue grouse, gray jays, woodpeckers, pine siskins, Clarke's nutcrackers, mountain chickadees, white breasted and pygmy nuthatches, yellow-rumped warblers and ruby-crowned kinglets.

MILE

3.8

(0.1)

—Goshawks and western red-tailed hawks hunt small birds and mammals.

CROSS CACHE LA POUDRE RIVER.
El.10,725 ft.

—The headwaters of Cache la Poudre River—here just a small creek ("crick" to local old-timers) is Poudre Lake.
—This small stream becomes a major river by the time it joins the South Platte River near Greeley, Colorado.

MILE

3.9

Mileage to next point of interest:

(0.4)

TRAILHEAD to the CRATER.
El. 10,740 ft. Parking area on right.

THINGS TO DO:
—To view the Crater, a topographic depression on the southwestern flank of Specimen Mtn., follow the steep trail 0.6 mi. northwestward. Beyond the Crater, the trail is closed to hikers to protect the habitat of bighorn sheep.
—The POUDRE RIVER TRAIL begining at Poudre Lake descends about 1000 ft. in 9.3 mi. to Long Draw. Parts of the trail cross wet, marshy ground.

PLANTS:
—Many **subalpine** wildflowers grow around Poudre Lake and on the open grassy slope above the parking area.
—During July, tall chiming bells, rosy paintbrushes, arrow-leaved groundsels, stiff, dark-headed sages, Drummond's rushes and little red elephants are easy to find—and to photograph.
—Spikes of bistort wave in the wind like tufts of white to light-pink cottonballs. Blackfoot and Cheyenne Indians used the starchy bistort roots in soups and stews. When roasted, the roots have a sweet, nutty flavor. They are also a favorite food of bears and rodents.

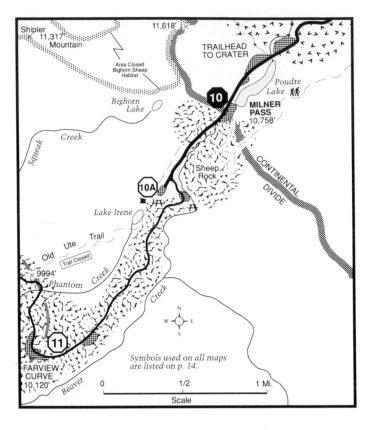

Indian paintbrush, the Wyoming State Flower, in close detail.

CONTINENTAL DIVIDE at top of MILNER PASS.
El. 10,758 ft.

10

MILE

4.3

Mileage to next point of interest:

(0.5)

Use caution when turning left into large parking area.
—RESTROOMS.

SCENERY:
—Normally the Continental Divide is thought of as a sharp, high ridge that divides water so that it flows either eastward or westward.
—Here, the low hillside behind the marker sign is the Continental Divide. Poudre Lake is on the eastern slope; its water begins a long trip to the Mississippi River and the Gulf of Mexico. Southwest of the hill, Beaver Creek begins its long westward journey down the Continental Divide to the Gulf of California.
—Poudre Lake is to the northeast.
—Sheep Rock is on the southern skyline.

THINGS TO DO:
—A trail climbs 740 ft. in about 2 mi. along part of the Old Fall River Road and ends at Forest Canyon Pass.

GEOLOGY:
—The low hill behind the marker sign is glacial debris that a Middle Pinedale-age glacier deposited between 50,000 and 35,000 years ago.
—The Colorado River Glacier, the largest in the Park, extended almost 20 mi. from an elevation of 12,000 ft. near the Continental Divide north of LULU CITY (p. 69, 227), to about 8400 ft. at the south end of SHADOW MTN. RESERVOIR south of Grand Lake.
—Glacial ice, about 2,000 ft. thick, filled the Kawuneeche Valley and left only the tops of peaks exposed on each side. Because of its great depth, ice over-flowed northeastward across Milner Pass and down the Cache la Poudre valley. The ice smoothed and polished the southwest side of SHEEP ROCK which juts up in the middle of the valley just south of the parking area. At the same time, ice quarried rock from the northeast side of Sheep Rock, leaving it rough and jagged. Sheep Rock is a classic **roche moutonnèe** (photos, p. 62, 96).

Yellow lady slipper orchid.

Fairy slipper orchid.

Wood lily.

View northward of Poudre Lakes from Stop 10 at Milner Pass, September 1988. Fall colors were softened by deepening smoke from huge forest fires in Yellowstone National Park

Remains of a large mudflow at the edge of the meadow at Specimen Mtn. Trailhead. The "skirts" around some of the conifers growing on the light-colored mudflow are created by heavy snows pressing down the lower branches which then begin to take root.
(F. W. Osterwald)

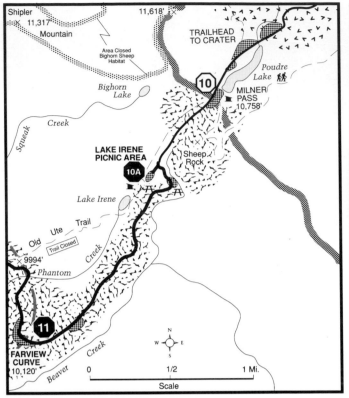

The southwestern end of Sheep Rock from Lake Irene Picnic Area. The glacial ice flowed northeastward over this surface rounding and smoothing it.

10A
MILE 4.8

Mileage to next point of interest:

(1.8)

LAKE IRENE PICNIC AREA.
El. 10,650 ft. Entrance on right.
—RESTROOMS.

SCENERY:
—The rounded, smoothed southwestern side of Sheep Rock is best seen from the picnic area.

THINGS TO DO:
—Great picnic area in a beautiful **subalpine** spruce-fir and lodgepole pine forest. Identify the different trees using the key on page 253.
—Lake Irene, a short distance down the hill to the southwest, is the source of PHANTOM CREEK. The lake formed behind a small landslide from a Middle Pinedale-age moraine.

WILDLIFE:
—Clarke's nutcrackers, gray juncos, western mule deer, chipmunks and ground squirrels.
—DO NOT FEED THE WILDLIFE. It is against Park regulations because it causes them to become over-abundant and unable to adapt to wild conditions.
—Bighorn sheep frequent the area around Sheep Rock.

PLANTS:
—Marsh marigolds and globeflowers bloom in the wet meadow beyond the building in June and early July.
—Ramshorn louseworts, Whipple's penstemons, alpine goldenrods, pearly everlastings, Jacobs ladders and fireweeds are among many flowers that bloom during July.
—Fireweed *(Epilobium angustifolium)* is common throughout the Park from July until frost. It is valuable forage for deer and elk. The pink to magenta-colored blossoms grow on tall spikes. It is one of the first plants to grow on disturbed soils and burned areas, hence the name.

HISTORY:
—The Ute Trail into the Kawuneeche Valley passed Lake Irene but it is now closed below the lake.
—Before the Old Fall River Road between Grand Lake and Estes Park was completed in 1920, many tourists followed the trail on foot or horseback.
—Lake Irene was named by Squeaky Bob Wheeler (p. 69) for a guest at his dude ranch in the Kawuneeche Valley.
—In 1926 a mess hall, residence and stable were built here for road crews. A bunkhouse, built in 1930, was the only building still standing in 1988.

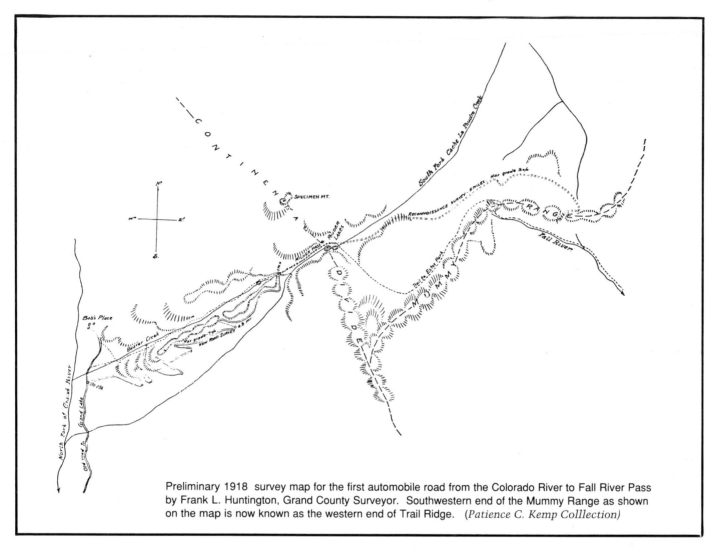

Preliminary 1918 survey map for the first automobile road from the Colorado River to Fall River Pass by Frank L. Huntington, Grand County Surveyor. Southwestern end of the Mummy Range as shown on the map is now known as the western end of Trail Ridge. *(Patience C. Kemp Colllection)*

Lake Irene in 1891. Little evidence remains today of the fire that destoyed this forest in 1871. The hill on the left is a Middle Pinedale -age moraine. (NPS)

In 1929 the road just east of Farview Curve looked like this. The rock outcrop on the hill was called Indian Head Rock. (Dunn, NPS)

Panoramic view westward from Farview Curve.

BEYOND LAKE IRENE:

The road descends the northwest side of Beaver Creek Valley to Farview Curve.

GEOLOGY:
—**Precambrian metamorphic gneisses** and **schists** crop out in roadcuts from here to Grand Lake Entrance Station.
—Loose, rounded boulders, cobbles and gravels litter the bedrock surfaces above many roadcuts—evidence that glaciers once passed this way.

11

MILE

6.6

Mileage to next point of interest:

(0.2)

FARVIEW CURVE.
El. 10,120 ft.

Please be careful when turning across traffic into the parking area on the left. It is on a sharp, blind curve.

SCENERY:
—Panorama, p 92-93, identifies landscape features.
—Never Summer Mtns. are directly west. The reddish rocks near the summits result from oxidation and alteration of metallic minerals.
—The Kawuneeche Valley of the Colorado River is below the overlook.
—The GRAND DITCH, the second oldest water diversion project in northern Colorado, winds along upper slopes across the valley.
—VASQUEZ MTNS. near Berthoud Pass are about 36 miles away on the southern skyline.
—JACKSTRAW MTN. (p. 95) is on the skyline east of the upper end of the parking area.

PHOTO HINTS:
—Best time for photos of the mountains to the west is in the morning.

WILDLIFE:
—Clarke's nutcrackers, gray jays, chipmunks and ground squirrels may greet your arrival at the overlook.

Building retaining walls for the road about 3/10 mi. east of Farview Curve, Stop 11. (NPS)

Ruins of prospector Hitchens cabin; Hitchens Gulch was named for him. August 14, 1958.   (NPS)

Site of Dutchtown, a small mining camp in the Never Summer Mtns. near the Continental Divide, August 14, 1958.   (NPS)

ADDITIONAL HISTORICAL NOTES

The Arapaho Indians called the Never Summer Mtns. *"Ni-chebe-chii"* which means "never no summer," an appropriate name because winter snows melt very slowly. The Arapahos called the Kawuneeche Valley *"Haquihana,"* meaning "valley of the wolves." Early non-Indian settlers called it simply the "North Fork Valley." About 1915 the Colorado Geographic Board changed the name to "Kawuneeche" for the Arapaho word,*"cawoonache," w*hich means coyote, even though "coyote" does not equal "wolf" even in English. The Geographic Board believed "Kawuneeche" was easier for non-Indians to pronounce.

The Colorado River was originally named the Blue River by very early trappers and traders. Later the name Grand River came into use, because some lost Mexicans thought they had reached the Rio Grande, not realizing they were on the wrong river.

THE GRAND DITCH:

In 1891, The Water Supply and Storage Company was incorporated to build a series of ditches, canals and reservoirs to collect water on the eastern slope of the Never Summer Mtns. and move it by gravity across the Continental Divide to the Cache la Poudre River and down to the plains to irrigate fields near Loveland and Ft. Collins, Colorado.

Chinese, Japanese and Mexican laborers did the early construction by hand, earning 22.5 cents per hour, from which 25 cents was deducted for each meal. Men lived in crude ditch camps strung out along the route.

When tons of snow had to be shoveled from the ditch each spring so water could start flowing toward the plains, the workers were often ill-equipped and poorly clothed.

Subsequently the ditch was extended south from Dutch Creek to Bakers Gulch in 1934, using heavy equipment for the first time.

The scar from construction remains unhealed for several reasons. Most of it was dug through loose, unsorted glacial debris in the tree-covered **lateral moraine**. At several places, where the ditch crosses hard **Precambrian** rocks, construction spoil was dumped down the steep hillsides below the ditch. Vegetation is slow to return in such areas. In past years during the spring ditch cleaning, rocks and soil also were merely dumped over the edge of the ditch.

The Grand Ditch is on the National Register of Historic Places.

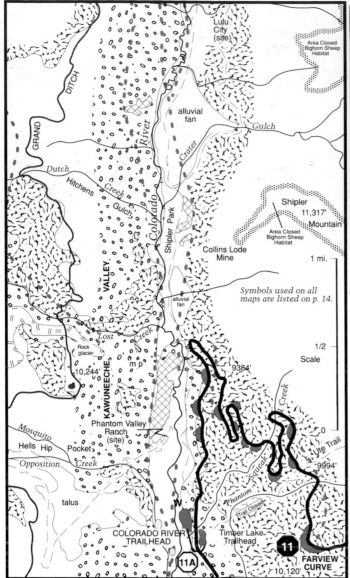

Aerial view southwestward of the Grand Ditch and the beautiful U-shaped side valleys and cirques near Bowen Mtn. *(Alcorn and Marold, U.S. Forest Service)*

PLANTS:
—Lodgepole pines *(Pinus contorta* var. *latifolia)* are the most common conifer in the Kawuneeche Valley. The tall slender trees with straight pole-like trunks are easy to identify because their needles are yellow-green color. Plains Indians used lodgepole trunks as poles to support their lodges (tepees).
—Lodgepole pines grow quickly in dense forests which have little undergrowth because little sunlight reaches the forest floor. This in turn attracts few mammals and birds. because food supplies are reduced.
—Forest fires open the forests, burn away the undergrowth and leave bare soils on which lodgepole pine seeds can easily sprout in full sunlight.
—Lodgepole cones, if not destroyed by fire, open up and release their seeds

when heated to temperatures between 113° and 122° F. which are then spread by winds, birds and mammals.

GEOLOGY:
—The Kawuneeche Valley is a large down-dropped **fault block**. Hot solutions deposited small mineral-bearing **veins** in some of these **faults**.
—This valley was V-shaped long before the Colorado River Glacier carved it into its present U-shape. The original V-shape was the result of the river rapidly eroding its channel into the weakened rocks along the north-trending **faults** of the valley. As the glacier retreated it partially filled the valley floor with rock debris, reducing the slope so that it is too gentle for the modern river to flow directly down-valley. This makes the river wander (meander) back and forth across the valley floor. Some of its meanders have been cut off where the river decided to take short cuts, forming **oxbow lakes**.

BETWEEN FARVIEW CURVE and GRAND LAKE:

The highway descends about 1,100 ft. in a series of switchbacks to the floor of the Kawuneeche Valley. The road winds through **upper montane** zone forest containing mostly lodgepole pines.

Much of the Grand Ditch was dug by men using picks, shovels and a few horses.   (NPS)

Primitive camp cabins along the Grand Ditch.   (NPS)

MILE **6.8** Mileage to next point of interest: **(0.1)**	**RHYOLITE PORPHYRY in ROADCUT on right.** ***There is no place to stop.*** GEOLOGY: —Dark brown, very fine-grained **rhyolite porphyry** was injected as molten rock into a **fault** in the surrounding **schists** during the Miocene Epoch between 24 and 5.3 million years ago. —Later, the rocks were faulted again and hot, mineral-bearing solutions deposited **quartz** and iron oxide minerals along the **faults**. —Just beyond the **rhyolite** outcrop, very soft, light-colored clay-like material crops out in another roadcut. This was once solid rock, but it was crushed and ground up by movements along the **faults** and was changed by circulating hot water. Such soft, fine-grained rock material is called **fault gouge**.
MILE **6.9** **(0.6)**	**CROSS PHANTOM CREEK.** El. 10,020 ft. The stream flows southwest from Lake Irene.
MILE **7.5** **(0.2)**	**CROSS SQUEAK CREEK.** El. 9,870 ft. Bighorn Lake above Milner Pass is the source of Squeak Creek.

MILE **7.7** **(0.4)**	**GABIONS on the hillside to the left.** ***No stopping place.*** —Heavy steel-wire baskets, filled with rocks, were placed above the steep roadcut to stabilize loose glacial debris which otherwise would move downward under the weight of snow in small avalanche tracks. —As soil and seeds are blown or washed onto the gabions, plants start to grow, further stabilizing the slope. —Gabions were first used in Europe and since have come into use in North America.
MILE **8.1** **(1.4)**	**CROSS SQUEAK CREEK.** El. 9700 ft.
MILE **9.5** **(0.9)**	**NORTHERN-MOST SWITCHBACK.** El. 9320 ft.
MILE **10.4** Mileage to next point of interest: **(0.3)**	**FAULT ZONE.** El. 9090 ft. GEOLOGY: —Beside a small, narrow parking area on the right, **schist** was broken up by movement along another small **fault**. Later the broken rock was altered to yellow-brown, soft, crumbly, iron-rich **fault gouge**. —Across the road on the left is Middle Pinedale-age glacial debris that is between 50,000 and 35,000 years old.

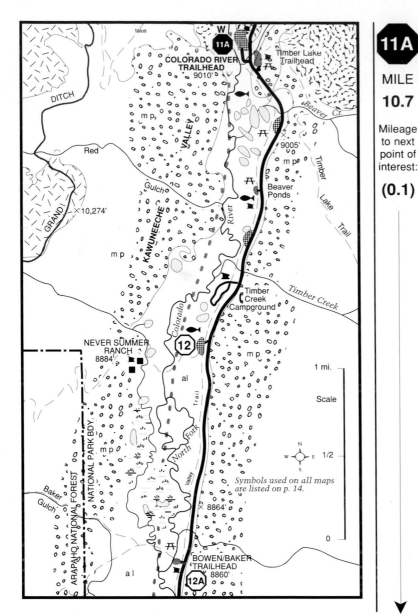

11A MILE 10.7

Mileage to next point of interest:

(0.1)

COLORADO RIVER TRAILHEAD.

El. 9010 ft

Large parking area. Entrance on right.

—RESTROOMS. DRINKING WATER.

SCENERY:

—The highway has reached the floor of the Kawuneeche Valley and the North Fork of the Colorado River.

THINGS TO DO:

—Picnic area.

—The COLORADO RIVER TRAIL goes north 0.5 mi. to the former site of Squeaky Bob's Place. At 2.1 mi. are the site of Shipler's mine and the ruins of his cabin. The site of Lulu City is 3.6 mi. from the trailhead.

—About 5.0 mi. north, the trail passes the spectacular cliffs of **Tertiary volcanic rock** cliffs aptly called Little Yellowstone Canyon. The trail climbs about 1200 ft. in 7.3 mi. to reach the Grand Ditch and La Poudre Pass.

—THUNDER PASS TRAIL starts from Lulu City and climbs about 4.0 mi., crossing the Continental Divide and descends to Michigan Lakes west of the Never Summer Mtns. This is a steep climb.

—RED MTN. TRAIL branches from the Colorado River Trail at the site of Squeaky Bob's Place. From there it climbs 1200 ft. in 2.8 mi. to the Grand Ditch, crossing Opposition Creek twice.

—VALLEY TRAIL winds southward along the Colorado River to the National Park boundary.

Lulu City was already falling into disrepair when this picture was taken in 1889. (Denver Public Library, Western History Dept.)

The main lodge at Camp Wheeler, August 22, 1916. This picture was taken by U.S. Geological Survey geologist W. T. Lee, who wrote the first geological publication about the new National Park. Squeaky Bob and his trained terrier are in the left foreground. Lee probably stayed at Camp Wheeler and enjoyed Squeaky Bob's famous cooking. *(USGS)*

ADDITIONAL HISTORICAL NOTES

CAMP WHEELER, HOTEL DE HARDSCRABBLE, or SQUEAKY BOB'S PLACE, as the resort was variously and affectionately known (p. 215), was about 0.5 mi. north of the picnic area. Robert Wheeler started the resort in 1907 as one of the earliest dude ranches in the Kawuneeche Valley and for whom Squeak Creek is named. Wheeler spoke in a high, squeaky falsetto voice because of severe bronchitis as a youngster.

Squeaky Bob sold Camp Wheeler to Lester Scott in 1925, who rebuilt it as PHANTOM VALLEY RANCH. Phantom Creek was named for Scott's ranch. Later the property was sold to the Park Service and by 1970 all the buildings were gone.

One of the earliest prospectors was Joseph Shipler who staked the Collins Lode Claim on the west-facing slope of a mountain that later was named for him. He spent his summers prospecting—and mining a little ore—until the early 1900s.

Lulu City was once a booming mining camp about 3.1 mi. north of Squeaky Bob's

Place. William B. Baker and Benjamin Franklin Burnett discovered silver-bearing veins on the upper slope of Lead Mtn. in 1879. In 1880 the men organized the Middle Park and Grand River Mining and Land Improvement Company, and laid out a 160-acre townsite, Lulu City, named for Burnett's beautiful daughter. It is interesting to note how many early western mining camps added the word "city" to their names. Perhaps this somehow conveyed the image of a more permanent settlement than actually existed.

By the fall of 1880, Lulu City boasted a post office, hotel, real estate agency, butcher shop, blacksmith shop and several cabins. In spite of much prospecting in the Lead Mountain Mining District, little ore was ever produced and by 1885 Lulu City was abandoned. Today, only a few fallen logs mark the site of the camp.

Dutchtown, another mining camp with only three or four cabins, was west of Lulu City near treeline. It was occupied until 1884.

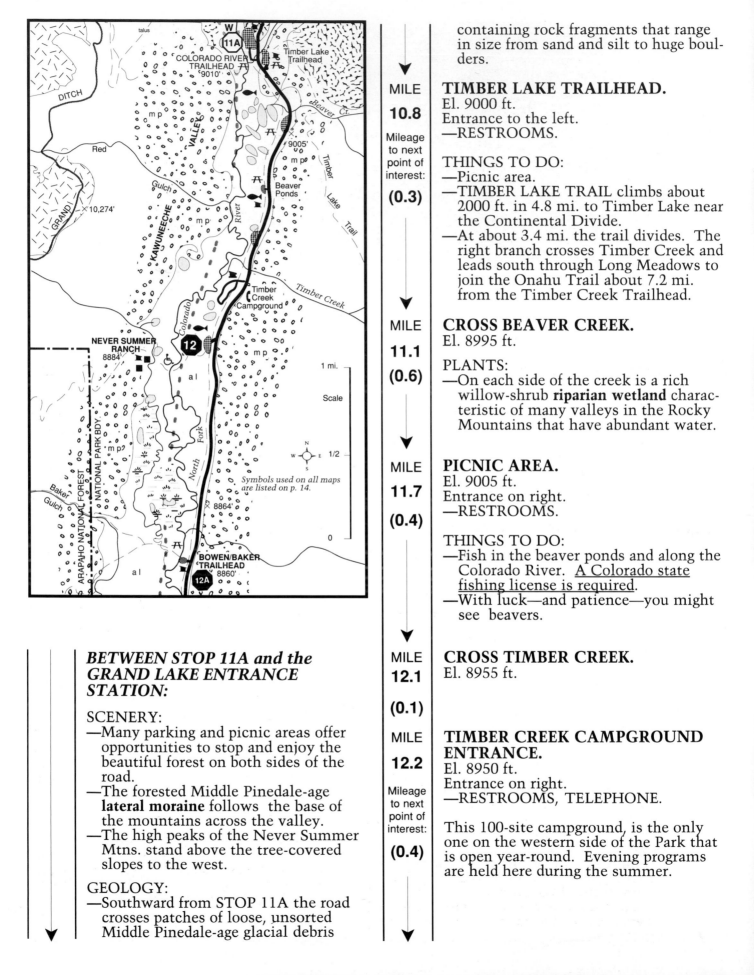

containing rock fragments that range in size from sand and silt to huge boulders.

TIMBER LAKE TRAILHEAD.
El. 9000 ft.
Entrance to the left.
—RESTROOMS.

THINGS TO DO:
—Picnic area.
—TIMBER LAKE TRAIL climbs about 2000 ft. in 4.8 mi. to Timber Lake near the Continental Divide.
—At about 3.4 mi. the trail divides. The right branch crosses Timber Creek and leads south through Long Meadows to join the Onahu Trail about 7.2 mi. from the Timber Creek Trailhead.

CROSS BEAVER CREEK.
El. 8995 ft.

PLANTS:
—On each side of the creek is a rich willow-shrub **riparian wetland** characteristic of many valleys in the Rocky Mountains that have abundant water.

PICNIC AREA.
El. 9005 ft.
Entrance on right.
—RESTROOMS.

THINGS TO DO:
—Fish in the beaver ponds and along the Colorado River. A Colorado state fishing license is required.
—With luck—and patience—you might see beavers.

CROSS TIMBER CREEK.
El. 8955 ft.

TIMBER CREEK CAMPGROUND ENTRANCE.
El. 8950 ft.
Entrance on right.
—RESTROOMS, TELEPHONE.

This 100-site campground, is the only one on the western side of the Park that is open year-round. Evening programs are held here during the summer.

MILE
10.8
Mileage to next point of interest:
(0.3)

MILE
11.1
(0.6)

MILE
11.7
(0.4)

MILE
12.1
(0.1)

MILE
12.2
Mileage to next point of interest:
(0.4)

BETWEEN STOP 11A and the GRAND LAKE ENTRANCE STATION:

SCENERY:
—Many parking and picnic areas offer opportunities to stop and enjoy the beautiful forest on both sides of the road.
—The forested Middle Pinedale-age **lateral moraine** follows the base of the mountains across the valley.
—The high peaks of the Never Summer Mtns. stand above the tree-covered slopes to the west.

GEOLOGY:
—Southward from STOP 11A the road crosses patches of loose, unsorted Middle Pinedale-age glacial debris

Main lodge of Holzwarths Neversummer Ranch as it looked in 1959. Part of the Grand Ditch shows on the mountainside above the lodge.   (NPS)

12

MILE

12.6

Mileage
to next
point of
interest:

(1.2)

NEVER SUMMER RANCH.
El. 8884 ft.
Entrance on right.
—RESTROOMS.

THINGS TO DO:
—Picnic area.
—A 0.5 mi. path, suitable for people using wheelchairs, leads to the Holzwarth Homestead, one of the early ranches in the valley. The path to the ranch crosses the Colorado River and winds through a grassy meadow with many **montane zone** wildflowers.
—Between 9 AM and 4 PM during the summer months, the Holzwarth home and one of the restored "tourist" cabins are open to the public.
—A National Park Service pamphlet, <u>Never Summer Ranch</u> has more information about the Holzwarth family and their dude ranch.
—The views of the western slope of the Front Range on the eastern skyline are dramatic.
—An access road starting from the ranch climbs about 1500 ft. in 2.2 mi. along the lateral moraine to the Grand Ditch. This steep road may be hiked to see the ditch.

HISTORY:
—John Holzwarth Sr. first visited the North Fork Valley in 1883 and returned in 1918 to start a cattle ranch. He and his wife bought a homestead owned by Joe Fleshuts.

—Soon friends and travelers discovered Mrs. Holzwarth's marvelous cooking and the couple started building rustic cabins along the road for their guests. First called Holzwarth Trout Lodge, the name was changed to Neversummer Ranch in 1929.
—John Holzwarth Jr. operated the dude ranch until 1974 when The Nature Conservancy bought it. The property was transferred to Rocky Mountain National Park in 1975.
—Page 215 has more information on the Holzwarth family.

MILE

13.8

(0.2)

BOWEN MTN. (left) and BAKER MTN. (right) are on the western skyline.

12A

MILE

14.0

Mileage
to next
point of
interest:

(1.3)

BOWEN-BAKER GULCH TRAIL-HEAD.
El. 8860 ft. Entrance on right.
—RESTROOMS.

SCENERY:
—To the west, the pyramid-shaped peak is Baker Mtn.
—The upper end of the Grand Ditch is high on the slope of Baker Mtn.
—The flat-floored, U-shaped Kawuneeche Valley, is a large **wetland**.
—From a spot about 0.3 mi. to the south there are good views of Bowen Mtn., along the western skyline.

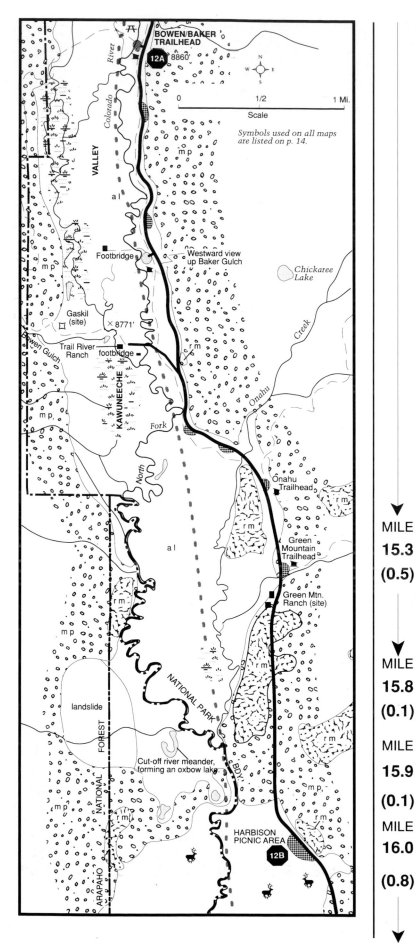

THINGS TO DO:
—Picnic area.
—From a concrete bridge across the Colorado River, a trail leads westward up BAKER GULCH to remote areas in the Never Summer Wilderness Area of Arapaho National Forest. This trail climbs 2400 ft. in 5.5 mi. to Baker Pass on the Continental Divide. At 3.6 mi., a trail branches to the left, continuing 1.3 mi. to Paprika Lake, just east of the Continental Divide. <u>This is a very steep trail.</u>
—BOWEN GULCH TRAIL climbs 2200 ft. in 7.5 mi. to Bowen Lake, just east of the Continental Divide. From Bowen Lake, the trail leads south to the site of the Wolverine Mine on the slope of Porphyry Peaks.

HISTORY:
—Baker Mtn. was named for John R. Baker, a trapper and miner who is credited with being the first non-Indian to climb the mountain. He staked a claim on the upper slopes in 1875.
—Bowen Mtn. and Gulch were named for Jim Bourn who staked the Wolverine Claim in 1875. The county clerk misread his handwriting and recorded the claim in the name of "Bowen".

MILE 15.3 (0.5)

SMALL, UNPAVED PARKING AREA, at bridge with wooden gate. Road leads to private property.

SCENERY:
—From here are fine views of Baker Mtn., Baker Gulch and the Grand Ditch.

MILE 15.8 (0.1)

Best view of BOWEN MTN. (left), BOWEN GULCH and BAKER MTN. (right) on the western skyline.

MILE 15.9 (0.1)

ROCHE MOUTONNEE: is directly ahead as the road curves to the right (photo, p. 73).

MILE 16.0 (0.8)

TRAIL RIVER RANCH: Road on right leads to Trail River Ranch, to other privately owned land and to the site of **Gaskil.**

Coyote. (Chase Swift©)

Black bear. (Chase Swift©)

Mountain lion. (Chase Swift©)

View westward from mile 15.8 showing Bowen Mtn. (left), Bowen Gulch and Baker Mtn. (right). The conifers were killed because beaver dams raised the water table in the valley floor.

Small tree-covered roche moutonnée at mile 15.9.

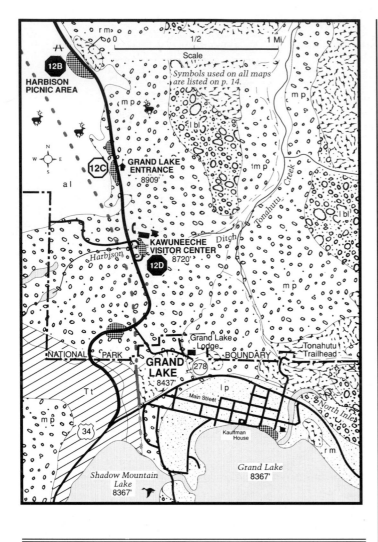

ADDITIONAL HISTORICAL NOTES

GASKIL, another small mining camp, was across the river at the foot of Bowen Gulch (see map). It was named for L. D. C. Gaskill, engineer, surveyor, accountant, promoter and manager of the Wolverine Mine. How and why the name of the town was spelled differently is not known.

The "town" started in 1880 when Al Warner, an enterprising businessman, opened a saloon and liquor store for miners going and coming from their prospects in the Campbell Mining District on the upper slopes of Bowen and Baker Mtns.

By 1882, when the Grand Lake Mining and Milling Company announced plans for a mill at Gaskil, miners moved to the new town. The mill never materialized but a general store, two-story hotel, post office and some storehouses were built.

The Wolverine Mine, the largest in the district, closed in 1886 and the town soon faded away.

MILE 16.8

Mileage to next point of interest:

(0.2)

CROSS ONAHU CREEK.
El. 8755 ft.
A small parking area is on the right just before the bridge.

PLANTS:
—A wide variety of plants grow on each side of the stream in a characteristic **mountain riparian ecosystem**.
—Alders, willows, birches, and aspens grow abundantly interspersed with a few blue spruces.
—Many different species of grasses and sedges, bittercresses, cow parsnips and arrow-leaf senecios thrive in such moist areas.

WILDLIFE:
—Many species of birds nest in **riparian wetlands** including tree swallows, warblers, vireos, dippers and belted kingfishers.
—Cottontail rabbits, muskrats, western jumping mice, water shrews, chipmunks, and squirrels live in such areas because of the abundant undergrowth. Other residents include several species of voles, long-tailed weasels, coyotes, red foxes, raccoons and beavers.
—Beavers recently moved into the area south of the road. Their dams raised water levels and drowned some of the conifers.

HISTORY:
—First called Fish Creek by non-Indians, the name of this stream was changed in 1914 to an Arapaho Indian word that means "warms himself."
—According to legend, Onahu was an Indian pony who stood close to campfires to warm himself on cold winter nights. Onahu died somewhere along the creek, hence the name.

MILE 17.0

Mileage to next point of interest:

(0.6)

ONAHU TRAILHEAD.
El. 8790 ft.
Parking area entrance on left.

THINGS TO DO:
—ONAHU TRAIL climbs 850 ft. in 3.1 mi. to a junction. From this junction, another trail goes south 2.2 mi. to the TONAHUTU TRAIL in the Big Meadows. The Tonanahutu Trail leads southward 4.3 mi. to Grand Lake or eastward about 10 mi. to Bighorn Flats and the Continental Divide.

The Onahu Creek bridge was far different in 1922 than the modern highway completed in 1985.   *(NPS)*

MILE
17.6

Mileage
to next
point of
interest:

(0.4)

GREEN MOUNTAIN TRAILHEAD.
El. 8780 ft.
Parking area entrance on left.
—RESTROOMS.

THINGS TO DO:
—From the trailhead, it is 1.8 mi. to the junction with the Tonahutu Trail.
—Bear Lake is 16.0 mi. over the Divide from the Trailhead.

HISTORY:
—The cabins across the highway, southwest of the trailhead, were part of the GREEN MTN. RANCH, another popular dude ranch in the Kawuneeche Valley (page 216).
—First homesteaded in 1888, the ranch was sold to Henry Schnoor in 1897. The property fell into decline and was sold for taxes in 1934. Carl Nelson bought it and built up a dairy herd of Guernsey cattle and an outstanding dude ranch. He sold the property to the National Park Service in 1972.
—The remaining buildings are now used to house Park Service personnel.

ROCHE MOUTONNEE on right.
GEOLOGY:
—The rounded hill on the right, densely covered with trees, is all that remains after the Colorado River Glacier ground away most of a hard outcrop of **Precambrian** rock.

MILE
18.0

(1.4)

12B

MILE

19.4

Mileage
to next
point of
interest:

(0.8)

HARBISON PICNIC AREA.
El. 8720 ft.
Large parking area is on right is at a wide curve in the Harbison Meadow.

SCENERY:
—Byers Peak (right) and Vasquez Mtn. (left) near Berthoud Pass are about 25 miles away on the southern skyline.

WILDLIFE:
—Deer and elk frequently browse in the meadow during the early morning and at dusk.
—Moose were transplanted to North Park, Colorado from the Uinta Mtns. of Utah in 1977. Some moose migrated into the Kawuneeche Valley and may be seen among the willows along the Colorado River.

PLANTS:
—Sagebrush, shrubby cinquefoils, green gentians, white yarrows, and willows are interspersed with grasses and sedges.
—Yarrow *(Achillea lanulosa)* was important to some Indians who made an extract by boiling the plant, for use as a stimulant, a tonic and cough remedy. Tea made from either fresh or dried leaves was used to relieve nausea and colds.

View northward from the summit of Shadow Mtn., showing Grand Lake, the Kawuneeche Valley and the Grand Ditch. Peaks of the Never Summer Mtns. are on the skyline. (Union Pacific R.R. photo, Denver Public Library, Western History Dept.)

12C

MILE

20.2
(0.4)

12D

MILE

20.6

GRAND LAKE ENTRANCE STATION.
El. 8709 ft.

KAWUNEECHE VISITOR CENTER.
El. 8720 ft.
Entrance on left.
—RESTROOMS and TELEPHONE.

Road to WINDING RIVER CAMP-GROUND on right.

THINGS TO DO:
—Park activity schedules are available.
—Park Service personnel are on duty to answer questions.
—Camping and hiking permits are issued.
—Books and maps for sale.

—TONAHUTU SPUR TRAIL connects with the main Tonahutu Trail 0.6 mi. east of the Visitor Center.

HISTORY:
—The HARBISON RANCH was across the highway (p. 216). The Harbison family, including sisters Annie and Kittie started a small dairy ranch in 1895. By 1905, the sisters began catering to tourists and were well-known for their delicious fried chicken dinners. The sisters died within a week of each other in November 1938.
—The property was eventually sold to the National Park Service and is now used as a utility area for Government equipment. No ranch buildings remain.

Grand Lake is 1.5 mi. south of the Visitor Center.

GRAND LAKE

This drive starts at the Grand Lake Chamber of Commerce Visitor Information Center at the junction of U.S. 34 and the road leading east into Grand Lake (Colorado Highway 278).

Southeastward view across Grand Lake showing glaciated valley of East Inlet Creek and Mt. Craig. (O. Roach photo, Western History Dept., Denver Public Library)

"He who feels the spell of the wild, the rhythmic melody of the falling water, the echoes among the crags, the bird songs, the wind in the pines and the endless beat of waves upon the shore—is in tune with the universe."

——Enos A. Mills, <u>Your National Parks,</u>
1917.

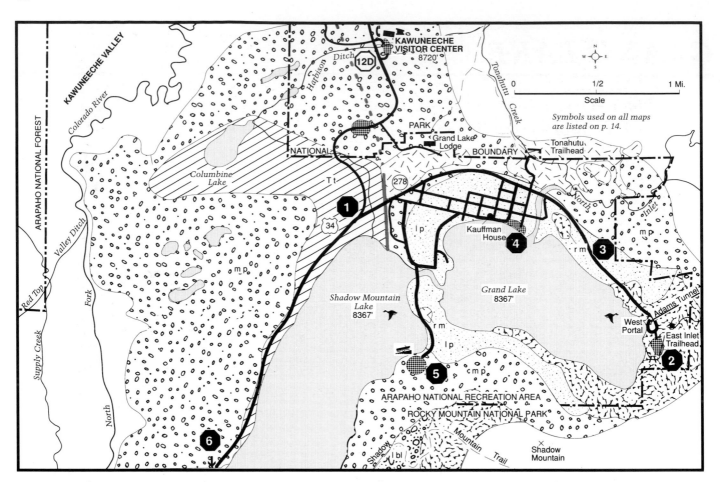

Symbols used on all maps
are listed on p. 14.

① GRAND LAKE CHAMBER of COMMERCE VISITOR INFORMATION CENTER is at the junction of **U.S. 34** with **Colo. 278**, the road leading east into **GRAND LAKE VILLAGE.**

—Open during the summer months, the Center has literature and information on points-of-interest, accomodations and the wide variety of recrecreational activities in the Grand Lake area.
—Grand Lake also hosts many wintertime events including snowmobiling and cross-country ski races.

BEYOND THE VISITOR CENTER: follow Colo. 278 that leads 2.5 mi. eastward around the northern edge of Grand Lake Village to the West Portal of the Adams Tunnel.

Mileages between stops are not shown for this log.

② WEST PORTAL of ADAMS TUNNEL and EAST INLET TRAILHEAD.
—RESTROOMS. Small picnic area.

THINGS TO DO:
—ADAMS FALLS, on East Inlet, is about 0.3 mi. east of and 79 ft. higher than the parking area. The falls were named for Jay E. Adams, a long-time summer resident of Grand Lake.
—The EAST INLET TRAIL climbs 1809 ft. in 6.9 mi. to Lake Verna on the northern slope of Mt. Craig.

SCENERY:
—Grand Lake, el. 8367 ft., the largest natural lake in Colorado, is about 1.5 mi. long and 0.5 mi. wide.
—It formed behind a Late Pinedale-age **terminal moraine**[1], remnants of which can be seen on the return drive at STOP 3.

---

[1]Terms in **bold-face** type are defined in the Glossary, p. 256.

Early southward view of Grand Lake with the shoulder of Shadow Mtn. on the left. Many trees have grown since the picture was taken.　　*(Colorado Historical Society)*

—The low, nearly level, tree-covered hill to the west above Grand Lake is a large Middle Pinedale-age moraine.

— APIATAN MT. is on the western skyline. Apiatan was an Arapaho Indian whose name meant "Wooden Lance" in English.

—From the East Inlet Trailhead are glimpses of PORPHYRY PEAKS to the northwest.

HISTORY:

—The Colorado-Big Thompson Project was started in 1938 by the U.S. Bureau of Reclamation. This multi-purpose project collects about 240,000 acre-feet of water per year from the upper parts of the Colorado River Basin. Water is stored in Lake Granby and Willow Creek Reservoir to be pumped 125 ft. uphill into Shadow Mtn. and Grand Lakes.

—The water is transported under the Continental Divide via the 13.1 mi. Alva B. Adams Tunnel to Estes Park. The tunnel was named for an early Colorado Governor. The western portal of the diversion tunnel is under the paved parking area.

—Construction of the Adams tunnel was started at both ends on July 15, 1940 and crews met on July 10, 1944 with the two bores almost perfectly aligned.

—The 9.7-ft. wide tunnel is lined with steel-reinforced concrete. On July 23, 1947 the first western slope water flowed through the tunnel and into the Big Thompson River at Estes Park.

—When water flows into the tunnel, the equal levels of Grand and Shadow Mtn. Lakes are maintained by pumping water into them from Lake Granby.

—Power to run the pumping stations is generated at power plants near Estes Park and transmitted back through the Adams tunnel in a large electrical conduit suspended from the roof of the tunnel and filled with nitrogen gas. The nitrogen serves as an insulator.

—From Estes Park the water flows through tunnels and canals to irrigate about 720,000 acres of farmland on the plains.

RETURN to GRAND LAKE:

GEOLOGY:

— Beyond Tonuhutu Drive, 1.0 mi. from the Adams Tunnel Parking Area, is an ideal place to see the jumbled rocks and soil in a **glacial moraine**.

—Roadcuts at that point expose loose, rounded **boulders**, **cobbles**, **sand** and fine-grained soils of a Late Pinedale-age **terminal moraine** that encircles the western half of Grand Lake Village.

CROSS TONAHUTU CREEK.

Tonahutu is an Arapaho Indian word meaning "big meadows."

Unsorted rock debris in Late Pinedale terminal moraine along Colo. Highway 278.

Main Street of Grand Lake, Colorado.

ROAD to TONAHUTU and NORTH INLET TRAILHEADS on right, a short distance west of Tonahutu Creek, at a sign to SHADOWCLIFF CAMP.

—The TONAHUTU TRAIL leads northward up Tonahutu Creek, joining the spur trail from the Kawuneeche Visitor Center and continues to the Continental Divide at Flattop Mtn. crossing.

—The NORTH INLET TRAIL climbs 300 ft. in 3.5 mi. to Cascade Falls. Beyond, the trail continues to Lake Nanita which is 2240 ft. higher and 11.0 mi. from the trailhead. A branch of the North Inlet Trail continues eastward and also crosses the Continental Divide at Flattop Mtn.

STOP SIGN. TURN LEFT to GARFIELD STREET.
Drive down the hill. Cross Grand Avenue, the main business street of Grand Lake. Continue to the lake front where there is a large parking area.

④

THINGS TO DO:
—Large picnic area along the lake is below the KAUFFMAN HOUSE (p. 215) at the foot of Pitkin Street. This early Grand Lake hotel has been restored by the Grand Lake Area Historical Society.

—It is open for tours from 1 to 5 PM from June through August.

—The log building is on the National Register of Historic Places.

—The Historical Society has a walking-tour pamphlet about other interesting historic buildings and sites in Grand Lake.

—PUBLIC RESTROOMS are east of the Kauffman House, near the Grand Lake Yacht Club.

SCENERY:
—The rounded mountain above treeline on the east-southeastern skyline is MT. CRAIG, el. 12,007 ft.

—This peak has also been called "Middle Mountain," "Round Mountain," "Round Top," "Baldy," "Old Baldy" and "Mt. Wescott".

—Many early-day residents thought the proper name should be Mt. Wescott to honor Grand Lake's first permanent non-Indian settler, Joseph L. Wescott, who lived along the western shore of the lake from 1867 until he died in 1914.

—The peak was finally named for William Bayard Craig, pastor of Central Christian Church in Denver, who came to Colorado in 1882. Craig spent his summers in the the area and opened a real estate office in Grand Lake.

—MT. WESCOTT, el. 10,421 ft. is the lower, tree-covered mountain to the right of Mt. Craig.

—The rocky cliffs to the left of Mt. Craig and across the glaciated valley are part of MT. CAIRNS, named for James Cairns, who built the first store in Grand Lake in 1881 after the townsite was surveyed and platted. Cairns operated his general store until 1924 when he sold his business to Matilda G. Humphrey.

Early boatmen on Grand Lake. One hardy sailor is experimenting with a crude sail. Judge Wescott is seated on the stump. *(NPS collection)*

—Timber-covered SHADOW MTN., el. 9923 ft. is across the lake to the south.

HISTORY:

—Grand Lake was called "Spirit Lake" by the Arapaho Indians because steam rises from the water on cold winter days. They also believed a supernatural buffalo lived in the lake.

—The lake is named for the Grand River, a former name for the Colorado River (p. 65).

—Joseph L. Wescott, who came to Grand Lake in 1867, settled in a crude cabin that trapper Philip Crawshaw had built ten years earlier.

—Wescott, a bachelor, filed for a homestead around the western shore of Grand Lake and supported himself by hunting and fishing. He occasionally rented the Crawshaw cabin to visiting hunters, fishermen, prospectors and tourists. Later he subdivided his homestead into lots, was appointed Grand Lake's first postmaster in 1877 and also served as Justice of the Peace.

—Between 1875 and 1885 Grand Lake grew "glacially slow" but stout-hearted tourists began arriving to enjoy the excellent fishing and hunting. The first hotel, the Waldron House was built in 1878; the Grand Central Hotel and restaurant followed in 1880.

—By 1879, the townsite of Grand Lake was platted and the village was the county seat of Grand County for several years during the height of the mining boom.

—Grand Lake has always been a summer resort and in 1902 sailing enthusiasts started the Grand Lake Yacht Club. The annual Regatta Week is a major event each summer. In recent years, wind surfing has grown in popularity.

—More historical information about Grand Lake is in the History Section, p. 210.

After visiting Grand Lake, follow Grand Avenue west.

Kauffman House in Grand Lake, 1987. (Ellen Hansen)

GEOLOGY:
—Near the western end of town, the highway has been cut through the Late Pinedale-age **terminal moraine**, another place to see the unsorted debris in a moraine.
—The Columbine Realty office building sits on a flat area excavated from the moraine.

Make a sharp left turn just beyond Sombero Stables.

5

—This road crosses the inlet between Grand Lake and Shadow Mtn. Lake and leads to picnic areas and Hilltop boat launch.
—Many species of water birds frequent the lake.

Retrace your route, returning to Grand Avenue and the junction with U.S. 34. TURN LEFT ONTO U.S. 34 to follow the rest of the drive .

—A 5.8 mi. drive southward leads to the GRANBY PUMPING STATION of the U.S. Bureau of Reclamation.
—Along both Shadow Mtn. Lake and Lake Granby are many picnic areas, campgrounds and boat docks.

GEOLOGY:
—Opposite the road junction, a roadcut exposes Troublesome Formation, a soft, tan to light-gray, fine-grained sedimentary rock of **Tertiary** age also containing some layers of volcanic ash.

—Streams washed old volcanic debris out of the mountains and deposited it in the lowlands where it became mixed with new ash from still active volcanos west and northwest of the Park.
—About 2.0 mi. south of the junction, opposite Blue Bird Motel, are good views southeastward of several small tree-covered islands in Shadow Mtn. Lake.
—These are remnants of a Middle Pinedale-age **terminal moraine** that were partly submerged when the reservoir was built.
—This marks the southern limit of the Colorado River Glacier during the Middle Pinedale Glaciation.
—During Pre-Bull Lake and Bull Lake Glaciations, the Colorado River Glacier extended even farther south.

The GRANBY PUMP CANAL is along the left side of the highway about 3.5 mi. south of the junction. This canal carries water pumped uphill from Lake Granby to Shadow Mtn. Lake.

6

Entrance Road to GRANBY PUMPING STATION is 4.7 mi. south of the junction into Grand Lake Village.

Turn left onto County Road 64 that leads 1.1 mi. to the Pumping Station and to Cutthroat Bay Campground.

—Tours of the pumping plant are 9 AM to 5 PM from Memorial Day to Labor Day. No admission is charged.
—Water from Lake Granby is pumped uphill 125 ft. to the Granby Pump Canal and into Shadow Mtn. Lake.

Retrace your route back to U.S. 34. Continue south to the junction with the road that crosses Granby Dam and leads to Arapaho Bay Campground, several picnic areas and to the Indian Peaks Wilderness Area trailhead at Monarch Lake .

U.S. 34 continues south to the junction with U.S. 40, 1.0 mi. west of Granby, Colo .

TRAIL RIDGE ROAD EASTBOUND—

Part 1 — Kawuneeche Visitor Center to Fall River Pass.

Ptarmigan basking in the sun on the tundra, wearing their summer plumage.

"The rugged peaks of Rocky Mountain National Park are not barren and lifeless, although viewed from a distance they appear so."

——Enos A. Mills, <u>Rocky Mountain National Park</u>, Memorial Edition, 1932

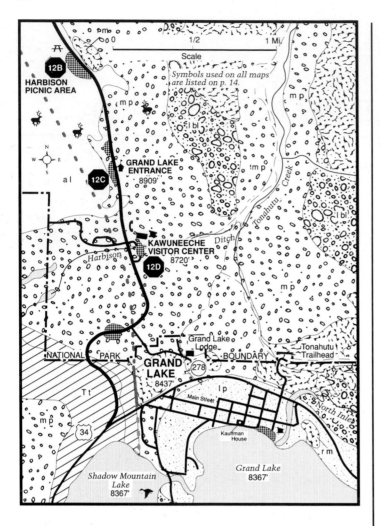

KAWUNEECHE VISITOR CENTER.

12D

MILE

0.0

Mileage to next point of interest:

(0.4)

El. 8720 ft. Entrance on right. Road to WINDING RIVER CAMPGROUND on left.
—RESTROOMS, TELEPHONE.

THINGS TO DO:
—Park activity schedules are available.
—Park Service personnel are on duty to answer questions.
—Camping and hiking permits issued.
—Books and maps for sale.
—TONAHUTU SPUR TRAIL connects the Visitor Center with the main Tonahutu Trail 0.6 mi. to the east. The main trail leads north from Grand Lake along Tonahutu Creel to cross the Continental Divide at Flattop Mtn.

PLANTS:
—Surrounding the Visitor Center is a dense **upper montane life zone**[1] (6000

[1] Terms in **bold-face type** are defined in the Glossary, p. 256.

to 9000 ft. elevation) lodgepole pine forest that includes some aspens, blue spruces and mountain alders.
—Lodgepole pines (*Pinus contorta* var.*latifolia*) are the most common conifers in the Kawuneeche Valley. The tall slender trees with straight pole-like trunks are easy to identify because of their yellow-green needles. Many Plains Indians used the trunks as poles to support their tepees.
—Lodgepole pines grow quickly in dense forests that have less undergrowth because little sunlight reaches the forest floor. This in turn attracts few animals and birds because food supplies are reduced.
—Wildfires open the forests, burn off the undergrowth vegetation and leave bare soils on which lodgedpole pine seeds easily sprout in full sunlight. Lodgepole cones, if not destroyed by fire, open and release their seeds when heated to between 113° and 122° F. These seeds then are spread by wind, birds and mammals.

HISTORY:
—Across the highway from the Visitor Center was the HARBISON RANCH (p. 216). The Harbison family, including sisters Annie and Kittie, started a small dairy ranch in 1895. By 1905, the two sisters began catering to tourists and were well-known for their delicious fried chicken dinners. They died within a week of each other in November 1938.
—The property eventually was sold to the Park Service and is now used as a utility area for Park equipment. No ranch buildings remain.
—A primitive road between Grand Lake and Lulu City was rebuilt as far as Squeaky Bob's Place (p. 90, 215) in the early 1900s.
—The route for the first road between Squeaky Bob's and Fall River Pass was surveyed in 1912 by Frank L. Huntington, Grand County Surveyor.
—Construction started in 1913 and by 1918 had reached MILNER PASS. In 1920 the road reached FALL RIVER PASS.

Stops in this guide are keyed to the National Park Service pamphlet Trail Ridge Road Guide. Numbered arrowhead-shaped road signs identify these major stops.

Traveling to Grand Lake in style. (NPS collection)

During the winters Rob Harbison delivered milk to customers in the Grand Lake area using this wagon mounted on skis.
(NPS collection)

Additional stops in this text are identified with a number–letter combination, ie. STOP 12C. All parking areas are shown on the maps.

Set your odometer to 0.0 or write down your mileage at the parking area exit. Turn right and follow U.S. 34 east toward Estes Park.

NO *service stations are between Grand Lake and Estes Park.*

The road climbs 3400 ft. between here and Fall River Pass.

12C

GRAND LAKE ENTRANCE STATION.
El. 8709 ft. Stop to pay entrance fees.

BETWEEN ENTRANCE STATION and STOP 11A:

SCENERY:
—Many parking and picnic areas offer opportunities to stop and enjoy the beautiful forest on both sides of the road.
—The tree-covered Middle Pinedale–age **lateral moraine** is across the valley along the base of the mountains.
—Vistas of the high peaks of the NEVER SUMMER MTNS. are on the western skyline.

MILE 0.4

Mileage to next point of interest:

(0.3)

GEOLOGY:
—North of the Entrance station, the road crossed patches of loose, unsorted Middle Pinedale–age glacial debris from 50,000 to 35,000 years old. Rock fragments range in size from sand, silt and clay to huge boulders.

12B

HARBISON PICNIC AREA.
El. 8720 ft.
Large parking area is on the left at a wide curve.

BE CAREFUL WHEN TURNING ACROSS THE ROAD.

SCENERY:
—Byers Peak (right) and Vasquez Mtn. (left) are on the southern skyline about 25 mi. away.

WILDLIFE:
—Deer and elk frequently browse in the large meadow in the early morning and at dusk.
—Moose were transplanted to North Park from the Uinta Mtns. in Utah in 1977. Some of them migrated from North Park into the Kawuneeche Valley and possibly may be seen among the willows along the Colorado River.

PLANTS:
—Sagebrush, shrubby cinquefoils, green gentians, white yarrows and willows are interspersed with grasses and sedges in the meadow.
—Yarrow *(Achillea lanulosa)* was an important plant to Indians. An extract made by boiling the plant was used as a stimulant, a tonic and a cough remedy. Tea made from fresh or dried leaves was used to relieve nausea and colds.

MILE 0.7

Mileage to next point of interest:

(1.9)

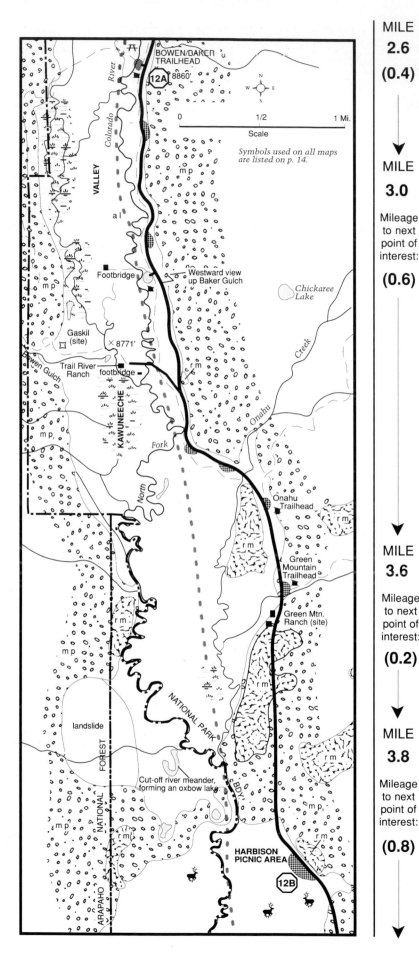

MILE 2.6 (0.4)

ROCHE MOUTONNEE on left.

GEOLOGY:

—The rounded, tree-covered hill left of the road, labelled "r m" on the map, is a resistant outcrop of **Precambrian** rocks. The Colorado River Glacier ground away much of this outcrop, leaving it smooth and polished.

MILE 3.0

Mileage to next point of interest:

(0.6)

GREEN MOUNTAIN TRAILHEAD.
El. 8780 ft. Parking area entrance on the right. RESTROOMS.

THINGS TO DO:

—From the trailhead, it is 1.8 mi. up the trail to its junction with the Tonahutu Trail and 16.0 mi. over the Divide to Bear Lake.

HISTORY:

—The cabins across the highway, just south of the trailhead, were part of the GREEN MTN. RANCH, another formerly popular dude ranch.

—First homesteaded in 1888, the ranch was sold to Henry Schnoor in 1897 (p. 216). The property declined and was sold for taxes in 1934. Carl Nelson bought it and built up a dairy herd of Guernsey cattle and an outstanding dude ranch. He sold the property to the Park Service in 1972.

—Remaining buildings now house Park Service personnel.

MILE 3.6

Mileage to next point of interest:

(0.2)

ONAHU TRAILHEAD.
El. 8790 ft.
Parking area entrance on right.

THINGS TO DO:

—ONAHU TRAIL climbs 850 ft. in 3.1 mi. to a junction with Timber Lake Trail. From the junction, the Onahu Trail leads south 2.2 mi. where it joins TONAHUTU TRAIL beyond Big Meadows. The trails continue south 4.3 mi. to Grand Lake.

MILE 3.8

Mileage to next point of interest:

(0.8)

CROSS ONAHU CREEK.
El. 8755 ft.

PLANTS:

—On each side of the stream is a characteristic **mountain riparian eco-system** where a wide variety of plants grows.

—Alders, willows, birches and aspens are common, but there are some blue spruces.

—Many different species of grasses, sedges, bittercresses, cow parsnips and arrow-leafed senecios thrive in these moist areas.

WILDLIFE:
—Many species of birds nest in riparian wetlands, including tree swallows, warblers, vireos, dippers and belted kingfishers.
—Cottontail rabbits, muskrats, western jumping mice, water shrews and several species of voles live in such areas because of abundant food supplies and good cover in the trees and undergrowth. Other residents include long-tailed weasels, coyotes, red foxes, raccoons and beavers.
—Shortly before 1988 beavers moved into the area south of the road. Their dams raised water levels, which killed some of the trees.

HISTORY:
—First called Fish Creek, the name was changed in 1914 to an Arapaho Indian word that means "warms himself."
—According to legend, Onahu was an Indian pony who stood close to campfires on cold evenings to get warm. Onahu died somewhere along the creek.

MILE 4.6 (0.1)

TRAIL RIVER RANCH: road on left leads to the ranch, to other private property and to the site of **Gaskil.**

MILE 4.7 (0.1)

ROCHE MOUTONNEE—the small tree-covered hill on the right also was ground off, smoothed and polished by glaciers.

MILE 4.8 (0.5)

First good view of BOWEN GULCH and BOWEN MTN. to the west.

MILE 5.3

Mileage to next point of interest:

(1.3)

SMALL, UNPAVED PARKING AREA at bridge with wooden gate leads to private property.

SCENERY:
—This spot provides the first good views of BAKER MTN. above BAKER GULCH and the GRAND DITCH (p. 94) in the Never Summer Mtns. to the northwest.

HISTORY:
—Baker Mtn. was named for John R. Baker, a trapper and miner who is credited with being the first non-Indian to climb the mountain. He staked a claim on the upper slopes in 1875.
—Bowen Mtn. and Gulch were named for Jim Bourn who staked the Wolverine Claim in 1875. The county clerk misread his handwriting and recorded it in the name of "Bowen."

ADDITIONAL HISTORICAL NOTES

GASKIL, a small mining camp, was across the river at the foot of Bowen Gulch (see map). It was named for L. D. C. Gaskill, engineer, surveyor, accountant, promoter and manager of the Wolverine Mine. How and why the town's name was spelled differently than his name is not known. The "town" started in 1880 when Al Warner, an enterprising businessman, opened a saloon and liquor store for miners traveling to and from their prospects in the Campbell Mining District on the upper slopes of Bowen and Baker Mtns.

By 1882, when the Grand Lake Mining and Milling Company announced plans to build a mill at Gaskil, miners moved to the new town. The mill never materialized but a general store, two-story hotel, post office and some storehouses were built.

The Wolverine Mine, the largest in the district, closed in 1886 and the town soon faded away.

Across the concrete bridge at STOP 12A is this westward view up Baker Gulch. The peaks (from left to right) are Mineral Point, el. 11,488 ft., Bowen Mtn., el. 12,524 ft. an unnamed peak on the Continental Divide and Baker Mtn., el. 12,397 ft. The tree-covered slope below baker Mtn. is part of Green Knoll, el. 12,225 ft. The scar of the Grand Ditch crosses the upper slope of Green Knoll and Baker Mtn.

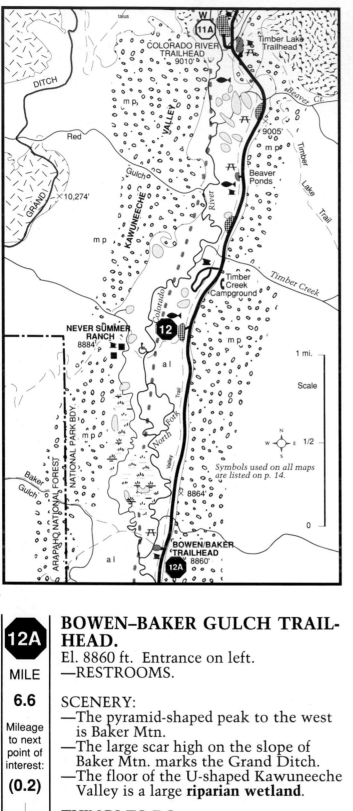

Symbols used on all maps
are listed on p. 14.

Pass on the Continental Divide. At 3.6 mi., a trail branches left, continuing 1.3 mi. to Paprika Lake, just east of the Continental Divide. <u>This is a very steep trail</u>.

—BOWEN GULCH TRAIL climbs 2200 ft. in 7.5 mi. to Bowen Lake, just east of the Continental Divide. From Bowen Lake, the trail extends southward to the site of the Wolverine Mine on the slopes of Porphyry Peaks.

Good view of the top of BOWEN MTN. (left) and **BAKER MTN. (right)** on the skyline to the west.

MORE HISTORICAL NOTES

The Arapaho Indians called the Never Summer Mtns. *"Ni-chebe-chii"* which means "never no summer," an appropriate name because winter snows melt slowly.

Kawuneeche Valley was first called *"Haquihana"* in Arapaho, meaning "Valley of the Wolves." Early non-Indian settlers simply called it "North Fork Valley," but about 1915 the Colorado Geographic Board changed the name to "Kawuneeche" for the Arapaho word *"Cawoonache"* which means coyote, not wolf. The Board thought Kawuneeche was easier for non-Indians to pronounce.

The Colorado River was orginally named the Blue River. It was later changed to Grand River by early trappers and traders, who thought it was the Rio Grande.

MILE 6.8

Mileage to next point of interest:

(1.2)

12A

MILE 6.6

Mileage to next point of interest:

(0.2)

BOWEN–BAKER GULCH TRAILHEAD.
El. 8860 ft. Entrance on left.
—RESTROOMS.

SCENERY:
—The pyramid-shaped peak to the west is Baker Mtn.
—The large scar high on the slope of Baker Mtn. marks the Grand Ditch.
—The floor of the U-shaped Kawuneeche Valley is a large **riparian wetland**.

THINGS TO DO:
—Picnic area.
—From a concrete bridge across the Colorado River, a trail leads westward up BAKER GULCH to remote areas of the Arapaho National Forest in the Never Summer Wilderness Area. The trail climbs 2400 ft. in 5.5 mi. to Baker

---

12

MILE 8.0

Mileage to next point of interest:

(0.4)

NEVER SUMMER RANCH.
El. 8884 ft.
Entrance to parking area on left.
—RESTROOMS.

USE CAUTION WHEN TURNING ACROSS TRAFFIC.

THINGS TO DO:
—Picnic area.
—A 0.5 mi.-path, suitable for people in wheelchairs, leads to the Holzwarth Homestead, one of the early ranches in the valley.
—The path crosses the Colorado river and winds through a grassy meadow with many montane wildflowers.
—Between 9 AM and 4 PM during the summer months, the Holzwarth home and a restored tourist cabin are open to the public.

View northward of Neversummer Ranch and the scar of the Grand Ditch high on the mountainside. September 1959.   (NPS)

—The Park Service pamphlet, <u>Never Summer Ranch</u>, has more information about the Holzworth family and their dude ranch.

—The views of the Front Range on the eastern skyline are dramatic.

—An access road to the Grand Ditch, starting at the ranch, climbs about 1500 ft. in 2.2 mi. One can hike this steep road on the **lateral moraine** to see the ditch.

HISTORY:

—John Holzwarth Sr. first visited the North Fork Valley in 1883 and returned in 1918 to start a cattle ranch. He and his wife bought a homestead owned by Joe Fleshuts.

—Soon friends and travelers discovered Mrs. Holzwarth's marvelous cooking, so the couple built rustic cabins along the highway for their guests. First called Holzwarth Trout Lodge, the name was changed to Neversummer Ranch in 1929.

—John Holzwarth Jr. operated the dude ranch until 1974 when it was purchased by The Nature Conservancy who transferred it to Rocky Mountain National Park the next year (p. 215).

MILE 8.4

TIMBER CREEK CAMPGROUND ENTRANCE.
El. 8950 ft. Entrance on the left.
TELEPHONE.

Mkileage to next point of interest: **(0.1)**

This campground, with 100 campsites, is the only one on the western side of the Park that is open all year.
Evening programs are held during the summers.

MILE 8.5 (0.4)

CROSS TIMBER CREEK.
El. 8955 ft

MILE 8.9

PICNIC AREA.
El.9005 ft.
Entrance on left.
—RESTROOOMS.

***BE CAREFUL** when turning across traffic.*

THINGS TO DO:

—Picnic area.

—Fish in the beaver ponds and along the Colorado River. <u>A Colorado state fishing license is required</u>.

—With luck and patience you may see beavers.

Mileage to next point of interest: **(0.6)**

MILE 9.5

CROSS BEAVER CREEK.
El. 8995 ft.
The headwaters of this stream are at the summit of MILNER PASS.

PLANTS:

—On each side of the creek is rich willow-shrub **riparian wetland**, a characteristic of many Rocky Mountain valleys having abundant water.

Mileage to next point of interest: **(0.3)**

MILE 9.8

TIMBER LAKE TRAILHEAD.
El. 9000 ft.
Entrance road on the right.
—RESTROOMS.

Mileage to next point of interest: **(0.1)**

THINGS TO DO:

—Picnic area.

—TIMBER LAKE TRAIL climbs about 2000 ft. in 4.8 m i. to Timber Lake near the Continental Divide. At about 3.4 mi. the trail branches and crosses Timber Creek. One branch leads south through Long Meadows to a junction with the Onahu Trail, about 7.2 mi. from the Timber Creek Trailhead.

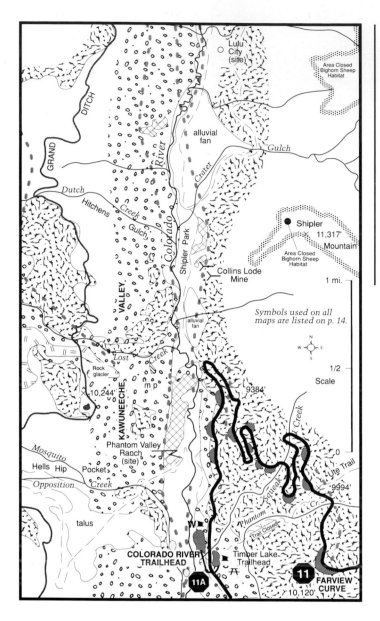

Symbols used on all maps are listed on p. 14.

1 mi.

1/2 Scale

0

11A

MILE

9.9

Mileage to next point of interest:

(0.3)

COLORADO RIVER TRAIL-HEAD.

El. 9010 ft.

—RESTROOMS. DRINKING WATER.

SCENERY:
—The triangularly shaped peak directly ahead on the skyline is Mt. Neota, on the Continental Divide.

THINGS TO DO:
—Picnic area.
—COLORADO RIVER TRAIL goes north 0.5 mi. to the site of Squeaky Bob's Place. At 2.1 mi. are the sites of Shipler's Tiger mine and cabin. The site of Lulu City is 3.6 mi. north from the trailhead. About 5.0 mi. north, the trail passes the spectacular **Tertiary volcanic** rock cliffs aptly called Little

Yellowstone Canyon. The trail climbs about 1200 ft. in 7.3 mi. to the Grand Ditch and La Poudre Pass.
—THUNDER PASS TRAIL starts at Lulu City and climbs about 4.0 mi. to cross the Continental Divide, then descends to Michigan Lakes on the west side of the Never Summer Mtns. This is a steep trail.
—RED MOUNTAIN TRAIL branches from the Colorado River Trail at the site of Squeaky Bob's Place and climbs 1200 ft. in 2.8 mi. to the Grand Ditch. It crosses Opposition Creek twice.
—VALLEY TRAIL winds southward along the Colorado River to the National Park boundary.

ADDITIONAL HISTORICAL NOTES

CAMP WHEELER, HOTEL DE HARDSCRABBLE, or SQUEAKY BOB'S PLACE (p. 215), as the resort was affectionately known, was about 0.5 mi. north of the picnic area. Robert Wheeler started the resort in 1907 as one of the earliest dude ranches in the Kawuneeche Valley and for whom Squeak Creek is named. Wheeler spoke in a high, "squeaky" falsetto voice because of severe bronchitis as a youngster.

Squeaky Bob sold Camp Wheeler to Lester Scott in 1926, who rebuilt it as the PHANTOM VALLEY RANCH. Phantom Creek was named for Scott's ranch. The property was sold to the Park Service and by 1970 all buildings were removed.

One of the earliest prospectors along the North Fork was Joseph Shipler who worked there as early as 1873. In 1876, he located the Collins Lode Mine on the west-facing slope of a mountain that was later named for him. He spent his summers prospecting—and mining a little ore—until the early 1900s.

As other prospectors joined the search for gold and silver, S. B. Stewart started the first toll road between Grand Lake and Ft. Collins in 1880. It crossed La Poudre Pass at the northern end of the Kawuneeche Valley and went down the Cache la Poudre Valley. This primitive wagon road was rebuilt as far as Squeaky Bob's Place in the early 1900s.

LULU CITY was once a booming mining camp about 3.1 mi. north of Squeaky Bob's Place. William B. Baker and Benjamin Franklin Burnett discovered silver-bearing veins on the upper slopes of Lead Mtn. in 1879 (photo p. 68).

In 1880 the men organized the Middle Park and Grand River Mining and Land

and Land Improvement Company and laid out the 160–acre townsite of Lulu City. The name honors Burnett's beautiful daughter. It is interesting to note how many early western mining camps added the word "city" to their names. Perhaps this projected the image of a more permanent settlement.

By the fall of 1880, the town boasted a post office, hotel, real estate agency, butcher shop, blacksmith shop and several cabins. In spite of much prospecting in the Lead Mountain Mining District, little ore was ever produced and by 1885 Lulu City was abandoned. Today, only a few fallen logs mark the site of the camp.

Dutchtown, another mining camp with only three or four cabins, was west of Lulu City near treeline. It was occupied until 1884.

Where Nature is Still Unspoiled

Camp Wheeler

THE DIFFERENT RESORT

ON THE

Grand River
Colorado

"HOTEL DE HARDSCRABBLE"

Brochure cover for "Squeaky Bob" Wheeler's Camp Wheeler located along the Colorado River until 1926.

(Collection of Patience C. Kemp)

BETWEEN STOP 11A and FARVIEW CURVE, STOP 11:

The road climbs the side of the Kawuneeche Valley in a series of switchbacks that presented major challenges to drivers in the 1920s before the road was widened.

Numerous parking areas offer glimpses of the valley and of the Vasquez Mountain on the southern skyline.

GEOLOGY:
—**Precambrian metamorphic gneisses** and **schists** crop out in roadcuts from here to Milner Pass.
—Above many roadcuts loose, rounded boulders litter the **bedrock** surfaces— evidence that a glacier passed this way.

MILE 10.2

FAULT ZONE.
El. 9090 ft.

Mileage to next point of interest: **(0.9)**

GEOLOGY:
—A small **fault zone** on the left illustrates how **schist** was sheared, broken and ground up by movements along the faults. Later the broken rock was altered to soft, crumbly, yellow-brown, iron-rich clay, called **fault gouge**.
—On the right is Middle Pinedale–age glacial debris from 50,000 to 35,000 years old.

MILE 11.1

(1.4)

NORTHERN-MOST SWITCHBACK.
El. 9320 ft.

MILE 12.5

(0.4)

CROSS SQUEAK CREEK.
El. 9700 ft.
Squeak Creek flows from Bighorn Lake north of Milner Pass.

MILE 12.9

Mileage to next point of interest: **(0.2)**

GABIONS.
No stopping place.

—Heavy steel wire baskets, filled with rocks, were placed above the steep roadcut to stabilize loose glacial debris which otherwise would move under the weight of snow down small avalanche tracks and landslides.
—As soil and seeds are blown or washed onto the gabions, plants start to grow, further stabilizing the slope.
—Gabions were first used in Europe and since have been used in North America.

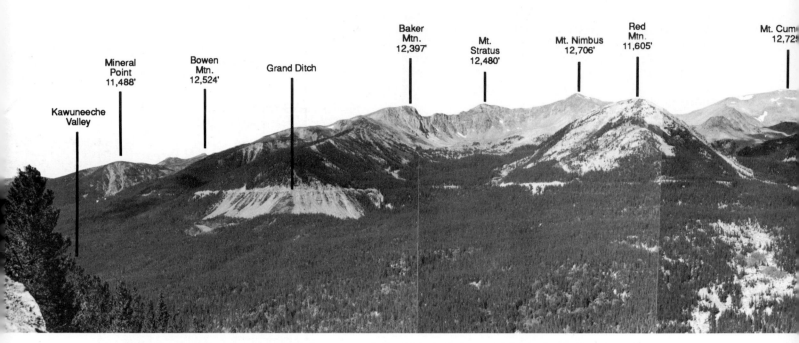

Kawuneeche Valley · Mineral Point 11,488' · Bowen Mtn. 12,524' · Grand Ditch · Baker Mtn. 12,397' · Mt. Stratus 12,480' · Mt. Nimbus 12,706' · Red Mtn. 11,605' · Mt. Cum... 12,72...

Panoramic view toward the west of the Never Summer Mtns. from Farview Curve.

MILE 13.1

CROSS SQUEAK CREEK.
El. 9870 ft.

MILE 13.7

CROSS PHANTOM CREEK.
El. 10,020 ft.
The stream flows southwest from Lake Irene near Milner Pass.

(0.1)

MILE 13.8

RHYOLITE PORPHYRY in ROAD-CUT on left.

No place to stop.

Mileage to next point of interest:

(0.2)

GEOLOGY:
—Just beyond Phantom Creek, a mass of very soft, light-colored clay-like material is in the roadcut on the left. This clay was once solid rock, but was ground up along a moving **fault** and altered by circulating hot water. Such material is called **fault gouge**.
—A short distance beyond, dark-brown, very fine-grained **rhyolite porphyry** crops out in the roadcut. This rock was injected as molten fluid into a fault cutting the schists during the Miocene Epoch between 24 and 5.3 million years ago. Later fault movement and circulating hot water deposited quartz and iron oxides in the porphyry.

11

FARVIEW CURVE.
El. 10,120 ft.
Parking area on right—at a curve.

MILE 14.0

Mileage to next point of interest:

(0.5)

SCENERY:
—Panorama above identifies landscape features.
—Never Summer Mtns. are directly west. The reddish rocks near the summits of the peaks result from oxidation and alteration of metallic **minerals**.
—Kawuneeche Valley of the Colorado River is below.

Fault gouge just east of Mile 13.8.
(F. W. Osterwald)

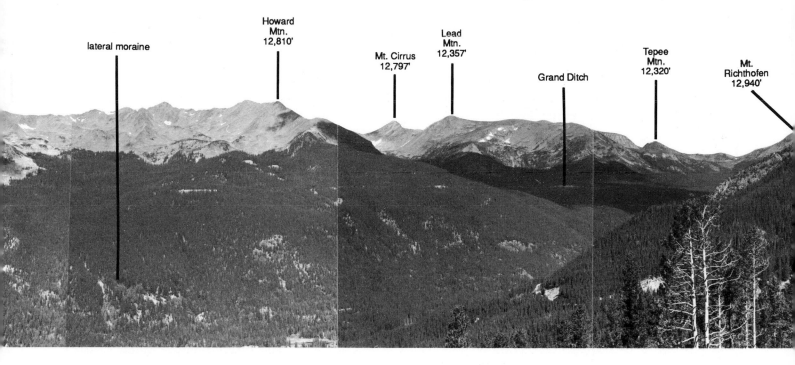

lateral moraine

Howard
Mtn.
12,810'

Mt. Cirrus
12,797'

Lead
Mtn.
12,357'

Grand Ditch

Tepee
Mtn.
12,320'

Mt.
Richthofen
12,940'

—The Grand Ditch (p. 94), part of the second oldest water diversion project in northern Colorado, winds along the upper slopes across the valley.
—Vasquez Mtns. are on the southern skyline.
—Jackstraw Mtn. (p. 95) can be seen on the eastern skyline from the upper end of the parking area.

PHOTO HINTS:
—Best time for pictures of the mountains to the west is in the morning. Good pictures of the Never Summer Mtns. are difficult to take from here because of the great range of light values between the dark forest below and the light-colored rocks above.

PLANTS:
—This stop is in the **subalpine life zone** that extends from 9000 ft. upward to **treeline**.
—Dominant trees are Engelmann spruces and subalpine firs. Use the key on p. 253 to identify the conifers around the parking area.

WILDLIFE:
—<u>DO NOT FEED THE WILDLIFE</u>. It is against Park regulations because it causes over-population of animals that are unable to adapt to wild conditions.
—Chickaree squirrels chatter and scold if you enter their territories. They collect pine cones into large piles called **middens**.
—Deer mice, least and Uinta

chipmunks, southern red-backed voles and pine martens live here and raid the squirrels' middens. Snowshoe hares and long-tailed weasels are common.
—Deer and elk feed in forest openings.
—Clarke's nutcrackers, gray jays, mountain chickadees, white-breasted and pygmy nuthatches, juncos, yellow-rumped warblers, several species of woodpeckers, blue grouse, pine grosbeaks and ruby-crowned kinglets are common.
—Goshawks and western red-tailed hawks hunt small birds and mammals.

GEOLOGY:
— A series of north-trending **faults** borders the Kawuneeche Valley. Hot mineral-bearing solutions deposited small veins containing ore minerals in and near some of these faults.
—Long before the Colorado River Glacier carved this valley into its present flattened U-shape, it was V-shaped because the stream rapidly eroded its path downward along the faults.
—Because the glacier partially filled the valley with rock debris, the gradient of the Colorado River is too low for the amount of water in the stream so the river **meanders** back and forth across the valley floor to compensate for its lack of slope. In some places **meanders** have been cut off as the river sought new channels, leaving **oxbow lakes**.

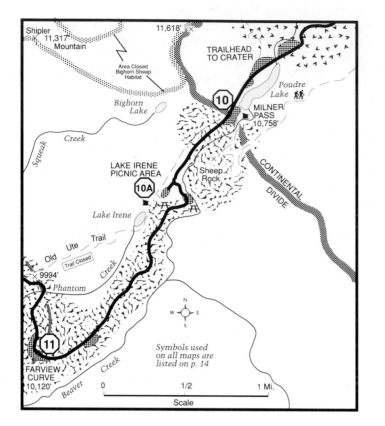

Close-up of the Grand Ditch.
(W. F. Wunsch photo, NPS collection)

Constructing a protective structure where the Grand Ditch crosses a landslide.
(NPS collection)

ADDITIONAL HISTORICAL NOTES

THE GRAND DITCH:

In 1891 the Water Supply and Storage Company was incorporated to build a series of ditches, canals and reservoirs. The objective was to collect water from the Never Summer Mtns. and to move it by gravity across the Continental Divide to the Cache la Poudre River, so that fields on the plains near Loveland and Fort Collins, Colorado could be irrigated.

Early construction was done by hand with Chinese, Japanese and Mexican laborers who were paid 22.5 cents per hour, from which 25 cents was deducted for each meal. Men lived in crude camps along the ditch route. The workers were often ill-equipped and poorly clothed. Tons of snow had to be shoveled from the ditch each spring so water could start flowing.

The ditch was extended south from Dutch Creek to Bakers Gulch in 1934 using heavy equipment for the first time.

The scar from ditch construction remains unhealed for several reasons. Most of the ditch was dug through loose, unsorted glacial debris in the tree-covered **lateral moraine**. At several places the ditch crosses hard **Precambrian** rock outcrops; in those places spoil was dumped down the steep hillside. Vegetation is slow to return in such areas. In past years, rocks and soil removed from the ditch during spring cleanings also were dumped over the cliffs.

Northward aerial view of the Kawuneeche Valley showing the Grand Ditch on the left and the western part of Trail Ridge Road on the extreme right. Specimen Mountain is on the right skyline.
(Joe Marold, NPS)

MILE

14.5

Mileage to next point of interest:

(1.3)

JACKSTRAW MOUNTAIN.
El. 10,280 ft.
Parking area on the right. Features are hard to see on the westbound drive.

SCENERY:
—Jackstraw Mtn. is to the south-south-east.
—Continental Divide along the Front Range is east and northeast.

NATURE:
—Dead trees near the top of the mountain look like a giant's pile of jack-straws. They were either killed by a fire or died as the climate cooled during the Arapaho Peak Glaciation between 100 and 350 years ago.
—When such trees are killed or removed, wind and solar radiation on the ground increase, while snow cover and soil moisture decrease. Thus modern, young Engelmann spruces and sub-alpine firs grow much more slowly and at lower elevations than did the trees in the old forest.

—GEOLOGY:
—The hummocks on the slopes of Jack-straw Mtn. are landslides in Middle Pindedale–age debris.

Jackstraw Mtn. to the east from Farview Curve has three summits that all are over 11,000 ft. in elevation. The rounded, hummocky slopes below treeline are landslides in loose glacial debris.

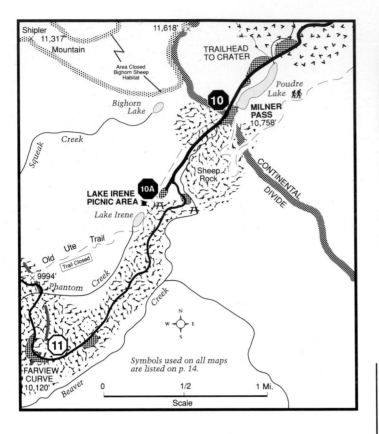

The Cache la Poudre Glacier flowed over Sheep Rock. The ice ground and polished the southwest end, but plucked rocks away from the other end, leaving it rough and jagged.

10A
MILE
15.8

Mileage to next point of interest:

(0.5)

LAKE IRENE PICNIC AREA.
El. 10,650 ft. Entrance on left.
—RESTROOMS:

Use caution when turning left into the picnic area.

SCENERY:
—SHEEP ROCK, another interesting **roche moutonnèe**, is northeast of the picnic area. Another picture of the rock is on p. 62.
—Lake Irene, a short distance down the hill to the southwest, is the source of Phantom Creek. The lake formed behind a small landslide from a Middle Pinedale moraine.

WILDLIFE:
—Clarke's nutcrackers, gray juncos, chipmunks, deer and ground squirrels. Bighorn sheep frequent the area around Sheep Rock.
—<u>DO NOT FEED THE WILDLIFE</u>. It is against Park regulations because it causes over-population of animals that are unable to adapt to wild conditions.

PLANTS:
—Marsh marigolds and globeflowers bloom in the wet meadow beyond the building in June and early July.
—Ramshorn louseworts, Whipple's penstemons, alpine goldenrods, pearly everlastings, Jacobs ladders and fire-weeds are a few of the many flowers that bloom during July.
—Fireweed (*Epilobium angustifolium*) is common throughout the Park from July until frost. It is valuable forage for deer and elk. The pink to magenta–colored blossoms grow on tall spikes. It is one of the first plants to sprout on disturbed soils, hence its name.

GEOLOGY:
—The southwestern side of Sheep Rock was smoothed and polished by glaciers that moved northeastward over it in each of the three Great Ice Ages.

HISTORY:
—The Ute Trail passes Lake Irene but below the lake is closed for revegetation. Before the Old Fall River Road between Grand Lake and Estes Park was completed in 1920, many tourists followed the trail on foot or horseback.
—Lake Irene was named by Squeaky Bob Wheeler for a guest at his dude ranch in the Kawuneeche Valley.
—In 1926 a mess hall, residence and stable were built here for road crew. A bunkhouse, built in 1930, was the only building still standing in 1988.

The trail to Forest Canyon Pass from Milner Pass traverses this cliff of Precambrian metamorphic rocks. Poudre Lake is in the background.

View northeastward from The Crater Trailhead showing the dip in road across the headwaters of the Cache la Poudre River. Light-colored Tertiary volcanic rocks are along the road and in the hill beyond.   (F. W. Osterwald)

10

MILE

16.3

Mileage to next point of interest:

(0.4)

CONTINENTAL DIVIDE at top of MILNER PASS.

El. 10,758 ft. Large parking area on right.
—RESTROOMS.

SCENERY:
—Normally the Continental Divide is thought to be a sharp, high ridge dividing water so that it flows either eastward or westward.
—Here, the low hillside behind the marker sign is the Continental Divide. Poudre Lake is on the eastern slope; its water begins a long trip to the Mississippi River and the Gulf of Mexico. Southwest of the hill, the water of Beaver Creek begins its westward journey down the west slope to the Gulf of California.
—Poudre Lake is to the northeast.
—Sheep Rock is on the southern skyline.

THINGS TO DO:
—A trail climbs 740 ft. in about 2 mi. along part of the Old Fall River Road and ends at Forest Canyon Pass.

GEOLOGY:
—The low hill behind the marker sign is a moraine that a Middle Pinedale–age glacier deposited from

50,000 to 35,000 years ago.
—The Colorado River Glacier, the largest in the Park, flowed almost 20 mi. from an elevation of 12,000 ft. along the Continental Divide north of Lulu City (p. 69, 227), to about 8400 ft. at the southern end of Shadow Mtn. Lake south of Grand Lake.
—Glacial ice, 2,000 ft. thick, filled the valleys and left only the tops of peaks exposed. Because of the great depth, ice over-flowed northeastward across Milner Pass and down the Cache la Poudre River valley.
—The ice smoothed and polished the southwest side of Sheep Rock and quarried rock away from the northeast side, leaving it rough and jagged (photo p. 62, 96,).

MILE

16.7

Mileage top next point of interest:

(0.1)

TRAILHEAD to THE CRATER.

El. 10,740 ft. Parking area on left.
Be careful turning left into the parking area.

THINGS TO DO:
—To see The Crater, follow a steep trail northwest about 0.6 mi. The Crater is a topographic depression on the southwestern flank of Specimen Mtn. Beyond The Crater the trail is closed to hikers to protect the habitat of bighorn sheep.

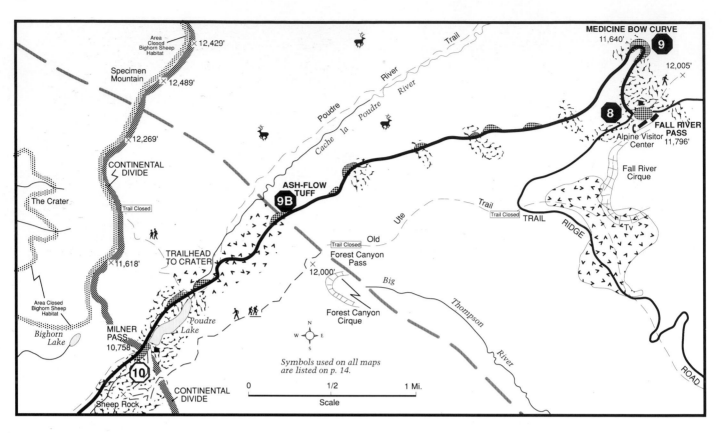

—The POUDRE RIVER TRAIL begins at Poudre Lake and descends about 1000 ft. in 9.3 mi. to Long Draw. Parts of the trail cross wet, marshy ground.

PLANTS:
—Many subalpine wildflowers grow around Poudre Lake and on the open grassy slope above the parking area.
—During July, tall chiming bells, rosy paintbrushs, arrow-leaved groundsels, stiff dark-headed sages, Drummond's rushes and little red elephants are easy to find—and photograph.
—Spikes of bistort wave in the wind and look like tufts of white to light-pink cottonballs. Blackfoot and Cheyenne Indians used the starchy bistort roots in soups and stews. When roasted, the roots have a sweet, nutty flavor. The are also a favorite food of bears and rodents.

CROSS CACHE LA POUDRE RIVER.
El. 10,725 ft.
—The headwaters of Cache la Poudre River—here just a small creek ("crick" to local old-timers) is Poudre Lake.

MILE
16.8
Mileage to next point of interest:
(0.7)

—This small stream becomes a middle–sized river by the time it joins the South Platte River near Greeley, Colorado.

BETWEEN CACHE LA POUDRE RIVER and MILE 17.5 (STOP 9B):

GEOLOGY:
—Rocks along the right side of the road are light-colored **welded ash-flow tuffs**.

ASH-FLOW TUFF OUTCROPS.
El. 10,920 ft. Small Parking area on left.

USE CAUTION, if you stop here.

GEOLOGY:
—Light-gray to cream-colored welded ash-flow tuff in roadcuts opposite the parking area were deposited 28 to 26 million years ago when a volcano in the Never Summer Mtns. exploded.
—It spewed hot, gaseous and nearly molten rock debris in an old valley.
—Older volcanic rocks in the lower part of Specimen Mtn. (directly west) and in the Never Summer Mtns. are from 55 to 54 million years old. They were partially buried by the younger ash-flow tuffs that make up the top part of the mountain.

9B
MILE
17.5
Mileage to next point of interest:
(2.7)

Red-tailed hawk. (NPS)

Golden eagle with chicks. (NPS)

Great gray owl. (NPS)

*Female saw-whet owl in nesting cavity.
(Chase Swift©)*

Great horned owl. (C.O. Harris, NPS)

Birds of prey.

View northeastward toward Medicine Bow curve showing the forest–tundra transition zone.

PLANTS:
—This stop is at the upper limit of the **subalpine life zone**, which extends from 9000 ft. to **treeline**.
—Large Engelmann spruces grow around the parking area. Ground cover in spruce forests includes tiny blueberry shrubs. Many birds and mammals (including humans) enjoy the sweet berries. They are a favorite food of the few black bears that live in the Park.
—Precipitation on the western side of the Continental Divide is about 6 in. more than on the eastern side and more water is available for plants. Wilflowers grow profusely on these **subalpine** slopes.
—When the snow melts in June and early July, white marsh marigolds and cream-colored globeflowers bloom first, followed by yellow alpine avens and paintbrushes.
—By late July and August, scarlet paintbrushes, goldenrods, sky pilots, geums, bistorts, kings crowns, green-leaved chiming bells and Rocky Mountain thistles bloom along the edge of the road.

BEYOND STOP 9B: There are no parking areas on the right side of the road in which to stop and see the irregular treeline along the sides of the Cache la Poudre River valley.

PLANTS:
—Treeline is between 11,400 and 11,500 ft. elevation in the Park.
—A **krummholz** (crooked wood) spruce-fir forest grows on the slope above the road (photo above).
—This is the **forest–tundra transition zone**. Because the areas in which species of both the **tundra and subalpine zones** overlap, a great variety of plants grows.
—Elevation of treeline varies according to wind direction and speed, snow depth, angle of slope, and the angle at which sunlight strikes the ground.
—Spruces and firs, which grow straight and tall at lower elevations, are gnarled and twisted by fierce winds as they battle to survive in the severe Alpine climate. They grow closely together in "islands" of dwarfed trees.

HISTORY:
—The road continues to climb the side of Cache la Poudre River valley, so named because in November 1836, some French trappers buried (*cached*) their supplies, including gunpowder, somewhere along the river. The next spring they returned to the spot and dug up their "cache" of powder (*Cache la poudre*) and other supplies.

Aerial view southeastward showing Medicine Bow Curve in the foreground, Fall River Pass in the middle distance and Trail Ridge Road in the distance. The ice-carved, high peaks of the Continental Divide are above Fall River Pass. The Front Range shows dimly on the skyline. (Joe Marold, NPS)

⑨

MILE

20.2

Mileage
to next
point of
interest:

(0.4)

MEDICINE BOW CURVE.
El. 11,640 ft.
BE CAREFUL entering the parking area on the left at a switchback.

SCENERY:
—Panorama (p. 56–57) identifies landscape features.
—Cache la Poudre River valley is below the parking area.
—Never Summer Mtns. are west and southwest of the overlook.
—Specimen Mtn., with its three rounded summits, is directly west across the valley.
—MEDICINE BOW PEAK (62 mi. away), CENTENNIAL RIDGE and the LARAMIE BASIN in Wyoming arc to the north.
—The rocky crags above the Alpine Visitor Center are on the eastern skyline.
—MUMMY RANGE is to the east and northeast.

PHOTO HINTS:
—Best time for photos to the west is in the morning.

PLANTS:
—Tundra plants include mountain dryads *(Dryas octopetala)*, a dwarf creeping shrub with cream-colored 8-petaled flowers whose seeds are plume-like and wave in the wind during August and September.
—Yellow alpine avens, western yellow paintbrushes and white bistorts are abundant.

WILDLIFE:
—Watch for herds of elk or deer in the open meadows above **treeline** on the opposite slope to the west.

GEOLOGY:
—During both Bull Lake and Pinedale Glaciations, ice was so thick in the Colorado River Glacier that it overflowed northeastward across Milner Pass. The same ice carved the broad, U-shaped Cache la Poudre River valley below Medicine Bow Curve.

Early attempts to clear snow from the Old Fall River Road were primitive— and slow. Here two teams of horses try to pull a bus carrying laborers through a drift in 1928 or 1929.
(Roger W. Toll, NPS)

⑧

MILE

20.6

ALPINE VISITOR CENTER and TRAIL RIDGE STORE at FALL RIVER PASS.
El. 11,796 ft. Entrance on left.
—RESTROOMS.
—EMERGENCY TELEPHONE.

<u>REVIEW PRECAUTIONS CONCERNING ELECTRICAL STORMS, P. 262.</u>

SCENERY:
—Don't miss the views into FALL RIVER CIRQUE and of FALL RIVER CANYON to the east from the overlook between the two buildings.
—MT. CHAPIN and the Mummy Range are to the east and northeast.
—From the parking area exit, Specimen Mtn. and the Never Summer Mtns. are directly ahead on the skyline.

THINGS TO DO:
—VISITOR CENTER has a small museum devoted to the **alpine tundra**. Park Service personnel are on duty to answer questions.
—Books and maps are for sale.
—TRAIL RIDGE STORE has a lunch counter, a fine collection of authentic Indian souvenirs, as well as books, film gifts and general souvenirs for sale.

—Near Trail Ridge Store, a 0.4-mi. trail leads to a scenic overlook at 12,005 ft. elevation. The steep trail climbs about 200 ft. but visitors are rewarded with magnificent vistas in all directions. Fall River Cirque is to the south, the Mummy Range to the east and northeast and the Medicine Bow Mtns. in northern Colorado and Wyoming are to the north and northwest. Along the trail are several masses of **pegmatite** with large crystals of **albite**, **microcline**, **quartz** and **mica**.

HISTORY:
—Fall River Pass is on one of six ancient trans-mountain Indian trails in the Park, Many other trails crossed the Front Range outside Park boundaries.
—Since 1920, when the Old Fall River Road was completed from Estes Park to Fall River Pass, this has been a favorite stop for travelers.
—When Trail Ridge Road was built, the route from Fall River Pass to Milner Pass was redesigned. Portions of that first road can still be traced across the **tundra** slopes below the entrance to the Visitor Center and on the slope above STOP 9.

To reach Estes Park,
follow Trail Ridge Road Eastbound Guide, Part 2, p. 103

To return to Grand Lake,
follow Trail Ridge Road Westbound Guide, Part 1, p. 53.

TRAIL RIDGE ROAD EASTBOUND—

Part 2 — Fall River Pass to Deer Ridge Junction.

Sunrise on the Tundra World Nature Trail.

"There are stupendous views of mountains, architecture, snowfields, emerald lakes, terraces, sweeping tablelands, bristling tooth-like peaks, titanic hexagonal towers, buttes and canyons—each gigantic and all effectively arranged on a tremendous scale."

——Enos A. Mills, <u>Rocky Mountain National Park</u>, Memorial Edition, 1932

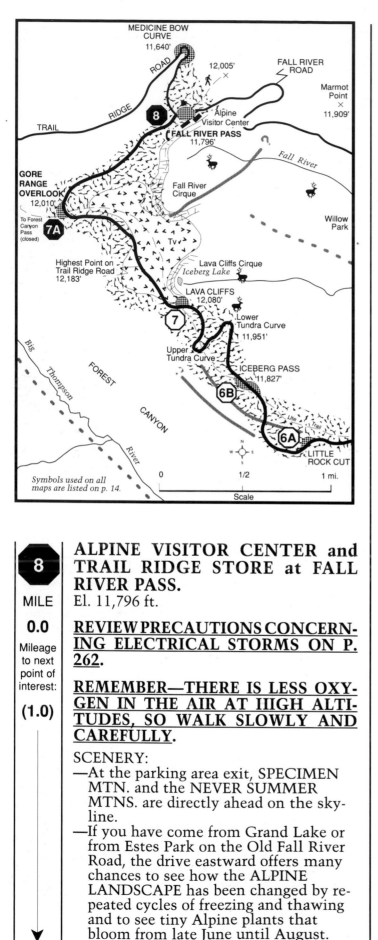

Symbols used on all maps are listed on p. 14.

Scale

8

MILE

0.0

Mileage to next point of interest:

(1.0)

ALPINE VISITOR CENTER and TRAIL RIDGE STORE at FALL RIVER PASS.
El. 11,796 ft.

<u>**REVIEW PRECAUTIONS CONCERNING ELECTRICAL STORMS ON P. 262.**</u>

<u>**REMEMBER—THERE IS LESS OXYGEN IN THE AIR AT IIIGH ALTITUDES, SO WALK SLOWLY AND CAREFULLY.**</u>

SCENERY:
—At the parking area exit, SPECIMEN MTN. and the NEVER SUMMER MTNS. are directly ahead on the skyline.
—If you have come from Grand Lake or from Estes Park on the Old Fall River Road, the drive eastward offers many chances to see how the ALPINE LANDSCAPE has been changed by repeated cycles of freezing and thawing and to see tiny Alpine plants that bloom from late June until August.

PLANTS:
—This harsh, windswept, treeless area is called **tundra**[1], a Lapp word that describes vast treeless Arctic and Alpine regions.
—Plants that survive such a forbidding climate are low-growing mats or cushions; some have deep tap roots.
—Plants in these communities are small, complex and delicate.
—Cushions of pink moss campions, three species of alpine clovers, white sandworts, alpine phlox and blue phlox, yellow alpine avens, white bistorts, sky pilots and blue greenleaf chiming bells may be in bloom in front of the Visitor Center during your visit.

PERIGLACIAL FEATURES: These are processes and topographic features found near glaciers or former glaciers and in glacial climates.
—With repeated cycles of freezing and thawing, rocks near the surface are broken and thrust up out of the ground. The jumbled mantle of rocks and soil surrounding the parking area formed in this way. The process is termed **frost heaving** or **up-freezing.**
—The ground <u>below</u> the layer exposed to freezing and thawing remains perennially frozen, and so is termed **permafrost.**
—Much of the **tundra** on Trail Ridge was underlain by permafrost during the Great Ice Ages. Permafrost still remains at a few sites.
—When thin, near-surface layers of rock and soil thaw during spring and summer, the soil particles become mixed with meltwater and flow downslope to form low ridges called **solifluction terraces.** There are many terraces along Trail Ridge Road. Large ones are easy to find, especially in late summer, because plants growing on the terraces stay green.

HISTORY:
—The road between Fall River Pass and Deer Ridge Junction was started in the fall of 1929 and opened for travel, July 16, 1932.
—This spectacular drive, the highest continuous paved highway in the U.S., has gentle grades with wide, sweeping curves and magnificent mountain vistas in all directions.

---

[1]Terms in **bold-face** type are defined in the Glossary, p. 256.

Travel on the Old Fall River Road in the early 1920s was a real adventure. (NPS)

—Paving was completed in 1938. Total cost of the road was less than $2 million.

Set your odometer at 0.0 or write down your mileage at the parking area exit. Turn left, following U.S. 34 to Estes Park.

Fall River Pass is also STOP 8 on the National Park Service pamphlet Trail Ridge Road Guide. Numbered arrowhead road signs identify these major stops.

Additional stops are identified in this text, and on the maps, by number-letter combinations, ie. STOP 7A. All parking areas are shown on the maps.

Alpine Visitor Center (right) and Trail Ridge Store (left) from the overlook after a snowstorm, September 1987.

Forest Canyon

Mt. Ida
12,280'

Gore Range
(60 miles away)

Baker
Mtn.
12,397'

Mt.
Stratus
12,480'

Red
Mtn.
11,605'

Mt.
Nimbus
12,706'

Forest
Canyon
Pass

Mt.
Cumulus
12,725'

Panoramic view southwestward from Gore Range Overlook.

7A

GORE RANGE OVERLOOK.
El. 12,010 ft.
Parking area entrance on the right.

MILE

1.0

Mileage
to next
point of
interest:

(0.5)

—This overlook gets the full force of strong westerly winds that sweep across the Never Summer Mtns. and blast the western end of Trail Ridge.
—Summertime gusts have been measured at 79 mph. The temperature is also cooler here than at lower elevations because air cools from 3 to 5 degrees Fahrenheit for every 1000 ft. increase in altitude.

SCENERY:
—Panorama above identifies landscape features.
—GORE RANGE is 60 mi. to the southwest.
—Peaks of Continental Divide are to the south and southeast.
—Forest Canyon Pass is below the overlook to the southeast.
—Never Summer Mtns. are to the west.
—Medicine Bow Mtns. in Wyoming are to the north.

PHOTO HINTS:
—Many photo possibilities at any time of the day, but lack of shadows at noonday may make pictures appear flat.
—Even on cloudy and stormy days, dramatic photos are possible. Don't put your camera away.

GEOLOGY:
—On the hillside east of this stop is the boundary (contact) between **Precambrian metamorphic gneisses** and **schists** and dark, reddish-brown **Tertiary welded ash-flow tuffs**, (photo, p. 107).
—About 28 to 26 million years ago, a volcano exploded in the Never Summer Mtns. about 8 mi. to the northwest. It spewed white-hot, glowing clouds of gas, rock fragments and ash onto a broad, shallow valley of the old upland surface. This old surface also extended to Milner Pass and La Poudre Pass.
—After cooling, the explosive volcanic material compacted into the welded ash-flow tuffs seen today.
—Later, water and glacial ice eroded most of the tuffs away, leaving only small patches today (see map).
—Where these volcanics crop out in roadcuts to the east, just west of Lava Cliffs, they are rusty-red in color. Heat from the hot volcanics baked and altered iron-bearing minerals in the ancient **Precambrian schists** to **hematite**, a red iron-oxide mineral.
—There are no stopping places to see these altered rocks unless one walks back toward the west 1/10-mile from the Lava Cliffs parking area.

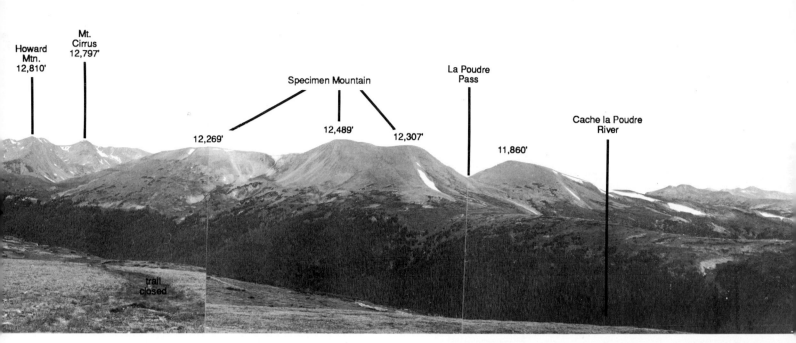

Howard
Mtn.
12,810'

Mt.
Cirrus
12,797'

Specimen Mountain

La Poudre
Pass

Cache la Poudre
River

12,269'

12,489'

12,307'

11,860'

trail
closed

PERIGLACIAL FEATURES:
—Also on the open, rounded hillside above the road are examples of freeze-thaw processes at work.
—Millions of broken pieces of the ash-flow tuffs have been arranged by freezing and thawing into distinctive piles of rock and soil making up what is called **patterned ground**.
— These piles called **rock circles, polygons, nets, garlands, stripes** and **felsenmeers** may be seen on the hill above the road as you drive east.
—Illustrations of these interesting and unusual features are on p. 113, 247 and 248.

HISTORY:
—The Ute Trail descended from this point to the Kawuneeche Valley floor and the Colorado River but is closed from here to Forest Canyon Pass for re-vegetation.
—The Gore Range was named for Scottish baronet Sir St. George Gore. In 1854 he led a notorious three-year hunting expedition from Ft. Laramie, Wyoming, southwestward into North and Middle Parks, Colorado. He tried to cross Gore Pass but was stopped by a band of Gros Ventre Indians, so the party returned to Wyoming.
—Gore's entourage included his fancy yellow-wheeled carriage, 21 two-wheeled Red River carts, 4 Conestoga wagons, 2 large freight wagons, a fur-lined commode and a portable bath-tub.

View eastward from Gore Range Overlook showing dark colored, welded, ash-flow tuffs of volcanic origin.

Felsenmeer in tuffs on summit above Lava Cliffs.
(F. W. Osterwald)

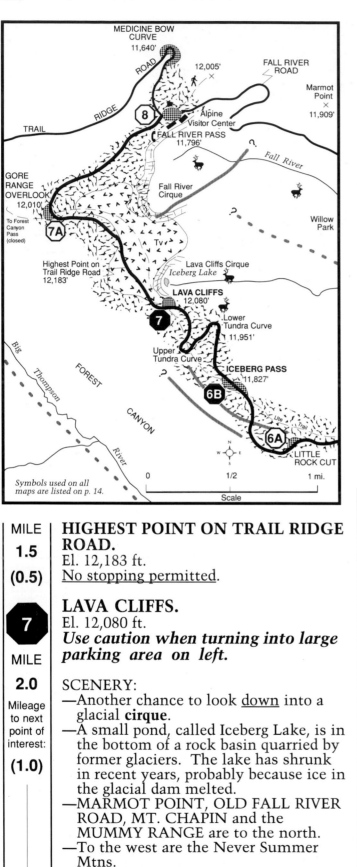

Iceberg Lake in Lava Cliffs cirque in 1927. (NPS)

Iceberg Lake was much smaller in August 1985
(Becky Osterwald)

MILE **1.5** (0.5)	**HIGHEST POINT ON TRAIL RIDGE ROAD.** El. 12,183 ft. <u>No stopping permitted.</u>
7 MILE **2.0** Mileage to next point of interest: (1.0)	**LAVA CLIFFS.** El. 12,080 ft. *Use caution when turning into large parking area on left.* SCENERY: —Another chance to look <u>down</u> into a glacial **cirque**. —A small pond, called Iceberg Lake, is in the bottom of a rock basin quarried by former glaciers. The lake has shrunk in recent years, probably because ice in the glacial dam melted. —MARMOT POINT, OLD FALL RIVER ROAD, MT. CHAPIN and the MUMMY RANGE are to the north. —To the west are the Never Summer Mtns. PHOTO HINTS: —Morning is the best time for photos into the cirque.

WILDLIFE:
—Brown-capped rosy finches, horned larks, swallows and ravens nest in the cracks and crevices of Lava Cliffs. Water pipits and white-crowned sparrows also nest on the **tundra**.
—White-tailed ptarmigans live year-round on the tundra. Summer plumage blends so well with the lichen-covered rocks, they are hard to find. Winter plumage is white.
—American kestrals (sparrow hawks), prairie falcons, gray jays, Clarke's nutcrackers and western red-tailed hawks are frequent summer visitors.
—Nine species of butterflies live on the tundra during their entire life cycle. Meade's sulfur and the gray variety of Phoebus parnassian have "solar collectors" on their wings and survive the Alpine climate by converting solar radiation into heat.
—Foxes, coyotes, martens, mountain lions, deer, elk, and bighorn sheep are summer visitors to the tundra.

BEYOND LAVA CLIFFS:
The road descends 250 feet on the beautiful, wide, sweeping TUNDRA CURVES to ICEBERG PASS. The scenery is breath-taking in all directions.

Aerial view eastward of Trail Ridge Road in September 1986. The rough, jagged outcrops of vertically dipping metamorphic rocks along the northeast side of Forest Canyon are cut by several faults, and contrast sharply with the smooth upland tundra surfaces. (D. B. Osterwald and J. B. Bennetti, Jr.).

6B
MILE

3.0

Mileage to next point of interest:

(0.7)

ICEBERG PASS.
El. 11,827 ft.
Large parking areas on each side of the road.

DO NOT CROSS DOUBLE–YELLOW LINE.

This divide, between Lava Cliffs to the northwest and the ridge above Rock Cut to the east, is blown free of snow most of the winter.

SCENERY:
—Tundra Curves and Lava Cliffs are to the northwest.
—The rocky crags at the summit of SUNDANCE MTN. are to the east.
—Great views of the ice-carved peaks of the Continental Divide are to the south and southeast.
—Never Summer Mtns., also on the Continental Divide, are to the west.
—Marmot Point, the rounded hill below the Mummy Range and Old Fall River Road are to the north.

THINGS TO DO:
—A wide variety of wildflowers bloom here from late June to August.
—PLEASE step on rocks if you walk away from the parking area to photograph the wildflowers and scenery. It takes hundreds of years for **tundra** plants to recover from being trampled by countless footsteps.

—Be careful not to drop any trash. Even a tissue dropped carelessly on a plant will kill it.
—See more examples of changes in the landscape wrought by cycles of freezing and thawing.

PLANTS:
—The largest and most striking plant on the tundra is the bright yellow sunflower *(Hymenoxys grandiflora).* "Compass flower" might be another good name for these plants because the blossoms always face toward the rising sun. After blooming, it dies.

PERIGLACIAL FEATURES:
—An active **solifluction terrace** (photo p. 49) with ponds is over the brow of the hill to the north where snow accumulates in huge drifts.
—Examples of **frost boils, hummocks, ponds** and **turf-banked terraces** (p. 247) are on both sides of the road.
—Processes that formed these periglacial features during the Ice Ages now are mostly dormant nearly everywhere on Trail Ridge because of less precipitation and warmer temperatures. These processes are still active in polar regions, however, because the sun strikes the ground at a higher angle in Colorado than it does near the poles. Thus the ground surface generally is warmer here than in high, polar latitudes where temperatures and sun angles are much lower.

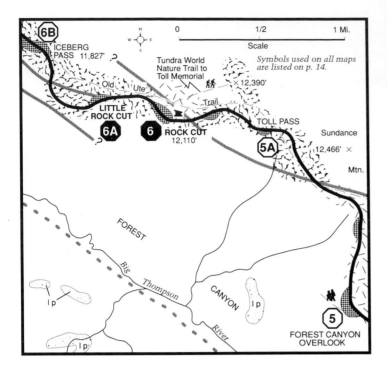

Little Rock Cut in early June 1989, before the snow had melted in the nivation depression.

After the snow melts, the residual rocks on the floor of the basin appear, interspersed with greening tundra plants.

6A LITTLE ROCK CUT.
El. 12,000 ft.

MILE
3.7

Mileage to next point of interest:
(0.4)

Use caution when turning into parking area on left.

THINGS TO DO:
—During the early summer, a boardwalk leads to a large snowbank in **a nivation depression** (see PERIGLACIAL FEATURES below).
—After the snow melts, the boardwalk is removed to protect the floor of the depression.

SCENERY:
—Never Summer Mtns. are to the west.
—Continental Divide is to the south.
—Chance to see more **periglacial features.**
—ROCK CUT, STOP 6, is to the east.

PLANTS:
—Distinctive communities of alpine wildflowers grow where thick snowbanks cover the ground all winter.
—As the snowbank melts, sedges and yellow snow buttercups bloom on the wet, boggy surface, followed by sibaldias and snowlovers.
—By late July and August, white-flowered black-headed daisies bloom. The "black" heads are actually dark purple hairs on the underside of the blossoms.

GEOLOGY:
—Outcrops of **schist** and **gneiss** break into angular, slab-like pieces during freeze-thaw cycles because of their layered structure. This contrasts with the way granite breaks into rough blocks.

PERIGLACIAL FEATURES:
—The **nivation depression** beyond the rail fence appears to be active. Nivation depressions form where deep snowbanks pile up in winter. As the snow melts, soil-water mixtures flow away from the snowbanks like syrup or honey, leaving residues of rocks near the margins of the snowbanks.
—Gradually the nivation depression is enlarged. If this process is carried far enough, a **cirque** forms.

Do not walk in the moist, boggy depression after the snow melts.

6

MILE

4.1

Mileage
to next
point of
interest:

(0.5)

ROCK CUT.

El. 12,110 ft.
Large parking areas on both sides of the road.
—Solar-powered RESTROOMS.

REVIEW PRECAUTIONS CONCERNING ELECTRICAL STORMS, p. 262.

SCENERY:
—Panorama on p. 46-47 identifies landscape features.
—More vistas of glaciated mountains along the Continental Divide to the southwest.
—Never Summer Mtns. are to the west.
—TUNDRA CURVES and LAVA CLIFFS, are to the northwest.

THINGS TO DO:
—TUNDRA WORLD NATURE TRAIL starts at the northwest end of the parking area. The asphalt pathway climbs 200 ft. in 0.5 mi. to the TOLL MEMORIAL PEAK FINDER. The steepest part of the trail is near the parking area where it crosses the Old Ute Trail.
—The peak finder, at the top of the larger crag, honors Roger Toll, the third Superintendent of "Rocky," who served from 1921 to 1929. He vigorously promoted and helped design Trail Ridge Road.
—Loose rocks on the ground along the trail arc sorted into distinctive geometric forms and shapes, making what is termed **patterned ground**. Many examples are close to the trail.
—Signs along the trail identify and explain unique features of the tundra.
—**Precambrian granite** crops out along the trail, but the crags are **Precambrian metamorphic gneisses** and **schists** with several irregular **dikes** and pods of light-colored **igneous pegmatites**.
—Views from the crags are spectacular in all directions.
—Watch for pikas, marmots and the usual birds of the tundra.

PHOTO HINTS:
—Dramatic photos of many subjects are possible any time of the day.
—Telephoto lenses help bring the mountains closer.
—Macro lenses are useful for close-ups of the tiny wildflowers.
—If you take close-ups, step on rocks— NOT on the plants.

PLANTS:
—Alpine wildflowers abound.
—A fenced plot along the left side of the parking area is used to study how long it takes for tundra plants to recover from countless footsteps. No new clumps of elk sedges (*Kobresia myosuroides*) have started to grow since the plot was fenced in 1959.

WILDLIFE:
—Pikas and yellow-bellied marmots are often seen along the parking areas.
—PLEASE DO NOT FEED THE WILDLIFE. It is against Park regulations because it causes over-population of animals that are unable to adapt to wild conditions.

GEOLOGY:
—Outcrops are **schist** and **gneiss**. Some small **pegmatite dikes** cut through the metamorphic rocks along the road.

PERIGLACIAL FEATURES:
—Above the rail fence and along the Tundra World Nature Trail are spectacular examples of **rock circles, polygons, nets, garlands** and **stripes**. These distinctive arrangements of rocks and soil are called **patterned ground**.
—Illustrations of these interesting but strange features are on p. 107, 113, 246, 247).

HISTORY:
—Trail Ridge Road was carefully designed not to scar the landscape and to blend with the natural surroundings.
—Rock Cut was the only location where much blasting was needed and great care was used to keep loose rocks from tumbling down the hillside (photo, p. 45).
—Minimum damage to the landscape by the equipment and crews is evident by how well the roadbed blends into the natural sites.
—Construction equipment included 5 gasoline-powered shovels, 3 roadgraders, 20 trucks and 8 horses. The contractor, W. A. Colt and Sons of Las Animas, Colorado, hired 6 foremen, 8 shovel operators, 5 cooks, 3 blacksmiths, 2 mechanics and 150 laborers to handle all construction.

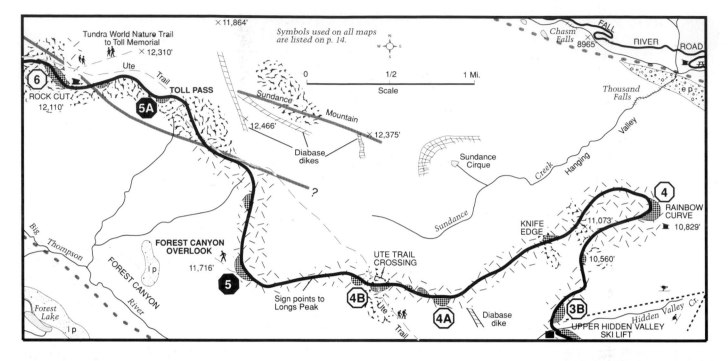

MILE

4.6

(0.3)

PARKING AREA on right is closed in mid-summer to protect tundra vegetation after a large snowbank on the hillside above the road melts.

5A

MILE

4.9

Mileage to next point of interest:

(1.3)

TOLL PASS.
El. 11,920 ft. Parking area on right. During winter, snowdrifts 30 to 40 ft. deep pile up on this small divide.

SCENERY:
—Continental Divide is to the south.
—Sundance Mtn. is on eastern skyline.
—Forest Canyon Overlook can be seen to the south-southeast.

THINGS TO DO:
—Another fine place to see a few of the more than 100 species of wildflowers that bloom on the **alpine tundra**.
—See a **solifluction terrace** along the parking area on the right.
—Many solifluction terraces on the slopes of Sundance Mtn. are visible from here.
—Another active **nivation depression** is across the road in the small depression.

Do not walk into this moist, boggy depression after the snow melts.

Clouds build up over the Continental Divide on most summer afternoons. View southwestward from Rock Cut toward the Never Summer Mtns. (F. W. Osterwald)

Mushroom rock near the Tundra World Nature Trail. Upper part of the pillar is schist, lower part is pegmatite. Continental Divide is on the skyline.

Black-headed daisy.

Koenigia islandica, one of the few annual plants that grow on the tundra. The tip of a ball-point pen indicates the tiny size of the blooms.

Big-rooted spring beauty.

Alpine sunflower.

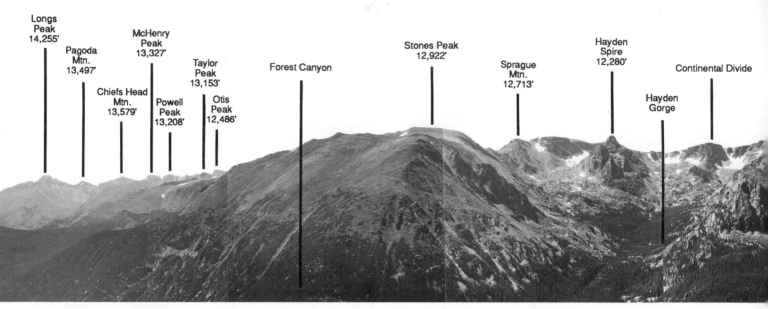

Longs Peak 14,255'
Pagoda Mtn. 13,497'
McHenry Peak 13,327'
Chiefs Head Mtn. 13,579'
Powell Peak 13,208'
Taylor Peak 13,153'
Otis Peak 12,486'
Forest Canyon
Stones Peak 12,922'
Sprague Mtn. 12,713'
Hayden Spire 12,280'
Hayden Gorge
Continental Divide

Panoramic view southwestward from Forest Canyon Overlook.

⬣ 5

MILE
6.2

Mileage to next point of interest:

(0.4)

FOREST CANYON OVERLOOK.
El. 11,716 ft.
Large parking area entrance on right.

REVIEW PRECAUTIONS CONCERNING ELECTRICAL STORMS, p. 262..

SCENERY:
—Panorama above identifies landscape features.
—Peaks of the Continental Divide on the southwestern skyline include STONES PEAK and TERRA TOMAH.
—Below the divide are HAYDEN GORGE, HAYDEN SPIRE and the GORGE LAKES.
—Never Summer Mtns. are to the west.
—Sundance Mtn. is to the north.
—FOREST CANYON, below the overlook, was filled with ice during each of the three major glaciations.
—One of best places to see how glaciers carved and sculpted the landscape.
—Another chance to see how the rolling, upland surface of Trail Ridge was reshaped by repeated cycles of freezing and thawing.

THINGS TO DO:
—Walk to the overlook to see awesome FOREST CANYON.
—PLEASE STAY ON THE PATH.
—Be careful not to drop any trash. Even a tissue dropped carelessly on a tundra plant will kill it.
—Signs explain glacial history and identify peaks.
—During the short summer, this is a great place to see many species of alpine wildflowers.

PLANTS:
—Because this area is swept by strong winds, little snow remains on the ground all winter.
—The test plot near the parking area was fenced in 1958, to study how **tundra** vegetation recovers from abuse by visitors after this stop was built in 1957. Hundreds of years may pass before the plants fully recover.

WILDLIFE:
—Pocket gophers burrow beneath the ground in search of food, mainly roots of plants. Signs of these animals are piles of loose, disturbed soil meandering through clumps of alpine plants along both sides of the path (photo p. 42).
—Yellow-bellied marmots —also called "rock chucks."
—Pikas.
—Long-tailed and montane voles.
—Deer and elk sometimes appear on distant hillsides.

Terra Tomah
12,718'

Mt. Ida
12,280'

Gorge Lakes

Forest Canyon

Baker
Mtn.
12,397'

Mt. Stratus
12,480'

Mt. Cumulus
12,725'

Mt. Nimbus
12,706'

Howard
Mtn.
12,810'

Lead
Mtn.
12,357'

GEOLOGY:

—Forest Canyon was filled with about 2000 feet of ice during Bull Lake Glaciation and probably by more ice during Pre-Bull Lake Glaciations. Later glaciations were less extensive because the climate was warmer.

—Examples of **cirques, horns, tarns, morainal lakes** and **U-shaped valleys** carved by Forest Canyon Glacier and its tributary glaciers are visible across the canyon in the peaks and valleys of the Continental Divide.

—Banded and layered **metamorphic** rocks crop out in glaciated rock walls across the canyon.

—Forest Canyon follows an ancient **fault zone** (see map) that first moved about 1.4 billion years ago.

—Blocky **granite** boulders surround the parking area.

HISTORY:

—STONES PEAK was named for G. M. Stone, a geology professor at Colorado College in Colorado Springs from 1881-1888. In the summer of 1886, while climbing with F. H. Chapin and William Hallett, he confirmed that actual flowing glaciers were in the Park.

—TERRA TOMAH MTN. was named by a group of Colorado Mountain Club members who came upon a previously unnamed lake while climbing in the Gorge Lakes area in 1914 . One member, an alum of Pomona College in California, sang out a portion of the

Hayden Gorge with Hayden Spire from Forest Canyon Overlook, July 1985. The foreground is covered by solifluction mantle.   *(Becky Osterwald)*

school's yell, *"He ne terratoma"* and the climbers decided to give the small lake that name.The words were from a Cohuila Indian chant. But the Colorado Geographic Board misread their handwriting, and assigned the name to the mountain. The lake was later named Doughnut.

—Abner Sprague (p. 130, 204) named HAYDEN SPIRE and JULIAN MTN. for Al and Julian Hayden in 1911 while the three friends were on a fishing trip. The Hayden brothers then named the peak south of Hayden Spire, SPRAGUE MTN.

—MT. IDA appeared on the 1915 USGS map, but the source of the name is unknown.

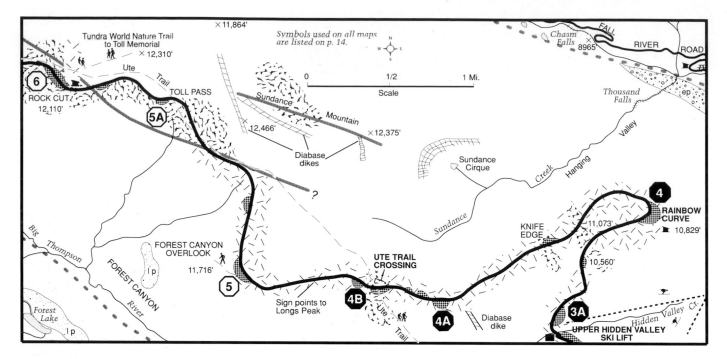

MILE **6.6**	**SIGN POINTS TO LONGS PEAK.** El. 14,255 ft., 11 miles away.

SIGN POINTS TO LONGS PEAK.
El. 14,255 ft., 11 miles away.

MILE 6.6

4B

TREELINE.
El. 11,480 ft.
Small parking area on right. If this one is full, two more are on the right side of the road west of RAINBOW CURVE.

MILE 7.0

Mileage to next point of interest;

(0.1)

SCENERY:
—Longs Peak is to the southeast.
—Forest Canyon is below parking area.

PHOTO HINTS:
—From here, majestic Longs Peak is photogenic at any time.
—The **krummholz** forests are also interesting subjects for your camera.

PLANTS:
—Along both sides of the road are **krummholz** (crooked wood) spruce-fir **tree islands** marking the **forest-tundra transition life zone**.
—Because species of both zones overlap, types of vegetation vary widely.

OLD UTE TRAIL CROSSING.
El. 11,440 ft.
Small parking area on right.

MILE 7.1

(0.4)

THINGS TO DO:
—A good hiking trail descends 3000 ft. in about 6.0 mi. to Upper Beaver Meadows. The trail leads along Tombstone Ridge to Timberline Pass

and around Beaver Mountain to the trailhead. Only one section is rough.

PLANTS:
—Across the road to the north are several dead **tree islands** that were alive as recently as the late 1970s.

HISTORY:
—Cairns (piles of rocks used as markers) were built to guide early settlers, prospectors and tourists on horseback who followed the Ute Trail. Most have been removed and in some places the present trail diverges from the older one because it was rebuilt during the 1920s.
—Trail Ridge Road generally follows a route used for thousands of years by American Indians and their ancestors to cross the Front Range. These early visitors came to hunt deer, elk, bighorn sheep, bison and possibly, at an earlier time, mammoths.
—Prehistoric people built a rock game-drive wall on a flat area along Tombstone Ridge so the animals could be channeled into a small enclosure and easily killed.
—Three small, rock-faced cabins stood against the hillside north of the highway from 1931 until the mid-1970s. One was used as a garage and two for emergency shelters to house road-clearing crews and Park Service personnel doing high-altitude research.

Construction of Trail Ridge Road in 1930 or 1931 had reached the Knife Edge east of Alternate Stop 4B.   (NPS)

By August 1987 coniferous trees were gradually filling in the openings on the mountainside that resulted from the pre-1860 forest fire at the Knife-Edge.

4A

MILE

7.5

Mileage to next point of interest:

(1.6)

ALTERNATE STOP:
El. 11,280 ft.
Small parking area on right.

SCENERY:
—Eastward are dramatic views of the KNIFE EDGE, a sharp, narrow divide between Sundance Creek (on the left) and Hidden Valley Creek (behind the ridge on the right).
—Mt. Chapin in the Mummy Range is to the north.
—The small SUNDANCE CIRQUE at the head of Sundance Creek is at the head of the steep valley on the left.

PHOTO HINTS:
—Photos of gnarled, twisted, dead trees can be dramatic, especially at sunrise, sunset or during storms.

PLANTS:
—Fire destroyed much of a very old spruce-fir forest sometime before 1860; only isolated patches of this old forest remain.
—Before the fire, the dense forest stood straight and tall. Today, however, Engelmann spruces, subalpine firs and limber pines grow very slowly at this elevation and are twisted and bent by fierce winds. They grow best in the shelter of rocks and fallen timber.
—The fire may have changed the local climate because when trees are killed or removed, wind and solar radiation on the ground increase, thus decreasing snow cover and soil moisture.
—Alternatively, the change in the forest may also be the result of cold weather and climate during the second advance of the **Arapaho Peak Glaciation** which reached its maximum between 1850 and 1870.
—Low, compact clumps of subalpine willows *(Salix)* growing along the roadside are regularly pruned by savage winds carrying ice and soil particles.
—Purple fringes *(Phacelia sericea)* bloom along the edge of the road here in July. They bloom earlier at lower elevations and literally climb the mountain as summer progresses.
—Raspberry bushes and the Colorado State Flower, the blue columbine, bloom along the right side of the road beyond the Knife Edge in July, before the road reaches RAINBOW CURVE.

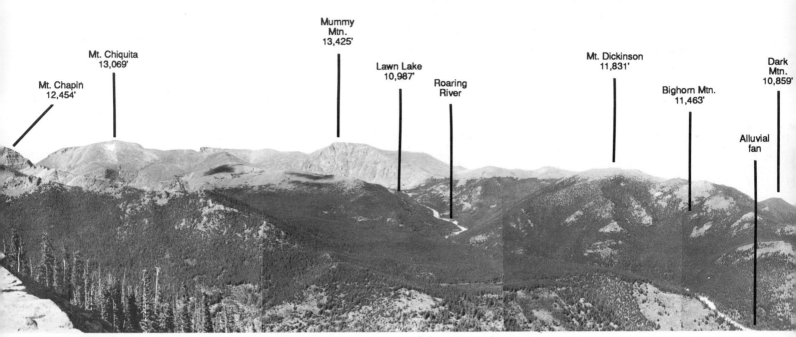

Mt. Chapin
12,454'

Mt. Chiquita
13,069'

Mummy
Mtn.
13,425'

Lawn Lake
10,987'

Roaring
River

Mt. Dickinson
11,831'

Bighorn Mtn.
11,463'

Dark
Mtn.
10,859'

Alluvial
fan

Panoramic view eastward from Rainbow Curve.

4

MILE

9.1

Mileage
to next
point of
interest:

(0.6)

RAINBOW CURVE.
El. 10,829 ft.
***Use caution to reach large parking
area on left—on an outside curve.***
—Solar-powered RESTROOMS.

SCENERY:
—Panorama above identifies landscape
features.
—Summer showers often produce rainbows in the eastern sky.
—HORSESHOE PARK is below the
overlook.
—HIDDEN VALLEY is directly below
the overlook.
—DEER MTN. is the flat-topped mountain beyond Hidden Valley.
—The scar and **ALLUVIAL FAN** deposited almost instantly on July 15, 1982
when Lawn Lake dam failed, are on
the northern side of Horseshoe Park
valley (p. 150). Lawn Lake is just
above the trees at the top of the rock
debris.

PHOTO HINTS:
—Best time for photos is in morning and
late afternoon.

PLANTS:
—Below the overlook are vistas of the
subalpine life zone spruce-fir forests
that grow between **treeline** and 9000
ft. elevation.

WILDLIFE:
—Least and Colorado chipmunks,
golden-mantled ground squirrels,
Clarke's nutcrackers, gray jays and
Stellar's jays vie for your attention—
and pose for photographs.
—PLEASE DO NOT FEED THE WILD-
LIFE. It is against Park regulations
because it causes over-populations of
animals that are unable to adapt to
natural conditions.

GEOLOGY:
—**Granite**, about 1.45 billion years old, is
exposed in the the roadcut.
—Prominent **joints** (cracks) make this
rock easy to quarry. Retaining walls
along Trail Ridge Road were built with
blocks from this cut and from a quarry
west of Toll Memorial.
—Hidden Valley, below the overlook, is
bounded on its north side by a tree-
covered Early Pinedale-age **lateral
moraine** deposited by the Fall River
Glacier between 75,000 and 60,000
years ago. This moraine blocked Hidden Valley Creek from its former
course into Horseshoe Park.

McGregor Mtn. 10,486' | Horseshoe Park | Hidden Valley | Deer Mtn. 10,013' | Trail Ridge Road | Twin Sisters Mtn. 11,413' | "Iron dike"

New Lake (1982)

Alluvial fan

lateral moraine

MILE **9.7** **(0.6)**	**TWO MILES ABOVE SEA LEVEL.** El. 10,560 ft. Sign is on left at a small parking area.

3A

MILE
10.3

Mileage
to next
point of
interest:

(1.6)

UPPER HIDDEN VALLEY SKI LIFT.
El. 10,470 ft.

Be careful when turning into parking areas on the left on either side of ski lift.

SCENERY:
—Chance to enjoy the huge, old, **subalpine** spruce and fir trees that were not burned in the 1915 Hidden Valley forest fire (p. 120).
—To the east are glimpses of Hidden Valley and of Fall River Valley beyond.
—To the southwest is TOMBSTONE RIDGE above **treeline**.

PLANTS:
—During June and July, water from melting snow cascades down the steep hillsides.
—Many **subalpine** plants thrive in this moist area. Along rock retaining walls are white brookcresses, yellow heart-leaf arnicas and blue larkspurs. Also growing are tall clumps of chiming bells *(Mertensia ciliata)*, called "blue medicine" by Cheyenne Indians who treated smallpox and measles with it.
—The slopes are closed for revegetation.

WILDLIFE:
—Chickarees (gray squirrels) are common.
—Residents of the the spruce-fir forests include snowshoe hares and jack rabbits, a few bobcats, coyotes, long-tailed weasels, woodrats ("pack rats"), and elusive martens and ermines.

HISTORY:
—The Estes Valley Recreation and Park District operates this lift during the ski season.

BETWEEN UPPER HIDDEN VALLEY SKI LIFT and MANY PARKS CURVE:

PLANTS:
—Redberried elder shrubs grow along the roadsides. They have large clusters of small white flowers in June and July. By late August they bear many small, dark red berries that are a favorite food for deer, elk, bears and birds.
—The drive eastward passes through a beautiful virgin, unburned **subalpine** spruce-fir forest.
—Limber pines grow on rocky, wind-swept ridge crests. Tops of many of these trees are flat rather than spire-shaped as are spruces and firs (see key, p. 253).
—So many small conifers have sprouted along the roadsides since the 1950s that they look like a miniature forest below the older, taller trees.

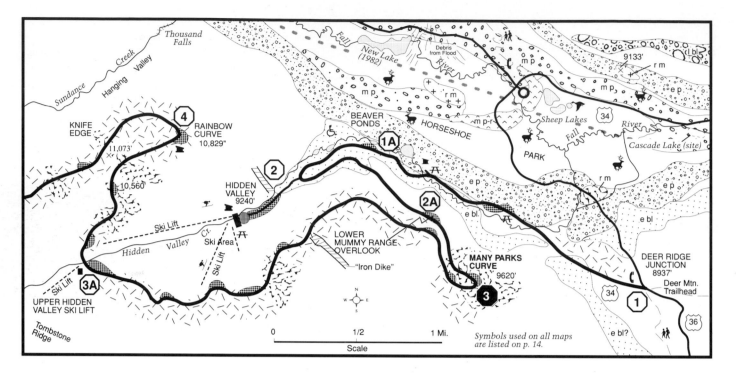

MILE
11.9
(1.4)

OUTCROP OF THE "IRON DIKE"
is on the right. There is no stopping place.

GEOLOGY:
—A dark rusty-brown, very fine-grained **igneous diabase** fills a **fault** or crack in the surrounding granite.
—Another outcrop of this dike at HIDDEN VALLEY SKI AREA is much easier to see.

MANY PARKS CURVE.
El. 9620 ft.

3

MILE
13.3

Mileage to next point of interest:

(0.5)

Follow sign to eastbound parking area.
A boardwalk connects the two parking areas.

SCENERY:
—Panorama (p. 121) identifies landscape features such as HORSESHOE PARK, MORAINE PARK, BEAVER BROOK PARK and ESTES PARK.
—The word "park" means many things to Coloradoans (p. 12).

PHOTO HINTS:
—Best time for photos to the east and south is in the afternoon.

PLANTS:
—Surrounding the parking areas are lodgepole pines and aspens that have grown since a fire started in a sawdust

pile at a sawmill in Hidden Valley on Halloween, 1915.
—These trees are interspersed with older Engelmann spruces and subalpine firs that survived the 1915 fire.

WILDLIFE:
—Golden-mantled ground squirrels, least and Colorado chipmunks scamper around the rocks begging for handouts.
—<u>DO NOT FEED THE WILDLIFE.</u>
—Clarke's nutcrackers, Stellar's jays, gray jays, chickadees and ravens are frequent visitors.

GEOLOGY:
—Most outcrops are **Precambrian metamorphic mica schist** and **granite gneiss**.

BETWEEN STOP 3 and STOP 2:
The highway descends about 400 ft. winding through lodgepole pine and aspen forests. The aspens are glorious in the fall when their leaves turn golden yellow and orange.

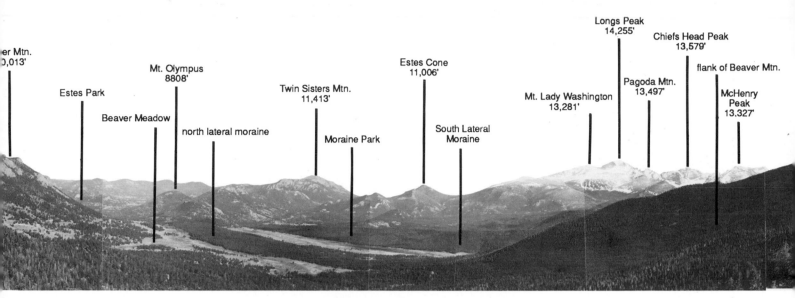

Longs Peak
14,255'

Chiefs Head Peak
13,579'

er Mtn.
0,013'

Estes Cone
11,006'

flank of Beaver Mtn.

Mt. Olympus
8808'

Estes Park

Pagoda Mtn.
13,497'

McHenry
Peak
13,327'

Beaver Meadow

Twin Sisters Mtn.
11,413'

Mt. Lady Washington
13,281'

north lateral moraine

Moraine Park

South Lateral
Moraine

Panoramic view southeastward from Many Parks Curve.

View eastward of the "Iron Dike" at Mile 11.9 on the eastbound drive.   (Becky Osterwald)

Wallflower.

Miners candle.

Indian paintbrushes.

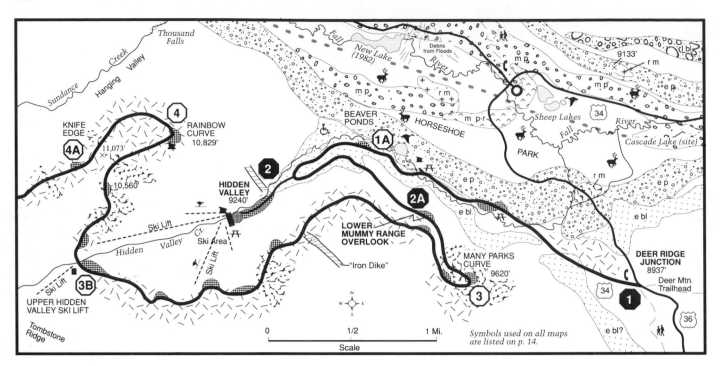

Symbols used on all maps are listed on p. 14.

2A — MILE 13.8

Mileage to next point of interest: **(0.9)**

LOWER MUMMY RANGE OVERLOOK.
El. 9540 ft.
Small parking area on right—on an outside curve.

SCENERY:
—Panorama (p. 123) identifies landscape features.
—Mummy Range is to the north.
—A closer view of the **alluvial fan** is below the overlook.
—Fall River valley and Horseshoe Park are to the north.

PHOTO HINTS:
—Best time for photos is in the morning or late afternoon.

PLANTS:
—Rocky Mountain maples growing along the edge of the parking area turn bright red in the fall.

HISTORY:
—MUMMY RANGE was named by either the Earl of Dunraven (p. 200) or by mountaineer William Hallett because its skyline supposedly resembles an Egyptian mummy lying on its back.
—MT. CHAPIN was named for Frederick Hastings Chapin, a mountain climber from Hartford, Conn., who first visited Estes Park in 1886 and returned to climb the peak the next year.

—MT. CHIQUITA probably was named by Enos Mills.
—YPSILON MTN. was named for the huge "Y" outlined by the cracks in its southeast face. Mrs. F. H. Chapin probably named the peak in 1887.
—FAIRCHILD MTN. was named for Lucius Fairchild, a governor of Wisconsin, a foreign minister to Spain, a Civil War veteran and a Commander-in-Chief of the Grand Army of the Republic, who visited Colorado in 1886. This is one of the few landmarks in the Park that are named for polictical figures.

2 — MILE 14.7

Mileage to next point of interest: **(0.5)**

ENTRANCE TO HIDDEN VALLEY PICNIC and SKI AREA.
El. 9240 ft.
—RESTROOMS in ski lodge.

Use caution when turning left.

THINGS TO DO:
—Picnic area.
—The Estes Valley Recreation and Park District opperates the ski area during the ski season.
—Ranger Station is in ski lodge.
—Headquarters for Rocky Mountain Nature Association seminars.
—First snow plow used on Trail Ridge Road is displayed.

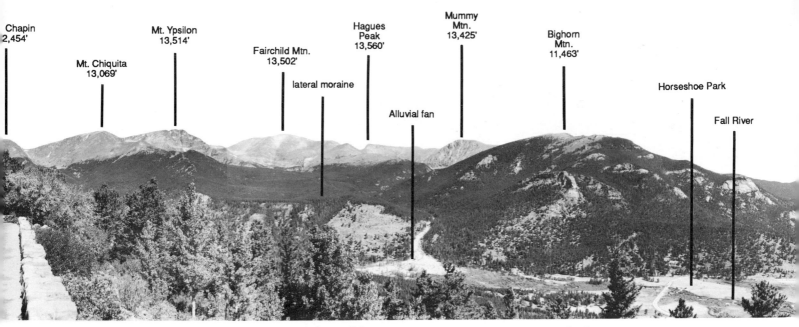

Chapin
2,454'

Mt. Chiquita
13,069'

Mt. Ypsilon
13,514'

Fairchild Mtn.
13,502'

lateral moraine

Hagues
Peak
13,560'

Alluvial fan

Mummy
Mtn.
13,425'

Bighorn
Mtn.
11,463'

Horseshoe Park

Fall River

Panoramic view northward from Lower Mummy Range Overlook

PLANTS:
—Ski lodge is at the lower limit of the **subalpine life zone** (9000 ft. to treeline).
—Aspens, subalpine spruces and firfs grow here in a lush forest on the hillsides above the ski lodge where winter snows reach 3 to 5 ft. deep. The steep upper slopes receive 10 to 15 ft. of snow.
—Yellow golden banners, lavender locoweeds and red Indian paintbrushes bloom throughout the valley in June and July.
—Indian paintbrushes (*Castilleja linariaefolia*), the Wyoming state flower, were named for Spanish botanist Domingo Castillejo. They have very small flower blossoms; the red color is in the upper bracts or leaves of the plant.
—Lavender to whitish Rocky Mountain locoweeds, pink wild roses, white pussytoes and yarrows bloom around the parking area during July and August.

GEOLOGY:
—A low, rounded ridge of rusty-brown, iron-rich, very fine-grained **igneous diabase** (photo p. 31) extends up the hill just above and across Hidden Valley Creek, 0.2 mi. west of the entrance to Hidden Valley Ski Area.
—Termed the "Iron Dike" by early Front Range miners because in some places

it contains valuable metallic minerals. The **intrusive igneous dike** was injected as a liquid into a **fault** in solid granite about 1.05 billion years ago.
—This is one of a series of northwest trending **dikes** in the the Park, but none contain economically valuable minerals.

HISTORY:
—Before 1900, Abner Sprague (p. 129), 130, 204) ran a sawmill near the present ski lift.
—From 1907 to the 1930s, Dan Griffith operated another sawmill here. The 1915 fire burned much of Hidden Valley. Aspen and lodgepole pine forests that sprouted since the fire are differently colored than the old spruce-fir forest so they clearly mark the fire area.
—The ski area started in 1935 when some Estes Park residents built rope tows. The present lodge and ski lifts were built in 1955.

BETWEEN STOP 2 and MILE 15.2:

WILDLIFE:
—The road passesHidden Valley Creek which has been dammed by beavers.
—Some beaver ponds and lodges can be seen to the left of the road.

Beavers rarely sun themselves on their lodges in the middle of the day.   (Enos A. Mills photo, collection of the Enos Mills Homestead Cabin)

MILE 15.2

Mileage to next point of interest:

(0.5)

BEAVER PONDS on left.
El. 9180 ft.
This is a fine stop for the westbound trip.

DO NOT CROSS DOUBLE–YELLOW LINE TO STOP:

—Greenback cutthroat trout, once thought to be near extinction, were successfully reintroduced to Hidden Valley Creek.
—Fishing is permitted from August 1 to December 31 on a catch-and-return basis only. <u>Colorado fishing license is required.</u>

GEOLOGY:
—The tree-covered hill on the left across Hidden Valley Creek, is an Early Pinedale-age **lateral moraine** that blocked the creek from its former direct course into Horseshoe Park.

MILE 15.7

(0.5)

PICNIC AREA, on left.
—RESTROOMS.
—No fishing permitted here.
—Picnic tables.

MILE 16.2

Mileage to next point of interest:

(1.0)

EASTERN END OF HIDDEN VALLEY.
El. 8940 ft. Parking areas on both sides of the road.

DO NOT CROSS DOUBLE–YELLOW LINE.

PLANTS:
—This stop is near the upper limit of the montane lifve zone which extends from 6000 to 9000 ft. elevation.

WILDLIFE:
—Beavers lived in the meadow on the right until the 1950s when they moved upstream looking for new sources of food and building materials.

GEOLOGY:
—Parking areas are build on an Early Pindedale-age **lateral moraine** left by the Fall River Glacier between 75,000 and 60,000 years ago (see map).

BETWEEN STOP 1A and STOP 1:

GEOLOGY:
—**Granite** ledges on the left just before reaching STOP 1 are deeply weathered and iron-stained.

①

MILE 17.2

DEER RIDGE JUNCTION.
El. 8937 ft.

An EMERGENCY TELEPHONE is in a dark green box on a post along the hillside northwest of the road junction.

SCENERY:
—Longs Peak and the Continental Divide are to the south on the skyline.
—Estes Cone is the lower, cone-shaped peak to the left of Longs Peak.

THINGS TO DO:
—Trailhead for Deer Mtn. is here. The trail rises about 1000 ft. in 2.5 mi.

**To reach Estes Park, follow U.S. 36 eastward
past the National Park Visitor Center,
or turn left and follow U.S. 34 eastward along Fall River
to Estes Park, using the Deer Ridge guide, p. 18.**

BEAR LAKE ROAD

**This drive starts 0.2 mi. west of Beaver Meadows entrance Station,
where the Bear Lake Road joins U.S. 36, the Deer Ridge Road.**

*Glacier Gorge, Bierstadt Lake, Bierstadt Moraine (right) with the Continental Divide on the skyline.
(F. W. Osterwald and J. B. Bennetti, Jr.)*

"The fascinating story left by the Ice King is for the most part
well-preserved and forms one of the Park's chief attractions.
No where in America are glacial records of such promin-
ence, more numerous, accessible and easily read."

——Enos A. Mills, <u>Your
National Parks</u>, 1917.

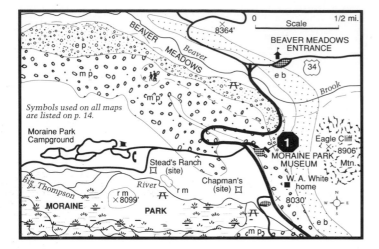

The main building of Moraine Park Lodge (now t*[...]* Museum) in 1936. This resort opened in 1908 on la*[...]* homesteaded by Imogene Green in 1899. Miss Gree*[...]* later Mrs. W. H. McPherson, ran the popular lodge f*[...]* many years and was active in community affairs. S*[...]* helped plan the dedication ceremony for the Nation*[...]* Park. *(Enwall, NP*

MILE **0.0** Mileage to next point of interest: **(1.2)**	# JUNCTION, BEAR LAKE ROAD with DEER RIDGE ROAD. El. 8325 ft. ***Turn left from Deer Ridge Road. Set your odometer at 0.0 or write down your mileage.*** ***If you take any side trips from the main road, your mileages will increase, so use the distance between stops (shown in the left column) to find the distances to your next stop or point of interest.*** **BETWEEN the JUNCTION and STOP 1:** SCENERY: —Very nice view of LONGS PEAK is directly ahead. —The road crosses a meadow along BEAVER BROOK and curves around a small hill of Early and Middle Pinedale-age **lateral moraines**[1]. PLANTS: —Montane **life zone**[2] wildflowers bloom in the meadow and in the aspen groves from April through June. —Most aspen trees have black scars on their trunks where deer and elk have eaten the soft aspen bark—sure signs of winter food shortages and of too many animals.

[1]Words in **bold-face type** are defined in the Glossary, p. 256.

[2]Life zones are communities of plants and animals characterized by dominant species living at particular climates and altitudes.

WILDLIFE:
—Deer and elk frequent this area in early morning or at dusk to feed on shrubs and grasses.

① MORAINE PARK MUSEUM.
El. 8240 ft.
—RESTROOMS.

MILE 1.2

Turn left WITH CAUTION into the large parking area above the road.

THINGS TO DO:
—The museum, open during summer months, features dioramas of the wildlife in the Park. It also has an excellent audio-tape and display on the Park's glacial history.
—Park Service employees are on duty to answer questions.
—Some naturalist-led hikes start here.
—Books and maps for sale.
—A public telephone is at MORAINE PARK CAMPGROUND, 0.5 mi. west.

SCENERY:
—Panorama (p. 127) identifies landscape features.
—Longs Peak, on far left, is east of the Continental Divide.

Panorama from Moraine Park Museum.

—Views westward of the high glaciated peaks along the Continental Divide.
—First chance to see TAYLOR, ANDREWS and TYNDALL glaciers.
—Along each side of Moraine Park are views of the tree-covered **lateral moraines** of the ancient THOMPSON GLACIER.

PHOTO HINTS:
—Best times for photos of the mountains to the west and south are in the mornings.

PLANTS:
—The Moraine Park Nature Trail starts at the museum and winds through the dry, sun-drenched ponderosa pine forest.
—Shrubs include wax currant, bitterbrush, rabbitbrush, serviceberry, thimbleberry and chokecherry.
—First wildflowers to bloom in spring are white candytufts, followed by lavender pasque flowers. Pearly everlastings, mountain pussytoes and sulfur flowers bloom during the early summer and by fall tall lavender asters and yellow gumweeds grace the hillsides.

WILDLIFE:
—Common mammals in **montane** ponderosa pine forests include four species of bats, Nuttall's cottontails, snow-shoe hares, yellow-bellied marmots, golden-mantled and Wyoming ("picket pin") ground squirrels. Others include Abert's squirrels, northern pocket gophers, deer mice, bushy-tailed voles, porcupines and long-tailed weasels. Larger mammals include coyotes, red foxes, badgers, skunks, a few cougars (mountain lions) and bobcats, as well as herds of deer and elk.
—Some of the birds that commonly nest in this life zone are mountain bluebirds, chickadees, pygmy and white-breasted nuthatches, Williamson's sapsuckers, dark-eyed juncos, pine siskins, Cassin's finches and broad-tail hummingbirds.

GEOLOGY:
—Three million years ago, before the Great Ice Ages, the mountains in Rocky Mountain National Park had rounded summits with broad ridges and stream-carved, V-shaped valleys.
—When the climate became colder heavy winter snowfalls did not melt in the summers. The weight of the ever-increasing depth of snow changed the lower parts of the snow to ice which began slowly flowing downhill.
—As glacial ice froze solidly to the **bedrock**, chunks of rock were plucked from the bedrock and carried away by the ice, leaving bowl-shaped depressions termed cirques (pronounced "serks").

*During the 1890's cattle grazed in Moraine Park and hay was cut for winter feed. On the right is a mowing machine. A well-known **roche moutonnèe**, is just behind the hay rake on the left. It somehow escaped being ground away when glacial ice filled Moraine Park.* *(NPS)*

An 1895 view of Spragues Hotel, the first in Moraine Park. *(NPS collection)*

By 1905 an expanded Spragues Hotel was providing the latest in transportation for its guests. Another picture of this ranch site by about 1930 is on p. 146.
(Lawrence "Con" Squires photo, NPS collection)

Golden banner.

Cottontail rabbit. (Chase Swift©)

Porcupine. *(Chase Swift©)*

Anemone.

Candytuft.

Red-shafted flicker.   *Red-naped sapsucker.*   *Pygmy nuthatch.*

(Bird pictures by Chase Swift©)

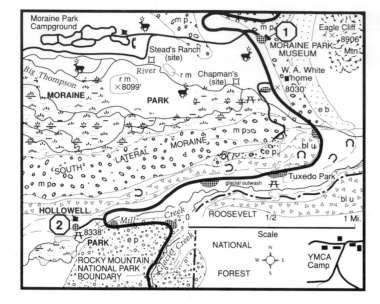

Party about to leave Chapmans' Store on a pack trip in the 1890s. The man in the center, probably a guide, is riding a mule and leading a pack animal. The man on the right has a rifle in a saddle scabbard. Chapmans' was the second post office in Moraine Park. (NPS collection)

—The loosened rocks carried in the ice also gouged, scraped, polished and hollowed out the valleys into their present-day U-shaped cross-sections.

—Moraine Park was the melting basin for the Thompson Glacier during each of the three major glaciations (chart, p. 230).

—The glacier left rock debris in huge piles along the sides and at the lower end of the ice-filled valley. The South Lateral Moraine is such a classic **lateral moraine** that it was given a proper geographic name. The floor of the valley was littered with **ground moraines**.

—Ice was 1500 to 2000 ft. thick in FOREST CANYON, SPRUCE CANYON and ODESSA GORGE to the west, but was much thinner in Moraine Park.

—As the large glacier finally melted during Middle Pinedale time, a large, shallow lake formed behind its **terminal moraine** at the eastern end of Moraine Park.

—After the huge glacier melted, the Big Thompson River breached the moraine and the lake drained, leaving thick lake-bottom muds upon which the beautiful meadow **wetland** grows today.

HISTORY:

—The first permanent settlers were brothers Abner and Fred Sprague (p. 204), who arrived in 1875. They spent their first winter in a crude, peat-roofed log cabin about 0.5 mi. west of the museum.

—The Spragues planned to ranch but passing tourists, prospectors and hunters needed lodging so they also became innkeepers. Fred Sprague operated the first stage coach between Moraine Park and Longmont.

—The sites of Sprague's Hotel (later Stead's Ranch), Moraine Park Lodge, Brinwood Hotel and Forest Inn are in Moraine Park, as were a post office, several stores, many summer cabins and a 9-hole golf course.

—Private inns, hotels and guest ranches within the Park boundaries gradually have been purchased and removed by the Park Service because there are ample accommodations outside the Park.

—The National Park Service's policy is to return the Park, as closely as possible, to its natural appearance.

—The present museum building, built in 1923, was the social center, assembly hall and tearoom for the Moraine Park Lodge.

—The log building is now on the National Register of Historic Places.

MILE **1.2** (0.4)

SIDE ROAD to MORAINE PARK CAMPGROUND, CUB and FERN LAKE TRAILHEADS:
Road begins on the right, <u>just</u> beyond the Museum entrance. Points-of-interest and trails are described on p. 144.

MILE **1.6** (0.3)

LARGE PARKING AREA ALONG BIG THOMPSON RIVER on right.
El. 8030 ft.

TOURIST: "IF THE GLACIERS DID ALL THIS STUFF, WHERE ARE THEY NOW?"
RANGER: "GONE BACK FOR MORE ROCKS!"

A dirt road leads across the river to several privately-owned cabins in the trees along the base of the South Lateral Moraine.

SCENERY:
—Different views of Moraine Park and the peaks of the Continental Divide.
—The MUMMY RANGE is to the north.
—EAGLE CLIFF MTN., to the east, kept the Thompson Glacier from flowing farther eastward.

THINGS TO DO:
—A nearly level hiking trail leads west for 2.0 mi. along the Big Thompson River. Beyond the first 2 mi., the trail climbs about 465 ft. in 1.0 mi. to Cub Lake.
—Fishing is permitted, but a <u>Colorado fishing is license required</u>.

HISTORY:
—Chapmans' ranch and store once stood west of the parking area along the river. Charles and Alson Chapman settled here in about 1895 and built a number of rental cabins. By 1903, rent was $10 for the season. In 1905, the price jumped to a whopping $25 a season—with outhouses and water pitchers included.

MILE
1.9
(0.1)

SMALL PARKING AREA on right. ***<u>DO NOT CLIMB ON THE BOULDERS ALONG THE RIVER.</u>*** **They can be very slippery—several people have fallen into the river and drowned.**

MILE
2.0
(0.8)

CROSS BIG THOMPSON RIVER on a curved concrete bridge. El. 7900 ft.

BEYOND THE RIVER:
the road curves around the South Lateral Moraine that was seen from Moraine Park Museum.

MILE
2.8

Mileage to next point of interest:
(0.8)

TUXEDO PARK PICNIC AREA. El. 8040 ft.
A picnic area that makes a nice stop for the return trip.

BETWEEN TUXEDO PARK and HOLLOWELL PARK:

GEOLOGY:
—The hill on the right is a Bull Lake-age moraine deposited by the Thompson Glacier at some time between 192,000 and 130,000 years ago.
— Most soils on Bull Lake-age moraines are rusty-brown. Boulders scattered on the surface of the moraine are badly weathered and covered with many lichens.

PLANTS:
—A mature ponderosa pine (*Pinus ponderosa*) forest grows on the moraine and in the picnic area.
—Deer and elk frequent this area. They browse on bitterbrush (*Purshia tridentata*) a low, olive-green shrub.
—Rocky Mountain maples and chokecherries grow along the left side of the road.

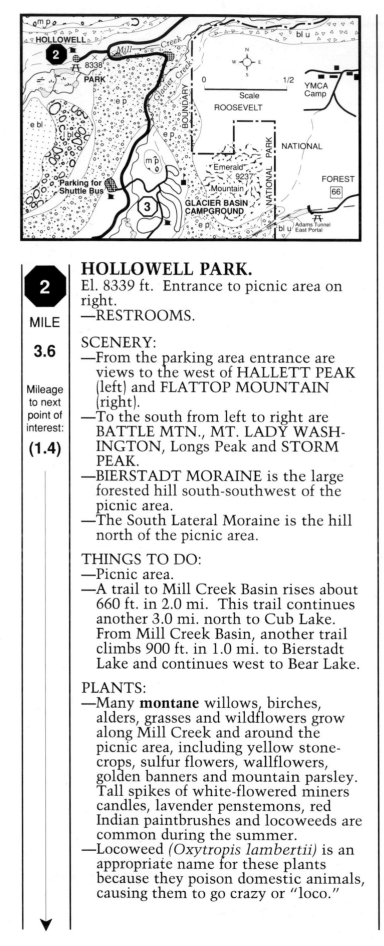

HOLLOWELL PARK.

2

MILE

3.6

Mileage to next point of interest:

(1.4)

El. 8339 ft. Entrance to picnic area on right.
—RESTROOMS.

SCENERY:
—From the parking area entrance are views to the west of HALLETT PEAK (left) and FLATTOP MOUNTAIN (right).
—To the south from left to right are BATTLE MTN., MT. LADY WASHINGTON, Longs Peak and STORM PEAK.
—BIERSTADT MORAINE is the large forested hill south-southwest of the picnic area.
—The South Lateral Moraine is the hill north of the picnic area.

THINGS TO DO:
—Picnic area.
—A trail to Mill Creek Basin rises about 660 ft. in 2.0 mi. This trail continues another 3.0 mi. north to Cub Lake. From Mill Creek Basin, another trail climbs 900 ft. in 1.0 mi. to Bierstadt Lake and continues west to Bear Lake.

PLANTS:
—Many **montane** willows, birches, alders, grasses and wildflowers grow along Mill Creek and around the picnic area, including yellow stonecrops, sulfur flowers, wallflowers, golden banners and mountain parsley. Tall spikes of white-flowered miners candles, lavender penstemons, red Indian paintbrushes and locoweeds are common during the summer.
—Locoweed *(Oxytropis lambertii)* is an appropriate name for these plants because they poison domestic animals, causing them to go crazy or "loco."

On the dry south-facing slopes are sagebrush and tall composites, including gumweeds.
— An open ponderosa pine forest grows on the dry, south-facing slope where many grasses, shrubs and wildflowers grow in a climate similar to that in the southwestern mountains of New Mexico and Arizona.
—A dense Douglas fir *(Pseudotsuga menziesii)* forest grows on the moist north-facing slope of Bierstadt Moraine in a climate similar to that in southern Alaska and Norway.
—Why the difference between the two forests on neighboring hillsides? The south-facing slope receives more direct sunlight all year so snow melts more quickly and water evaporates rapidly.
—Little direct sunlight strikes the north-facing slope with the Douglas fir forest. Winter snows accumulate and do not melt as fast, creating a moist environment. This growth pattern is world-wide, but in the southern hemisphere the roles are reversed; the moist hillsides face south.

HISTORY:
—Hollowell Park was named for G. C. Hollowell, a rancher from Loveland, who ran cattle here during the summers from 1893 until he gave up his homestead in about 1907.
—An old Indian Trail, called the "Big Trail" by Arapahos, passed through Hollowell Park on the way to Flattop Mountain and Ptarmigan Pass on the Continental Divide.
—Two lumbermen, Hill and Beckwith, started a sawmill here in 1876, but moved it to Teller City in North Park in 1880.
—During the 1890s, Abner Sprague operated a water-powered sawmill where the stream from Bierstadt Lake joins Mill Creek.
—Dan Griffith built a sawmill at Bierstadt Lake in 1907 to cut timbers for the Stanley Hotel in Estes Park.
—An old logging trail from Bierstadt Lake came down the northern side of the moraine; aspens have since grown at the mill site and along the skid trail.
—A Civilian Conservation Corps (CCC) camp was in the open park between 1933 and August 1942.
—Between 1921 and 1951, boys from the Chicago, Ill. area attended Rocky Mountain Boys Camp, located on the south-facing slope.

Westward view of north- vs. south-facing slopes at Hallowell Park. The line of yellow aspens on the tree-covered Bierstadt Moraine is the site of an old logging trail from Bierstadt Lake.

The dormitories and other buildings of the Hollowell Park Civilian Conservation Corps (CCC) camp in 1934. This camp operated until 1943. *(NPS)*

—From 1947 until the early 1960s some rental cabins stood where the picnic area is today. A Youth Conservation Corps camp also was at this site for several years during the 1960s.

BETWEEN HOLLOWELL PARK and the SHUTTLE BUS PARKING AREA:

The road curves to the right around the eastern end of the Bierstadt [**lateral**] **Moraine** and continues southward along the moraine, following Glacier Creek. This creek cut through an Middle Pinedale-age moraine.

GEOLOGY:
—Middle Pinedale-age glacial debris was deposited between 50,000 and 35,000 years ago.

—Soils in these Middle Pinedale-age moraines are light gray. Some boulders and cobbles still have glacial **scratches** and **striations** on their surfaces.

WATCH FOR SIGN ALONG RIGHT SIDE OF THE ROAD TELLING VISITORS IF BEAR LAKE PARKING AREA IS FULL.

If so, park in the Shuttle Bus Parking Area and take the free shuttle bus to Bear Lake. The bus also stops at trailheads along the way.

SHUTTLE BUS PARKING AREA.
El. 8595 ft.
Entrance on right.

MILE

5.0

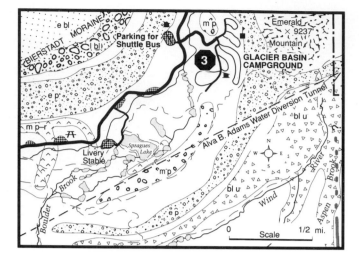

3

MILE

5.0

Mileage to next point of interest:

(0.7)

GLACIER BASIN CAMPGROUND.

Entrance on left.
—RANGER STATION, PUBLIC TELE-PHONE and RESTROOMS.

A short detour to the campground offers more beautiful views of the peaks of the Continental Divide as well as chances to see several interesting geologic features.

SCENERY:
—Panorama (p. 135) identifies landscape features.
—Mummy Range is to the north.

THINGS TO DO:
—A trail leads southwest 0.7 mi. to Sprague Lake where it joins the Storm Pass Trail.

PLANTS:
—The campground is near the northeastern edge of an area ravaged by fire in August 1900. Some picnickers on the north side of Bear Lake let a campfire get out of control. The fire spread rapidly and destroyed much of the forest in Glacier Basin and on the Bierstadt Moraine.
—No resources or man-power were available to fight the fire. As a result it alternately smoldered and flared up for many months.
—The campground is in a lodgepole pine (Pinus contorta var. latifolia) forest which sprouted after the fire. These trees are easy to identify because of their thin, straight trunks and yellow-green needles.
—Fires open the forests, remove the underbrush and leave bare soils on which lodgepole pine seeds can easily sprout in full sunlight. Lodgepole cones, if not destroyed by fire, open up and release their seeds when heated to temperatures between 113° and 122° F. The seeds are then spread by winds, birds and mammals.
—All the lodgepole pines here sprouted about the same time, so they grow closely together in a dense forest.
—Because so little vegetation grows on the forest floor, lodgepole pine forests are well-suited for use as campgrounds.

WILDLIFE:
—Lodgepole pine forests attract fewer animals and birds because of less ground cover and reduced food supply.
—Chickaree (red) squirrels chatter and scold if you enter their territories. They collect cones into large piles called **middens**.
—Pine martens, deer mice, southern red-backed voles and Uinta chipmunks live here and raid the squirrels' midden piles.
—Mountain chickadees, juncos, white-breasted and pygmy nuthatches, gray jays, ruby-crowned kinglets and several kinds of warblers are common in lodgepole pine forests.

GEOLOGY:
—The broad, flat, treeless area at the edge of the campground was the melting basin for the Pinedale-age Bartholf Glacier.
—The flat is an **outwash plain** of sand and gravel that was deposited by streams flowing from the base of the melting glacier as it retreated.
—The low, rounded ridges throughout the campground are small **recessional**

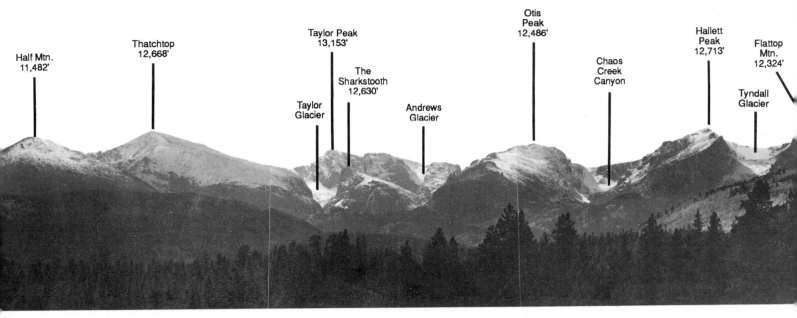

Half Mtn. 11,482'
Thatchtop 12,668'
Taylor Peak 13,153'
The Sharkstooth 12,630'
Taylor Glacier
Andrews Glacier
Otis Peak 12,486'
Chaos Creek Canyon
Hallett Peak 12,713'
Flattop Mtn. 12,324'
Tyndall Glacier

Panorama from Glacier Basin Campground

moraines that formed at the snouts of the retreating glacier as it stopped melting from time to time.

HISTORY:
—Glacier Basin originally was named "Bartholf Park" and the former glacier "Bartholf Glacier" by Abner Sprague in honor of his friend Frank G. Bartholf.
—In 1961, the name of the open flat was changed to Glacier Basin to "agree with common usage."
—The name Bartholf has precedence, however, for the huge glacier that carved out Glacier Gorge and Glacier Basin and should be retained.
—From 1922 until the mid-1950's, both the campground area and the Sprague Lake area were used each summer by hundreds of Highlander Boys, members of a Denver youth organization started by George W. Olinger, a Denver businessman.
—The campers built latrines, piped water to the campground and used the open area as a parade ground.

MILE

5.7

(0.4)

ENTRANCE to SPRAGUE LAKE PICNIC AREA and LIVERY STABLE.
El. 8680 ft. Another possible stop on the return trip.

BEYOND the SPRAGUE LAKE ENTRANCE:

SCENERY:
—Spectacular glimpses of the high peaks along the Continental Divide are seen through openings in the aspen forest, which has grown since the 1900 fire.
—This is a lovely drive in the fall when the aspen leaves turn bright yellow, orange and red.

PLANTS:
—Aspens *(Populus tremuloides)* reproduce from shallow roots which spread laterally. They send shoots upward to form a grove in which all the trees are related and are called "clones."
—The genetics of clone groves determine when the first leaves appear in the spring, when and to what color the leaves turn in the fall. Amounts of moisture, temperature and soil compositions also affect these traits.
—Genetics also determine the shapes of the branches and the color of the bark, which varies from light gray-green to brownish-green to white. Bark of old aspens normally is whitish because it has oxidized.

MILE

6.1

(0.4)

SMALL PARKING AREA on right.
El. 8790 ft.
—Picnic table.
—Best time for photos is in the morning.

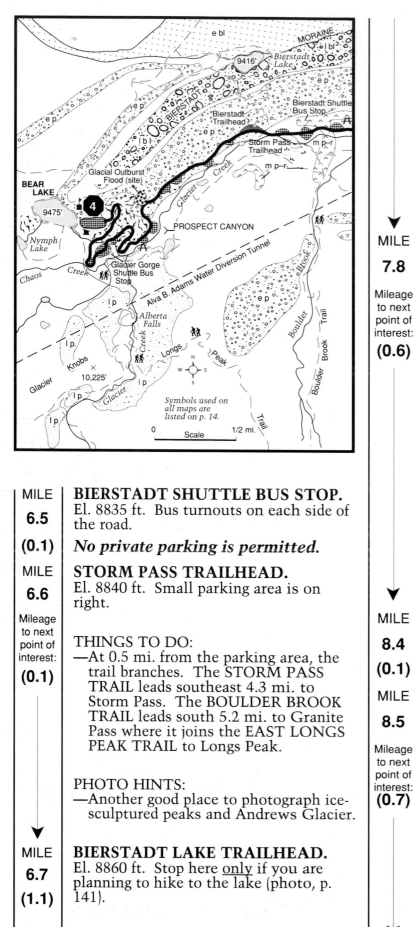

MILE **6.5** (0.1)

BIERSTADT SHUTTLE BUS STOP.
El. 8835 ft. Bus turnouts on each side of the road.

No private parking is permitted.

MILE **6.6**

Mileage to next point of interest: (0.1)

STORM PASS TRAILHEAD.
El. 8840 ft. Small parking area is on right.

THINGS TO DO:
—At 0.5 mi. from the parking area, the trail branches. The STORM PASS TRAIL leads southeast 4.3 mi. to Storm Pass. The BOULDER BROOK TRAIL leads south 5.2 mi. to Granite Pass where it joins the EAST LONGS PEAK TRAIL to Longs Peak.

PHOTO HINTS:
—Another good place to photograph ice-sculptured peaks and Andrews Glacier.

MILE **6.7** (1.1)

BIERSTADT LAKE TRAILHEAD.
El. 8860 ft. Stop here <u>only</u> if you are planning to hike to the lake (photo, p. 141).

THINGS TO DO:
—The trail climbs about 600 ft. up the Bierstadt Moraine in about 1.4 mi.

HISTORY:
—Bierstadt Lake and Bierstadt Moraine were named for Albert Bierstadt, a famous American landscape artist from Philadelphia. He was commissioned by the Earl of Dunraven in1877 to paint a picture titled "Estes Park" which now hangs in the Denver Public Library.

MILE **7.8**

Mileage to next point of interest: (0.6)

PROSPECT CANYON.
El. 9010 ft.
A stop for the return trip. Picnic tables are below the parking area.

BETWEEN PROSPECT CANYON and BEAR LAKE:
The road climbs about 400 ft. on a series of switchbacks.

GEOLOGY:
—Directly ahead are GLACIER KNOBS, a **giant's stairway** made up of a series of glacially polished, rounded cliffs resembling huge stairsteps. Glaciers flowing down the valley ground away parts of the ledges of **bedrock** to form these stairs.
—As the road continues toward Bear Lake there are views of **cirques** and glimpses of tiny TYNDALL GLACIER nestled between HALLETT PEAK (left) and FLATTTOP MOUNTAIN (right).

MILE **8.4** (0.1)

GLACIER GORGE SHUTTLE BUS STOP.
El. 9200 ft. Small turnout on each side of road for busses only.

MILE **8.5**

Mileage to next point of interest: (0.7)

GLACIER GORGE TRAILHEAD.
El. 9240 ft. Small parking area at a switchback.
—RESTROOM.

THINGS TO DO:
—From the parking area, one trail leads to Bear Lake and another climbs 160 ft. in about 0.6 mi. to Alberta Falls.
—From Alberta Falls, the trail leads south 1.4 mi. to a junction with North Longs Peak Trail. At 1.9 mi. the trail branches again.
—One branch leads southwest along Icy Brook past The Loch to Glass Lake, 3.9 mi. from the trailhead. Beyond Glass Lake is Sky Pond, a **tarn** below

Taylor Glacier. Andrews glacier is 5.0 mi. by trail and 2000 ft. above the parking area.

—The other branch leads south along Glacier Creek to Glacier Falls and to Mills and Jewell Lakes, ending at Black Lake, 4.4 mi. away from the trailhead and 1200 ft. in elevation above it.

PHOTO HINTS:

—Best time for photos of the mountains to the south is in the morning. Late afternoon light on the tops of the peaks also can result in very dramatic pictures.

PLANTS:

—June brings yellow golden banners, small lavender penstemons, loco-weeds, red Indian paintbrushes and pussytoes.

—During late summer, white yarrows, purple asters and bracken ferns are easy to spot along the roadside.

—Low junipers also are common.

Bear Lake, probably in the 1920s. Storm Peak is the pyramidal summit; to its right is The Keyboard of the Winds, a sharp, saw-toothed divide. (NPS)

Nymph Lake. (Margaret F. Boos)

Bear Lake Lodge was a popular resort with about 20 buildings and cabins accomodating about 75 guests. Frank Cheley operated his famous Bear Lake Trail School here from 1924 to 1926, before moving it outside the Park. All the buildings were removed after 1960, as part of the "return to nature" policy (NPS)

Kinnikinnick in bloom.

Yarrow.

Battle Mtn.
12,044'

Half Mtn.
11,482'

Pagoda
Mtn.
13,497'

Chiefs
Head
Peak
13,579'

That
12,

Panorama showing the Continental Divide from the Bear Lake parking area.

4
MILE
9.2

BEAR LAKE PARKING AREA.
El. 9475 ft.

SHUTTLE BUS STOP.
—RESTROOMS.

SCENERY:
—Panorama above identifies landscape features.
—The best views of the glaciated mountains along the Continental Divide are from the lower end of the parking area.
—Tyndall Glacier is nestled between Hallett Peak (left) and Flattop Mtn. (right) to the west.
—Longs Peak is behind Storm Peak.

THINGS TO DO:
—Take a leisurely 0.5 mi. walk around Bear Lake, using the National Park Service pamphlet Bear Lake Nature Trail.
—A nearly level trail leads 1.7 mi. east to Bierstadt Lake.
—The summit of Flattop Mtn. is 4.4 mi. from Bear Lake and Grand Lake is 16.5 mi. via the Flattop Trail.
—Fern Lake is 4.7 mi. northwest of Bear Lake.
—The popular (and often crowded) trail to NYMPH, DREAM and EMERALD LAKES leads west up Tyndall Gorge. Nymph Lake is 0.5 mi. from Bear Lake, and Dream Lake is 1.1 mi. Emerald Lake is 1.8 mi. and 625 ft.

above Bear Lake.
—From Dream Lake, another trail leads south 1.1 mi. to a junction with a trail from Glacier Gorge. From that junction, the trail leads southeast 0.2 mi. to Lake Haiyaha and 1.2 mi. to trails in the Glacier Gorge area. The name Haiyaha is an Indian word meaning "rock."

PLANTS:
—Bear Lake is in the **subalpine life zone** (9000 ft. to treeline). Dominant trees are Engelmann spruces *(Picea engelmanni)* and subalpine firs *(Abies lasiocarpa)*.
—A **climax** spruce-fir forest that escaped the 1900 fire remains on the western side of Bear Lake. Such forests represent the peak of plant succession and probably will not be succeeded by other tree species under normal conditions. One Engelmann spruce here is more than 400 years old.
—Use chart, p. 253, to identify the different conifers growing around the parking area and near Bear Lake.

WILDLIFE:
—Golden-mantled ground squirrels, least chipmunks, Nuttall's cottontail rabbits and snowshoe hares, martens and chickeree squirrels are common in subalpine spruce-fir forests.

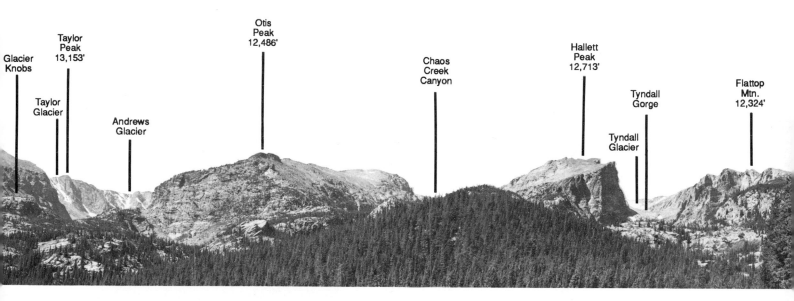

—DO NOT FEED THE WILDLIFE. It violates Park regulations because it results in over-population of animals that are unable to adapt to wild conditions.

—Stellar's jays, gray jays, Clarke's nutcrackers, mountain chickadees, dark-eyed juncos and olive-sided flycatchers are abundant. Mallard ducks frequent the lake.

GEOLOGY:

—Rocks around Bear Lake and along the Continental Divide are **Precambrian gneisses and schists**.

—The parking area is built on Early Pinedale-age glacial debris deposited between 75,000 and 60,000 years ago.

—Bear Lake fills a depression between glaciated **bedrock** cliffs on the west, and **moraines** that form a dam on the other three sides.

—Tyndall Glacier formerly flowed eastward through this area to join the main stream of the Bartholf Glacier below Glacier Gorge.

HISTORY:

—The first road to Bear Lake was built in 1921 by a private contractor harvesting dead timber from the 1900 fire.

—Shortly thereafter drivers began to negotiate the narrow, rutted road with 14 percent grades to visit and hike in the area.

—By 1928, tourist travel had increased so much that the present road was built.

—Bear Lake Lodge, built in 1922, lasted until 1960 when all buildings were removed and the area revegetated by the Park Service.

—TYNDALL GLACIER and TYNDALL GORGE were named by Enos Mills (p. 206) for John Tyndall, an English physicist and glaciologist, whose writings Mills admired.

—HALLETT PEAK was named for mountain climber William L. Hallett (p.169) who came to Colorado from Massachussetts in 1878. In 1896 he was one of 18 men who founded the Rocky Mountain Club, an organization of dedicated mountain climbers.

—OTIS PEAK, south of Hallett Peak, was named for another mountain climber, Dr. Edward O. Otis of Boston. Otis came west in the 1880s to climb with Fredrick H. Chapin (p. 33).

—TAYLOR PEAK and TAYLOR GLACIER were named by Sprague for Albert Reynolds Taylor, president of Kansas State Normal School in Emporia, Kansas. He spent the summer of 1895 in Estes Park and climbed with Sprague. Taylor Glacier, the largest in the Park, is not visible from Bear Lake.

—McHENRYS PEAK was named by Sprague for B. F. McHenry, a math and science teacher from Union Christian College in Meron, Ind.,who spent three summers near Estes Park in the 1890s.

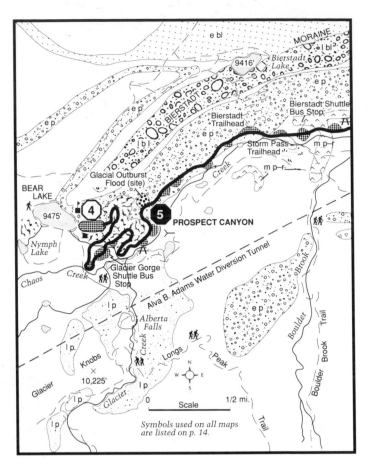

Sunlit golden aspens.

MILE

0.0

Mileage to next point of interest:
(0.7)

RETURN DRIVE to DEER RIDGE ROAD.

Several stops and points-of-interest have been saved for the return trip.

Set your odometer at 0.0 or write down your mileage at the lower end of the parking area.

BEYOND the FIRST SHARP SWITCHBACK:
Watch for glimpses of the giant's stairway to the south, across the valley.

This portion of the road is lovely in the fall when golden aspen leaves rustle and flutter to the ground.

MILE

0.1

GLACIER GORGE TRAILHEAD.

MILE

0.8

(0.6)

GLACIER GORGE SHUTTLE BUS STOP.

Small parking area on right.

PROSPECT CANYON OVERLOOK.

El. 9010 ft.
Parking area on right along a rail fence. Picnic tables are below the parking area overlooking Glacier Creek.

MILE

1.4

Mileage to next point of interest:
(0.2)

SCENERY:
—Views of tree-covered Bierstadt Moraine to the northeast.
—Half Mtn. is to the south and Battle Mtn. is on the southeastern skyline.

PLANTS:
—This forest of lodgepole pines and aspens sprouted since the 1900 fire.
—The tapered tops of some Engelmann spruces which survived the fire stand noticeably higher than the other younger trees.
—Very few aspen trunks have been gnawed by deer and elk. The animals seldom winter here because the snow is too deep.

GEOLOGY:
—A number of **perched erratics**, dropped by the melting glacier, are above the road on the left and atop the cliffs across Glacier Creek.

—Glacier Creek eroded its narrow, crooked channel along joints (cracks) in the **metamorphic bedrock**.

—Across the creek and below the overlook is a small opening (called an **adit**) for a gold prospect driven along a **fault** in the metamorphic rocks.

HISTORY:

—About 1909, prospector Albert Schwilke staked a claim along the fault zone, drove the adit across the creek and sank a vertical shaft about 100 ft. deep that is now covered by the road.

—He hoped to find rich gold-bearing quartz veins in the faults. Schwilke did find traces of gold but they were too low in grade to warrant further exploration.

—He deeded the claim to the National Park Service before 1921.

0.2 MI. BEYOND PROSPECT CANYON OVERLOOK:

Watch for a large pile of boulders on the left side of the road at a sharp right-hand curve.

MILE 1.6

GLACIAL OUTBURST FLOOD.
El. 8980 ft.

Mileage to next point of interest: **(0.9)**

GEOLOGY:

—With the sudden release (outburst) of meltwater from a glacier or because of the sudden failure of a glacier-dammed lake above, a catastropic flood dumped these boulders on the hillside.

—The floodwaters and subsequent rains at the end of the Late Pinedale Glaciation, perhaps between 14,600 and 7,600 years ago, washed fine-grained sand, silt and soil from a glacial moraine rapidly down the hillside.

—This manner of failure is similar to the Lawn Lake flood of 1982 (p. 150) that catastrophically deposited a new alluvial fan along the side of Horseshoe Park.

MILE 2.5

BIERSTADT LAKE TRAILHEAD.
El. 8860 ft.

MILE 2.6

STORM PASS TRAILHEAD.
El. 8840 ft.

MILE 2.7

BIERSTADT SHUTTLE BUS STOP.
El. 8835 ft.
No stopping is permitted.

(0.8)

Glacial outburst flood debris is easily seen at mile 1.5 on the return trip.

Camping at Bierstadt Lake, probably in the 1920s.
(NPS)

This winter scene of Spragues Glacier Basin Lodge was taken in 1940. *(NPS)*

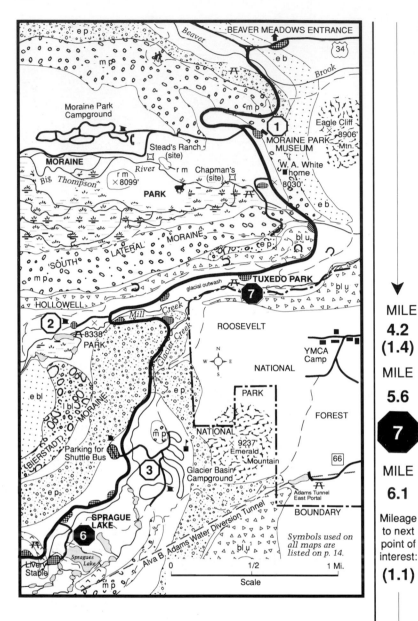

HISTORY:
—After Abner Sprague sold his property in Moraine Park, he built Spragues Glacier Basin Lodge here between 1910 and 1914. The lodge was reached by a road from the YMCA Camp about 2.0 mi. to the northeast outside the National Park Boundary.
—Sprague dammed a breach in a Middle Pinedale-age moraine and stocked the resulting lake with trout for his guests.
—Sprague, an expert guide and unofficial Park historian, wrote many interesting articles about his life in Rocky Mountain National Park.
—The fishing lodge, which operated until 1958, was removed about 1960.

MILE 4.2 (1.4)

GLACIER BASIN CAMPGROUND ENTRANCE.
El. 8595 ft.

MILE 5.6

HOLLOWELL PARK PICNIC AREA.
El. 8339 ft.

7

TUXEDO PARK PICNIC AREA.
El. 8040 ft.
Entrance on right. There are more picnic tables down the hill along Glacier Creek.

MILE 6.1

Mileage to next point of interest:

(1.1)

GEOLOGY:
—Picnic area is on an **outwash terrace** from the Bartholf Glacier.
—This area has a very long and complicated glacial history. The Thompson and Bartholf glaciers merged downstream from here during Bull Lake time, and a **medial moraine**, part of the South Lateral Moraine, was deposited where the two glaciers met. Much evidence of this merging has been washed away, however.

HISTORY:
—This area was named by F. O. Stanley (p. 208) who owned it at one time. He named it for a posh resort north of New York City.
—In June 1935, a fossilized skeleton of a young prehistoric woman was uncovered by a sudden cloudburst along the old Bear Lake road at the eastern end of Tuxedo Park.
—The body apparently had been cremated on the glacial outwash flat and was covered later by glacial debris washed down from the hill above, perhaps as much as 12,000 to 11,000 years ago.
—The skull is in the Rocky Mountain National Park Museum.

6

SPRAGUE LAKE PICNIC AREA and LIVERY STABLE.
El. 8680 ft.
Entrance on right across Glacier Creek.

MILE 3.5

Mileage to next point of interest:

(0.7)

THINGS TO DO:
—A 0.5 mi. path encircles the lake. It is wide enough for wheelchairs for about $^2/_3$ of the way.
—Picnic area.
—Horses are available for hire at the livery stable.
—Fishing is permitted in the lake, but a <u>Colorado state fishing license is required</u>.

PHOTO HINTS:
—Reflections of the mountain skyline in the lake make dramatic photographs, especially in the morning.

MILE **7.2** (0.4) ↓
MILE **7.6**
Mileage to next point of interest: (0.4)
↓
MILE **8.0**
↓
MILE **8.0**
MILE **9.0**

CROSS BIG THOMPSON RIVER.
El. 7900 ft.

GEOLOGY:
—The huge boulders in the river channel were rounded by glacial ice and dumped here in **terminal moraines**.

WILLIAM ALLEN WHITE CABINS are on the hillside above the road.

HISTORY:
—White was a nationally recognized writer, political activist, editor and publisher of the <u>Emporia Gazette</u> of Emporia, Kansas. He first visited Moraine Park in 1889 and returned many times before purchasing the large cabin with the rock-faced porch in 1912.
—Many famous people visited the Whites at their summer home, including lawyer Clarence Darrow, orator William Jennings Bryan and Chief Justice of the Supreme Court Charles Evans Hughes.
—White died in 1944. The family sold the property to the Park Service in 1973.
—The main cabin is now used for an artist-in-residence program.
—The buildings are on the National Register of Historic Places.

ROAD TO MORAINE PARK CAMPGROUND, and to CUB and FERN LAKE TRAILHEADS on left.

The guide for points-of-interest on this road is on p. 144.

MORAINE PARK MUSEUM.
Entrance on right.

JUNCTION with DEER RIDGE ROAD.

W. A. White cabin.

William Allen White with President Theodore Roosevelt in front of the White cabin, probably in 1912 when Roosevelt was running for president on the Bull Moose party ticket. (NPS)

Elk grazing in the early spring of 1986, near Mile 9.0. (Becky Osterwald)

ROAD TO CUB AND FERN LAKE TRAILHEADS IN MORAINE PARK

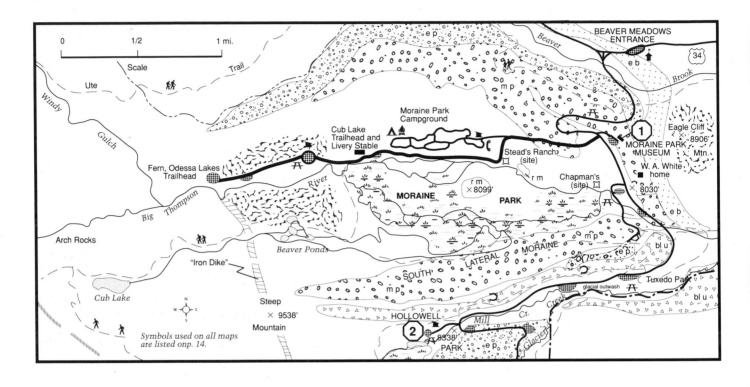

MILE	
0.0	***Turn west off the Bear Lake Road a short distance south of the entrance to the MORAINE PARK MUSEUM.***
	Set your odometer to 0.0 or write down your mileage at the turn-off.
0.5	**MORAINE PARK CAMPGROUND.** Entrance straight ahead. —RESTROOMS, PUBLIC TELEPHONE.
	Turn left to follow the road west to Cub and Fern Lake Trailheads. Stop only in designated parking areas.
	SCENERY: —The campground is among gently-rolling hills on the north lateral moraine of the ancien Thompson Glacier.

BEYOND THE CAMPGROUND, the road descends a gentle hill of the moraine to the Big Thompson River.

0.7 — **SITE OF SPRAGUES' HOMESTEAD** and hotel, later called Stead's Ranch.

HISTORY:
—A 9-hole golf course and livery stable also were in the meadow.
—Brinwood Inn was a short distance to the west.

GEOLOGY:
—The small, rounded rock outcrop to the left, in the center of the valley, is a remnant of a large mass of bedrock. The Thompson Glacier ground away the rest of the rock.
—This is a classic ***roche moutonnèe***, meaning "fleecy rock," a term first used by early French geologists to describe glacially polished, resistant, bedrock outcrops that look like huge, fleecy-backed sheep, when a group of them are seen from a distance.

—To the west are a number of huge, rounded **erratic** boulders. These are not bedrock outcrops, but are rocks carried in the ice of the Thompson Glacier from near the Continental Divide. When the glacier melted the boulders were simply dropped here.

1.6 CUB and FERN LAKE TRAILHEAD.
Parking area on left. LIVERY STABLE on right. More parking areas for hikers are to the west.

THINGS TO DO:
—CUB LAKE is south and then west 2.5 mi. from the trailhead. From Cub Lake, a trail continues 0.8 mi. to The Pool, on the Fern Lake Trail.
—West of Cub Lake a trail leads south almost 2.0 mi. to Mill Creek Basin and Hollowell Park on the Bear Lake Road, which is 4.0 mi. from this trailhead.
—Cub Lake is noted for its yellow pond lilies that bloom in July and August.
—This is a great bird-watching area.

1.7 *END OF PAVED ROAD.*

2.0 PICNIC AREA.
—RESTROOM. Circular parking area.

THINGS TO DO:
—Picnic tables.
—Fish in Big Thompson River. Colorado fishng license is required.
—Several beaver lodges are near the road. Dawn and dusk are the best times to see these busy, primarily nocturnal mammals.

PLANTS:
—This is one of the few areas within Rocky Mountain National Park where Rocky Mountain junipers grow, see key, p. 253. They are common at lower elevations and in Estes Park.
—Aspen groves and willow thickets are good sources of food and building materials for a beaver colony.
—Beyond this parking area many tall bracken ferns grow. They turn a beautiful light-brown in the fall.

2.4 *PARKING AREA on left.*

2.6 FERN LAKE TRAILHEAD.
El. 8150 ft.

THINGS TO DO:
—An easy trail climbs less that 200 ft. in 1.7 mi. to The Pool, which is near the junction of Spruce Creek, Fern Creek and the Big Thompson River.
—Fern Lake is 3.5 mi. from the trailhead and Odessa Lake is 1.0 mi. beyond.
—From Odessa Lake a steep trail continues 3.8 mi. south around Joe Mills Mountain to Bear Lake.
—This is a popular cross-country skiing and snowshoeing area in the winter.

PLANTS:
—**Montane life zone** trees include aspens, cottonwoods, willows, birches, alders and Rocky Mountain maples.
—Shrubs include chokecherries, bitterbrush, rabbitbrush, Rocky mountain thimbleberries and wax currants.

GEOLOGY:
—Beyond the trailhead, the valley narrows into the steep, U-shaped Forest Canyon of the Big Thompson River.
—Bare, glacially-polished rock surfaces glisten on both sides of the valley.
—It is difficult to visualize this canyon filled with 1500 to 2000 ft. of slowly moving ice, yet it filled repeatedly during the Great Ice Ages.

Retrace your route back to the Bear Lake Road.

Steads Ranch accommodated about 200 guests during the 1930s. After it was sold to the National Park Service in 1963 for $750,000, the buildings were demolished. (L. C. McClure photo, Denver Public Library, Western History Dept.)

The main lodge of Brinwood Inn about 1915. (Estes Park Area Historical Museum

Oblique aerial view southeast across Moraine Park showing the forested South Lateral Moraine of the Thompson Glacier. Hollowell Park is in the lower far right. Glacier Basin Campground is in the right center, beyond Hollowell Park. Twin Sisters Peaks are on the center skyline.

(D. B. Osterwald and J. B. Bennetti, Jr.)

OLD FALL RIVER ROAD

This drive starts in Horseshoe Park
at the junction of Deer ridge Road with the Old Fall River Road.

Oblique aerial view westward up Fall River canyon in September 1986. The Old Fall River Road is in the bottom of the canyon in the lower center of the picture. The "Iron Dike" on the south face of Mt. Chapin stands out clearly. Lava Cliffs cirque and Fall River cirque are in the center distance above treeline. Beyond Fall River cirque is the rounded summit of Specimen Mtn. The Never Summer Mtns. are on the skyline.   (F. W. Osterwald and J. B. Bennetti, Jr.)

"Below timberline the purple robe of coniferous forest drapes
and flows over the slopes, ridges and basins."

——Enos A. Mills, <u>Rocky Mountain National Park</u>,
Memorial Edition, 1932.

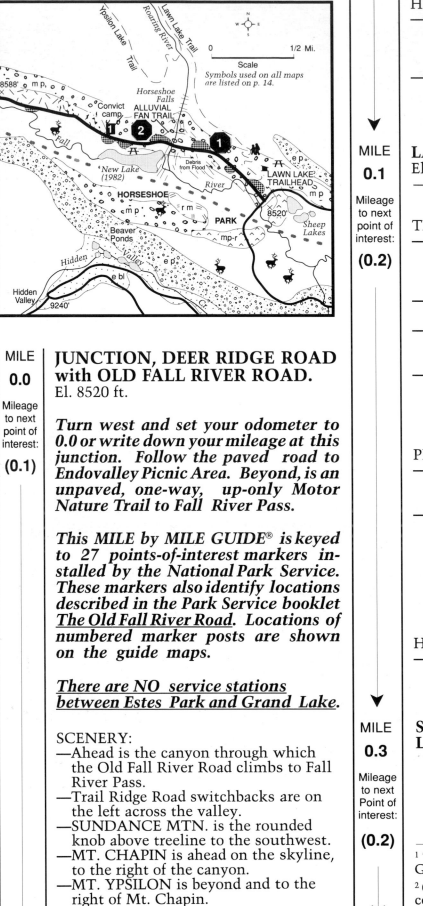

Scale
Symbols used on all maps
are listed on p. 14.

JUNCTION, DEER RIDGE ROAD with OLD FALL RIVER ROAD.
El. 8520 ft.

MILE 0.0
Mileage to next point of interest:
(0.1)

Turn west and set your odometer to 0.0 or write down your mileage at this junction. Follow the paved road to Endovalley Picnic Area. Beyond, is an unpaved, one-way, up-only Motor Nature Trail to Fall River Pass.

This MILE by MILE GUIDE® is keyed to 27 points-of-interest markers installed by the National Park Service. These markers also identify locations described in the Park Service booklet The Old Fall River Road. Locations of numbered marker posts are shown on the guide maps.

There are NO service stations between Estes Park and Grand Lake.

SCENERY:
—Ahead is the canyon through which the Old Fall River Road climbs to Fall River Pass.
—Trail Ridge Road switchbacks are on the left across the valley.
—SUNDANCE MTN. is the rounded knob above treeline to the southwest.
—MT. CHAPIN is ahead on the skyline, to the right of the canyon.
—MT. YPSILON is beyond and to the right of Mt. Chapin.

HISTORY:
—Begun in 1913, the road was completed in 1920. It connected Estes Park with Grand Lake and was the first trans-mountain road in northern Colorado.
—The Old Fall River Road offers chances to stop often and explore many natural features and several historic sites.

MILE 0.1
Mileage to next point of interest:
(0.2)

LAWN LAKE TRAILHEAD.
El. 8525 Ft. Entrance on right.
—RESTROOMS. EMERGENCY TELEPHONE.

THINGS TO DO:
—The first 1.5 mi. to the junction with the Ypsilon Lake Trail is a very steep climb along the Middle Pinedale-age north **lateral moraine**[1].
—The LAWN LAKE TRAIL climbs 2400 ft. in 6.2 mi. to Lawn Lake.
—The YPSILON LAKE TRAIL climbs about 2000 ft. in 6.0 mi. from the trailhead.
—About 0.6 mi. below Lawn Lake, the BLACK CANYON TRAIL joins the Lawn Lake Trail, and leads down Black Canyon to the McGregor Ranch Museum.

PLANTS:
—This drive starts near the upper limit of the **montane life zone** which extends from 6000 to 9000 ft. elevation.
—During August and September, many ragged, yellow gumweeds bloom around the parking area. The young leaves and flowering heads of these composite[2] plants were used by Indians as medicines such as sedatives, antispasmodics, expectorants and anti-irritants to treat poison ivy.

HISTORY:
—Rocky Mountain National Park was formally dedicated in ceremonies held September 4, 1915 on the open hillside east of the trailhead.

Small PICNIC AREA and HORSE-LOADING RAMP on left.

MILE 0.3
Mileage to next Point of interest:
(0.2)

---

[1] Terms in **bold-face type** are defined in the Glossary, p. 256.

[2] Composites are the largest and most complex family of flowering plants, and the most difficult to identify.

Fall River Lodge stood near Lawn Lake Trailhead until the mid-1940s.   (Estes Park Historical Society)

Close-up view of aspen trees near the Alluvial Fan parking area. The trunks are badly scarred where deer and elk ate the soft bark when their other preferred foods were scarce.

The audience assembled for the dedication of Rocky Mountain National Park in Horseshoe Park, September 4, 1915.   (NPS photo)

View west of the washed-out Fall River Road in August 1982.

① ALLUVIAL FAN TRAILHEAD.

MILE 0.5

Mileage to next point of interest: **(0.2)**

El. 8560 ft.
Parking area on right.

THINGS TO DO:
—An asphalt-paved path crosses an **alluvial fan** deposited almost instantaneously on July 15, 1982 when the Lawn Lake Dam (el. 10,987 ft.) in the Mummy Range failed.
—Features along the 0.4 mi. walk across the fan dramatically demonstrate the enormous impact of rushing flood water on the landscape.

HISTORY:
—Lawn Lake, a natural lake, was enlarged in 1903 to hold irrigation water for farmland on the Plains.
—When the dam failed, a wall of water 25 ft. to 30 ft. high rushed down Roaring River (a very apt name that day!). Large trees and huge glacially-rounded **boulders** in the path of the flood were washed away. The debris was dumped along the steep slope and against the lower side of Horseshoe Park when the flood water slowed as it reached the flat valley floor.
—Rubble and debris in the alluvial fan is as much as 44 ft. deep. Huge boulders, weighing up to 452 tons, were carried several miles down Roaring River before they were deposited in the fan.
—Finer-grained **sand**, **silt** and **soil** were carried outward from the fan and deposited on the floor of Horseshoe Park.

MILE 0.7

CROSS ROARING RIVER.

② MILE 0.8

PARKING AREA for WESTERN SIDE of the ALLUVIAL FAN:

SCENERY:
—A new lake, formed when debris from the flood dammed Fall River, can be seen through the trees on the left.
—Damaged and partiallly buried trees that were in the path of the flood continue to die and stand as stark reminders of this disaster.
—No attempt was made to clean up the debris from the flood. The scar and alluvial fan serve as dramatic examples of the destructive force of running water in the mountains. It will be interesting to see how many years pass before vegetation completely covers them. Thirty-five species of grasses and willows had sprouted on the fan after the first season.

MILE 0.9

SMALL PARKING AREA on left.
—Picnic table.

PLANTS:
—The road passes a small grove of balsam poplars *(Populus balsamifera)*, which are quite rare in the Park, but common to the north in Wyoming and Montana. These trees are distinguished from narrowleaf cottonwoods by their broader, ovate leaves and fragrant, sticky buds.

The force of the flood water stripped all the bark and branches from this conifer. August 1982.

Fine-grained sand, silt and clay were washed farther out into Horseshoe Park from the toe of the fan. A new lake formed when this fine-grained debris dammed part of Fall River. August 1982.

Lawn Lake Dam failed because water seeping through the earth fill around the outlet pipe (lower center) began washing away fine-grained material from the body of the dam, creating a channel through which water, mud and rocks eventually poured. (1982 photo, Estes Park Trail Gazette)

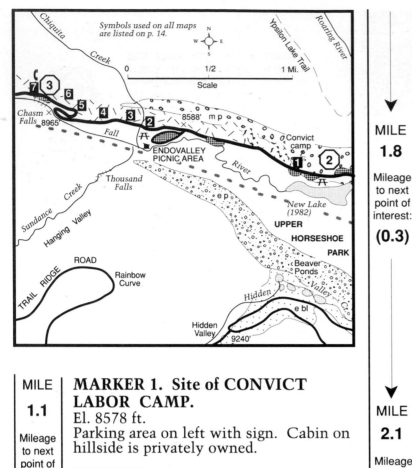

Symbols used on all maps are listed on p. 14.

MILE **1.1**

Mileage to next point of interest:

(0.7)

MARKER 1. Site of CONVICT LABOR CAMP.
El. 8578 ft.
Parking area on left with sign. Cabin on hillside is privately owned.

HISTORY:
—Because the infant Colorado State Highway Department had little manpower and money for road-building in the early 1900s, state prison convicts were put to work building part of the Fall River Road.
—During summers of 1913 and 1914, 38 convicts lived in log cabins and tents in the aspen grove on the right.

PLANTS:
—The aspen grove is being slowly invaded by Engelmann spruce trees which normally grow in the higher **subalpine life zone**.
—Cold air draining down Fall River Canyon in the late afternoons and at night creates a locally colder climate in which Engelmann spruces thrive.
—Such cold air drafts blowing down canyons at the bases of high mountain divides are common in the Rocky Mountains.

WILDLIFE:
—Deer and elk frequent this area in early morning and at dusk to feed on shrubs and grasses. Many aspen trees have black scars on their trunks where hungry deer and elk ate the soft aspen

bark—sure signs of winter food shortages and too many animals for the available food supplies.
—Beaver are active along this part of Fall River. Watch for their ponds and lodges. Willows and aspens are their favorite foods and building materials.

ENTRANCE to ENDOVALLEY PICNIC AREA on left.
El. 8588 ft.
Many picnic sites in the forest along Fall River are open from 8 AM to 8 PM.

FROM HERE to FALL RIVER PASS, the road is an unpaved, one-way, up-only adventure with plenty of small parking areas in which to stop and enjoy the sights. Speed limit is 15 mph.

Drive in low gear—it is easier on your engine, transmission, cooling system and tires. No motor homes over 25 ft. long or trailers are permitted.

MILE **1.8**

Mileage to next point of interest:

(0.3)

MILE **2.1**

Mileage to next point of interest:

(0.1)

MARKER 2. VIEW EAST of HORSESHOE PARK.
Small parking area on left.

SCENERY:
—Horseshoe Park and the new lake formed in 1982 by the Lawn Lake flood are to the east. Flat-topped Deer Mtn. is on the eastern skyline. (photo p. 155)

PHOTO HINTS:
—Best time for photos to the east is in the afternoon.

GEOLOGY:
— The **hanging valley** of Sundance Creek is across the the canyon to the southwest. A small glacier flowed down this valley from Sundance Cirque. It was too small, however, to gouge out as deep a valley as did the main Fall River Glacier. Thus, the valley was left "hanging."
—Rocks along the road are **Precambrian granite .**

PLANTS:
—Douglas firs on both sides of the valley were killed by spruce budworms that feed on the tips of green fir or spruce needles.
—The National Park Service does not use pesticides or other methods to interfere with this natural and self-limiting thinning process.

This log cabin that housed convicts building Fall River Road in 1913 and 1914 was still standing during the summer of 1940. (NPS)

Streams make potholes the same way pharmacists grind material for medicines—using a loose stone as a pestle they swirl it around and around until it wears a hole in the rock.

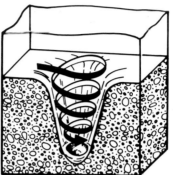

MILE **2.2** El. 9000 ft.

Mileage to next point of interest:

(0.3)

MARKER 3. CROSS CHIQUITA CREEK.
El. 9000 ft.

HISTORY:
—Chiquita Creek, as well as Chiquita Mtn., probably were named by Enos Mills. These names first appeared on a map of the Estes Park area that he published in 1905.

PLANTS:
—Waxflower shrubs are common along the road. They have waxy, white, slightly fragrant blossoms in the spring.

MILE **2.5**

(0.2)

MARKER 4. LARGE GLACIAL POTHOLE.
A large **pothole** in **granite** is behind the marker post on the right.

GEOLOGY:
—This **pothole** probably formed when meltwater flowing down a nearly vertical hole in the glacier, eroded the granite at the edge of or under the ice. The swirling water, aided by the grinding action of loose stones in the water, gradually wore this hole in the solid granite.

MILE **2.7**

(0.2)

LOWER TRAILHEAD to CHASM FALLS.
El. 8965 ft.
Parking for several cars at the first of many switchbacks.

THINGS TO DO:
—A trail, less than 0.1 mi. in length leads to Chasm Falls which drops about 25 ft.

PHOTO HINTS:
—Morning is the best time for photos of the falls.

GEOLOGY:
—The falls were formed when the stream wore its channel through a chain of **potholes** in the granite. These **potholes** were formed by high water as the Fall River Glacier melted at the end of the Middle Pinedale Glaciation.
—Stones swirling around with the water ground out the hole in the granite just as a pharmacist grinds up material with his mortar and pestle.

MILE **2.9**

Mileage to next point of interest:

(0.1)

MARKER 5. SWITCHBACK.
These switchbacks offered a real challenge to drivers when this was a two-way road!

A large **talus slope**, across the canyon to the south, resulted from **periglacial weathering** as the glacier retreated beyond this point.

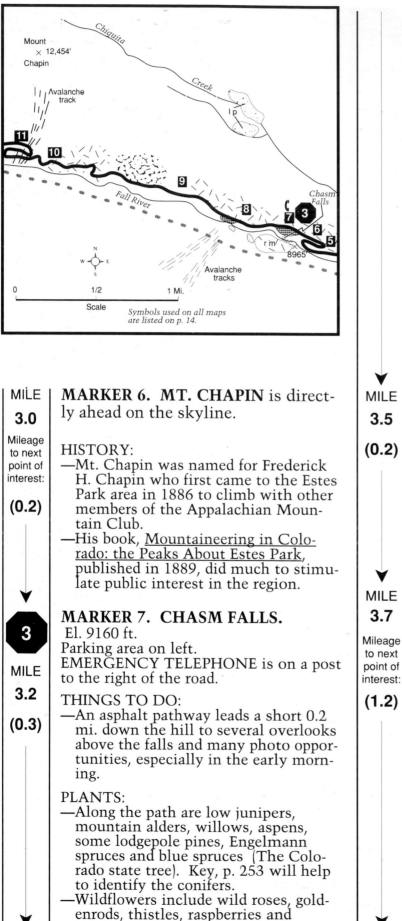

Mount
× 12,454'
Chapin

Chiquita

Creek

Avalanche
track

l p

11

10

9

Fall River

8

7 **3**

Chasm
Falls

6

5

r m

8965

Avalanche
tracks

N
W ◆ E
S

0   1/2   1 Mi.

Scale

*Symbols used on all maps
are listed on p. 14.*

---

alumroots. Alumroots grow in dense
mats on rocky ledges during July and
August. Their small, greenish, bell-
shaped flowers grow on short, dense
spikes. The leaves are scalloped with
sharply toothed edges.

GEOLOGY:
—Across the stream, opposite the path,
is a rounded tree-covered hill, termed a
roche moutonnèe.
—Fall River follows an ancient **fault
zone** (see map) that probably moved
for the first time about 1.4 billion
years ago during **Precambrian** time.
—Stream-formed **potholes** along the path
were made by stones swirling around
in eddies of the river channel after the
last glacier melted.

BEYOND MARKER 7:
There are occasional glimpses through
the trees of the *roche moutonnèe* across
the stream on the left.

MILE

3.5

(0.2)

MARKER 8. GLACIAL ACTION.
Drive past the marker post to a
small parking area on the left.

SCENERY:
—From there, look back to the east to
see a large, **perched erratic** boulder on
a glacially polished granite ledge.
—Snow avalanche chutes down the steep
slope of Sundance Mtn. are visible
across the canyon.
—The crags and spires of Mt. Chapin are
on the western skyline.

MILE

3.7

Mileage
to next
point of
interest:

(1.2)

MARKER 9. SUBALPINE LIFE ZONE.
El. 9305 ft.

PLANTS:
—This life zone extends from about 9000
ft. in elevation to **treeline**.
—Engelmann spruces and subalpine firs
are the dominant trees.
—Aspens, a few mountain alders and
lodgepole pines grow in narrow bands
along the road where the ground was
disturbed during road construction.
—Lodgepoles and aspens grow easily on
disturbed soils, whereas the spruces
and firs prefer undisturbed sites.

BEYOND MARKER 9:
There are several places to stop and to
enjoy the beautiful **subalpine** spruce-fir
forest.

MILE

3.0

Mileage
to next
point of
interest:

(0.2)

3

MILE

3.2

(0.3)

MARKER 6. MT. CHAPIN is direct-
ly ahead on the skyline.

HISTORY:
—Mt. Chapin was named for Frederick
H. Chapin who first came to the Estes
Park area in 1886 to climb with other
members of the Appalachian Mountain Club.
—His book, <u>Mountaineering in Colorado: the Peaks About Estes Park,</u>
published in 1889, did much to stimu-
late public interest in the region.

MARKER 7. CHASM FALLS.
El. 9160 ft.
Parking area on left.
EMERGENCY TELEPHONE is on a post
to the right of the road.

THINGS TO DO:
—An asphalt pathway leads a short 0.2
mi. down the hill to several overlooks
above the falls and many photo opportunities, especially in the early morning.

PLANTS:
—Along the path are low junipers,
mountain alders, willows, aspens,
some lodgepole pines, Engelmann
spruces and blue spruces (The Colorado state tree). Key, p. 253 will help
to identify the conifers.
—Wildflowers include wild roses, goldenrods, thistles, raspberries and

View eastward down Fall River from Marker 2.

Pothole (glacial mill) in granite at Marker 4.

Alumroot.

Waxflower.

Chasm Falls at Marker 7.

*Glacially polished granite at Marker 8. A **perched erratic** is on top of this outcrop.*

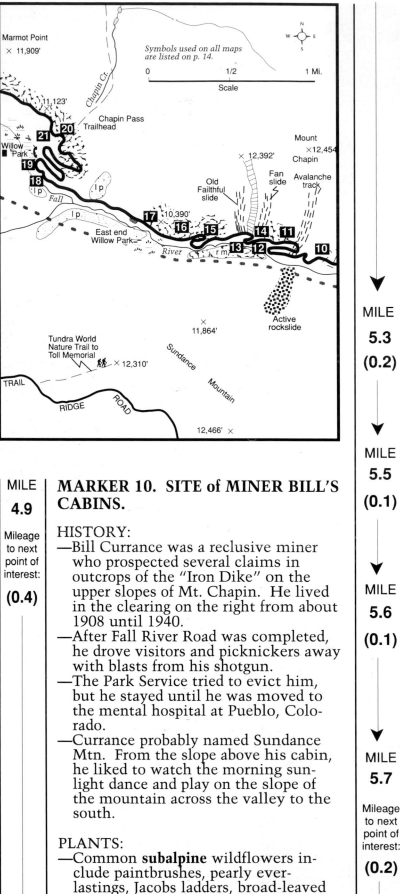

Marmot Point
× 11,909'

Chapin Cr.

Symbols used on all maps
are listed on p. 14.

0   1/2   1 Mi.
Scale

× 11,123'

Chapin Pass
Trailhead

20
21

Willow
Park

19

18

Fall

l p

l p

East end
Willow Park

River

Mount
×12,454
Chapin

× 12,392'

Old
Faithful
slide

Fan
slide

Avalanche
track

17 ×10,390'

16   **15**

14   **11**

13   **12**

10

Active
rockslide

×
11,864'

Tundra World
Nature Trail to
Toll Memorial
× 12,310'

Sundance

Mountain

TRAIL

RIDGE   ROAD

12,466' ×

—By August the main floral display is over, but tall spikes of reddish-purple fireweeds, lavender aspen daisies and leafy-bract asters bloom.
—Throughout the **subalpine zone**, ground cover in spruce-fir forests includes tiny blueberry shrubs whose leaves turn yellow-brown or reddish in late summer and fall.

BEYOND MARKER 10:
Bedrock outcrops from here to Fall River Pass are **Precambrian gneisses** and **schists** (see map).

From here to WILLOW PARK, patches of loose, rounded cobbles (glacial debris) are perched on bedrock surfaces.

MILE
5.3
(0.2)

LOWER END of AVALANCHE TRACK.

SCENERY:
—During the winter of 1985-6, an avalanche from Mt. Chapin flattened many trees along the steep slope to the left.

MILE
5.5
(0.1)

ROAD AGAIN CROSSES AVALANCHE TRACK.

SCENERY:
—Some aspens, small spruce and fir trees survived the snowslide and the hillside is beginning to turn green again.

MILE
5.6
(0.1)

MARKER 11. ACTIVE ROCKSLIDE is across the valley.

SCENERY:
—An active **rockslide** that moves nearly every year is across the valley on the steep slope of Sundance Mtn.
—Very little vegetation can grow in this track because rocks come down frequently.

MILE
5.7

Mileage to next point of interest:
(0.2)

MARKER 12. GABIONS.
El. 11,000 ft.

SCENERY:
—From here to Marker 15 is the most difficult part of the road to maintain.
—Snow avalanches and rockslides from Mt. Chapin have destroyed the road many times. After the road was blocked by slides during the 1970s, it was rebuilt using gabions to stabilize the slope.

MILE
4.9

Mileage to next point of interest:

(0.4)

MARKER 10. SITE of MINER BILL'S CABINS.

HISTORY:
—Bill Currance was a reclusive miner who prospected several claims in outcrops of the "Iron Dike" on the upper slopes of Mt. Chapin. He lived in the clearing on the right from about 1908 until 1940.
—After Fall River Road was completed, he drove visitors and picknickers away with blasts from his shotgun.
—The Park Service tried to evict him, but he stayed until he was moved to the mental hospital at Pueblo, Colorado.
—Currance probably named Sundance Mtn. From the slope above his cabin, he liked to watch the morning sunlight dance and play on the slope of the mountain across the valley to the south.

PLANTS:
—Common **subalpine** wildflowers include paintbrushes, pearly everlastings, Jacobs ladders, broad-leaved arnicas, yarrows, hairbells and thistles.

View eastward of "Miner Bill" Currance's home, the pyramid-shaped building on the right. Several other buildings stood against the hillside to the left when the picture was taken about 1930.   (NPS)

View down slope at Mile 5.5 where the road crosses a recent avalanche track.

Fall River Road camp at some time between 1913 and 1920.   (NPS)

Building the Fall River Road. Horses, fresnoes and back-breaking manual labor were the order of the day.   (NPS)

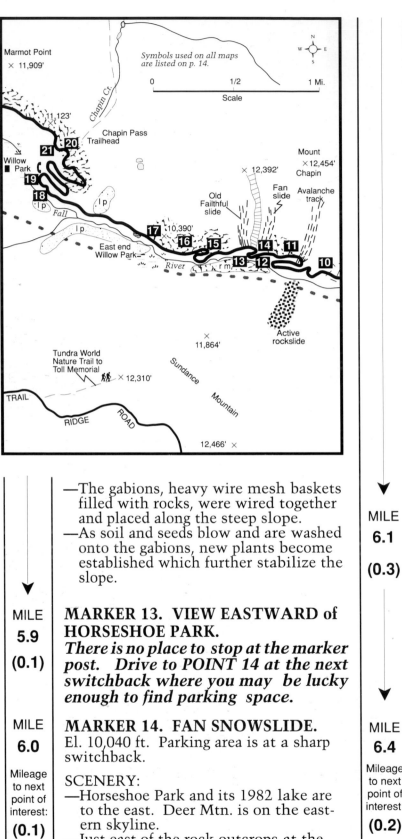

—The gabions, heavy wire mesh baskets filled with rocks, were wired together and placed along the steep slope.
—As soil and seeds blow and are washed onto the gabions, new plants become established which further stabilize the slope.

MARKER 13. VIEW EASTWARD of HORSESHOE PARK.
There is no place to stop at the marker post. Drive to POINT 14 at the next switchback where you may be lucky enough to find parking space.

MILE 5.9 (0.1)

MARKER 14. FAN SNOWSLIDE.
El. 10,040 ft. Parking area is at a sharp switchback.

MILE 6.0

Mileage to next point of interest: (0.1)

SCENERY:
—Horseshoe Park and its 1982 lake are to the east. Deer Mtn. is on the eastern skyline.
—Just east of the rock outcrops at the switchback, look down the steep gorge to see the track of the Fan Avalanche which runs nearly every winter.
—More views of Mt. Chapin are above the parking area to the north.

WILDLIFE:
—Clarke's nutcrackers, Stellar's and gray jays ("Camp Robbers"), chipmunks and golden-mantled ground squirrels may greet your arrival. <u>PLEASE DON'T FEED THE WILDLIFE</u>. It causes over-population of animals that are unable to adapt to their natural living conditions.

GEOLOGY:
—Another outcrop of the **diabase dike** is about 100 ft. west of the switchback along the right side of the road.
—It was called the "Iron Dike" by early Front Range miners because in some places the iron-rich **diabase** contains metallic minerals in economically mineable quantities.
—The dike was injected as a molten liquid into a fault in solid **metamorphic** rocks about 1050 million years ago.

HISTORY:
—During the 1920s and 1930s, large touring cars and open-topped tour buses had to back around this curve and other sharp switchbacks—and hopefully get up enough speed to continue up the hill.
—Imagine how thrilling this drive must have been when the road was two-way!

MILE 6.1 (0.3)

OLD FAITHFUL SNOWSLIDE.

SCENERY:
—Another snowslide track is visible on the steep slope to the right. It was named "Old Faithful" because every afternoon for 13 days, snowslides came down and blocked the road as crews were trying to open the road for the summer.
—Today the Park Service clears the drifts and slides and then lets the roadway dry before spring grading is done and the road opened for traffic.

MILE 6.4

Mileage to next point of interest: (0.2)

MARKER 15. AVALANCHES.

SCENERY:
—Across the valley to the left are more scars where snow avalanches wiped away great swaths of timber on Sundance Mtn.
—Many small willows and spruces have started to grow at the bases of these avalanche runs.
—Some snow remains in these tracks all summer.

Avalanche tracks on the north slope of Sundance Mtn. near Marker 15.

This westward view was taken in 1925 from the sharp switchback at Marker 14. One always honked before rounding blind curves to warn drivers of opposing traffic. Cars travelling uphill always had the right-of-way— cars headed downhill had to find the nearest wide spot.
(NPS)

W. T. Parke took this early photo looking eastward toward Marker 14 when the road was a thrilling adventure in a Stanley Steamer tour bus. The rock retaining walls were replaced by gabions.
(Collection of the Enos Mills Homestead Cabin)

Mt. Chapin on the skyline above the Old Fall River Road.

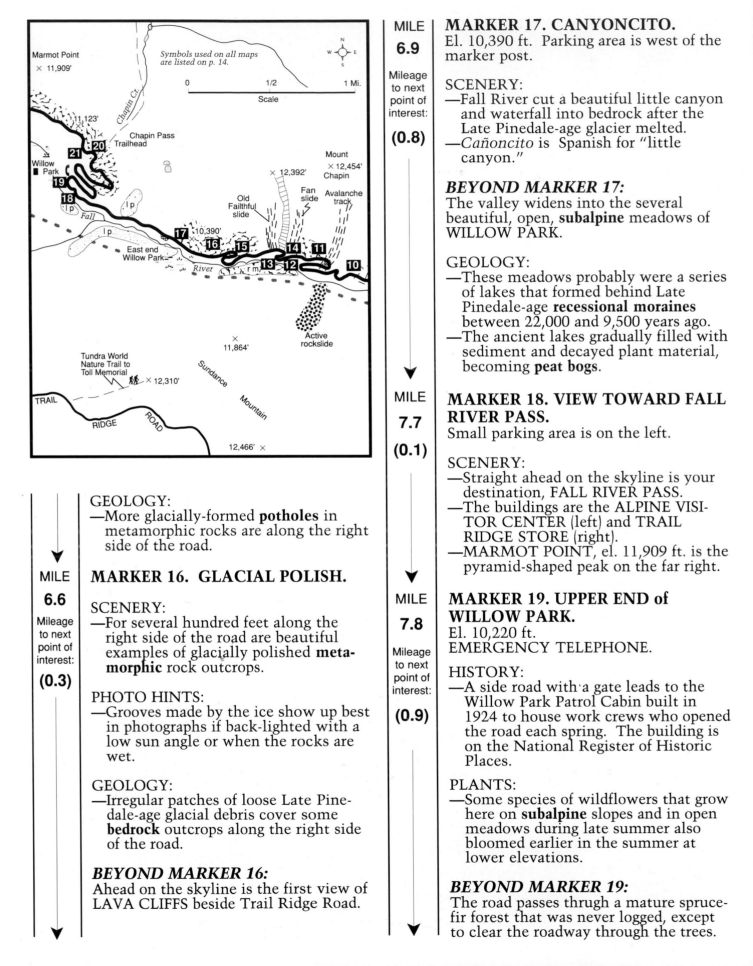

Marmot Point × 11,909'

11,123'

Chapin Pass Trailhead

21 20

Willow Park

19

18 lp

lp Fall

lp

East end Willow Park

17 10,390'

16 15

14

13 12

11

10

River r m

Mount × 12,454' Chapin

× 12,392'

Old Failthful slide

Fan slide

Avalanche track

Active rockslide

× 11,864'

Tundra World Nature Trail to Toll Memorial × 12,310'

Sundance Mountain

TRAIL RIDGE ROAD

12,466' ×

Chapin Ct.

Symbols used on all maps are listed on p. 14.

N W E S

0   1/2   1 Mi.
Scale

GEOLOGY:
—More glacially-formed **potholes** in metamorphic rocks are along the right side of the road.

MARKER 16. GLACIAL POLISH.

SCENERY:
—For several hundred feet along the right side of the road are beautiful examples of glacially polished **metamorphic** rock outcrops.

PHOTO HINTS:
—Grooves made by the ice show up best in photographs if back-lighted with a low sun angle or when the rocks are wet.

GEOLOGY:
—Irregular patches of loose Late Pinedale-age glacial debris cover some **bedrock** outcrops along the right side of the road.

BEYOND MARKER 16:
Ahead on the skyline is the first view of LAVA CLIFFS beside Trail Ridge Road.

MILE
6.6
Mileage to next point of interest:
(0.3)

MILE
6.9
Mileage to next point of interest:
(0.8)

MILE
7.7
(0.1)

MILE
7.8
Mileage to next point of interest:
(0.9)

MARKER 17. CANYONCITO.
El. 10,390 ft. Parking area is west of the marker post.

SCENERY:
—Fall River cut a beautiful little canyon and waterfall into bedrock after the Late Pinedale-age glacier melted.
—*Cañoncito* is Spanish for "little canyon."

BEYOND MARKER 17:
The valley widens into the several beautiful, open, **subalpine** meadows of WILLOW PARK.

GEOLOGY:
—These meadows probably were a series of lakes that formed behind Late Pinedale-age **recessional moraines** between 22,000 and 9,500 years ago.
—The ancient lakes gradually filled with sediment and decayed plant material, becoming **peat bogs.**

MARKER 18. VIEW TOWARD FALL RIVER PASS.
Small parking area is on the left.

SCENERY:
—Straight ahead on the skyline is your destination, FALL RIVER PASS.
—The buildings are the ALPINE VISITOR CENTER (left) and TRAIL RIDGE STORE (right).
—MARMOT POINT, el. 11,909 ft. is the pyramid-shaped peak on the far right.

MARKER 19. UPPER END of WILLOW PARK.
El. 10,220 ft.
EMERGENCY TELEPHONE.

HISTORY:
—A side road with a gate leads to the Willow Park Patrol Cabin built in 1924 to house work crews who opened the road each spring. The building is on the National Register of Historic Places.

PLANTS:
—Some species of wildflowers that grow here on **subalpine** slopes and in open meadows during late summer also bloomed earlier in the summer at lower elevations.

BEYOND MARKER 19:
The road passes thrugh a mature spruce-fir forest that was never logged, except to clear the roadway through the trees.

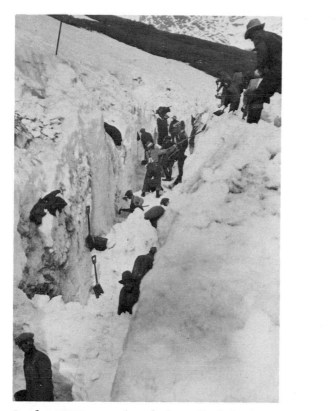

In the 1920s men hand-shovelled the huge drifts into benches, then cleared each bench in turn to finally open the road to Fall River Pass.   *(NPS)*

Opening day on Fall River road—almost a traffic jam!   *(NPS)*

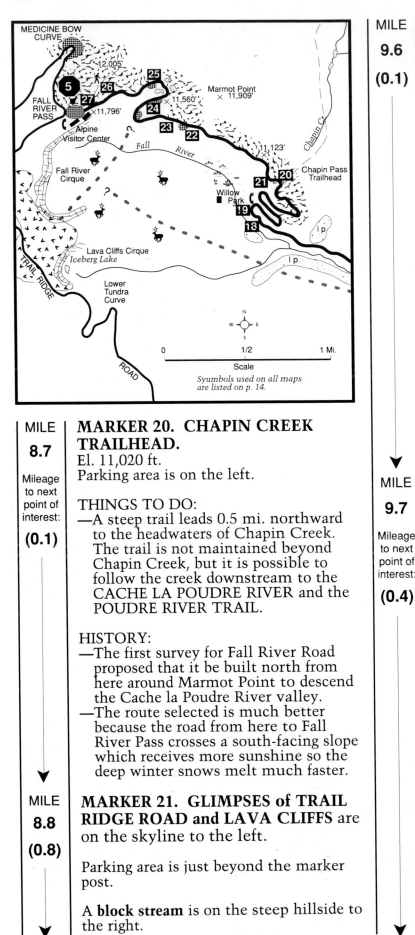

Syumbols used on all maps are listed on p. 14.

MILE

8.7

Mileage to next point of interest:

(0.1)

MARKER 20. CHAPIN CREEK TRAILHEAD.
El. 11,020 ft.
Parking area is on the left.

THINGS TO DO:
—A steep trail leads 0.5 mi. northward to the headwaters of Chapin Creek. The trail is not maintained beyond Chapin Creek, but it is possible to follow the creek downstream to the CACHE LA POUDRE RIVER and the POUDRE RIVER TRAIL.

HISTORY:
—The first survey for Fall River Road proposed that it be built north from here around Marmot Point to descend the Cache la Poudre River valley.
—The route selected is much better because the road from here to Fall River Pass crosses a south-facing slope which receives more sunshine so the deep winter snows melt much faster.

MILE

8.8

(0.8)

MARKER 21. GLIMPSES of TRAIL RIDGE ROAD and LAVA CLIFFS are on the skyline to the left.

Parking area is just beyond the marker post.

A **block stream** is on the steep hillside to the right.

MILE

9.6

(0.1)

MARKER 22. TREELINE.
El. 11,300 ft.
A parking area is on the left 0.1 mi. beyond the marker post.

PLANTS:
—Directly ahead is **treeline** which averages about 11,400 ft. at this latitude.
—Trees no longer grow straight and tall at this elevation but are much smaller, twisted and stunted because they struggle to survive in the Arctic-like climate.
—The gnarled trees, termed **krummholz**, mark the **forest-tundra transition life zone**.

WILDLIFE:
—This is a good place to look for pikas and yellow-bellied marmots sunning themselves on the rocks along the road.
—Pikas do not hibernate and spend the summers busily harvesting grass for their winter food supply.
—Marmots hibernate so they stuff themselves all summer, storing up a thick layer of fat for their long winter nap.

MILE

9.7

Mileage to next point of interest:

(0.4)

MARKER 23. VIEW of WILLOW PARK.
Small parking area is on the left; a larger one is ahead on the right, at a curve.

SCENERY:
—Vistas to the east include Willow Park, the west slope of Mt. Chapin and Sundance Mtn.
—To the west is FALL RIVER CIRQUE, the birthplace of the ancient Fall River Glacier.

PLANTS:
—Welcome to the **tundra** and the **alpine life zone**. Tundra is a Lapp word describing vast treeless areas in Arctic and Alpine regions.
—Here tiny, ground-hugging plants, grasses, sedges and arctic willows are especially adapted to survive in the harsh climate.
—During the short growing season kings crowns, little red elephants, dwarf clover, alpine clover, yellow alpine paintbrushes, bistorts and alpine avens are a few of the many flowers that grace the hillsides.

Western yellow paintbrush.

Parry primrose.

Whiproot or alpine clover.

Dwarf clover growing in front of gray and yellow lichens on pegmatite.

Mountain harebells.

Arctic gentian.

Typical subalpine and alpine wildflowers.

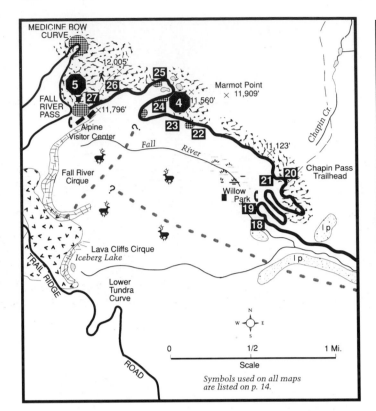

Symbols used on all maps
are listed on p. 14.

BETWEEN MARKER 23 and 24:
The road continues to climb the side of
the **cirque** and passes several small,
hollowed-out depressions filled with
water.

PHOTO HINTS:
—Best time for photos into the **cirque** is
in the morning.
—Deer and elk often feed on grass and
willows on the floor of the **cirque**.

GEOLOGY:
—These ponds are in **nivation depressions** that formed after the Late
Pinedale-age glacier melted.
—The ground adjacent to the former
glacier repeatedly froze and thawed, so
that rocks near the surface were broken and thrust up out of the
ground. This process is termed **frost
heaving** or **up-freezing**.
—The ground <u>below</u> the surface layer
that freezes and thaws may have
remained perennially frozen, and is
termed **permafrost**.
—When thin, near-surface layers of rock
and soil thaw during spring and summer, the soil particles become mixed
with meltwater. The mixtures of soil
and water flow downslope to form
solifluction terraces.

—Several such terraces, outlined by
stands of subalpine willows, are in the
cirque.
—**Nivation depressions** form under large
snowbanks. As the snow melts, soil-
water mixtures flow away from the
snowbank like syrup or honey. This
leaves residues of rocks piled near the
margins of the snow. Gradually the
depressions are enlarged. If this process is carried far enough, a new **cirque**
may form.
—The geology chapter, p. 243, has more
details about these processes.

MARKER 24. MARMOT POINT.
El. 11,560 ft.
A large parking area is on the right just
beyond the marker post.

SCENERY:
—On both sides of the marker are plenty
of parking areas in which to stop and
enjoy the views. Marmot Point, el.
11,909 ft, is the cone-shaped peak to
the east.

HISTORY:
—This is the site of the former Timberline Cabin, built in 1925 to house
crews who cleared the road of snow
each spring. The building was removed in 1988 to restore the area to
its original, natural condition.
—Men formerly worked here each spring
with shovels, picks, teams of horses,
wagons and even a steam shovel to
remove drifts up to 40 ft. deep.

BEYOND MARKER 24 :

GEOLOGY:
—Another water-filled **nivation
depression** is on the left.
—Many subalpine willows growing
along the bench-like **solifluction
terraces** are pruned on one side by the
fierce winter winds.
—On the hill above the sewage treatment ponds are several outcrops of
light-colored igneous **pegmatite**.

HISTORY:
—The fenced-in area encloses waste
water treatment ponds for the Alpine
Visitor Center and Trail Ridge Store at
Fall River Pass.
—Potable water for use at these facilities
is pumped from upper Willow Park.

4

MILE

10.1

Mileage
to next
point of
interest:

(0.1)

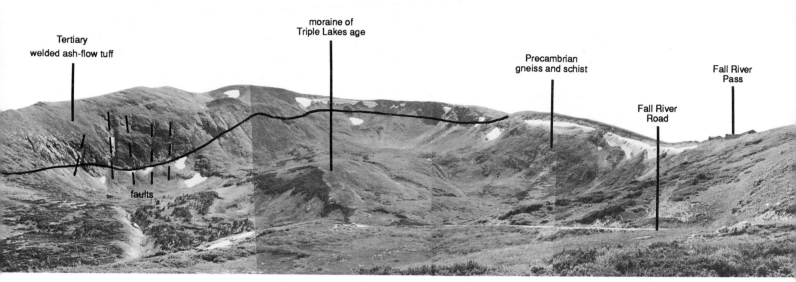

Tertiary
welded ash-flow tuff

moraine of
Triple Lakes age

Precambrian
gneiss and schist

Fall River
Pass

Fall River
Road

faults

Panoramic view southward of Fall River cirque and Fall River Pass between Markers 23 and 24.

MILE	
10.2	

Mileage
to next
point of
interest:

(0.3)

MARKER 25. VIEW NORTHWARD of CHAPIN CREEK VALLEY.
El. 11,123 ft.
There is no stopping place at the marker post, but a small one is 0.1 mi. to the west.

SCENERY:
—This small divide separates the tributaries of Fall River from those of Chapin Creek, which flows northward into Cache la Poudre River.
—On the south-southeastern skyline, the rough rock outcrops along the top of Sundance Mtn. are at the summit of the TUNDRA WORLD NATURE TRAIL on Trail Ridge Road.

BEYOND MARKER 25:
Small parking areas are on both sides of the road.

GEOLOGY:
—On the hill above the road are more patches of **pegmatite**.

MARKER 26. EARLY-DAY SNOW REMOVAL.

MILE	
10.5	

Mileage
to next
point of
interest:

(0.3)

HISTORY:
—This portion of the road was the most difficult to open each spring because winter winds blow snow from the western slopes across Fall River Pass and drop it in huge snowdrifts on the lee side of the pass.
—The snowbank at the top of the **cirque** south of the Visitor Center rarely melts completely away.

Horse power came to rescue the first bus of the season that tried to get through an 18-foot drift near the top of Fall River Pass on June 20, 1923.   (NPS)

Alpine Visitor Center and Trail Ridge Store are on the brink of Fall River cirque. September 1987.

MARKER 27. ALPINE VISITOR CENTER and TRAIL RIDGE STORE at FALL RIVER PASS.

(5)
MILE
10.8

El. 11,796 ft.
A large paved parking area is beyond the store.
—RESTROOMS.
  EMERGENCY TELEPHONE.

REVIEW PRECAUTIONS CONCERNING ELECTRICAL STORMS, p. 262.

REMEMBER THAT THE AIR AT HIGH ALTITUDES HAS LESS OXYGEN, SO WALK SLOWLY AND CAREFULLY.

SCENERY:
—From the overlook between the two buildings is another view down into Fall River Cirque.
—Mt. Chapin and the Mummy Range are to the east and northeast.
—From the parking area exit, SPECIMEN MTN. and the NEVER SUMMER MTNS. are directly ahead on the skyline.

THINGS TO DO:
—VISITOR CENTER has a small museum devoted to the **alpine tundra**.
—Naturalists are on duty to answer questions.
—Books and maps are for sale.
—TRAIL RIDGE STORE has a lunch counter, a fine collection of authentic Indian souvenirs, as well as a shop with books, film, gifts, and general souvenirs for sale.
—Near Trail Ridge Store, a steep 0.3-mi. trail climbs about 200 ft. to a scenic overlook.
—Visitors are rewarded with magnificent vistas in all directions. Fall River Cirque is to the south, the Mummy Range is to the north and northeast and the MEDICINE BOW MTNS. in Wyoming are to the north.
— Along the trail are several masses of **pegmatite** with large crystals of **albite**, **microcline**, **quartz** and **mica**.

HISTORY:
—Fall River Pass is on one of six ancient trans-mountain Indian trails in the Park. Many other trails crossed the Front Range outside Park boundaries (See The Trailmakers, in press).
—Since 1920, when the Old Fall River Road was completed from Estes Park, this has been a favorite stop.

To return to Estes Park,
follow Trail Ridge Eastbound, Part 2 Guide, p. 103.

To reach Grand Lake,
follow Trail Ridge Road Westbound, Part 2 Guide, p. 53.

PEAK TO PEAK HIGHWAY (COLO. 7) TO ALLENSPARK

**This 15-mile drive starts at the junction of
Colorado Highway 7 and U.S. 36,
opposite the U.S. Bureau of Reclamation hydro-electric power plant.**

Aerial oblique view southwestward of Mt. Meeker, The Notch on Longs Peak, Mt. Lady Washington and the U-shaped valley through which the ancient Mills Glacier flowed. On the right side of the valley is the Mills Moraine. At the head of the valley are The Diamond on Longs Peak and the modern Mills Glacier. (D. B. Osterwald and J. B. Bennetti, Jr.)

". . .side by side are two dominant peaks. These are Longs Peak,
14,255 feet high and Mt. Meeker, 14,000 feet above the sea.
These great summits were a landmark for the primitive
red man who saw them from the plains. He called
them the ' Two Guides'."

––Enos A. Mills, <u>Your National Parks</u>, 1917.

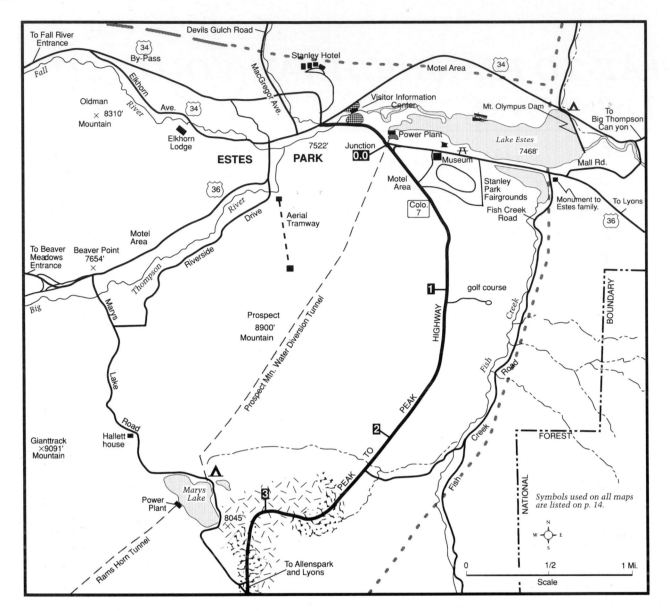

MILE	
0.0	**JUNCTION, COLO. 7 and U.S. 36.** El. 7530 ft.

Mileage to next point of interest:

(1.0)

Set your odometer at 0.0 or write down your mileage at this junction. Follow Colo. 7 southward to Allenspark, Colorado.

This guide is keyed to State Highway mile markers along the west (right) side of the road; marker locations are shown on the maps. Mile marker 0 is at this junction.

SCENERY:
—The highway passes a shopping center, a motel area and the road to the STANLEY PARK FAIRGROUNDS.

—Estes Park is a thriving, all-season vacationland and an attractive retirement community. Many motels, resorts and businesses remain open year-round.

MILE	
1.0	**MILE MARKER 1.** Opposite Eagle Landing Condominiums.

MILE	
1.1	**GOLF COURSE ROAD** to the east leads to ESTES PARK GOLF and COUNTRY CLUB. The golf course, started in 1909, is one of the oldest in Colorado.

(0.9)

SCENERY:
—Ahead, as the road curves to the southwest, are the first views (left to right) of TWIN SISTERS PEAKS, MT. MEEKER, LONGS PEAK and MT. LADY WASHINGTON.

Marys Lake in 1873. (W. H. Jackson photo, Colorado Historical Society collection)

HISTORY:
—Mt. Lady Washington was named either for or by Anna Dickinson, the first woman known to have climbed Longs Peak, with members of F. V. Hayden's Geological and Geographical Survey of the Territories (p. 199), on Sept 13, 1873.
—Miss Dickinson may have thought the peak resembled Mt. Washington in New Hampshire which she had climbed many times. Perhaps the term "Lady" was added by Ralph Meeker, her admirer, who also was on that memorable climb.

—Mt. Dickinson in the Mummy Range later was named for Anna Dickinson by Enos Mills.
—Mt. Meeker was also named on that day for Nathan Meeker, Ralph's father, and founder of the Union Colony at Greeley, Colo.

MILE 2.0

MILE MARKER 2.
Marker is between Twin Drive and Pinewood Lane.

MILE 3.5

MARYS LAKE ROAD JOINS COLO. 7 from the west.
El. 8081 ft.

ADDITIONAL NOTES ON MARYS LAKE ROAD

The Marys Lake Road is one of the oldest in the Estes Park area. This 2.2-mi. road joins U.S. 36 at BEAVER POINT, along the Big Thompson River.

The road passes MARYS LAKE, a natural lake that was enlarged to hold water from Ramshorn Tunnel. The lake was named for Mary I. Fleming, bride of Milton Estes, one of Joel Estes's sons (p. 198). The Marys Lake Power Plant generates about 50 million kilowatts of electricity annually from one generator.

About 0.5 mi. north of Marys Lake is HALLETT HOUSE (see map p. 168), built in 1881 by W. H. Hallett as a summer home. Hallett, a mining engineer from Springfield, Mass., came to Estes Park in 1878 to climb with Frederick H. Chapin. In time, each man named a mountain peak for the other.

Hallett and his family settled in Denver, but he also owned a ranch near Loveland for several years. He worked as a mining engineer, as a smelter manager and later for the Denver Water Board. An avid mountain climber, he helped found the Rocky Mountain Club in 1896.

The HIGHLANDS HOTEL once stood on the hillside west of the Hallett House. Horace W. Ferguson arrived in Estes Park in 1876 and built a two-room cabin. Like many other early settlers, Ferguson planned to ranch but soon realized that summer tourists, mountain climbers and adventurers needed lodging. Such visitors were a more lucrative source of income than cattle.

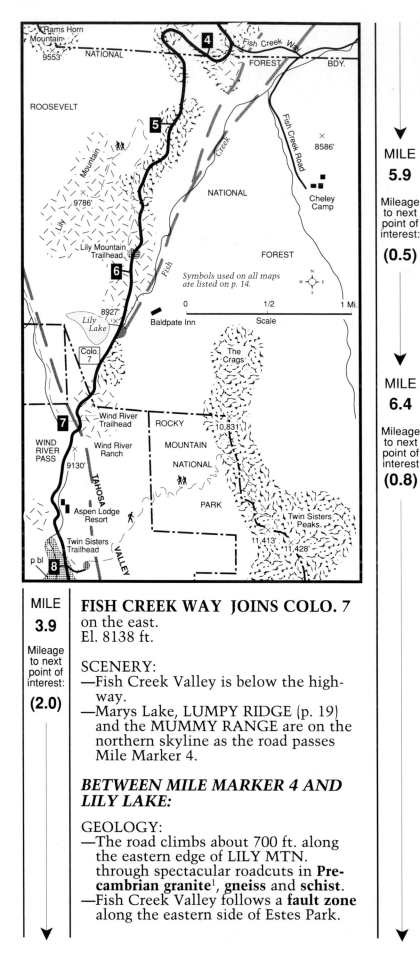

Symbols used on all maps are listed on p. 14.

MILE
3.9

Mileage to next point of interest:

(2.0)

FISH CREEK WAY JOINS COLO. 7
on the east.
El. 8138 ft.

SCENERY:
—Fish Creek Valley is below the highway.
—Marys Lake, LUMPY RIDGE (p. 19) and the MUMMY RANGE are on the northern skyline as the road passes Mile Marker 4.

BETWEEN MILE MARKER 4 AND LILY LAKE:

GEOLOGY:
—The road climbs about 700 ft. along the eastern edge of LILY MTN. through spectacular roadcuts in **Precambrian granite**[1], **gneiss** and **schist**.
—Fish Creek Valley follows a **fault zone** along the eastern side of Estes Park.

PLANTS:
—The drive to Allenspark passes through characteristic **montane life zone** forests of Douglas firs, ponderosa pines, lodgepole pines and aspens.
—Many Douglas fir trees recently were killed by spruce budworms.

MILE
5.9

Mileage to next point of interest:

(0.5)

LILY MTN. TRAILHEAD.
El. 8842 ft.
The trailhead is poorly marked with only small parking areas on each side of the highway.

THINGS TO DO:
—The trail climbs about 1000 ft. in 1.8 mi. to the summit of Lily Mtn., el. 9786 ft., and offers fine views of Estes Park, Fish Creek Valley and Twin Sisters Peaks.
—Numerous **potholes**, up to 8 ft, deep and 10 ft. in diameter are along the trail and elsewhere on the mountain.

MILE
6.4

Mileage to next point of interest

(0.8)

LILY LAKE.
El. 8927 ft. A large parking area is on the east.

SCENERY:
—The **gneiss** and **schist** crags at the northern end of Twin Sister Peaks are to the east.
—Another vista of Fish Creek Valley and eastern end of Estes Park Valley are to the north-northeast.
—Mt. Meeker and Longs Peak are to the west.
—Lily Lake fills a small meadow at the southern base of Lily Mountain.
—The Mummy Range is to the north.

PLANTS:
—South of Lily Lake the road enters a dense lodgepole pine forest. The tall slender trees are easy to identify because of their yellow-green needles. Indians used the trunks as poles to support their lodges (tepees).
—Lodgepole pines grow rapidly forming dense forests. These forests have little undergrowth because very little sunlight reaches the forest floor.
—This in turn attracts few mammals and birds because of food supplies are reduced.

[1]Terms in **bold-face** type are defined in the Glossary, p. 256.

View northward of Lily Lake and Rams Horn Mtn. The prominent rocks at the top were named Teddys Teeth for Theodore Roosevelt. During his presidency cartoonists commonly pictured him with a wide grin and protruding teeth. This feature stands out best from Moraine Park. September 1963. *(Margaret F. Boos)*

—Forest fires, although destructive, have beneficial effects on the ecosystem. Fires remove undergrowth and leave bare soils upon which lodgepole pine seeds can easily sprout in full sunlight.

—Lodgepole cones, if not destroyed by fire, open up and release their seeds when heated to temperatures between 113° and 122° F. The seeds are then spread by winds, birds and mammals.

HISTORY:

—Isabella Bird (p. 200) wrote in 1873 that the lake was "...fittingly called Lake of the Lilies."

—BALDPATE INN, a famous old hotel that proudly displays a collection of more than 1400 keys from all over the world, is a short distance down the road northeast of this stop. The Inn was named after the mystery novel, The Seven Keys to Baldpate.

MILE
7.2

Mileage to next point of interest:

(0.3)

SUMMIT, WIND RIVER PASS.

WIND RIVER RANCH is east of the road.
El. 9130 ft.
This gentle divide separates the Tahosa Valley from the valleys of Fish Creek and Aspen Brook.

HISTORY:

—Wind River Pass is named for Wind River, a northward-flowing stream from Battle Mtn. that joins Aspen Brook near the YMCA of the Rockies about 3.0 mi. northwest from here.

MILE
7.5
(0.5)

MILE
8.0

Mileage to next point of interest:

(0.1)

THE ASPEN LODGE RESORT and CONFERENCE CENTER is to the east.

TWIN SISTERS TRAILHEAD.

El. 9000 ft.
Entrance to the parking area for the trailhead is on the east.

THINGS TO DO:

—A steep trail climbs 2300 ft. in 3.7 mi. to the northern peak at 11,428 ft. elevation.

—From the summit are spectacular vistas to the west (left to right) of Mt. Meeker, Longs Peak, Mt. Lady Washington, Battle Mtn. and Estes Cone.

—The Great Plains spread out to the east.

—The Tahosa Valley stretches southward toward Allenspark.

HISTORY:

—In 1917 a small area surrounding Twin Sisters Peaks was annexed to Rocky Mountain National Park.

—The fire lookout station that had served for many years to spot forest fires was removed in July 1977 after it became more efficient to use aircraft for fire patrols.

—Although the two summits do indeed look like twins from the plains, they appear much differently from the Tahosa Valley.

—*Tahosa* was a famous Kiowa Indian chief whose name means "Little Mountain."

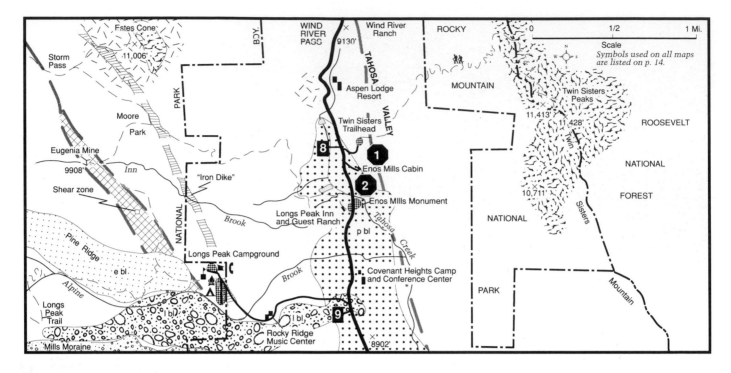

① ENOS MILLS' CABIN.

MILE **8.1**

Mileage to next point of interest:

(0.3)

El. 8960 ft.

Entrance road is on the left.

THINGS TO DO:

—Visit the "Homestead Cabin" built by Enos Mills in 1885. Enda Mills Kiley and her husband, Robert, have opened Mills' first one-room home in the Tahosa Valley as a museum filled with photographs, books and mementos of his life.

—A labeled nature trail leads from the Kileys' home to the cabin.

—The Homestead Cabin is on the National Register of Historic Places.

HISTORY:

—Enos Abijah Mills came to Colorado in 1884 at the age of 14. He visited his second cousin, the Rev. Elkanah Lamb, who owned a ranch just west of the Homestead Cabin. Mills fell in love with the Tahosa Valley and decided to make it his home.

—To support himself he worked as a ranch hand and at Rev. Lamb's Longs Peak House. During 1885 Mills climbed Longs Peak for the first time, helping Rev. Lamb's son, Carlyle, carry some bulky photographic equipment to the top for one of their guests.

—In 1887, Mills first climbed Longs Peak alone and decided to become the best nature guide in the Rocky Mountains.[2]

—During the winters he worked in the copper mines at Butte, Mont. or as a snow observer for the Colorado Irrigation Department.

—Summers were spent exploring the mountains and leading groups of tourists up Longs Peak. Through self-study and careful observation he soon became an outstanding nature guide.

—As his knowledge increased he began to write about his experiences and observations in the mountains.

—Mills was the driving force in convincing the Congress of the U.S. to establish Rocky Mountain as the thirteenth National Park in 1915. He lived in the Tahosa Valley from 1885 until he died in 1922. See p. 175, 206 for more information about Mills' life and work.

---

[2] Fazio, Patricia M., 1982, <u>Cragged crusade: the fight for Rocky Mountain National Park, 1909–1915</u>, Univ. of Wyo. M.A. thesis, p. 34.

Enos Mills with his daughter, Enda, at his homestead cabin in 1922, shortly before his death.   (Collection of Enos Mills Cabin).

Interior of Mills Homestead Cabin, now a museum.

Enos A Mills.   (W. S. Cooper photograph, NPS collection.)

Famous Longs Peak Inn on a bright, sunny morning, probably about 1915, against a backdrop of Mt. Meeker, Longs Peak, and Mt. Lady Washington. (Denver Public Library, Western History Dept.)

2
MILE
8.4
Mileage to nexct point of interest:
(0.4)

ENOS MILLS MONUMENT on left, at a large parking area east of present-day LONGS PEAK INN and GUEST RANCH.
Inscription on the monument reads:

> Enos A. Mills
> Father of
> Rocky Mountain National Park.
> Internationally known naturalist, author, lecturer and nature guide.
> Homesteaded on this site
> 1885.
> Erected by
> Namaqua Chapter,
> Daughters of the American Revolution
> 1982

SCENERY:
The Mills' "Homestead Cabin" is visible across the valley to the east.
—The view westward of Mt. Meeker, the Notch on Longs Peak and Mt. Lady Washington is spectacular.
—ESTES CONE, el. 11,006 ft. is to the northwest.
—Twin Sister Peaks are on the eastern skyline.

PHOTO HINTS:
—Best time for photos to the west is in the morning.

HISTORY:
—Reverend Elkanah Lamb and his family (page 204) settled in the lovely valley opposite this stop in 1875 and started LONGS PEAK HOUSE, one of the earliest resorts in the Tahosa Valley.
—Soon he found it more profitable to guide tourists to the top of Longs Peak

for $5 per person. "If they would not pay for spiritual guidance, I compelled them to pay for material elevation," Lamb wrote.

—In 1902 Enos Mills purchased the resort which he renamed Longs Peak Inn.

—In June 1906 fire destroyed the Inn but one month later Mills was able to re-open. The new structure was built of weathered logs killed by a forest fire because Mills did not want to cut live trees.

—To bring the natural beauty of the outdoors into the new Longs Peak Inn, Mills used many dead trees and curi-ous old stumps with interesting shapes for furniture and decorations. He wanted to bring the natural beauty of the outdoors into his inn.

—The lodge and surrounding cabins ac-commodated about 100 guests and was noted for its excellent food. The main structure burned in 1949.

—The present inn and guest ranch were built in 1950.

GEOLOGY:
—On the slope of Battle Mtn. directly to the west was the Eugenia Mine, the largest prospect on the eastern side of the National Park.

—Carl P. Norwall and Edward A. Cu-dahy staked a **claim** along a large **fault zone** and drove an **adit** about 1000 ft. into the mountain. No ore was ever produced but Norwell, his wife and two daughters lived in a comfortable house near the "mine" until about 1917.

—The mine site can be reached from Longs Peak Ranger Station. The trail climbs about 508 ft. in 1.4 mi.

—From here, southward for about 2.0 mi., thin, discontinuous patches of rounded **cobbles**, **gravel** and weathered reddish-yellow unsorted **sands** and dis-integrated rock debris cover many **bedrock** outcrops. These deposits are shown on the guide maps.

—This debris is all that is left of mater-ial deposited in the Tahosa Valley by an ancient Pre-Bull Lake-age glacier. This glacier flowed from the high mountains to the west between 2,400,000 and 245,000 years ago. Twin Sisters Peaks blocked the glacier from flowing farther eastward, turning it southward into the Tahosa Valley.

Just beyond Longs Peak Inn on the right is the entrance to HIGH PEAK CAMP operated by the Salvation Army.

MILE **8.8** (0.2)

MILE **9.0**

Mileage to next point of interest:

(0.7)

COVENANT HEIGHTS CONFERENCE CENTER on the east.

MILE MARKER 9.
El. 8952 ft.
One mile west of this junction is **LONGS PEAK CAMPGROUND, PICNIC AREA, RANGER STATION, and LONGS PEAK TRAILHEAD.**
—RESTROOMS, TELEPHONE.
Also along this road are ROCKY RIDGE MUSIC CENTER and CIRCLE C YOUTH CAMP.

THINGS TO DO:
—Longs Peak Campground has 27 camping sites for tents only. No campers, trailers or motorhomes are permitted.
—From the trailhead it is a 16.0 mi. round trip to the summit of Longs Peak.

DO NOT ATTEMPT TO CLIMB LONGS PEAK WITHOUT THE LAT-EST INFORMATION ON WEATHER AND CLIMBING CONDITIONS. MANY HAVE LOST THEIR LIVES BY NOT HEEDING THIS PRECAUTION.

HISTORY:
—Rocky Ridge Music Center, along the road to Longs Peak Campground, is a summer music camp at the former Hewes-Kirkwood Inn and Resort.
—Founded by Beth Miller Harrod in 1942, the Music Center has a distin-quished faculty and offers voice and instrumental instruction to high school and college students.

GEOLOGY:
—Just east of the final curve into the trailhead parking area is an outcrop of the "Iron Dike," a term used by early Front Range miners because in some places the iron-rich **diabase dike** contains abundant metallic minerals.
—The dike was injected as a liquid into **faults** in the surrounding rocks about 1050 million years ago.
—This is one of a series of northwest-trending dikes in the Park, but eco-nomically valuable minerals are rare in them.

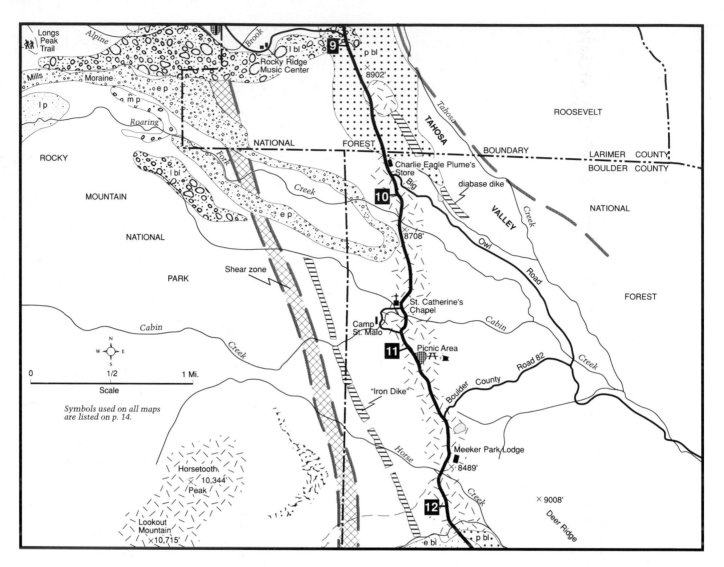

MILE	
9.7	**BOULDER-LARIMER COUNTY LINE and ROOSEVELT NATIONAL FOREST BOUNDARY.**
↓	
MILE **9.8**	**BIG OWL ROAD JOINS COLO. 7** from the east. El. 8800 ft.

Mileage to next point of interest:

(1.0)

—At this junction are Bishop's Antique Shop and Charlie Eagle Plume's Trading Post. Eagle Plume sells authentic Indian-made articles.

GEOLOGY:
—For the next 2.0 mi., **Precambrian granite** crops out on both sides of the highway.

MILE **10.8** **(0.3)**	**ST. CATHERINE'S CHAPEL, ST. MALO MOUNTAIN RETREAT and CONFERENCE CENTER and CAMP ST. MALO.** El. 8708 ft.

HISTORY:
—This historic Chapel on the Rock was built of local granite trimmed with Lyons Sandstone. Completed in 1936, the chapel seats 100 worshippers who have a breathtaking view of Mt. Meeker to the west.
—CAMP ST. MALO was started in 1916 on land owned by William McPhee, a Denver lumberman.
—McPhee and Monsignor Joseph J. Bosetti, a mountaineer and choir director of the Cathedral of the Immaculate Conception in Denver, combined their efforts to build a summer camp for choir boys of the church.
—During the 1930's, Mr. and Mrs. Oscar L. Malo of Denver financed a new dormitory and the chapel.
—The Conference Center opened in November 1987. The boys camp was closed for remodeling in 1986.

Meeker Park Lodge.

St. Catherine's Chapel.

MILE 11.1 (0.4)

MEEKER PARK PICNIC AREA.
This U.S. Forest Service picnic area, on the east side of the road, is in a lodgepole pine forest.

MILE 11.5 (0.2)

BOULDER COUNTY ROAD 82,
on the east, leads into Roosevelt National Forest along the Cabin Creek Road.

MILE 11.7

Mileage to next point of interest:

(0.4)

MEEKER PARK LODGE.
El. 8489 ft.

SCENERY:
—To the west is a lovely view of Mt. Meeker, el. 13,911 ft.
—HORSETOOTH PEAK, el. 10,344 ft. is to the southwest and LOOKOUT MTN., el. 10,715 ft., is left of Horsetooth Peak.
—ST. VRAIN MTN. is on the southern skyline.

HISTORY:
—Meeker Park, Meeker Lodge and Mt. Meeker were named for Nathan C. Meeker, a former editor of the New York Tribune who came west with Horace Greeley and helped found the Union Colony of Greeley in 1870.
—Later Meeker served as Indian Agent on the White River Reservation in northwestern Colorado. He was killed in 1879 by Ute Indians who resented his plowing up their horse-racing track and his efforts to make them settle in one place and learn to farm.

—Isaac S. Stapp probably was the first non-Indian settler in Meeker Park. After Stapp left this homestead, Franklin Hornbaker acquired the land in 1891. He operated a tollgate on the road to Estes Park and offered tourists, prospectors and hunters food and shelter at his Good View Ranch.
—Hornbaker had a herd of dairy cows, carried the mail, ran a stage coach line between Lyons and Estes Park and guided tourists up Longs Peak.
—Fred Robinson purchased the Hornbaker property about 1901 and owned it until 1922 when H. G. Nowels and O. L. Dever bought the Good View Ranch. Both men were high school teachers who wanted mountain property on which to spend their summers.
—The partnership lasted until 1929, when Mr. Nowels sold his interest to the Devers. The Dever family have owned and operated this well-known guest ranch and dining room since then.

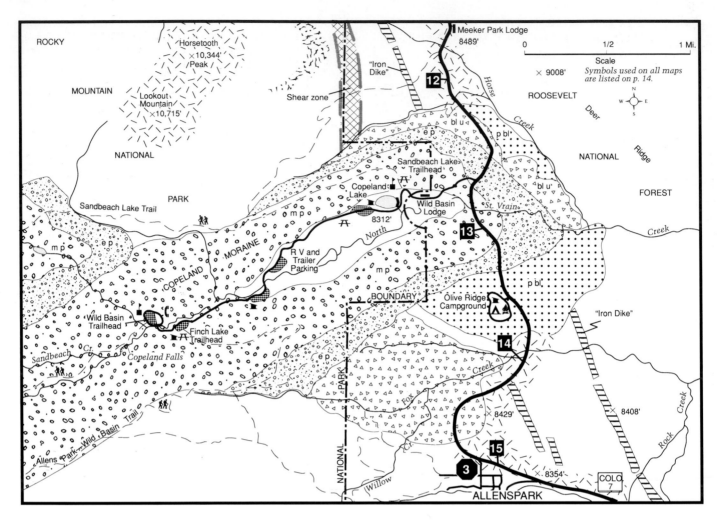

MILE	
12.2	**HIGHWAY CROSSES COPELAND LATERAL MORAINE of the WILD BASIN GLACIER.**

Mileage to next point of interest:

(0.5)

GEOLOGY:
—For the next 2.0 mi. the highway crosses Pre-Bull Lake, Bull Lake and Pinedale-age glacial debris (see map).
—Thin, discontinuous patches of rounded **cobbles**, **gravels** and weathered reddish-yellow unsorted **sands** with other disintegrated rock debris cover **bedrock** surfaces along the roadcuts.

MILE
12.7

ROAD TO WILD BASIN LODGE, COPELAND LAKE and WILD BASIN TRAILHEADS on the west.
Points-of-interest along this road and the trails are described on p. 182.

MILE
12.9

(0.7)

CROSS NORTH ST. VRAIN CREEK.
El. 8280 ft.

SCENERY:
—From left to right the mountains to the west are OGALALLA PEAK, el. 13,138 ft., COPELAND MTN., el. 13,176 ft. in the center and OUZEL PEAK, el. 12,716 ft. on the right.

PLANTS:
—Along both sides of North St. Vrain Creek is a rich bank-side habitat that is home to wide variety of birds and mammals.

GEOLOGY:
—South of North St. Vrain Creek, the highway cuts through the Middle Pinedale-age south **lateral moraine**.
—Boulders and cobbles are larger and not as weathered as the ones in older Bull Lake and Pre-Bull Lake moraines.

HISTORY:
—The stream was named for fur traders Ceran and Marcellin St. Vrain who built a trading post, Fort St. Vrain, along the South Platte River near its confluence with St. Vrain Creek in 1837.

MILE
13.6
Mileage to next point of interest:
(0.4)

OLIVE RIDGE CAMPGROUND and BOULDER COUNTY ROAD 84W.
Entrance on west.

THINGS TO DO:
—This U.S. Forest Service Campground in a ponderosa pine forest has 56 campsites for tents and RV's .

GEOLOGY:
—Throughout the campground, bedrock surfaces have thin, scattered patches of badly weathered, rusty-yellow, unsorted sands, gravels and cobbles. This is all that remains of Pre-Bull Lake-age glacial debris.
—Erosion by wind, water and younger glacial ice during the past 245,000 years has removed nearly all evidence of this ancient glaciation and in some places younger glacial debris covers the older deposits.
—Many of the large, rounded, glacial boulders that outline the roadways and campsites are of Pinedale age, brought in by the Forest Service.

MILE
14.0
(0.9)

MILE MARKER 14.
The sign is along the west side of the road just north of a gravel road leading west. Don't miss the views of the high peaks to the west.

GEOLOGY:
—More patches of ancient, rust-colored Bull Lake-age glacial debris litter the ground surface above roadcuts.

ROAD INTO ALLENSPARK.
El. 8520 ft.
Entrance on the west.

MILE
14.9
(0.1)

THINGS TO DO:
—Allenspark, a secluded mountain community of many year-round homeowners, has a number of restaurants, a grocery store, gift and antique shops.
—The livery stable has horses for rent.

HISTORY:
—This former mining community was named for Alonzo Nelson Allen, a prospector who built a cabin near here in 1864.
—George Mack filed for a homestead but later sold it and his mining claims to George Phifer, who formed the Allenspark Land and Townsite Company in 1896, at about the same time the first post office was established. Phifer built a 14-room hotel and slowly a town grew around the hotel.
—A flurry of mining activity was set off in 1903 when the Clara Belle Mine was "opened." This stock-promotion scheme lasted until 1910, when the property was sold for $300. No ore was ever shipped, but prospectors spent many more summers searching for the "mother lode."
—Allenspark is near the northeastern end of the Colorado Mineral Belt, a zone rich in ore deposits that extends southwestward across Colorado to the San Juan Mountains.

MILE
15.0

MILE MARKER 15.
Marker is 0.1 mi. southeast of the road junction into Allenspark, at the eastern end of the divided highway.

Colorado Highway 7 continues eastward to Lyons, Colo.
About 4.0 mi. southeast of Allenspark,
Colo. 7 joins Colo. 72 , which continues southward
as the Peak-to-Peak Highway.

This deeply weathered Pre-Bull Lake glacial debris crops out on the east side of Colo. 7 near the entrance road into Olive Ridge Campground. The light-brown rusty-looking soil containing small rock fragments overlies deeply weathered Precambrian granite ledges in the lower right of the photos. (F. W. Osterwald)

Allenspark, Colo. in 1985.

Snow-covered Mt. Meeker stands above tree-covere[d] Lookout Mtn. The nearly level line of aspens (arrow) [is] at the top of the north lateral (Copeland) moraine [of] the old Wild Basin Glacier.

This dramatic picture, taken in 1889 by famous mountain climber F. H. Chapin, shows the north wall of Mt. Meeker from the Mills Moraine. Layering in the ancient metamorphic rocks shows clearly in the huge ledges. Guide Carlyle Lamb is sitting in the foreground.   (NPS Collection)

Below is a William H. Jackson photo showing the flat-topped summit of Longs Peak on the right.   (Colorado Historical Society)

ROAD to WILD BASIN TRAILHEADS

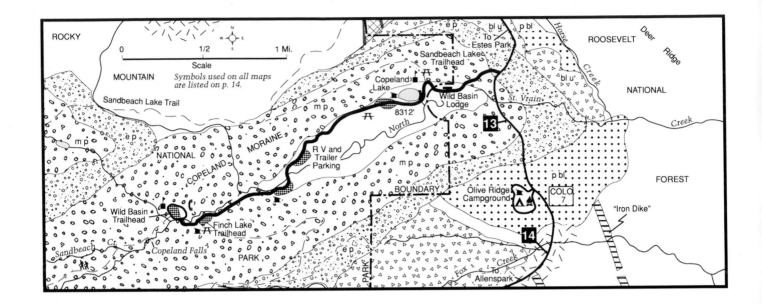

0.0 | *Turn west 2.2 mi. north of Allenspark and follow the road to WILD BASIN RANGER STATION. Set your odometer to 0.0 or write down your mileage at this junction.*

0.3 | **WILD BASIN LODGE** on left.

Beyond the lodge, turn right and follow the graveled road past the RANGER STATION.

0.4 | **TRAILHEAD TO SANDBEACH LAKE** is on the north side of Copeland lake.
El. 8400 ft. Parking area on right.

THINGS TO DO:
—The trail to Sandbeach Lake climbs 1971 ft. in 4.2 mi. A natural lake was enlarged many years ago to provide water for the city of Longmont, Colorado.
—In 1984 the National Park Service paid the city of Longmont $1.9 million for Sandbeach, Pear and Bluebird reservoirs in Wild Basin. The dams were removed in 1988 to return the areas to their natural states.

0.5 | **CROSS COPELAND LAKE DAM.**
El. 8312 ft.

THINGS TO DO:
—Fishing is permitted; a picnic area surrounds the lake. Colorado fishing license is required.

HISTORY:
—Copeland Lake was named for John B. Copeland who "proved up" on a 320-acre homestead around the lake in 1896.
—He dug a ditch to divert water into the lake from North St. Vrain Creek and enlarged the lake with an earth-fill dam.
—By 1903 the State Business Directory listed "Copeland Park" with J. B. Copeland as manager.
—He stocked his lake with trout and probably charged visiting fishermen to use his private preserve. Little else is known about this gentleman for whom a lake, a moraine and a mountain are named.
—In 1913, the city of Longmont bought Copeland's water rights, 129 acres around the lake and subsequently enlarged the original dam.

GEOLOGY:
—Copeland Lake is an ancient **kettle lake** within an oval basin created and outlined by an **esker**, a relic of the Great Ice Ages.

—**Kettles** and **eskers** are unusual in glaciated mountains, but are very common where the land formerly was covered by **continental** glaciers.

—A stream flowing within glacial ice deposited the **esker** around the eastern and southern sides of a large, stranded ice block that formed the **kettle** when it melted. The kettle later filled with water to become a **kettle lake**.

—When the dam was enlarged, the shape and composition of the esker were considerably modified.

—In June 1929, one wall of the basin was washed out, partially emptying the lake. Where the ridge was eroded out at least four distinct beds of water-laid, stratified glacial debris were uncovered. These beds indicate that the ridge is not a **glacial moraine**.

—If the break had not occurred, Copeland Lake would have been considered simply a kettle lake in glacial **till**, instead of the unusual combination of a kettle and an esker.

0.7 **PICNIC AREA** on the right.
—RESTROOMS. Many places to stop and more picnic areas are along both sides of the road from here to Wild Basin Ranger Station.

0.9 **NATIONAL PARK BOUNDARY SIGN.**

SCENERY:
—The road leads southwest along the south edge of the Middle Pinedale-age north **lateral** Copeland Moraine deposited by the Wild Basin glacier.

PLANTS:
—The **montane life zone** forest includes Douglas firs, ponderosa pines, low junipers and aspens.
—Mats of very low-growing dark green kinnikinnic shrubs are common.
—Along North St. Vrain Creek is a **wetland** of thick willows that attracts many birds and mammals.
—This is an outstanding area for birding; at least 27 species nest here.
—Many conifers have been killed by spruce budworms which feed on the tips of the green fir or spruce needles.
—The National Park Service does not use pesticides or other methods to interfere with this natural and self-limiting thinning process.

1.5 **RV and TRAILER PARKING.**
El. 8360 ft. Beyond here, the road is too narrow and winding for large vehicles.

1.6 **CROSS BRIDGE over NORTH ST. VRAIN CREEK**

SCENERY:
—The stream cascades through glacial debris and **outwash terraces** left by the Wild Basin Glacier.
—Huge, rounded boulders along the stream were carried down from the Continental Divide by glacial ice.

1.7 **PICNIC AREA and HORSE-LOADING RAMP** on left.
—RESTROOMS.

2.3 **FINCH LAKE TRAILHEAD.**
Parking area on left.

THINGS TO DO:
—The trail to Finch Lake climbs 1442 ft. in 4.5 mi., continuing on another 2.0 mi. to Pear Reservoir, which is 2112 ft. higher than the trailhead. The ALLENSPARK–WILD BASIN TRAIL joins the FINCH LAKE TRAIL about 1.5 mi. from the trailhead.

2.5 **CROSS NORTH ST. VRAIN CREEK** and start one-way loop road to the Ranger Station.

2.6 **WILD BASIN RANGER STATION and TRAILHEAD.**
El. 8630 ft.
—RESTROOM. EMERGENCY TELEPHONE.

THINGS TO DO:
—Hiking trails in Wild Basin lead to many glacial lakes, photogenic waterfalls and beautiful vistas. **Subalpine life zone** wildflowers are always a delight to find along the trails.
—An easy trail to COPELAND FALLS is 0.3 mi. from the trailhead.
—CALYPSO CASCADES is 700 ft. higher and 1.8 mi. from the trailhead. At Calypso Cascades, the trail branches. One branch leads east and then southwest to FINCH LAKE which is 1412 ft. higher and 5.3 mi. distant from the trailhead. This trail passes parts of forest burned in 1978.
—Another trail from Calypso Cascades leads west to OUZEL FALLS which is

Aerial oblique view southwestward across Wild Basin , September 1986. Large area of dead trees is the site of the Ouzel Lake fire. Copeland Mtn. is the rounded peak at left center.
(D. B. Osterwald and John B. Bennetti, Jr.)

950 ft. higher and 2.7 mi. distant from the trailhead. Beyond the falls is OUZEL LAKE, which is 1510 ft. higher and 4.9 mi. from the trailhead. It was near Ouzel Lake that lightning struck in 1978, starting the Ouzel Lake fire.

— Beyond Ouzel Lake the trail continues to BLUEBIRD LAKE, a **tarn** in a **cirque** near the Continental Divide. It is 2478 ft. higher and 6.0 mi. distant from the trailhead.

—BOULDER–GRAND PASS, across the Continental Divide, is 8.0 mi. from the trailhead and 3561 ft. higher. The trail over the pass leads to Grand Lake.

—Also for the adventurous, MT. ALICE, el. 13,310 ft., is along the Divide 9.0 mi. from the trailhead. COPELAND MTN., el. 13,376 ft. is 6.7 mi. from the trailhead.

HISTORY:

—Near Ouzel Lake on August 9, 1978, lightning started a forest fire that smoldered for weeks before flaring up and spreading.

—On September 1, high winds fanned the smoldering flames which spread to tree tops. The Park Service then acted to contain the fire on its eastern edge. But on September 15, wind gusts up to 60 mph fanned the flames to even greater intensity.

—National Park Service crews, the Allenspark Fire Department, Boulder County fire crews and the Interagency Fire Center in Boise, Idaho, all sent teams of experts to fight the fire; it was finally extinguished in mid-October.

—Since 1973 the Park Service policy has been to let some lightning-caused fires burn, within certain prescribed limits. The Ouzel Lake fire was considered low risk and allowed to burn until high winds threatened to spread the flames eastward to populated areas.

—Fire is a natural process that thins dense forests, making openings where deer and elk can return to feed on new plant growth. Aspens and lodgepole pines sprout quickly on the bare ground which contains nutrients derived from the ashes. A hike through the burned area offers a fascinating demonstration of natural plant succession. A greater variety of plants, and thus more mammals, will return to live in the burned areas.

END OF ROAD.
Return to Colorado 7.

DEVILS GULCH ROAD TO GLEN HAVEN

This drive starts at the exit of the U.S. Bureau of Reclamation Power Plant on U.S. 36 just east of the Estes Park Tourist Information Center, east of the main intersection of U.S.36, U.S.34 and U.S. 34 By-pass.

View northward of MacGregor Ranch and Twin Owls.   *(Denver Public Library, Western History Dept.)*

"Men who coped with wilderness were sturdy, steadfast. Matching their wits with nature, they learned a measure of her resourcefulness and drank her vigor."

——Enos A. Mills, <u>Rocky Mountain National Park</u>, Memorial Edition, 1932.

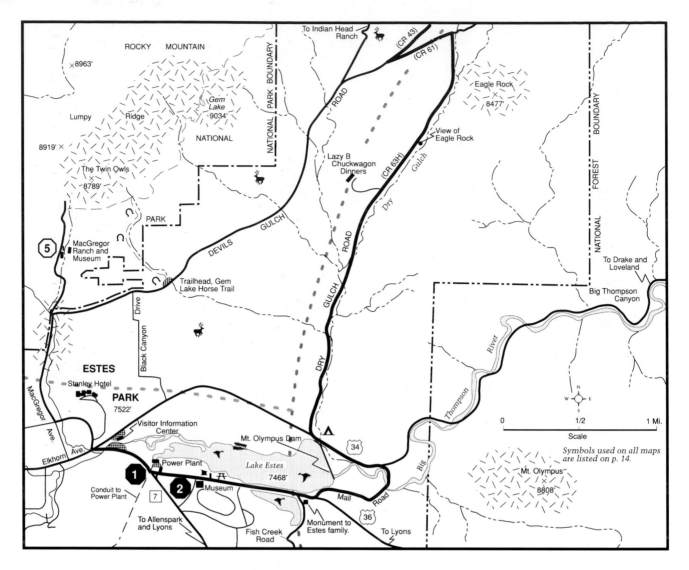

ESTES PARK VISITOR INFORMATION CENTER.

Entrance is on the left. Cross Big Thompson River on a foot bridge to the center. The main entrance is on U.S. 34, just east of the triple junction.

Information is available on motels, resorts, restaurants and activities in this year-round vacation community.

U.S. BUREAU of RECLAMATION POWER PLANT.

El. 7504 ft. Entrance on left.

THINGS TO DO:
—Visitors are welcome year-round at this power plant which generates 117 million kilowatts of power annually from its three generators.
—Water from the western slope is diverted to the eastern slope via the 13.1 mi. Alva B. Adams tunnel under the Continental Divide.

1

MILE

0.0

Mileage to next point of interest:

(0.2)

—From the east portal, water flows via Aspen Creek Siphon and Ramshorn Tunnel to Marys Lake and to the Marys Lake power plant.
—From Marys Lake, the water goes through Prospect Mountain Pressure Conduit and Tunnel and drops 482 ft. to the Estes Park power plant before flowing into Lake Estes. This lake was formed when MT. OLYMPUS DAM was completed in 1949.
—From Lake Estes water flows through tunnels, canals and reservoirs before reaching the Plains. The project was started in 1938. The first water was delivered through the Adams Tunnel in 1947 and the project completed in 1959.

Set your odometer at 0.0 or write down your mileage at the exit from the parking area. Turn left onto U.S. 36.

The Estes Park Visitor Center (foreground) and the Stanley Hotel (white) with Lumpy Ridge on the sky-line in 1984.

2

MILE
0.2

Mileage
to next
point of
interest:

(0.1)

ESTES PARK AREA HISTORICAL MUSEUM is on the right at 4th Street.

THINGS TO DO:
—Open daily from mid-May through September, the museum has an excellent collection of historic photographs documenting Estes Park history.
—Inside the front door is a shiny Stanley Steamer auto, the brainchild of twins Freelan O. Stanley and Francis E. Stanley. F. O. Stanley made Estes Park his summer home from 1903 until his death in 1940. More information about Stanley's many contributions to Estes Park is on p. 208.
—A collection of cameras and equipment used by early-day Estes Park photographer Fred Clatworthy are displayed as are many other facets of Estes Park history.
—Special group tours may be arranged in the off-season.
—A pamphlet for an historical walking-tour is available for those who wish to learn more about Estes Park history.

MILE
0.3

Mileage
to next
point of
interest:

(0.3)

ACCESS ROAD to LAKE ESTES. El. 7468 ft.
—RESTROOMS.

THINGS TO DO:
—The road on the left leads to picnic areas and boat docks. The lake is stocked with trout. <u>A Colorado fishing license is required</u>.

SCENERY:
—Directly ahead are MT. OLYMPUS (left) el. 8806 ft. and MT. PISGAH (right) el. 8630 ft.
—Mt. Olympus, the rounded, pyramid-shaped granite peak, was named by Fernando C. Willet, a teacher who came to Estes Park from Indiana in 1873 for his health. Because he taught Greek mythology to the few students then living in Estes Park, he named the mountain for the home of the Greek gods.
—The Arapaho Indians had a different, and probably more appropriate name for the mountain, which when translated meant "Faces to the Wind."
—Mt. Pisgah was named after the peak in Jordan from which Moses looked down upon the promised land.

MILE
0.6
(0.3)

↓

▼

MILE
0.9

Mileage
to next
point of
interest:

(0.1)

↓

▼

STANLEY PARK FAIRGROUNDS on right.

HISTORY:
—Land for the fairgrounds was donated to the town of Estes Park by F. O. Stanley.
—Each summer the Rooftop Rodeo and other shows attract large audiences.

FISH CREEK ROAD joins U.S. 36 on the right. Stay on U.S. 36 for another 0.1 mi.

SCENERY:
—To the south and southwest (left to right), the views of TWIN SISTERS PEAKS, MT. MEEKER and LONGS PEAK are spectacular.
—LUMPY RIDGE is to the northwest.

HISTORY:
—On the small hill southeast of the junction is a slender granite monument honoring the Joel Estes family who were the first permanent settlers in the park that bears their name.
—Joel Estes and his son Milton discovered the park in the fall of 1859 while on a hunting and prospecting trip. The family returned in 1860 and built two crude cabins at the confluence of Fish Creek and the Big Thompson River. The site is now under Lake Estes. See p. 198 for more about the Estes family.
—After the long, bitterly cold winter of 1865-66, Estes sold his squatters rights for a pittance and moved to southern Colorado. After several more changes of ownership, Griffith Evans acquired the property.
—It was to Griff Evans' ranch that the indominable Isabella Bird came in September, 1873. She paid Evans $8 per week for a one-room cabin and meals. See p. 200 for more about Bird and her adventures in Estes Park.[1]
—Southward along Fish Creek is the site of the first hotel built by the Earl of Dunraven in 1877.
—The Earl of Dunraven added spice and controversy to the history of Estes Park when he tried to acquire most of what is now Estes Park and much of the surrounding land for a private hunting preserve. More information about the Earl and his activities is on p. 200.

[1]Bird's fascinating book, <u>A Lady's Life in the Rocky Mountains</u>, first published in 1879, is still in print.

View southwestward of Griff Evans' ranch in the late 1870s or early 1880s. (W. G. Chamberlin photo, Denver Public Library, Western History Dept.)

Another southward view of Estes Park and the Big Thompson River taken by Enos Mills. (Collection of the Enos Mills Homestead Cabin)

View eastward of Lake Estes. Mt. Olympus is the peak on the right.

MILE
1.0

Mileage to next point of interest:

(0.4)

Just beyond Fish Creek Road, watch for MALL ROAD on the left.

JUNCTION, U.S. 36 and MALL ROAD.

Turn left and follow Mall Road 0.6 mi. to U.S. 34.

HISTORY:
—Mall Road was named for Dr. Jacob D. Mall, a practicing physician who came to Estes Park in the late 1930s.
—On the left is Mt. Olympus Dam, a structure of the massive Colorado-Big Thompson Project built by the U. S. Bureau of Reclamation.
—During the catastrophic Big Thompson flood of July 31, 1976, water from Dry Gulch swept across U.S. 34 and eroded the base of the dam. Gray rock was used to repair the damage.
—Heaviest rainfall, near Glen Comfort in the Big Thompson canyon, was 11.5 inches of rain in 4 hours.
—The town of Estes Park, west of the storm center, received only 1 inch of rain, while Olympus Heights, just east of Lake Estes received about 10 inches.
—Eastward through the Big Thompson Canyon, floodwater destroyed roads, 197 automobiles, and 93 propane gas tanks. Damaged beyond repair were 252 structures and 139 people were killed. To repair the damage, 319,863 cu. yds. of debris were removed from the path of the flood. Remarkably, six concrete highway bridges in the canyon survived.
—Today, little evidence remains of that natural disaster. Fewer lives would have been lost if warnings had been heeded and structures had not been built on the **floodplain** of the river.

MILE
1.4

ESTES PARK SEWAGE TREATMENT PLANT on left.

MILE
1.5

CROSS BIG THOMPSON RIVER below Mt. Olympus Dam.

MILE
1.6

(0.6)

JUNCTION, MALL ROAD and U.S. 34.

Turn left onto U.S. 34 opposite Olympus Motor Lodge.

MILE
2.2

(1.7)

JUNCTION, U.S. 34 and DRY GULCH ROAD.

Turn right onto Dry Gulch Road at Sombrero Ranch Stables.

MILE
3.9

ENTRANCE TO LAZY B CHUCK-WAGON DINNERS on left.

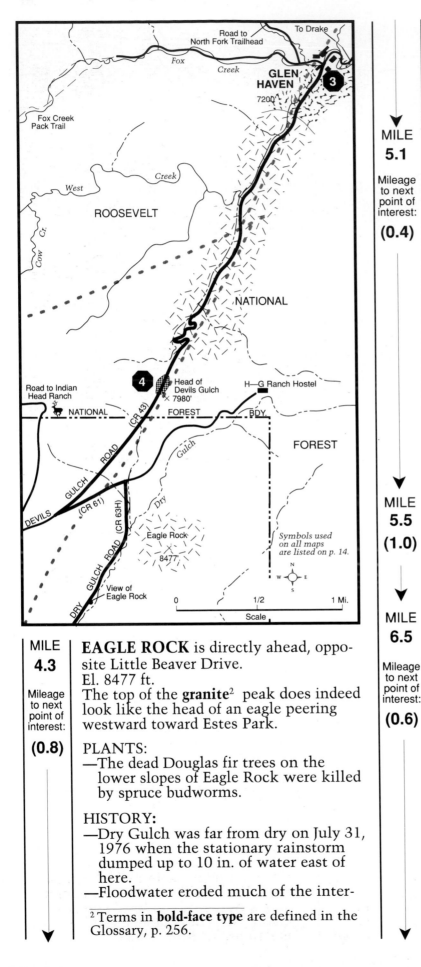

mittent stream channel. The U.S. Bureau of Land Management placed rip-rap at several locations along the stream bed and reseeded the slopes. Today, only subtle differences in the color and texture of the vegetation mark the reclamation efforts.

MILE 5.1

Mileage to next point of interest:

(0.4)

JUNCTION, DRY GULCH ROAD (County Road 63H) and COUNTY ROAD 61.

Turn left and follow gravel road 0.4 mi. to next road junction.

SCENERY:
—From a large parking area on the right are views to the southwest of Mt. Meeker, Longs Peak and the high peaks along the Continental Divide.
—Lumpy Ridge is to the west. The name comes from the Arapaho Indian term, *"Thath-aa-ai-atah"* which means "Little Lumps."

HISTORY:
—The H Bar G RANCH HOSTEL, to the east, was homesteaded by Shep Husted, an early-day rancher and guide.
—Husted climbed Longs Peak more than 800 times during the 52 years he lived in Estes Park.

MILE 5.5

(1.0)

JUNCTION, CR 61 with CR 43.

Make a sharp right turn onto the paved highway, (County Road 43) near the northeastern end of Estes Park. Follow County Road 43 to Glen Haven.

MILE 6.5

Mileage to next point of interest:

(0.6)

HEAD of DEVILS GULCH and ROOSEVELT NATIONAL FOREST BOUNDARY.
El. 7980 ft.
Small parking areas are on both sides of the road.

Beyond here, the road plunges down a steep canyon with four sharp switch-backs.

HISTORY:
—During the 1870s and 1880s, the route between Estes Park and Glen Haven was little more than a rough horseback trail.
—By 1899 the road was passable for wagons and teams of horses. It was "paved" with logs laid side by side making a "corduroy" road. The logs kept the road from washing away and gave the horses better footing.

MILE 4.3

Mileage to next point of interest:

(0.8)

EAGLE ROCK is directly ahead, opposite Little Beaver Drive.
El. 8477 ft.
The top of the **granite**[2] peak does indeed look like the head of an eagle peering westward toward Estes Park.

PLANTS:
—The dead Douglas fir trees on the lower slopes of Eagle Rock were killed by spruce budworms.

HISTORY:
—Dry Gulch was far from dry on July 31, 1976 when the stationary rainstorm dumped up to 10 in. of water east of here.
—Floodwater eroded much of the inter-

[2] Terms in **bold-face type** are defined in the Glossary, p. 256.

Examining flood damage in the Big Thompson Canyon east of Estes Park. This car was just one of 197 destroyed by the raging water on July 31, 1976.
(Estes Park Trail Gazette)

—The present road, built by Larimer County, was paved in the 1960s.
—In the 1877 Hayden Survey, <u>Atlas of Colorado</u>, this canyon was called "Devils Cañon". Some time since then the name was changed to "gulch", a typically western term for a steep, narrow gully or canyon.

GEOLOGY:
—Outcrops of **Precambrian granite** along the right side of the road have been broken into small, rust-colored pieces by movement along a fault (shown on map).

LOWEST SWITCHBACK.
El. 7668 ft.

PLANTS:
—On both sides of the road Douglas firs, killed by spruce budworms, have been removed. As a result, the hillsides are more open now so more light reaches the forest floor. This allows more plants and grasses to grow.
—Low-growing patches of kinnikinnic form carpets of bright, evergreen, glossy leaves.

MILE
7.1

Mileage to next point of interest:

(1.3)

HISTORY:
—The very severe, nearly stationary thunderstorm storm on July 31, 1976 dumped only about 6 inches of rain in 45 minutes along the North Fork of The Big Thompson River just west of Glen Haven.
—Torrents of water, however, poured into the narrow canyon from every drainage. Much of Glen Haven was damaged or destroyed. The road to Estes Park was washed away at several places.
—On the tree-covered slopes in Devils Gulch, **sheet-flooding** removed much of the soil cover, but little evidence of the flood remains today.

CONTACT BETWEEN PRECAMBRIAN GRANITE and MICA SCHIST.

GEOLOGY:
—On the right side of the road, just beyond a small cabin tucked against the hillside, is the contact (or boundary) between light-colored **igneous granite** and dark-colored, layered **metamorphic mica schist**.

MILE
8.4

Mileage to next point of interest:

(0.5)

This home in Glen Haven was swept from its foundation by the flood of July 31, 1976.
(Estes Park Trail Gazette)

Part of the road between Estes Park and Glen Haven was washed out by the storm. Temporary repairs had been started when this picture was taken. (Estes Park Trail Gazette)

Glen Haven Postmaster Roberta Speyer watches forlornly as mud and debris are shoveled from the Post Office.
(Estes Park Trail Gazette)

3

MILE
8.9

Mileage
to next
point of
interest:

(2.4)

GLEN HAVEN.
El. 7200 ft.

THINGS TO DO:
—Glen Haven has several interesting gift shops, restaurants and lodges.
—A livery stable has horses for hire.
—A gravel road between the General Store and Calico Kate's Gift Shop leads about 0.2 mi. west to a road junction.
—The left fork follows Fox Creek 1.2 mi. to the trailhead for FOX CREEK PACK TRAIL. From there it is about 3 mi. to the NORTH BOUNDARY TRAIL which leads about another 4 mi. northward to a patrol cabin along the North Fork of the Big Thompson River.
—The right fork follows the North Fork for 1.4 mi. to a trailhead. From this trailhead it is 1.5 mi. to the end of the Dunraven Glade road. Another patrol cabin is 3.7 mi. beyond the end of the road.
—A trail starting near the Livery Stable climbs 500 ft. in about 4.5 mi. to the summit of Crosier Mountain, southeast of Glen Haven.

HISTORY:
—The North Fork of the Big Thompson River and its surrounding area have always been noted for their excellent hunting and fishing. The Earl of Dunraven built a remote hunting lodge for his guests in Dunraven Glade, north of Glen Haven.
— George W. Ragan ran cattle here in the 1870s and probably was the first settler.
—By 1885, P. J. Pauley bought Ragan's ranch. His extensive holdings included the Indian Head Ranch.
—Lumberman Ira O. Knapp first visited the area in 1893. In 1896 he and his brother, O. S. Knapp, moved their sawmill to Glen Haven. For several years the cluster of cabins around the sawmill was known as Knappville.
—About 1900 George Dennis built the first summer tourist resort, the Dennis Hotel, at the foot of the canyon where West Creek enters Devils Gulch.
—In 1903 the Knapps sold some of their property to the Presbyterian Assembly Association of Boulder, Colo. for use as a summer resort known as Glen Haven.

Glen Haven, Colorado in 1985.

—Under the guidance of minister W. H. Schureman and Mason E. Knapp, the non-profit organization sold cabin sites for $50. In 1923, the association was reincorporated as the Glen Haven Resort and through the years many improvements, more cabins and year-round homes were built.

After your visit to Glen Haven, turn around and follow the Devils Gulch Road back up the hill.

4

11.3

Mileage
to next
point of
interest:

(1.0)

HEAD of DEVILS GULCH.
Small parking areas on both sides of the road.

SCENERY:
—Don't miss the magnificent vistas from this stop at the northern end of Estes Park.
—Eagle Rock is the nearby granite knob on the left.
—From left to right are Twin Sisters Peaks, and the Fish Creek Valley. To the right of the valley are Mt. Meeker, Longs Peak and MT. LADY WASHINGTON, which is the lower peak to the right of Longs Peak. On the southwestern skyline are the high peaks along the Continental Divide.

PLANTS:
—During June and July the meadows are a blaze of color when many **montane life zone** wildflowers bloom.

WILDLIFE:
—Watch for mountain bluebirds who raise their young in birdhouses placed on fence posts by thoughtful ranchers and homeowners.

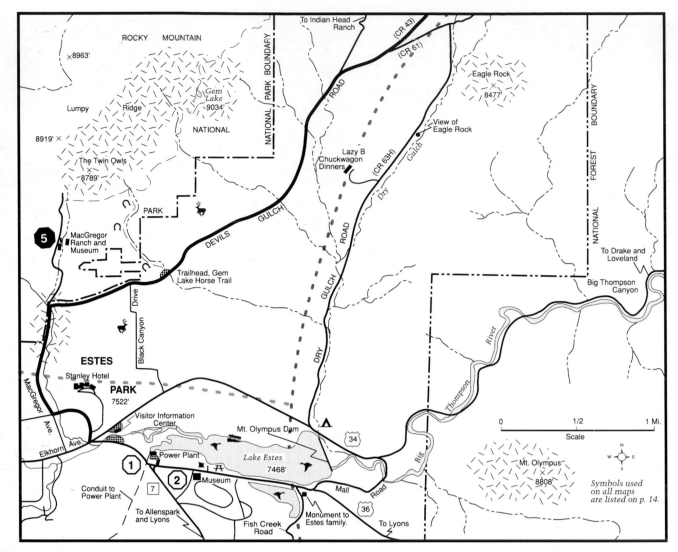

MILE	
12.3	**COUNTY ROAD 61 joins DEVILS GULCH ROAD 43, also called MacGregor Avenue.**

Mileage to next point of interest:

(0.3)

Continue southwest toward Estes Park on Devils Gulch Road.

GEOLOGY:
—Directly ahead are outcrops of granite that were formed by a process termed **exfoliation**. Their distinctive appearance gave rise to the name Lumpy Ridge.
—Thin shells of granite break from the outcrops when pressure in the rock is released as the overlying rock is worn away.
—Changes in temperature of the rocks, freezing and thawing of water, and chemical and physical reactions within the granite also aid in loosening both the onion-skin shells and the mineral grains in the granite.
—Similar processes formed both the spheroidal knobs and the arch-shaped over-hanging outcrops along the cliffs.

MILE	
12.6	**ROAD JUNCTION.**
(1.8)	Gravel road leads to Indian Head Guest Ranch that was purchased by the National Park Service in 1988 and is now part of Rocky Mountain National Park.

MILE	
14.4	**GEM LAKE HORSE TRAIL.**

Parking area on right.
Another hiking trail starts at the Mac-Gregor Ranch trailhead, about 1 mi. to the west.

Mileage to next point of interest:

(0.4)

SCENERY:
—More views of Eagle Rock to the east.
—The two metal conduits directly ahead along the side of Prospect Mountain carry water to the Estes Park Power Plant.
—The high peaks of the Continental Divide provide a lovely backdrop to Estes Park.

Black-billed magpie.

Male mountain bluebird.

Bird pictures by Chase Swift©.

Western tanager.

View southwestward of Longs Peak from MacGregor Ranch.

Fireweed.

Richardson geranium.

Fremont geranium.

MILE **14.8** | **BLACK CANYON DRIVE** joins the highway on the left.

MILE **15.0** | **HIGH FENCE on LEFT.**

Mileage to next point of interest: **(0.3)**

HISTORY:
—This fenced area was used to pen elk brought from Yellowstone National Park in 1913–14 to replenish animals killed by hunters before "Rocky" became a National Park.
—With the financial aid of F. O. Stanley, more than 60 elk were transported to Estes Park. Their descendants now roam the Park and the surrounding forests.

(5)

MACGREGOR RANCH and MUSEUM.
El. 7616 ft. Entrance on right.

MILE **15.3**

THINGS TO DO:
—The museum, in the old MacGregor family home, is open 11 AM to 5 PM, Tuesdays through Sundays from Memorial Day to Labor Day. It offers a fascinating view of life on an early-day Colorado cattle ranch.
—The GEM LAKE TRAIL starts at the MacGregor Ranch and climbs about 1300 ft. around Twin Owls to reach a small lake nestled in a pothole-like depression in granite. It is about 1.8 mi. from the ranch.[3]
—Technical rock climbers use a number of routes to reach the top of Twin Owls and other rocky summits along Lumpy Ridge.[4]
—The BLACK CANYON TRAIL leads 7.5 mi. northwest up Black Canyon Creek to join the Lawn Lake Trail along Roaring River.

Mileage to next point of interest: **(0.9)**

WILDLIFE:
—Wyoming ground squirrels ("picket pins") recently took up residence here.

[3]Check with Park service personnel for dates of special closures in this area, which is a nesting area for raptors.

[4]Lumpy Ridge: Estes Park Rock Climbs is a detailed guide for technical climbing in this area.

SCENERY:
—To the northwest, from left to right are McGREGOR MTN., el. 10,486 ft. and BLACK CANYON.
—MUMMY MTN. is on the skyline above Black Canyon.
—Twin Owls, two monoliths that stand as sentinels above Estes Park are directly behind the ranch buildings.
—Several marked nature trails start from the ranch.

HISTORY:
—Alexander Q. MacGregor, an attorney from Milwaukee, Wis., came to Colorado in 1869. In 1872, he first visited Estes Park on a camping trip and in 1874 returned with a new bride and mother-in-law to start the Black Canyon Ranch, now known as the MacGregor Ranch.
—His wife, a talented artist, was the first postmaster of Estes Park.
—Through the years the family continued to buy land and cattle, raised a large vegetable garden, built a water-powered sawmill on Black Canyon Creek, dug ditches to irrigate the hay meadows west of the ranch buildings and even built rental cabins for summer tourists.
—When Muriel L. MacGregor died in 1970, she was the last immediate survivor of the family. Her will stipulated that the cattle ranch should continue to operate and that the profits were to be used for charitable purposes.
—The 1210-acre ranch is now preserved as open space and as an outdoor laboratory for school children.
—More information about the MacGregor family is on p. 204.

After your visit to the MacGregor Ranch Museum, continue southward to Estes Park.

MILE **16.2** | **JUNCTION, MACGREGOR AVENUE AND U.S. 34 BY-PASS.**

To reach downtown Estes Park, continue straight ahead on MacGregor Avenue.

HISTORY

OF113. A BIT OF ESTES' PARK FROM THE STAGE WINDOW.-

A view of Estes Park taken by famed western photographer W. H. Jackson, probably during the 1880s. The pointed hill in the middle distance is Eagle Cliff Mountain, then called Sheep Mountain. Some of the peaks along the Continental Divide are in the background. (Colorado Historical Society).

"The frontier no longer exists, and the days of wilderness are gone forever. Yet in our magnificent National Parks we still have a bit of the primeval world and the spirit of the vigorous frontier."

——Enos A. Mills, <u>Your National Parks</u>, 1917.

EARLIEST VISITORS

The first known human residents of Colorado lived on the Great Plains east of the Front Range about 16,000 years ago. Although these first Coloradans aren't known to have come into what is now Rocky Mountain National Park, later peoples, who lived in the state between 11,500 and 11,000 years ago, probably were the first visitors to the Park and nearby parts of the Front Range. These first visitors came to hunt mammoths and other large animals near the end of the last major glaciation. They apparently followed ancient game trails across the Front Range in their never-ending search for food. Some of those earliest visitors made distinctive large stone weapon points called "Clovis" points. A few broken Clovis points have been found in the Park and on Trail Ridge but no permanent campsites of Clovis people have ever been found in the Park.

Over 2000 years ago, different early people followed the same ancient trails into and across the Front Range that the Clovis people had followed. Although the large game animals hunted by the Clovis people were extinct, these later hunters used more refined hunting techniques that included game-drive walls. They built low stone walls that enabled the hunters to herd animals into narrow enclosures where they could be easily killed.

During the past thousand years, Plains Indians and their ancestors from many different tribes frequently visited the Park to hunt or travel the ancient trails on warring or trading expeditions. The trading expeditions primarily went to and from the Pueblo Indian tribes in New Mexico. Among the Indians known to have come into the Park were the Plains Apaches, Snakes, Utes, Arapahos, Cheyennes, Kiowas and Comanches but none made permanent homes here. The Front Range, including what is now the National Park, was part of a large reservation set aside for the Arapahos and Cheyennes in 1851.

By the early 1700s, wide-ranging French fur trappers undoubtedly followed game trails into Estes Park or traveled a well-known trail along the western side of the Park near Grand Lake to trap or hunt. Few written journals remain to tell of their adventures but word was passed that the Rocky Mountains were fine places for hunters, adventurers and explorers.[1]

The first U.S. Government expedition to pass near Rocky Mountain National Park was the Long Expedition which followed the South Platte River southward in 1820. Although Longs Peak is named for the leader of the expedition, Major Stephen H. Long, none of his party attempted to climb the peak, although they did enter the mountains at several points. Major Long named it "James Peak" for the geologist and botanist of the expedition, but John C. Fremont changed the

name to Longs Peak.

Rufus Sage, one of the earliest tourists, spent several years exploring Colorado and camped several days in Moraine Park in 1843. He wrote an excellent journal with accurate, interesting descriptions of his travels. By the 1850s, other explorers, hunters, prospectors and tourists were arriving in the Rocky Mountains. Soon Estes Park and Grand Lake were settled and their histories became closely intertwined with the area that later became Rocky Mountain National Park.

ESTES PARK

THE FIRST SETTLERS

The open grassy meadowland surrounded by tree-covered mountains that is now called Estes Park was named for Joel Estes (1806-1875) who first visited this lovely **park** (p. 188) in the fall of 1859. Estes and his family came to Colorado from California where he had been moderately successful as a gold miner. After visiting the new prospects along Cherry Creek and Gregory Gulch, Estes concluded that the California gold fields had looked richer so he returned to his former profession of ranching. During the summer of 1859 the family settled on land along the South Platte River near present-day Ft. Lupton, Colorado .

In October, Estes and his 12-year old son, Milton, left their recently established "ranch" on a hunting and prospecting trip. They followed the same ancient Indian trail that Rufus Sage had trod. It led from the plains into the mountains generally along the route that is now U.S. Highway 36 from Lyons to Estes Park. Estes explored the "Longs Peak area" for several days and decided the rich parkland, with its abundant game, was better suited to ranching than their location on the plains. Estes, his wife Patsy, and six of their twelve children returned the next summer with about 60 head of cattle. They built two crude cabins in the valley where Fish Creek joined the Big Thompson River. The site is now under Lake Estes. A granite monument to the Estes family is on the hillside just east of the junction of U.S. 36 and Fish Creek Road.

Game was so plentiful in and around Estes Park that Estes supplied the Denver markets with wild game and dressed skins. In his memoirs, Milton Estes stated that one fall and winter he killed 100 head of elk along with some deer, bighorn sheep and antelope. The family supplemented their diet of deer, elk and beef with trout, wild berries and milk. Much of their clothing was made from animal hides.

It is not known when the Estes family opened their home to the first tourists, but in the fall of 1861, Henry M. Teller arrived and probably spent the winter at the Estes ranch. In later years, Teller served as a U.S. Senator from Colorado.

On August 18, 1864, the Estes family had their first visitors of the year when a party of men seeking

---

[1] The Trailmakers (In press) has a full account of the trails and earliest visitors to Rocky Mountain National Park.

to climb Longs Peak arrived at the Estes ranch. The adventurers, including William N. Byers, editor of the Rocky Mountain News in Denver, stayed with the Estes family before and after assaulting the peak. Byers, who is credited with naming the park for the Estes family, wrote several articles for his newspaper summarizing their adventures:

> "We are quite sure that no living creature, unless it had wings to fly, was ever upon its summit, and we believe we run no risk in predicting that no man ever will be, though it is barely possible that the ascent can be made."

Publicity resulting from that visit encouraged other sightseers and adventurers to venture into this little-known part of the Colorado Front Range.

The Estes family lived in their remote valley until April 15, 1866 when they sold their squatters rights to Michael Hollenbeck and a man named Buck for a pair of oxen. They moved to southern Colorado to start another ranch in a warmer and less isolated area. Joel Estes died in Farmington, N.M.. in 1875.

Hollenbeck and Buck stayed in Estes Park only a short time before selling the property to a man named Jacobs for $250. In 1867, Jacobs sold out to Griffith ("Griff") Evans for an unknown price. Evans, an amiable whiskey-loving Welshman, retained control of the property until November 1878, when he sold it to the Earl of Dunraven for $900. During those years, he built several small cabins to house the increasing numbers of hunters, tourists and hikers that began to arrive in this remote mountain park to enjoy hunting and fishing and the superb mountain scenery (photo, p. 188).

THE SCIENTISTS CAME TOO

Major John W. Powell was the first scientist to visit the area. Powell, a veteran of the Union Army in the Civil War, had lost an arm at the battle of Shiloh (Pittsburgh Landing). After the war he taught geology at Illinois Wesleyan University. In 1867, he brought a group of students to Colorado on a field trip that included a successful ascent of Pikes Peak. Favorable publicity from that climb encouraged Powell to return the following year to attempt an assault on Longs Peak. Byers heard of these plans and was eager to join in the venture.

For this attempt the party of climbers started from Grand Lake. On August 23, 1868, Major Powell, Walter Powell (the Major's brother), William Byers, Jack Summer (Byer's brother-in-law), and students L. W. Keplinger, Sam Garman and Ned Farrel finally reached the top of the famous landmark.

Byers later became a great publicity agent for Hot Sulphur Springs (which he owned), Grand Lake and Estes Park. Powell went on to lead the first expedition by boat down the Green and Colorado Rivers and through the Grand Canyon. Later, Powell's U. S. Geographical and Geological Survey of the Rocky Mountain Region (Powell Survey) mapped and described the geology and geography of the Colorado Plateau west of the Continental Divide. Lake Powell, upstream along the Colorado River from present-day Glen Canyon dam, is named for the Major.

Evans' ranch was the base camp in 1871 for geologist Clarence King's U. S. Geological Exploration of the Fortieth Parallel (King Survey). With the King party were two brothers, geologist Arnold Hague and civil engineer James Hague, for whom Hagues' Peak is named. King's topographic engineers had trouble making their triangulations that summer because huge smoke clouds from forest fires all over the West made accurate sightings through their surveying instruments very difficult.

While King was in Estes Park, Henry Adams, the wealthy grandson of President John Quincy Adams, arrived with topographer James T. Gardner. Gardner was in charge of one of King's surveying parties that had worked south from Fort Bridger, Wyoming into the Uinta Mountains of Utah. In August 1871, Gardner's party made their way to Estes Park and joined Clarence King for a climb up Longs Peak. Adams, who was on summer vacation from teaching history at Harvard, was fascinated with King's work and the two men became life-long friends after that chance meeting at Evans' ranch in Estes Park.

Members of the U. S. Geographical and Geological Survey of the Territories (Hayden Survey) also visited Estes Park. William H. Jackson, the official photographer for the Hayden Survey, arrived in Estes Park in late May or early June of 1873 with botanist H. M. Coulter and entomologist Lt. W. L. Carpenter (U.S. Army). Jackson spent several days taking the first known photographs of the Estes Park area before traveling on to central Colorado.

Dr. Ferdinand V. Hayden, director of the Hayden Survey, arrived in Estes Park in September 1873 to attempt to climb Longs Peak. Among the twelve climbers who reached the top with Hayden were topographer James Gardner, then with Hayden's Survey, James Stephenson and W. H. Holmes, a topographic artist who took a panoramic photograph from the top of Longs Peak. Also with Hayden were Anna Dickinson, her brother, Reverend John Dickinson, Ralph Meeker, son of Nathan Meeker, founder of Greeley, and William Byers—always ready for adventure and a story.

Because four different scientific surveys in the West were competing for government funds, Hayden and Gardner invited Anna Dickinson and William Byers, knowing that they would write of the trip and thus publicize the Hayden Survey. Anna, a well-known writer, lecturer and avid mountain climber, probably was the first non-Indian woman to reach the top of Longs Peak.

ISABELLA BIRD (1831-1904)

By 1873, the Estes Park area was well-known, due in part to the writings of Byers and Powell. It was so well-known that in September, Isabella Bird, a 42-year old British writer and world traveler made Estes Park a destination after a visit to New Zealand and Hawaii. Bird rode a hot, dusty, rattling railway coach from Cheyenne, Wyoming to Greeley, Colorado. She wrote of her first view of the Front Range before the train reached Greeley:

"After running on a down grade for some time, five distinct ranges of mountains, one above another, a lurid blue against a lurid sky, upheaved themselves above the prairie sea.... As I write I am only twenty-five miles from them, and they are gradually gaining possession of me. I can look at and _feel_ nothing else."

This determined tourist spent several days trying to find a guide to take her to Estes Park. In Longmont she rented a "gentle, but high-spirited" horse and accompanied two vacationing law students on the trip into the mountains. Her traveling companions were S. S. Downer, who later became a judge in Boulder, and Platt Rodgers, who became a well-known Denver mayor. The party followed Estes's trail from the plains.

Isabella Bird first saw Estes Park:

"...lying 1500 feet below in the glory of the setting sun, an irregular basin lighted up by the bright waters of the rushing Thompson, guarded by sentinel mountains of fantastic shape and monstrous size, with Longs Peak rising above them all in unapproachable grandeur."

She compared Longs Peak to Mont Blanc in France and was so enthralled that, in spite of chronic health problems, she managed to reach the top with much prodding and shoving by Mountain Jim Nugent. Nugent was the somewhat disreputable hunter and recluse she met when the party passed his cabin in Muggins Gulch on their way to Estes Park. An interesting friendship developed between Mountain Jim, whose face had been mauled by a bear, and the dumpy English spinster. Jim accompanied her to the plains when she left Estes Park to return to England.

Downer and Rodgers stayed only a few days with Evans after climbing Longs Peak, but Isabella remained at the ranch off and on until December. She paid $8 a week for a primitive one-room cabin and ate her meals with the Evans family. In 1879, Miss Bird's letters to a sister about her adventures in Colorado were published in England as A Lady's Life in the Rocky Mountains, which did much to publicize the Estes Park area.

THE LORD OF THE MANOR

No account of Estes Park's colorful history is complete without a glimpse of the Right Honorable Windham Thomas Wyndham-Quin, Fourth Earl of Dunraven (1841-1926). This immensely wealthy nobleman from County Limerick, Ireland, first visited Estes Park in 1872 after meeting Englishman Theodore Whyte, while both were imbibing at a fashionable Denver bar. The two men joined forces and went to the Evans' ranch to hunt in Black Canyon and along Fall River. The Earl was so impressed with the "sporting" possibilities that he decided to acquire all of Estes Park for a cattle ranch, private playground and hunting preserve for affluent English visitors. Griff Evans was one of the first settlers to be "influenced" to sell his land to the new English Company, but he continued to work for the Earl.

With Whyte's aid, the Earl had the area legally surveyed in February 1873. He found men who were willing (for a price!) to file on 160 acre homesteads. Dunraven, through his agent Whyte, then acquired the land for about $5 per acre. Between 1874 and 1880, Dunraven's company "purchased" 8200 acres and controlled another 7000 acres. When other homesteaders realized what the Earl of Dunraven was doing, the landowners banded together to oppose the Earl and his underhanded ways of doing business.

In 1876, Dunraven built the first real hotel in Estes Park along the eastern side of Fish Creek valley with a magnificent vista of Longs Peak. Named the Estes Park Hotel, it was always called the "English Hotel" by local residents. John Cleave, a master carpenter from Cornwall, in Britain, had settled in Estes Park and at Dunraven's request built the Earl a hunting lodge in Dunraven Glade on the North Fork of the Big Thompson River. He agreed to plan and build Dunraven's hotel. Upon completion, Cleave either homesteaded or was given a 160-acre homestead on Fish Creek by the Earl. He later traded that property for 160 acres at the junction of Big Thompson River and Fall River in what later became downtown Estes Park.

Cleave started the first general store near the present intersection of Elkhorn and Moraine Avenues. In 1877, he took over the job of postmaster from Mrs. Evans. The first schoolhouse was built near Cleave's store. In 1905, Cleave sold all his property to the newly-formed Estes Park Town Company for $8000 because he could not stand to see the "danged place overrun by tenderfeet tourists."

By the late 1880s the Earl grew tired of fighting other landowners, ceased visiting Estes Park and leased all his land and the hotel to Theodore Whyte. Whyte managed these holdings until 1896 when he went bankrupt and returned to England. In 1907, the Estes Park Company sold the Estes Park Hotel and 6000 acres to F. O. Stanley and B. D. Sanborn of Greeley. Thus ended the period of British influence in Estes Park.

MURDER!

The first murder in Estes Park probably was the result of the Earl of Dunraven's devious business affairs. According to eye-witnesses, Griff Evans fired two shotgun blasts at Mountain Jim Nugent on June 19, 1874, when Jim came into Evans' corral to water his horse. Although the reason for the shooting is vague, it is known that Griff did not approve of Jim or his interest in Evans' attractive daughter.

A more likely reason for the shooting was the fact Mountain Jim controlled the only route through Muggins Gulch (about 5 miles east of Estes Park on U.S. 36) to Estes Park and was known to have taken pot-shots at some of the Earl's friends on their way to the park. Jim lived until September with a shotgun pellet lodged in his brain. Before he died, he said the shooting was due to British greed and gold. Most Estes Park residents at the time were inclined to agree. And what happened to Griff Evans? He was acquitted for lack of evidence.

THE TOWN'S GROWING!

By 1875 there were perhaps 50 people living in Estes Park valley year-round. They came because of the beautiful surroundings, healthy climate, abundant fish and game, and grass for their cattle. Homesteads were filed and crude log cabins were built. The Spragues, MacGregors, Hupps, McCreerys, Rowes, Cleaves, Fergusons, James and Lambs were among the earliest settlers.

Estes Park was listed in the Colorado State Business Directory for the first time in 1878. No population was given and only MacGregor's Hotel and cheese factory and Dunraven's Estes Park Company were listed as businesses. Ed McLaughlin operated a sawmill. By 1880, MacGregor's sawmill was listed and McLaughlin must have moved to greener forests. The 1885 Business Directories stated that Estes Park had 75 permanent residents. Dr. S. Ellis was a physician, H. S. Gilbert ran the livery and McCabe had a general merchandise store. Fred Sprague was listed as a guide. By 1900, Estes Park had a year-round population of about 200 citizens.

WE HAVE TO GET NEW ROADS!

During the early 1870s, the only "road" to Estes Park from the plains was the somewhat improved ancient Indian trail that Rufus Sage, Estes and Isabella Bird followed on their memorable trips. A better road was needed if the area was to survive and grow. On September 11, 1874, attorney A. Q. MacGregor (p. 196, 204), Marshall Bradford and Georgianna Heeney filed incorporation papers with the State of Colorado for the Park Road Co.:

"...to go from the northwest bank of St. Vrain Creek in Boulder County, then northwest through Timber Gulch to Little Thompson Creek, then up this creek through Elk and Moose Parks to the source of the branch upon which Mountain Jim Nugent's ranch is situated. Thence in a northwest direction and down the gulch which heads on the opposite side of the divide between the Little and Big Thompson Creeks and heads near the head of the said branch of the Little Thompson Creek to the east side of the Big Thompson Creek in Estes Park."

Records in the Colorado State Archives also show that the Estes Park Wagon Road Co. was incorporated on March 13, 1875 by MacGregor, Henry C. F. Jensen, and G. Heeney. Just why there was a second incorporation is not known. But work continued all winter on the toll road that opened for business on July 27, 1875. This venture was never a financial success. Travelers resented having to pay the $1 per wagon toll charge. At least twice the toll gates were destroyed by irate users. In 1882, MacGregor sold the toll road to some businessmen in Longmont.

Present-day U.S. Highway 36 follows the general route of MacGregor's toll road and on both sides of the community of Pinewood Springs, rock work for the toll road still can be traced on the western side of the highway.

When F. O. Stanley (p. 208) drove his Stanley Steamer from Lyons to Estes Park in 1903, he realized a better road was a necessity. One of his first projects was to help raise money to rebuild that road. He purchased the right-of-way and then gave it to the county. After the Stanley Hotel was completed, a fleet of Stanley Steamers met the excursion trains at Lyons and then treated their guests to an exciting ride to Estes Park.

A 40-mile road (of sorts) between Estes Park and Loveland was built sometime after 1876 and is shown on maps published during the 1880s. Known as the Pole Mountain or Bald Mountain road, it went east from Estes Park between Mt. Pisgah and Mt. Olympus, passing the tiny community of Pinewood before reaching the plains.

The only other toll road built in the area was the Longs Peak Toll Road started in August 1877 by Elkanah J. Lamb (p. 204), John McMarble and Walter A. Buckingham. According to the articles of incorporation the road was:

"...to start in Estes Park and go south up the valley of Lilly Creek to Lilly Lake, then south by the best route to Lamb's Ranch, and then to the North St. Vrain Creek, with a branch from Lamb's Ranch by the most practicable route toward Longs Peak to or above timberline on the said mountain."

Little is known of how long tolls were collected along this road, but with its completion, business at Lamb's Longs Peak House increased dramatically.

This eastward view of Estes Park was taken from the top of Oldman Mountain in the 1880s. Nothing is known of the history of the wooden monument on the left or when it was removed.
(Estes Park Area Historical Society)

Eastward view of downtown Estes Park in 1908; the country road is now Elkhorn Avenue. (Photo by L. C. McClure, Denver Public Library, Western History Dept.)

Elkhorn Lodge as it looked during the summer of 1889.
(NPS collection)

Estes Park Hotel, built by the Earl of Dunraven in 187
(NPS collectio

The first rumor of railroad construction to the area was in 1881 when the Union Pacific surveyed a route, as reported by Abner Sprague, who assisted the surveyors:

"Union Pacific officials heard a survey had been made by a party working under the name of the Denver, Utah and Pacific—really the Santa Fe— [author's note: actually it was the Burlington and Missouri River Railroad] and they had found a line with easy grades to cross through Fall River Pass and over the Continental Divide via Milner Pass. To check the line the U.P. sent a party to the Park in November, 1881. They camped in my original cabin and took their meals with us."

The Denver Times reported on July 25, 1889:

"It is possible that in the not distant future a railway will meander up Muggins Gulch and through Estes Park, crossing the range northwest of Moraine and over into the undeveloped region of nature's richness in North Park."

Nothing more was every heard of this pie-in-the-sky scheme. It is quite interesting though, that one of Colorado's premier railroad entrepreneurs, David H. Moffatt, was one of the Earl of Dunraven's associates for a time.

The closest railhead to Estes Park is Lyons. The Denver, Utah and Pacific Railroad built a narrow gauge branch to Lyons in 1885 to serve nearby sandstone quarries. This branch was leased and converted to standard gauge in 1889 by the Burlington & Missouri River Railroad. It became the Lyons branch of of the Chicago, Burlington & Quincy in 1908. Tourists arriving in Lyons boarded 9-passenger Stanley Steamers for the drive to Estes Park. The beautiful sandstone depot in Lyons, built in 1885, is now on the National Register of Historic Places. Track beyond a cement plant at the east edge of Lyons was abandoned in 1984.

By 1915, the narrow-gauge Denver, Boulder & Western Railroad, known as the "Switzerland Trail of America", ran excursion trains from Denver into the mountains to Ward via Boulder. Passengers arrived in Ward in time for lunch and then were treated to an exciting ride in Stanley Steamers from Ward to Estes Park along the route now known as the Peak-to Peak Highway.

Rumors of an electric railroad through the Big Thompson Canyon to Estes Park surfaced in about 1900, but nothing ever came of this plan, probably because C. H. Bond proposed that an automobile road be built in the canyon. He raised money through private donations and then convinced Larimer County to do the construction. The narrow, dusty, almost one-way road was completed in 1904. The roadbed was rebuilt in 1919—and again in1976 after the Big Thompson flood.

An early view northeastward of Elkanah Lamb's Longs Peak House resort. Twin Sisters Mountains are on the skyline. *(Denver Public Library, Western History Dept.)*

SOME OF ESTES PARK'S LEADING CITIZENS

ELKANAH J. LAMB

The Reverend Elkanah J. Lamb, (1832-1915) a tall, energetic missionary for the United Brethren Church, first came to Colorado in 1860 with a group of prospectors, including Enos Mills' parents. The party prospected at Breckenridge and along the headwaters of the Blue and Arkansas Rivers but did not find any rich ore deposits, so they returned to Kansas. In 1871, Lamb returned to Colorado to serve as minister to families living on the plains along the St. Vrain River. During that summer he visited the Longs Peak Valley (now called Tahosa Valley) and climbed Longs Peak for the first time.

In 1878, Lamb homesteaded in the beautiful open valley east of Longs Peak. He borrowed $200 to start a resort and also guided tourists up Longs Peak for $5 a trip. When Lamb was busy administering to the needs of his church members, his hard-working wife and children were responsible for the growing Longs Peak House resort (photo, p. 203). Lamb was very outspoken about the land-grabbing techniques of the Earl of Dunraven and worked with attorney MacGregor and other early settlers to oppose the Earl and his henchmen.

During the 1890s, Lamb preached each Sunday to hundreds of summer visitors. In 1902, he sold his Longs Peak House to his second cousin, Enos Mills, and settled on a new ranch at the present site of Wind River Ranch where he lived for the rest of his life.

ABNER SPRAGUE AND OTHER INNKEEPERS

Abner Sprague (1850-1943), a native of Dundee, Illinois left home at the age of 14 and worked as a locating engineer for the Missouri Pacific Railroad. In later years, he served three terms as Larimer County Surveyor. He first visited the Estes Park area in 1868 and returned in 1874 when he climbed Longs Peak for the first of many times. Sprague and his brother Fred settled in Moraine Park in 1875. The Spragues planned to ranch, but soon they were busy guiding hikers up Longs Peak and providing primitive lodging for early tourists. By 1905, business had grown so much that the brothers opened Spragues' Hotel (p. 128). The Spragues built the first road to Moraine Park as well as the first trail from Moraine Park to Longs Peak via the Boulder Field.

In 1884, Fred Sprague started a stage line between Loveland, Estes Park and Moraine Park. He also contracted to carry the U.S. Mail, providing daily service in the summer and three times a week during the winter. In his later years, Abner Sprague wrote many articles about his early life.

Other homesteaders also started hotels and summer resorts. Horace W. Ferguson and his family homesteaded about 1/2 mile north of Marys Lake in 1875. They spent the first winter in a two-room log cabin with a sod roof. In 1876, four rooms were added and the Fergusons started a boarding house, known as The Highlands.

William E. James first visited Estes Park on a hunting trip in 1875 and was so impressed with the area he immediately filed for a homestead along what is now the Devils Gulch Road. His wife and family soon joined him from their former home in Syracuse, New York. In 1877, he traded this land and a one-room sod-covered log cabin for land belonging to Rev. William H. McCreedy along Fall River. James planned to ranch, but like Abner Sprague, he too found it more profitable to provide for tourists and the Elkhorn Lodge was born. Hunting, fishing and hiking were popular and often on summer afternoons and evenings, groups of guests hiked to the top of Oldman Mountain (photo, p. 202). Today this historic resort is one of the oldest in Estes Park.

THE MACGREGORS

Attorney Alexander Q. MacGregor (1845-1896) came to Colorado in 1869 from Wisconsin. He worked for a short time as a clerk in the Arapahoe County Court and in 1871 purchased land in Larimer County north of Ft. Collins. MacGregor first visited Estes Park in 1872 on a camping trip at which time he met Clara Heeney, an art student from the University of Wisconsin. Clara was with a group of students who had spent the summer traveling through the central Colorado mountains to sketch the scenery. Clara's mother, Georgianna Heeney, a wealthy widow and also an accomplished artist, was the chaperon for the trip. A romance soon developed and they were married on Christmas Day, 1873 at Black Earth, Wisconsin.

MacGregor returned to Estes Park in 1874 with his bride and mother-in-law and started the Black Canyon cattle ranch. The first post office in Estes Park opened in 1876 at the Macgregor ranch with Mrs. MacGregor as the postmaster. On March 22, 1877, Mrs. Griff Evans was awarded the job and the office was moved to the Evans ranch, probably because of the influence that the Earl of Dunraven wielded at the time.

For a number of years the MacGregor family spent their winters in Denver where their three sons, George, Donald and Halbert were born. MacGregor served as Larimer County judge from 1883 to 1885 and also practiced law in Denver, Ft. Collins and Estes Park.

The MacGregors continued to expand the Black Canyon Ranch buying more land and cattle and also built rental cabins for summer visitors. They planted a large vegetable garden, harvested hay from the rich meadows, built a water-powered sawmill on Black Canyon Creek and dug ditches to irrigate the meadows. The family worked hard, but still took time to

Clara, Halbert, Donald, Alexander and George MacGregor in front of their ranchhouse at some time before 1896. (NPS Collection)

enjoy music, painting and other pleasures. Many of the paintings by Clara and Georgianna are displayed at the MacGregor Ranch Museum.

MacGregor invested in mining properties in North Park and frequently went prospecting. On July 17, 1896, while he and his son, George, were doing assessment work on a mining claim near Poudre Lakes, he was struck by lightning and killed. His obituary in the Ft. Collins Courier of June 25, 1896 stated:

> "They were in the act of drilling a hole for a shot and while the father was leaning back again the wall with the steel drill in hand, and the boy on his knees charging the hole, the fatal shock came. The young boy (21 years old) though within a few feet of his father was prostrated for some time. When George regained consciousness, he found his father still sitting in an upright position against the side of the hole."

Clara MacGregor continued to manage the ranch after the death of her husband and even bought more land. When she died in 1901, 18-year old Donald took over management of the ranch. His two brothers were never interested in ranching and he eventually purchased their shares of the estate. In 1903 Donald married Minnie Maude Koontz of Denver and Muriel Lurilla MacGregor was born the following year. Donald

was a careful and frugal manager. He bought more land, increased the size of the cattle herd from 150 to 200 head and harvested up to 3000 tons of hay per year.

Donald and Minnie MacGregor were in poor health in later years and Muriel took over responsibility for running the ranch. She had earned a Bachelor of Arts degree in mathematics from Colorado College in Colorado Springs in 1925, a Master of Arts degree from the University of Colorado in 1931, and in 1934 was awarded a Bachelor of Laws degree from the University of Denver. By 1936 she was one of two women admitted to practice law before the Colorado Supreme Court. She practiced in both Denver and Estes Park, but helping on the ranch was more important to her. She used her legal skills mainly for the benefit of the family's interests and to aid a few local friends.

The year 1950 was a tragic one for Muriel MacGregor. Her father died in March and her mother in December. The shy and reserved spinster was left alone to operate the 2000-acre ranch, with few friends and little help. For the next 20 years she struggled to hold together all that the MacGregor clan had acquired. Cash-poor Muriel was unable to hire help to keep the ranch from deteriorating, but through those difficult years she never considered selling out. Ranching was her life, and like her father and grandfather, she valued the land above all else.

On October 22, 1970 Muriel MacGregor died in a Denver hospital. Her body was interred in the private mausoleum on the ranch where her parents are buried. In her will Muriel stated quite clearly her plans for the future of the Black Canyon Ranch.

"It is my wish that my ranch shall be maintained and retained insofar as is possible, and that my cattle herd be preserved and maintained insofar as is possible, and that the new proceeds of the productions of my ranch and cattle herd be used for charitable and educational purposes."

Muriel MacGregor named William Albion Carlson, Victoria Gross and Jane Carlson trustees to carry out her wishes. The will was contested, however, and after three years of costly legal battles with distant family members, 20 distant cousins were awarded 325 acres in the Fish Creek area and 50 acres around Dollar Lake. About 1200 acres were left in the Trust.

In 1917, the boundaries of the National Park were revised to include 400 acres of the MacGregors' land but neither Donald or Muriel would consider selling the land to the Park Service. In 1976, however, after lengthy legal negotiations with W. A. Carlson, executor of the MacGregor estate, the Park Service bought the 400 acres for $500,000 and gave the Trust a 25-year lease so that the pasture could still be used for cattle grazing. By the time the legal expenses were paid for the two disputes, little was left to set up the Trust and operate the ranch in the way Muriel MacGregor desired.

Finally in February, 1980, the National Park Service proposed including the western part of the ranch within the Park under a conservation easement designation. This designation would ensure that the Trust could continue to operate the ranch and that the Park would guarantee preservation of the property. It would also allow the government to purchase the rest of the ranch, if it were ever put up for sale.

After lengthy discussions, Congress gave the necessary approval in September 1983 and the MacGregor Trust received $3,935,000 for an easement on 1200 acres. The administrators of the Trust are working to restore the ranch to its former appearance as the interest on this money becomes available. The MacGregor Ranch will continue as a working cattle ranch, a living museum and an environmental education center.

ENOS ABIJAH MILLS

Enos Mills (1870-1922) (p. 172) came to Colorado from his Kansas home in 1884. He worked at a ranch on the plains and later that same year helped move a herd of cattle to the Lamb Ranch in the Longs Peak Valley (now called the Tahosa Valley). Overwhelmed by the majesty and beauty of the mountains, Mills decided to stay in Colorado.

In 1885 he worked for Lamb, first climbed Longs Peak and began hiking and exploring. Also during that year he acquired a rock and timber claim, on which he completed his "Homestead Cabin" the following year. To support himself, he worked during the winters in the Anaconda Copper Co. mines at Butte, Montana where he ultimately qualified as a stationary engineer. He decided he would rather work in the mines than live off the land by hunting game as so many others did. Many winters were spent tramping through the Colorado mountains measuring snow depths for the Colorado Irrigation Department. Summers were spent exploring, observing nature, guiding tourists up Longs Peak and leading nature hikes.

From the time Mills left home, he kept a journal of his experiences and observations which were invaluable resources in later years. After meeting California's well-known naturalist and conservationist, John Muir, on a beach in San Francisco in 1889, Mills' life took on a whole new purpose and direction. Through his friendship with Muir and the knowledge he had gained through years of self-study, he began to write and lecture about his experiences. Mills was a careful observer and a good storyteller. He was able to explain complex concepts in simple terms. His articles and books were very popular and helped shape the attitudes of his readers to better understand and appreciate the wilderness.

In 1902, Mills purchased Lamb's Longs Peak House and renamed it Longs Peak Inn. He used one room at the Inn for nature study and a museum. He loved to spend evenings talking to his guests and never tired of answering their questions. There was no piano in the sitting room and he asked his guests not to play cards in the lobby. His message was that the wilderness is a friendly place and that time spent in the wilderness is vital for physical and spiritual health.

Mills became a nationally recognized naturalist, conservationist, writer, lecturer, photographer, explorer and nature guide. He wrote 16 books and many articles for newspapers and magazines. Mills also began to train others as nature guides, a program that was the forerunner of the work later done by trained National Park Service naturalists. Considered "the Father of Rocky Mountain National Park," he spent about 6 years traveling and lecturing all over the United States to promote the formation of the Park. He was particularly proud of the fact he had camped in Alaska, Canada, Mexico and every state of the United States. On all these travels he made a point of meeting various experts in many fields of study.

Among many visitors and guests who enjoyed Mills' hospitality was Esther Burnell, an artist, poet and interior decorator. She fell in love with Enos, gave up her work in the east and moved to Colorado where she filed for a homestead along Fall River north of the

Enos A. Mills in his study at Longs Peak Inn. (Collection of the Enos Mills Cabin).

Geologist W. T. Lee, U. S, Geological Survey, conferring with Enos Mills at Longs Peak Inn, July 27, 1916.
(U.S. Geological Survey)

fish hatchery. She assisted Enos in his many projects and in 1918 the couple were married at the "Homestead Cabin." The following year their daughter, Enda, was born. She was named for author Edna Ferber, a frequent guest at Longs Peak Inn. When the birth was recorded by the county two letters were transposed so she became Enda.

The years together for Esther and Enos were few, however. In September 1922, following surgery to treat an abscessed tooth, he died at the Inn September 22. Enos Mills was buried near his "Homestead Cabin." A year later Esther Mills had her husband's body exhumed and cremated so that his ashes could be spread in the valley he loved so well. She feared vandals might desecrate his grave.

Esther Mills continued to operate Longs Peak Inn, completed editing four of his books which were published posthumously and wrote a biography of her husband. She sold the Inn in 1945 and retired to the house near Enos Mills "Homestead Cabin" where she lived until her death in 1964.

FREELAN O. STANLEY

F. O. Stanley (1849-1940) was 54 years old and suffering from tuberculosis when his doctors suggested that a trip to Colorado might give him a few more months to live. He shipped one of his steam-powered automobiles to Lyons, Colorado from his home in Boston, Massachusetts and then drove the vehicle alone up the steep, primitive, rutted road to Estes Park. Stanley spent the summer of 1903 resting and enjoying the scenery and pleasures Estes Park had to offer its visitors. By the end of the summer, the dry climate had worked its magic. His health restored, Stanley returned to Estes Park each summer for 37 years.

Stanley and his twin brother, Francis E. Stanley, had invented the Stanley Steamer automobile and also a machine to coat glass photographic plates with light-sensitive emulsions. This process produced plates that could be stored dry and eliminated the old, cumberson collodion-coated wet plates. They sold their patents to Eastman Kodak Company in 1904. As early as 1898 the brothers built a mass-production plant to assemble Stanley Steamers, thus preceeding Henry Ford by 11 years. Stanley was also an architect, designer, engineer, teacher and an astute businessman. He also enjoyed building and playing violins and shooting billards.

Estes Park enchanted Stanley and he soon realized that the area needed a first-class hotel for the increasing numbers of tourists visiting the area. The Stanley Hotel was completed in 1909 and boasted a fully equipped electric kitchen, including a dishwasher that Stanley designed. As demand increased, the year-round Stanley Manor was built just east of the hotel.

Perhaps because he felt a great sense of gratitude for his restored health, he took an active part in the affairs of the village.

Stanley was president of Estes Park's first bank, that opened in 1908. He built the first electric plant and water works and donated land (purchased from the Dunraven Ranch) for the town's high school, fairgrounds and sewage disposal plant. He arranged for elk to be transported from Yellowstone National Park to replace the herds destroyed by the Earl of Dunraven and his hunting friends. No wonder he was known as the "Grand Old Man of Estes Park."

THE TOWN CONTINUES TO GROW!

The Estes Park Town Company was formed in August 1905 by Cornelius H. Bond, J. B. Anderson, W. L. Beckfield, J. Y. Munson and F. M. Wright for the express purpose of acquiring land for the village of Estes Park. This group of investors then bought the quarter-section of land owned by John Cleave (p. 200) for $8000. Abner Sprague surveyed the property into lots. Ones along Elkhorn Avenue sold for $50, while those farther east went for $35. It was not long before the first service station opened, new hotels and summer cottages appeared, and Elkhorn Avenue was lined with shops catering to the ever-growing number of tourists. By 1910, 74 businesses were listed in the State Business Directory and the permanent population had grown to about 400 people.

Also in 1905, B. D. Sanborn, a developer from Greeley, succeeded where others had failed. He was able to buy the 6400 acres of land still owned by the Earl of Dunraven's company. When Stanley heard about this deal, he offered to buy a half interest in Sanborn's Estes Parks Development Company and agreed to build a hotel and power plant. Final payment of some $80,000 to the Dunraven company was made in 1907 and the partnership began the first of many civic improvements and land developments that set the tone for the future.

Stanley Steamer automobiles were very popular in Estes Park in the early 1900s. These were lined up for departure from the main lodge at the YMCA of the Rockies. (YMCA of the Rockies Collection)

YMCA OF THE ROCKIES

During the summer of 1908, Estes Park and Wind River Lodge were hosts to members of the Young Men's Christian Association's (YMCA) first Western Conference. This organization, founded in England in 1844 for social welfare and religious study, proved to be very popular and quickly spread around the world. Each summer, encampments are held for members to meet and study. Members wanted to establish a permanent summer training center in the Rocky Mountains and after a lengthy search, decided that Wind River Lodge met their needs perfectly. The fact that the first group of members to visit the Lodge noticed that the "Y" notched in the steep face of Ypsilon Mountain could be seen from the lodge grounds, only confirmed their convictions that the Western Conference had found a new home.

Wind River Lodge was started in 1902 by Guy Robert LaCoste, a St. Louis journalist. By 1908 the property was owned by the Estes Park Land and Development Co., which in turn sold it to the YMCA in 1909 for $8500. The price included 334 acres, the lodge, hotel equipment and 11 horses. For many years a dirt road connected the camp with the Bear Lake Road inside the Park boundary.

Among the many benefactors of the YMCA was A. A. Hyde, founder of the Mentholatum Co., who first visited Estes Park in 1876 and helped William James put a new roof on the Elkhorn Lodge. Very active in the YMCA, Hyde donated 125 acres to the Conference in 1915 and continued to be active in the organization until he died in 1936 at the age of 86.

A new honor for the YMCA of the Rockies came in 1980 when the camp was designated an International YMCA. The World Council of YMCA's and a World Youth Conference were held in Estes Park in 1981. Today this 1400-acre camp is used as a training school for YMCA workers, as well as a very popular convention and training site for many other organizations Many schools along the Front Range use the camp year-round for outdoor education programs. More than 200 cabins are available and the many lodges and dorms can accomodate more than 2000 guests.

GRAND LAKE VILLAGE
THE FIRST SETTLERS

Across the Continental Divide from Estes Park, nestled along the eastern edge of the North Fork of the Colorado River is the largest natural lake in Colorado. Grand Lake, a beautiful morainal lake, was called "Spirit Lake" by some Indian tribes because of the way steam rises off the water during cold winter days and also because they believed a supernatural white buffalo lived in the lake.

The first recorded non-Indian settler at Grand Lake was Phillip Crawshaw, a hunter and trapper, who built a cabin at the western end of the lake in 1857 or 1858. He stayed until 1861. In 1867 Joseph L. Wescott (1838-1914) moved to Grand Lake and lived in Crawshaw's cabin until he built one of his own nearby. Wescott had served with Company G of the First Colorado Cavalry during the Civil War but was discharged with rheumatism. Somehow he heard that Hot Sulphur Springs was the place for a cure and arranged to be carried in a hammock across Berthoud Pass to the hot springs. Wescott recovered his health and spent the rest of his life in Grand Lake. Never married, he homesteaded and supported himself by hunting, fishing and offering lodging to occasional visitors. He was well-educated, recited and wrote poetry and served as Postmaster and Justice of the Peace. Judge Wescott also was remembered for his yearly drinking sprees.

Wescott wrote a long lyric poem entitled "Legend of Grand Lake" reprinted in Mary Lyons Cairn's excellent history, Grand Lake in the Olden Days. The poem describes a fierce battle that supposedly took place near Grand Lake between a band of Ute Indians and their enemies the Cheyennes and Arapahos. In order to save their women and children from the attack, the Utes put them on a crude raft and pushed it out from the shore of Grand Lake. A sudden wind gust capsized the raft and all were drowned. Most of the Ute warriors supposedly were killed in the battle.

"Judge" Wescott's cabin on the shore of Grand Lake, probably in 1874. (W. H. Jackson, NPS collection)

THE FIRST SUMMER RESIDENTS

Alexander Proctor, a Denver businessman and his two sons George and A. Phimister, spent the summer of 1875 with Judge Wescott. The boys, aged 14 and 12 respectively, had a wonderful time with the Judge who taught them much about hunting, fishing and living in the mountains. Between 1876 and 1885 Proctor, his wife and 8 children spent each summer and one winter in a cabin they built near Wescott's place. Proctor spent most of his time prospecting but never made a strike. All the children loved to be with the Judge who was an important part of their lives. A. Phimister became a famous sculptor; two of his more famous works, "The Buckaroo" and "On the Warpath" are in the Civic Center in Denver, Colorado.

THE SCIENTISTS CAME TO GRAND LAKE TOO

Geologist John W. Powell (p. 199) stayed with Wescott in 1868 before his successful climb of Longs Peak. Knowing Byers had failed in his attempt to reach the top from Estes Park in 1864, he decided to try an ascent from the west.

Dr. F. V. Hayden, Director of the U. S. Geological and Geographical Survey of the Territories (p. 199), came to the Grand Lake area during the summer of 1874. He was in charge of geological and topographical surveying in the region. Hayden's Atlas of Colorado, published in 1877, is still a valuable resource that shows many old trails and long-forgotten towns. Photographer William H. Jackson was with Hayden that summer and made the first known photographs of Grand Lake and its surroundings.

GRAND LAKE NEEDED ROADS TOO

While Estes Park continued to attract tourists throughout the 1870s, Grand Lake grew at a glacially slow pace. Judge Wescott's isolated fishing camp only attracted the stout-hearted and adventurous who neither worried about Indian attacks or minded a long horseback ride across a high mountain pass. During August 1874 between 200 and 300 tourists entered Middle Park but most came to enjoy William N. Byers' well-publicized spa and resort at Hot Sulphur Springs, the county seat of Grand County.

The early routes to Grand Lake followed old Indian trails that were gradually improved by settlers, miners, hunters and tourists. The Ute Trail along Trail Ridge and over Fall River Pass to the Colorado River is one of three major routes across the Continental Divide. One of the earliest routes into Middle Park went up South Boulder Creek and over Rollins Pass. Still another route led up Mill Creek and over Flattop Mtn.

A group of old Arapaho Indians returned to the Park in 1914 to tell members of the Colorado Mountain Club their tribal place names for many of the geo-

OLDTOWN GRAND LAKE. COLO.   DALGLEISH PHOTO

Grand Lake village in the mid-1880s.   *(Colorado Historical Society)*

graphic features. The club was hoping to preserve many of the Indians' names. The Arapahos reportedly called the Trail Ridge route the "Childs Trail" but their words may have been mis-translated. They probably said that the trail was used by short, stocky people (Utes); but their words were interpreted to mean that the trail was so steep the children (little people) had to walk. French fur trappers, as well as other Indian tribes, always referred to the Utes as *"la tribe des enfants"* because of their short stature. The Ute Trail is relatively easy to travel.

Abner Sprague stated that he found no well-worn trail when he first came to the area, but when miners headed for the North Fork Mining District, deep ruts were soon worn across the tundra on what is now called the Ute Trail. Many of the miners built piles of rocks (cairns), as had many ancient Indians, to mark the trail in bad weather. In 1923 the trail was realigned, cleared and marked with new cairns by National Park Rangers Shep Husted and Jack Moomaw. This was done, in part, to mark the Windy Gulch trail and also to direct horseback riders to Squeaky Bob's Camp Wheeler (p. 69) in the Kawuneeche Valley. Most cairns have now been removed.

Other routes to Grand Lake included wagon roads across Boulder (Rollins) Pass, which was completed in 1864, and Berthoud Pass which was opened ten years

later. By 1874, roads in Middle Park were still so poor, however, that it took two days to drive a team and wagon 25 miles between Hot Sulphur Springs and Grand Lake. No wonder few tourists ventured over the mountains from the eastern slope towns.

THEN CAME THE MINERS

Judge Wescott's quiet, remote fishing village was jolted in July 1875 when Alexander Campbell and James H. Bourn rode into town with the news of their silver, lead and copper strike high in the Rabbit Ears Range (now called the Never Summer Mountains) north of Grand Lake. Their claim, the Wolverine, promised its owners more than it ever paid them and the following year a Georgetown grocery store owner who had grub-staked the miners took over the claim. Between 1875 and 1885, Grand Lake forgot about hunting and fishing and became the supply and transportation center for mining companies, miners, prospectors, promoters, entrepreneurs, store and saloon keepers, gamblers and prostitutes.

The Middle Park, Grand Lake and North Park Wagon Road Co. was incorporated August 3, 1878 to build a road to the mining camps. On August 27, 1878 the Grand Lake, North Fork and Rabbit Ears Range Wagon Road Co. also filed incorporation papers to build a road to the mines. On Feb. 25, 1880 the Loveland and Northwestern Toll Road Co. was formed to build a toll road from the plains to Hot Sulfur Springs and to Crescent City in North Park. In 1880 The Stewart Toll Road was completed, but no incorporation papers are in the State Archives.

Soon Grand Lake had a sawmill. Its first hotel, the Grand Lake House, or Waldron House, as it was also known, opened in 1878. Built by Mr. and Mrs. Wilson Waldron, it immediately became the social center of the growing village. The Grand Lake House was also the scene of the first murder in Grand Lake which occurred during an 1882 New Year's Eve dance. Waldron had been drinking heavily and began to tease his wife who was nursing their baby—the first non-Indian child born in Grand Lake. When he became more abusive, Mrs. Waldron asked Bob Plummer, a miner from the Ruby Mine who was in town for the evening, to take Waldron outside to sober up. Waldron resisted Plummer's attempts to remove him from the hotel and in a drunken rage went for his gun hanging on the wall.

Plummer immediately left and walked across the street to a small log building; but as he entered, Waldron fired a shot that killed him instantly. Waldron was arrested and put in the year-old jail where he awaited trial. In September he knocked the jailer unconscious and escaped but no attempt was ever made to track him down. Mrs. Waldron finally gave up trying to run the hotel and moved away. The building remained the town's haunted house until 1919 when it was torn down and the Pine Cone Inn built on the site.

In 1880, the Grand Central Hotel and Restaurant opened its doors. Built by Mr. and Mrs. Winslow Nickerson, the Grand Central (or Nickerson House) was very popular and because the Nickersons had three children, they offered a room at one end of the hotel for the first school. The couple died within a few months of each other in 1884 and the July 24 issue of the Grand Lake Prospector reported that Mrs. Nickerson's sister, Mrs. Melhorn of Oakman, Minnesota, had arrived to take her nieces and nephew to live with her. The hotel was operated until 1919 when it was sold and turned into the Corner Cupboard Restaurant.

Although Grand Lake was surveyed and platted in August 1879, it was not incorporated until 1944. The 1880 census showed 31 year-round residents, while all of Grand County had some 417 settlers. Grand Lake was listed in the State Business Directory for the first time in 1881 with a population of 300. During the summers, stage coaches operated between Grand Lake, Georgetown, Ft. Collins and the mining camps of Lulu City, Gaskil and Teller City. By 1883 the village boasted 400 residents and Grand County had about 2000 optimistic residents.

The year 1881 was important because two more hotels, the Grandview and the Fairview, were built,

the first school building opened and James Cairns opened the first general store. More importantly, Grand Lake mustered enough votes to have the Grand County seat moved from Hot Sulphur Springs to Grand Lake. The town was so anxious to have the county seat that they built a courthouse and adjoining jail in the record time of 48 hours. All of this activity was the direct result of promising mining claims staked in the Lead Mountain and Campbell Mining Districts.

By 1882, mining activity was feverish and on July 27, the first issue of the Grand Lake Prospector was published. Each new strike was reported in the paper, which fueled even more prospecting and promoting. The Campbell Mining District was located west and northwest of Gaskil on the upper slopes of Bowen Mountain and in Baker Gulch at or near treeline. Some of the larger prospects, in addition to the Wolverine, were the Toponas, Hidden Treasure, Rustic and Southern Cross. No production totals are known. The Lead Mountain Mining District, located high on Lead Mountain west of Lulu City, also yielded small amounts of gold, silver, lead and copper. Prospects included the Lulu, Crystal, Silver Star, Eureka, Baker, Bonanza, Fairplay, Pioneer, Reindeer, Galena, Mountain Gorge, Rocky Falls and Snow Flake. Fairfax, at the Ruby Mine, boasted a post office from June, 1884 to July, 1885. It was above the Wolverine Mine almost at treeline.

Vague references to mining camps called Dutchtown, Teller City, Crescent City, Pearl and Tyner have appeared in the literature, but little is known of their histories. In both the Campbell and Lead Mountain districts ore deposits were small and no rich lodes were ever found. Throughout this period, the main products from the mines and prospects were the manufacture and sale of hope and expectation of future wealth.

AVALANCHE!

Finding a rich ore deposit was not the only problem the miners faced. In December 1881, Jules C. Harmon, the well-liked Superintendent of the Hidden Treasure Mine in Bowen Gulch was killed in a snowslide he started while trying to make a new path between the mine portal and the bunkhouse. His body was not recovered until the snow melted the following June.

In February 1882, a huge snowslide roared down the mountainside above the Toponas Mine, also in Bowen Gulch, and hit a cabin in which four miners were resting. Two other men, C. W. Royer and a Mr. Stokes, were returning from a hunting trip and were almost engulfed by the slide. Although they were partly buried by snow, they were uninjured and went to the Wolverine Mine for help. Mike Flynn lay buried in the snow some 13 hours before being rescued—he suffered only frostbite. The bodies of Jack Williams,

Thomas Booth and E. R. "Doc" Duty were finally recovered and buried in the Grand Lake Cemetery at Sagebrush Flat.

AND MORE MURDER

If those tragedies were not enough for the townspeople of Grand Lake, a bloody shoot-out shocked them on the morning of July 4, 1883 as the town was preparing to celebrate Independence Day. In fact people thought the first shots fired were part of the holiday celebration. This account is a brief summary of various conflicting reports of the massacre.

Attorney E. P. Weber, Superintendent of the Wolverine Mine, was also a Grand County Commissioner. With him that fateful morning were two friends, rancher and County Commissioner Barney Day and County Clerk, T. J. "Cap" Dean of Hot Sulphur Springs. These three men were trying to gain control of the Republican Party and thus of Grand County.

Opposing Weber was Attorney John G. Mills (no relation to Enos Mills) and an unknown number of men. Mills, who lived in Teller City, was Chairman of the County Commissioners and had been feuding with Weber for several months. Mills and Weber had known each other in Chicago and had come to Colorado to invest Illinois money in the mines. Mills' reputation was questionable; he was reported to have been involved in a Cook County, Illinois killing before coming to Colorado.

Mills enlisted the aid of Charles Royer, the respected but somewhat weak Grand County sheriff, and William Redman, an aggressive deputy sheriff, to help settle his dispute with Weber. Royer had survived the snowslide at the Toponas Mine the previous February. Redman had a personal grudge against Weber and was anxious to join Mills in his plan. Mills reportedly said: "We are going to give Weber a little scare and scare him so good he will have to get out of Grand County for good and never come back."

Weber, Day and Dean left the Fairview Hotel and started walking toward town. A short distance down the road, the three men were ambushed. Weber was hit first. As Dean and Day attempted to assist him, two masked men jumped from their hiding place and one pistol-whipped Dean about the face and fired more shots. Day dodged around the ice house where he fired at one of the masked men, who turned out to be John Mills. Day hit Redman in the arm before being hit by a bullet fired by Royer, the third masked man. Day fell into the lake mortally wounded. Mills died in a pool of blood in the dusty road.

When help arrived, both Weber and Dean were still alive and were carried back to the hotel. Weber never regained consciousness, but Dean lived until July 17 and was able to give a legal deposition of the shooting. He could not identify any of the assailants, although he did describe the clothes worn by one of them. His description matched Redman's attire that day.

In a strange turn of events, both the sheriff and his deputy disappeared shortly after the shooting. Sheriff Charles Royer arrived in Hot Sulphur Springs the same day on a well-lathered horse and reported he had been chasing the murderers. Several days later Royer told his friend, Adam Kinney, of his part in the massacre and admitted killing his best friend, Barney Day. Later the distraught Royer rode to Georgetown, rented a room in the Ennis Hotel and committed suicide.

Deputy Sheriff Redman was last seen heading for North Park leaving a trail of blood behind. Efforts to track Redman down were unsuccessful but in August, a body believed to be his was found along the Thornburgh Road about 4 miles from the Colorado-Utah border. It was first thought he had committed suicide, but later rumors suggested that friends of Dean and Day had tracked him down and committed one more murder. Still others thought Redman escaped to Arizona where he later led a band of outlaws known as the Redman Gang.

Fallout from the tragedy lingered for many years and hindered the growth of Grand Lake. Tourists believed the village was too wild and stayed away.

THE BOOM WENT BUST

Living down the massacre was bad enough for Grand Lake residents, but an additional crisis arose because the mining boom was ending. Miners finally realized that neither the Lead Mountain nor the Campbell Mining Districts would ever be another Leadville. Mines shut down, miners drifted away to the next camp following glowing rumors of rich ores lying on the ground. Grand Lake village, the principal supply center for the mines, all but closed down. Many businesses folded; only Cairn's general store stayed open. By 1886 all mining had ceased and the mining camps of Lulu City, Teller City and Gaskil were abandoned, their post offices closed forever.

In 1886, the Grand Lake Prospector proposed that a road be built between Estes Park and Grand Lake to entice tourists back to the community. But it was another 34 years before the first dirt road crossed Milner and Fall River Passes.

The struggling village was dealt another hard blow in 1888 when the county seat was moved back to Hot Sulphur Springs where more people lived. In 1885 Grand Lake had 600 permanent residents, 400 in 1886 and by 1890, only 80 permanent residents, according to the State Business Directories.

THE TOURISTS RETURN

Grand Lake gradually returned to what it had been—a resort town that welcomed and provided for its summer visitors who built summer homes and helped establish churches and other essential town facilities. The Bellevue, largest of the early hotels, was built in 1892 by Preston H. Smith. It was destroyed by

James Cairns general store in Grand Lake sometime during the 1880s. (NPS Collection)

By the 1890s or early 1900s, Cairns had rebuilt his store, complete with an awning.
(L. C. McClure photograph, Denver Public Library Western History Dept.)

fire in 1912. Another early hotel, The Rustic, stood on the western shore of the lake.

The Kauffman House was built in 1892 by Ezra Kauffman, who had spent several years prospecting and packing supplies to miners at Lulu City and Teller City. When the mining boom ended, he joined the growing list of innkeepers. Kauffman operated his hotel continuously until his death in 1920. From 1921 to 1946, his widow and daughters operated the hotel during the summer months. In 1946, the family sold the hotel to Henry Rhone, owner of the Corner Cupboard. Later, the Grand Lake Historical Society acquired the log building which they restored. It is now on the National Register of Historic Places and open as a museum during the summer months.

The closest railroad passenger connection to Grand Lake was at Granby. The Denver Northwestern & Pacific Railway (Moffat Road), now part of the Denver & Rio Grande Western, built track over Rollins Pass to Hot Sulphur Springs in the summer of 1905. Many special excursion trains ran from Denver to the famous spa, with stops at Corona (the summit) and Granby. Stage coaches or jitney buses were available for the 15-mile ride from Granby to Grand Lake.

Some visitors spent their vacations hunting, fishing and hiking, while others began to convert rowboats to sailboats, using lodgepole pine trunks for masts and bed sheets for sails. This led to the formation of the Grand Lake Yacht Club in 1902 by a group of Denverites who spent their summers at Grand Lake. The club has the distinction of having the highest yacht anchorage in the world.

Each summer, Regatta Week is a major event for sailing enthusiasts. A clubhouse was built in 1912 on land donated by Jacob N. Pettingell, an early-day resident and postmaster. That same year members invited Sir Thomas Lipton, of Lipton tea fame, to a dinner in his honor at the old Denver Club in Denver. The members hoped to persuade Sir Thomas, a world-famous yachtsman, to visit and race at Grand Lake. Although he declined the honor, Sir Thomas did give the club a beautifully ornate silver cup that is still its most sought-after trophy. A number of other cups are awarded as trophies each year during Regatta Week. Wind surfing is growing in popularity, in spite of the inevitable spills into the frigid lake water.

TOURIST ACCOMMODATIONS
Camp Wheeler

No account of accommodations for guests in the North Fork area would be complete without recalling Camp Wheeler, a tent resort begun in 1907 along the North Fork of the Colorado River about 10 miles north of Grand Lake, in what now is known as Phantom Valley. Camp Wheeler, one of the first dude ranches, was also affectionately known as "Hotel de Hardscrabble" or simply "Squeaky Bob's Place," for its owner, Robert Wheeler (1865-1946) who spoke in a high falsetto voice, the result of severe bronchitis as a youngster.

Before a road was built across the Continental Divide, travelers on horseback always tried to plan their trips between Grand Lake and Estes Park to include an overnight stay with Wheeler. His primitive tent cabins and lumpy mattresses were soon forgotten by his guests who enjoyed his lively yarns, excellent food, hunting and fishing. He spun tall tails about his life as a rancher, miner and soldier in the Spanish-American war in which he "...charged up San Juan Hill." His actual military service, however, was spent as a horse wrangler in Jacksonville, Florida.

In 1926, Squeaky Bob sold Camp Wheeler to Lester Scott who rebuilt and renamed it Phantom Valley Ranch for the imagined phantoms and spirits of Indians, trappers, miners, laborers and others who had visited the valley in the past. Phantom Creek in turn was named for Scott's ranch. The Park Service bought the ranch in 1959 and all traces of the resort were removed by 1970.

Never Summer Ranch

Another early dude ranch in the Kawuneeche Valley was Holzwarth's Trout Lodge—later called the Neversummer Ranch. John Holzwarth came from Germany in 1879 when he was 14 years old. He finally found his brother who had homesteaded near Granby. Holzwarth fell in love with the Colorado mountains and in 1883 filed for a homestead on land that is now under Shadow Mountain Reservoir. He supported himself by hunting, hauling freight and breaking horses—skills he learned on his brother's ranch.

After his marriage, he moved to Denver and ran a saloon until prohibition forced him out of business. John and his wife, Sophia, decided that working a cattle ranch would be a better life for their young family so they returned to the North Fork in 1918 and purchased a homestead along the Colorado River owned by Joe Fleshuts.

Their cabin became the site of the Holzwarth Trout Lodge after Sophia decided they should charge those who came to visit. The dream of a working cattle ranch died when John was injured in a wagon accident and was unable to do the heavy work a successful ranch needed. After the road over Fall River Pass was completed in 1920 business boomed; the Holzwarths charged $2 a day for a room and Sophia's magnificent home-cooked meals. As early as 1922, the family used the Fleshuts cabins near the highway to accommodate guests and finally decided to move the dude ranch to that location. The first year tent houses were built and in 1929 the main lodge of their Neversummer Ranch was completed.

In later years the son, John Holzwarth Jr., took over running the guest ranch and like his parents was a genial host. His packtrips were always popular and guests sometimes spent several leisurely days riding to Central City to attend the opera and stay at the Teller House. John Jr. sold the ranch to the Nature Conservancy in 1973 with the understanding that the land would be preserved as open space. The property was sold to the Park Service the following year. All the buildings near the highway were removed but the log buildings of the original Trout Lodge along the Colorado River have been preserved. Several cabins are open for tours to show Park visitors what life was like on an early-day western dude ranch.

Green Mountain Ranch

The Green Mountain Ranch was about 4 miles south of the Never Summer Ranch. Charles F. Hertel homesteaded here in 1888, but in 1897 rancher Henry Schnoor bought the property. Schnoor built a fine cabin with a bay window in about 1898. He hoped to marry Kittie Harbison who lived 3 miles south of Schnoor's place. He thought the bay window would be a fine place for the geraniums Kittie liked to grow.

After Kittie turned down his proposal of marriage, Henry finally married someone else but his wife was never happy in the remote valley and one day she simply walked away leaving Henry with their two small children. Kittie Harbison and her sister, Annie, took in the two children and raised them as their own. When the sisters died, the surviving Schnoor daughter inherited the Harbison Ranch.

Henry Schnoor sold his ranch in 1906, moved to Grand Lake and became a successful contractor and builder. The property changed hands several times before it was purchased by Carl and Ada Nelson in 1934 at a tax sale. Nelson spent about $2100 to pay off delinquent taxes and a mortgage. He built up a dairy herd of 325 registered Guernsey cattle and also developed the Green Mountain Ranch into an outstanding dude ranch. Because of poor health, the Nelsons sold the ranch to the Park Service in 1972. The remaining buildings are used to house Park personnel.

Harbison Ranch

On down the road toward Grand Lake, the Harbison sisters, Kittie and Annie, homesteaded on adjoining 160-acre sites in 1895. They were accompanied by their parents and a younger brother, Rob, who had the reputation of being extremely lazy. The homestead laws required that the owner reside upon the land for a certain number of days per year. To meet this provision, the sisters first built two cabins about 10 yards apart on each side of the boundary line between their homesteads. In 1898 they built a large cabin that straddled the property line. It is said that the sisters used Annie's cabin as a kitchen and Kittie's cabin for bedrooms!

The two women never married and worked very hard to run their small dairy ranch. They did manage,

Henry Schnoor's homestead cabin with its bay window.
(NPS collection)

however, to get their brother to deliver milk. In 1905, the ambitious sisters began catering to tourists and were well-known for their delicious fried chicken dinners. The Harbison sisters died of pneumonia within a week of each other in November, 1938. The main ranch buildings, just west of the Kawuneeche Visitor Center, were eventually sold to the Park Service and all have been removed.

Grand Lake Lodge

Another well-known guest ranch, once within the National Park, is the Grand Lake Lodge situated in the lodgepole pine forest above Grand Lake. The lodge was started in 1920 by Mr. A. D. Lewis. The Park Service approved construction so they could control the facility. The hotel opened with a grand ball on July 3, 1920 and through the years has been enlarged and many cottages built around the main building. Through an exchange of properties, the southern boundary of the Park was recently revised to exclude Grand Lake Lodge from the National Park.

By 1900, Grand Lake had grown to a whopping 100 permanent residents and for the next 15 years the number of year-round inhabitants did not increase. During the summers, however, more than 1000 summer residents and visitors flocked to Grand Lake to vacation. When Fall River Road was officially opened for travel in September 1920, a new era began for Grand Lake. A popular tour then—as today—started in Denver, went to Estes Park, across the Continental Divide to Grand Lake and returned to Denver across Berthoud Pass.

Today about 400 year-round residents and at least 2000 summer residents live in Grand Lake. Because Grand Lake has remained a small resort town, tourists are welcomed in a relaxed way.

Part of the enthusiastic crowd that assembled for the formal dedication ceremonies for Rocky Mountain National Park, September 4, 1915.   *(NPS Collection)*

ROCKY MOUNTAIN NATIONAL PARK

On the rainy, late-summer afternoon of September 4, 1915, between 1000 and 2000 enthusiastic citizens from all over Colorado took part in the formal dedication ceremonies for Rocky Mountain National Park. As reported by the <u>Loveland Daily Herald</u>, 267 cars were parked "in the natural amphitheater of Horseshoe Park." The <u>The Denver Post</u> stated that a caravan of about 100 cars, which left Denver at 7:15 A.M., arrived in Estes Park at noon. Most of the dignitaries were in this procession. Others came by car, wagon, carriage, horseback or on foot.

The Estes Park Women's Club served box lunches and coffee to the visiting dignitaries. At 2 P.M. Master of Ceremonies Enos Mills convened the formal ceremonies to dedicate the nation's thirteenth National Park. He read congratulatory messages from President Woodrow Wilson and Franklin K. Lane, Secretary of the Interior.

Assistant Secretary of the Interior, Stephen T. Mather, gave the principal address. Other speakers included Colorado Governor George A. Carlson, Colorado State Representative Edward T. Taylor, Colorado

Congressman C. B. Timberlake, T. B. Stearns, president of the Denver Chamber of Commerce, H. V. Edmunds of the Ft. Collins Chamber of Commerce, F. O. Stanley of Estes Park and Boston, Mass. and Leonard A. Curtis of the State Highway Commission. Mrs. John D. Sherman of Chicago, Chairperson of the Conservation Department of the General Federation of Women's Clubs, spoke of the Federation's efforts to have the area proclaimed a National Park.

Mills concluded the program with the following remarks:

> "This is the proudest moment of my life. I have lived to see the realization of a great dream come true. It means great things for Colorado and the nation. There is nothing more inspiring than the vast chain of mountains which are connected in the Rocky Mountain National Park."

Since the dedication, the number of visitors has steadily increased from about 51,000 in 1916 to 2.5 million in 1988. Two years after the dedication, the Park boundaries were enlarged for the first of several times. Deer Mountain, Gem Lake and Twin Sisters Peaks became part of the National Park.

ROADS—STILL A PROBLEM

The new National Park had many problems. There was little overall policy because the National Park Service was not formed until the following year. High on the agenda was the need for better transportation in the Park. The first road across Fall River Pass, started by the State of Colorado in 1913, was finally completed and opened for travel between Estes Park and Grand Lake in 1920.

In 1921, a private contractor was permitted by the Park Service to build a road to Bear Lake to harvest dead timber from the 1900 fire in Glacier Gorge. After Bear Lake Lodge was built in 1922, traffic increased so much that a new, wider road with reduced gradients was built in 1928. Today this is one of the most popular drives in the Park.

The most spectacular of all the roads is Trail Ridge. The original Fall River Road is too narrow and steep for a two-way route. Park Service officials wanted a new scenic highway to connect Estes Park and Grand Lake. They dreamed of a new road across the Front Range with gentle grades, wide, sweeping curves and magnificent vistas of snow-capped mountain peaks in all directions.

The route selected generally follows the Ute Trail used thousands of years ago by Paleoindians to cross the Continental Divide. When the State of Colorado relinquished control of the roads within the National Park in the fall of 1929, construction of Trail Ridge Road began. It was completed to Fall River Pass by July, 1932. The route from Fall River Pass to Milner Pass was realigned and was opened for travel in August, 1932. Paving of the entire route was completed in 1938. The total cost was less than $2 million.

On July 17, 1982, the 50th anniversary of the opening of Trail Ridge Road was held in Hidden Valley. A big celebration was planned, complete with a special band. Unfortunately because of the Lawn Lake Dam failure (p. 150-151) two days earlier the celebration was almost cancelled and only a small group of citizens attended the ceremony.

VISITOR FACILITIES

To provide for the increasing numbers of visitors throughout the 1920s, campgrounds were built or enlarged, several shelters were constructed for road-clearing crews and new entrance stations were built. Many resorts within the Park boundaries were enlarged and some new ones were built. Winter sports enthusiasts also began visiting the Park to ski, snowshoe and toboggan. Until the drought years of the 1930s, the Colorado Mountain Club held annual winter outings at Fern Lake Lodge.

To help visitors enjoy and better understand the Park, educational programs were expanded. They were patterned after Enos Mills' nature guide schools. Ranger Naturalist–guided hikes and evening campfire programs proved to be very popular. Rangers helped fight fires, rescued mountain climbers, guarded the wildlife from poachers, built trails, explained to tourists how to drive safely in the mountains and most of all, attempted to help visitors enjoy and appreciate the Park while ensuring its conservation.

Between May 12, 1933 and July 29, 1942, Rocky Mountain National Park was home to hundreds of young men in the Civilian Conservation Corps (CCC). From their camps in Little Horseshoe Park and at Hollowell Park, the men built and improved trails, campgrounds and picnic areas, removed beetle-infested dead trees, planted trees and shrubs, fought forest fires, built fish-rearing ponds, installed sod along roadways, built telephone lines, removed old structures and even helped rescue stranded mountain climbers.

In 1956 a ten-year program, called "Mission 66", was started to improve visitor facilities in all the National Parks. "Rocky" received over $9 million to repair roads, enlarge parking areas, build new maintenance shops and housing for employees, and construct the new Visitor Center and Park Headquarters building. Much money was also used to purchase private land within the Park. Gone were the days when tourists enjoyed all their vacation in the area. More visitors arrived, but they were not likely to remain long in one place. Many planned to see all the West during a two-week vacation!

WILDLIFE MANAGEMENT

The term "wildlife management" was coined in the early part of the 20th-century when some people realized that new programs and new laws were needed to protect wildlife and manage the sizes of animal populations. Outside the National Parks, the goal of wildlife management is to maintain an optimum number of those birds, fish and mammals that are thought to benefit man. This policy results in high populations of those species that are not dangerous to humans. It tends to upset nature's balance by eliminating predators that naturally control the mammal and bird populations.

During the late 18th- and early 19th-centuries, the western Great Plains were populated with innumerable thousands of buffalo, deer, elk, bighorn sheep, antelope and wolves. Bears were numerous and the streams were full of fish and beaver. Problems started when pioneer hunters and trappers slaughtered thousands of these animals and traders encouraged Indians to do likewise. Most of the remaining animals lived in the mountains. It is hard to visualize today how many animals were harvested. The Ft. Collins Express of December 29, 1880 reported that Luke Wheeler (Squeaky Bob Wheeler's brother) and Frank Ainsworth had come through town from North Park with a load of game and reported on the season's kill:

"The two hunters, during the season, brought to market fourteen large loads of elk, antelope and deer. They killed 500 antelope and 250 elk. They sold all the meat readily in Denver and Boulder. Elk sold from 7 to 10 cents per pound; antelope from 7 to 8 cents, and deer from 10 to 12 1/2 cents. The season was a very profitable one. They made two shipments of hides, the last being 3,500 pounds."

The first non-Indian settlers in Estes Park harvested deer and elk as a livelihood. They supplied meat to markets in towns on the plains and to mining camps in the mountains. The hides were sold for clothing. By contrast, the Earl of Dunraven and his "sportsmen" friends killed many game animals just for thrills and trophies. When Joel Estes' son, Milton, returned to Estes Park after many years absence, he remarked over and over about how few wild animals were left in the area.

In 1887, the State of Colorado finally passed a law to stop the commercial sale of game animals, but by that time the damage to herds was almost irreversible. The first settlers and homesteaders also raised cattle which competed with game animals for forage and winter feeding grounds. The wild game were forced to move to the high mountains where less food was available, especially during the winter.

By the 1890s, the United States finally realized that all its natural resources should be conserved. Questionable mining practices, overgrazing, harvesting of timber on public lands with no thought to reforestation, and the destruction of animals and their habitats caught the attention and concern of many people. President Theodore Roosevelt was an ardent conservationist, as well as a hunter, and during his terms of office many effective laws were passed to protect the land and the wildlife.

Also during the 1890s, the government established the first forest reserves, four of which were in Colorado. In 1905, the Medicine Bow Forest Reserve in Wyoming was extended into Colorado and included land within the future National Park. By 1910, the Colorado portion of the forest was separated administratively and renamed the Colorado National Forest. In 1932, the name was changed again to Roosevelt National Forest to honor Theodore Roosevelt. Slowly Forest Rangers convinced people that they should preserve and protect the forests and all the animals living in them.

The Estes Park Protective and Improvement Association, founded in 1906, began an extensive advertising campaign for the area. In 1907, H. N. Wheeler, first Supervisor of Medicine Bow National Forest, gave a talk to the Association about wildlife protection and suggested that "...if they (Estes Park) wished to increase the value of their playground they should create a game refuge." The first refuges or reserves were established by state or federal governments to provide adequate protection, suitable habitats and dependable food supplies for all types of wildlife. Members of the Association, impressed by Wheeler's ideas, began seriously to consider forming such a refuge. By 1909, Enos Mills and the Protective Association were enthusiastic about establishing a game refuge and also the formation of Estes National Park.

Estes Park residents realized that the elk herd was nearly extinct and raised money to transport elk from Yellowstone National Park to reestablish the herd. In 1913, 25 elk were brought from Wyoming but only 12 survived the trip. In 1914, 22 more elk were released in the Park area. They made the long trip by train from Gardner, Montana to Lyons, Colorado where they were loaded onto trucks for transport to Estes Park. The following year, about 30 elk were estimated to be living within the Park. The elk thrived because all hunting was prohibited.

In 1922, the first predator control program was started to further protect the deer and elk in the Park. Grizzly bears, gray wolves and mountain lions are predators that prey on elk and deer, particularly the old, weak or ill animals. Since grizzlies had been all but eradicated earlier, Park Rangers began a full-scale program to eliminate wolves, mountain lions (cougars or pumas), bobcats, foxes, black bears, lynx and coyotes. When humans do not upset the natural balance between predator and prey animals, the predators generally live on surplus populations and have little effect on the breeding stock.

Between 1917 and 1925, 17 mountain lions, 74 bobcats, 65 coyotes, 6 badgers and 26 foxes were killed within the National Park. By 1930 the deer herds had increased so much that Superintendent Edmund Rogers wrote in his monthly report of his problems in feeding the animals during the winter months.

Private lands in Beaver Meadows, Horseshoe Park and along Mill Creek were purchased in 1932 and all livestock were removed from those areas, which somewhat increased the amount of winter range available to deer and elk. During 1933 and 1934, the first study plots were fenced in Upper Beaver Meadows to exclude deer and elk. Comparisons of the grasses, shrubs and trees in the fenced and unfenced areas showed quite graphically that grasses would slowly recover from the effects of overgrazing, but little or no improvement was noted in the growth of aspen, willow, sagebrush and bitterbrush. The natural balance between predators and non-predators at this time was completely upset and a few voices were raised to urge that the remaining predatory animals be protected.

While the deer and elk populations continued to increase, the number of bighorn sheep declined drastically. Studies were started in 1935 to determine the reason. Many hundreds of sheep died between 1878 and 1906 because much of their winter range was used by domestic stock, which weakened the sheep so much that they fell prey to infections such as scabies and lungworm. When elk populations declined during the early 1900s, the bighorn sheep made a come-back because of increased forage. A study made during the 1960s showed a high mortality rate among new-born lambs, a factor which has kept (and continues to keep) the size of the bighorn sheep herds quite stable.

During the 1940s, deer and elk were killed within the National Park by Park Rangers and special hunting seasons were allowed within the Park boundaries. Damage to native grasses and browse plants continued with some species actually disappearing. Aspen groves along the eastern side of the Park also died because they were weakened by drought during the 1930s. This drought did not extend to the western side of the Continental Divide because of greater precipitation. Deer and elk living on the western slope entered legal hunting areas and excess animals were eliminated.

By the 1960s, deer and elk populations were still too high and hunters were encouraged to hunt just outside the eastern Park boundaries. Many elk were trapped, tagged and moved to other parts of Colorado.

As elk and deer populations continue to increase, there is renewed talk of re-introducing gray wolves that effectively prey on these animals. In addition to preying on them, the wolves may also break up groups of elk so that the animals move to other winter ranges. Today about 60 percent of the winter habitat for deer, elk and bighorn sheep is outside the Park, and because of rapid land development around Estes Park, many of these grazing lands are rapidly disappearing.

Other animals that were trapped relentlessly for fur in the late 1700s and 1800s were beaver. Recent studies have shown just how valuable beavers are as reclamation engineers. When beavers are re-introduced into badly eroded or washed-out streams and left a supply of cut aspen trees, the animals use the wood to build lodges and dams. This is the first step in erosion control. Silt in streams is reduced dramatically below beaver dams and the rate of water flow is slowed. As ponds form and become stabilized, a previously destroyed ecosystem gradually returns. Muskrats and deer, as well as many bird species, migrate back into these stablized areas as willows and other vegetation begin to grow. Thus beavers create a renewable and dependable food supply for themselves as well as for many other animals. In the Park, beaver populations seem to run in cycles and are increasing at the present time.

The National Park Service is committed by Federal law to protect the wildlife and yet assure that future generations will be able to see and enjoy these animals. Through the years this paradoxical mandate to provide a balance between protecting the wild creatures and providing for their well-being has proved to be a difficult and unending task.

THE PARK TODAY

During the 1930s, the Park Service started a program to acquire land. Private inns, hotels and cabins within the Park boundaries gradually were purchased and removed by the National Park Service. This policy is practical in Rocky Mountain National Park because of adequate accommodations in Estes Park and in Grand Lake. The Park Service's policy is to return the Park to its original appearance as closely as possible. That policy continues, and by 1988 less than 11,000 acres of privately-owned land remains within the Park boundary.

As a result of the Wilderness Act of 1964, which-established the National Wilderness Preservation System, the Park was evaluated to see how much land should be left undeveloped and how much of the Park's 265,679 acres should be reserved for roads, campgrounds and public uses. After much study and discussion, 240,000 acres or about 90 percent of the Park are now proposed as wilderness. Wilderness areas are places where man is a visitor and does not remain. This policy dictates that no more roads will be built in the Park and the ones now in use will become even more important to those visitors who are unable to hike into the remote back country. As a result of the Wilderness Act, there is a new awareness of the importance of our National Parks, both today and for future generations.

As of 1989, historic buildings and sites within the Park that have been placed on the National Register of Historic Places include the William Allen White cabins, Moraine Park Museum, Bear Lake Ranger Station, Fern Lake Patrol Cabin, and Glacier Basin Ranger station. On the western side of the Park are the Grand and Specimen Ditches, Lulu City and Dutchtown mining sites, the Holzwarth historic district, Shadow Mountain Lookout and the Kauffman House in Grand Lake. Fall River Pass Ranger Station, Trail Ridge Road, Fall River Road, the Milner Pass Road Camp, Mess Hall and House and the Willow Park Patrol Cabin also are listed. In and near Estes Park, places on the National Register include the Stanley Hotel, the Elkhorn Lodge and the Leiffer House just east of Longs Peak Campground.

Since the first Paleoindians crossed Trail Ridge, change is the only constant in the long and colorful history of Rocky Mountain National Park. Man has changed the Park is many ways—animal populations are altered; roads and buildings were built, rebuilt and removed; man-made lakes have failed with dramatic results; visitor-trampled trails and "short-cuts" have damaged the tundra and wet meadows in the back country; and in more subtle ways man has left many imprints on the Park. For future generations, the challenge is to allow use while restraining abuse and protecting the integrity of the Park.

HISTORY REFERENCES

Abbott, Carl, 1979, The active force—Enos Mills and the National Park Movement: Colo. Mag., no. 1, 2, v. 56, p. 58-73.

Alberts, E. C., 1954, Rocky Mountain National Park, Colorado: Nat. Hist. Handb. Ser., no. 3, Washington, D. C., 66 p.

Anonymous, undated, Colorado—Big Thompson project: Unpub. report, Rocky Mtn. Natl. Park Library.

_____, undated, Historical guide, Grand Lake, Colo.: Grand Lake Hist. Soc. folder.

_____, 1962, The story of the Colorado—Big Thompson project: U.S. Bureau of Reclamation, Washington, D.C., 56 p.

_____, 1968, A pictorial history of Estes Park, Colorado: Estes Park, Colo., (2nd printing) 64 p.

_____, 1975, Bear Lake Nature Trail: Rocky Mtn. Nature Assoc., Estes Park, Colo., 16 p.

Arps, L. W. and Kingery, E. E., 1972, High Country Names: Rocky Mtn. Nature Assoc., Estes Park, Colo., 212 p.

Arthur, Clare, 1984, The MacGregors and the Black Canyon Ranch, three generations of tradition: Unpub. report, Rocky Mtn. Natl. Park Library, 35 p.

Atkins, D. F., 1972, The Old Fall River Road Motor Nature Trail: Rocky Mtn. Nature Assoc., Estes Park, Colo., 16 p.

_____, Unpub. files, Rocky Mtn. Natl. Park Library.

Bancroft, Caroline, 1967, Trail Ridge Country: Johnson Publishing Co., Boulder, Colo., 71 p.

Bartlett, R. A. 1962, Great surveys of the American West: Univ. of Okla. Press, Norman, Okla., 410 p.

Bird, I. L., 1879, A lady's life in the Rocky Mountains: Univ. of Okla. Press, Norman, Okla., (repr. 1965), 249 p.

Black, R. C., III, 1977, Island in the Rockies: Grand County Pioneer Soc., Granby, Colo., 436 p.

Buchhholtz, C. W., 1983, Rocky Mountain National Park, a history: Colo. Associated Univ. Press, Boulder, Colo., 256 p.

Cairns, M. L., 1971, Grand Lake in the olden days: The World Press, Denver, Colo., 308 p.

Cargo, D. N., 1978, Exploring Rocky Mountain National Park: David N. Cargo, printed by Johnson Publishing Co., Boulder, Colo., 80 p.

Carothers, J. E., 1951, Estes Park past and present: Univ. of Denver Press, Denver, Colo., 90 p.

Colorado Prospector Newspaper, Highlights from early day newspapers, v. 8, no. 4; v.11, nos. 3, 6; v. 13, no. 3,; v.14, no. 6, Denver, Colo.

Colorado Archives, List of Toll Road Incorporation.

Colorado State Business Directories, 1875—1920.

Crofutt, G. A., 1885, Crofutt's grip-sack guide of Colorado: Cubar Associates, R3, Golden, Colo. (repr. 1966), 266 p.

Dannen, Kent, and Dannen, Donna, undated, Fire: Rocky Mtn. Nature Assoc., and Natl. Park Service leaflet, Estes Park, Colo.

Devers, C. C., 1970, Meeker Park and the Dever family: Privately publ., 24 p.

Dunning, H. M., 1956, Over hill and vale: Johnson Publishing Co., Boulder, Colo., v, 1, 605 p.

_____, 1962, Over hill and dale—In the evening shadows of Colorado's Longs Peak: Johnson Publishing Co., Boulder, Colo., v. 2, 605 p.

_____, 1967, The history of Estes Park: Johnson, Publishing Co., Boulder, Colo., 64 p.

_____, 1967, The history of Trail Ridge Road: Johnson Publishing Co., Boulder, Colo., 60 p.

_____, 1971, Over hill and dale—history of Larimer County, Johnson Publishing Co., v. 3, Boulder, Colo., 511 p.

Eberhart, Perry, 1959, Guide to the Colorado ghost towns and mining camps: Swallow Press, Inc., Chicago, Ill., 496 p.

Estes, Milton, 1939, Memoirs of Estes Park: Colo. Mag., v, 16, no. 4, p. 121-132.

Fazio, P. M., 1982, Cragged crusade: the fight for Rocky Mountain National Park: Univ. of Wyo., M. S. thesis. 235 p.

Glidden, D. E., 1981, Summer wind studies near Alpine Visitor Center, Rocky Mountain National Park: Rocky Mtn. Nature Assoc., Estes Park, Colo., 53 p.

_____, 1982, Winter wind studies in Rocky Mountain National Park: Rocky Mtn. Nature Assoc., Estes Park Colo., 29 p.

Harvey, Mr. and Mrs. J. R., 1947, "Squeaky" Bob Wheeler's hunting and ranch life in the North Park country: Colo. Mag., v. 24, no.4, p. 145-158.

Hicks, Dave, 1976, Estes Park from the beginning: Egan Printing Co., Denver, Colo., 60 p.

Holland, F. R., Jr., 1971, Rocky Mountain National Park, historical background data: Unpubl. Report, Rocky Mtn Natl. Park Library, 87 p.

Huntington, F. L., 1912, Written communications in files of Patience C. Kemp, Grand Lake, Colo.

Jackson, C. S., 1947, Picture maker of the Old West: Charles Scribner's Sons, New York, 307 p.

Jarrett, R. D., and Costa, J. E., 1984, Hydrology, geomorphology and dam-break modeling of the July 15, 1982, Lawn Lake Dam and Cascade Dam failures, Larimer Co., Colo.: U.S. Geol. Survey Open-file Rept. 84-612, 109 p.

Kaye, Glen, 1982a, Longs Peak: Rocky Mtn. Nature Assoc., Estes Park, Colo., 20 p.

_____, 1982b, Trail Ridge: Rocky Mtn. Nature Assoc., Estes Park, Colo., 10 p.

_____, 1983, Lulu City: Rocky Mtn. Nature Assoc., Estes Park, Colo., 12 p.

_____, 1986, Moraine Park Nature Trail: Rocky Mtn. Nature Assoc., Estes Park, Colo., 13 p.

_____, undated, Never Summer Ranch: Rocky Mtn. Nature Assoc., Estes Park, Colo., 8 p.

Kiley, Enda, and Kiley, Robert, 1986, Personal interview concerning the life of Enos Mills.

_____, 1989, Personal inerview concerning the life of Enos Mills.

Knapp, J. G., undated, The Glen Haven story: Johnson Publ. Co., Boulder, Colo., 81 p.

Lamb, E. J., 1906, Memories of the past and thoughts of the future: Press of the United Bretheran Publ. House, 257 p.

Mattes, M. J., 1986, The Boulderfield Hotel, in Colorado Heritage: Colo. Hist. Soc., Issue 1, Denver, Colo., p. 30-41.

Melton, J. R., and Melton, Lulabeth, 1982, YMCA of the Rockies; Seventy-five years of history 1907–1982: Lula W. Dorsey Mus., YMCA of the Rockies, Estes Park, Colo., 105 p.

Mills, E. A., 1909, Wild life on the Rockies: Univ. of Neb. Press, Lincoln, Neb. (repr. 1988), 271 p.

_____, 1911, The spell of the Rockies, Houghton-Mifflin

Co., Boston, Mass., 356 p.

_____, 1913a, In beaver world: Houghton-Mifflin Co., Boston, Mass., 228 p.

_____, 1913b, The story of a thousand-year pine, and other tales of wild life: Houghton-Mifflin Co., Boston, Mass.,119 p.

_____, 1915, The Rocky Mountain wonderland, Houghton-Mifflin Co., Riverside Press, Cambridge, Mass., 363 p.

_____, 1917, Your national parks: Houghton-Mifflin Co., Boston, Mass., 431 p.

_____, 1921, Waiting in the wilderness: Doubleday, Garden City, N. Y., 241 p.

_____, 1931, Bird memories of the Rockies: Houghton-Mifflin Co., Boston, Mass., 263 p.

_____,1932, The Rocky Mountain National Park, Memorial Ed., Houghton-Mifflin Co., 239 p.

_____, 1939, Early Estes Park, with foreword and biographical sketch by Esther B. Mills: 3rd Ed., Denver, Colo., 60 p.

Mills, Joe, 1926, A mountain boyhood: Univ. of Neb. Press, Lincoln, Neb. (repr. 1988), 311 p.

Musselman, L. H., 1971, Rocky Mountain National Park administrative history, 1915—1965: Natl. Park Service Open-file Report, 235 p.

Nilson, Erik, 1978, Rocky Mountain National Park Trail Guide: Anderson World Books, Inc., Mountain View, Calif., 189 p.

Prosser, Glen, 1971, The saga of Black Canyon, the story of the MacGregors of Estes Park: Privately published, 48 p.

Ramaley, W. C., 1975, Trails and trail builders of the Rocky Mountain National Park: Unpub. Report, Rocky Mtn. Natl. Park Library, 117 p.

Shroba, R. R., Schmidt, P. W., Crosby, E. J., and Hansen, W. R., 1979, Geologic and geomorphic effects in the Big Thompson Canyon area, Larimer County, Colorado, U.S. Geol. Survey Prof. Paper 1115, 103 p.

Shoemaker, F. J., 1947, The pioneers of Estes Park: Colo. Mag., v. 24, no. 1, p. 15-23.

Sprague, A. E., 1935, Pioneering on the Big Thompson and in Estes Park: Colo. Mag., v.12, no. 3, p. 92-97.

_____, 1938, My first winter in Estes Park: Colo. Mag., v.15, no. 4, p. 153-157.

Stauffer, Ruth, 1979, Historical vignettes of early days in Estes Park: Estes Park Area Hist. Mus., Estes Park, Colo., 64 p.

Trenholm, V. C., 1970, The Arapahoes, our people: Civilization of the American Indian Ser., Univ. of Okla. Press, Norman, Okla., 367 p.

Trimble, Stephen, 1984, Rocky Mountain National Park in The Sierra Club Guides to the National Parks, Rocky Mtns. and the Great Plains: Stewart, Tabori and Chang, p. 109-149.

Wild, Peter, 1979, Enos Mills: Boise State Univ., Western Writers Ser. no. 36, Boise, Idaho, 47 p.

Yandell, M. D.,1975, ed., National parkways, a photographic and comprehensive guide to Rocky Mountain and Mesa Verde National Parks: World-wide Research and Publishing Co., Casper, Wyo., 88 p.

GEOLOGY

How the Scenery in Rocky Mountain National Park was formed.

Aerial view of the northeast face of Mt. Ypsilon from an altitude of 13,200 feet. Metamorphic rocks are about 1.75 billion years old. Spectacle Lakes are tarns filling bedrock basins in the cirque.
(F. W. Osterwald and J. B. Bennetti, Jr., September 1986)

"Gray and red granite form a larger portion of its surface.
Here and there are mixtures of schist, gneiss, and
porphyry. The northwest corner is volcanic and
is made up of rhyolite, obsidian, and lava."

——Enos A. Mills, <u>The Rocky Mountain
Wonderland</u>, 1915.

GEOLOGY
by
Dr. Frank W. Osterwald

THE SETTING

Rocky Mountain National Park, in the high mountains of the Front Range in central Colorado, is west of the Great Plains, straddles the Continental Divide, and extends westward nearly to Colorado's unique intermontane parks. It is a magnificent part of America's snow-capped backbone.

Colorado can be divided roughly into three parts. The eastern one-third is part of the huge expanse of the Great Plains that stretch from northern Mexico to Saskatchewan in Canada and from the Rocky Mountains almost to the Mississippi River. The Great Plains slope gently eastward from the Front Range to the Mississippi River. The eastern margin is obscure, marked in some places by a low, east-facing excarpment and elsewhere merely by a change from rolling wooded hills on the east to grass-covered plains on the west. This gentle eastward slope is broken in some places by hills as much as a few hundred feet high along major stream divides. Here and there a few steep-sided buttes rise above the plains and some streams have eroded their beds deeply into the land surface. General George A. Custer likened the Great Plains to an ocean because when one climbs a hill up from a stream valley only another valley and hill lie ahead.

Beneath the Great Plains are thick layers of geologically young sedimentary rocks that were deposited as nearly horizontal layers during the Cretaceous and Tertiary Periods of geologic time. In places these layers are covered by even younger sediments left by streams and winds as well as by glaciers during the Ice Ages. The sedimentary rocks tilt gently toward the west in eastern Colorado but near the Front Range they were bent up sharply and broken by faults as the mountains rose.

Central Colorado is a north-south belt of many individual mountain ranges that is interrupted by four large, open, high-altitude prairies called "parks." Between the mountain ranges, north-south rivers flowing in long open valleys provide convenient travel routes. Other river valleys cut completely across the ranges, furnishing rugged east-west routes as well.

Many mountain ranges, parks and valleys are bordered by faults. Most ranges have cores of very old, hard, igneous and metamorphic rocks that are rimmed by tilted sedimentary rocks. Within some of the mountain ranges volcanoes poured out lava and blew out huge amounts of debris in violent explosions. The most recent volcanic eruption in Colorado was only about 4000 years ago near Dotsero along the Colorado River east of Glenwood Springs.

A major flaw in the earth's crust, the Rio Grande **rift**, passes along the Kawuneeche Valley in Rocky Mountain National Park. This rift, a narrow belt of down-dropped fault blocks extending from northern Mexico to southern Wyoming, is a weak, sagging strip where the earth's crust is slowly being pulled apart.

Western Colorado is a land of spectacular mesas, canyons and buttes. This land comprises several large plateaus capped by nearly horizontal layers of hard sedimentary or volcanic rocks isolated by long, deep river valleys. The San Juan Mountains in the southwestern corner of Colorado are an oval-shaped bulge in the earth's crust with a core of hard Precambrian and Paleozoic rocks, plastered by thick volcanic rocks.

GEOLOGIC TIMETABLE

Percent of Geologic Time	Eras	Periods	Epochs	How Many Years Ago?
1.0%	CENOZOIC	Quaternary	Holocene	today / 14,000
			Pleistocene	2.4 million+
		Tertiary	Pliocene	11 million
			Miocene	24 million
			Oligocene	37 million
			Eocene	59 million
			Paleocene	66 million
4%	MESOZOIC	Cretaceous		144 million
		Jurassic		208 million
		Triassic		245 million
8%	PALEOZOIC	Permian		286 million
		Pennsylvanian		320 million
		Mississippian		360 million
		Devonian		408 million
		Silurian		438 million
		Ordovician		505 millon
		Cambrian		570 million
87%	PRECAMBRIAN	Proterozoic Eon		2.5 billion
		Archean Eon		3.8 billion?

IT WAS A LONG TIME AGO!

To think about geology one needs to think of huge mind-boggling amounts of time. Very old rocks almost 2 billion years old make up most of the mountains of the northern Front Range, so when one looks at the alpine scenery in the National Park one really looks backward in time about 2 billion years. Geologists subdivide time into large units called Eras (the longest), Eons, Periods, and Epochs (the shortest). Eons and Periods are subdivisions of Eras while Epochs are subdivisions of Periods (see Timetable). The very old rocks in the National Park belong to the earliest part of geologic time, the Precambrian Era. Units of geologic time are summarized in the chart.

For example, 1.8- to 2-billion-year-old rocks belong to the latter part of the Precambrian known as the Proterozoic Eon, but deposits from the 1982 Lawn Lake flood belong to the Holocene Epoch of the Quaternary Period.

THE OLDEST ROCKS IN THE PARK— THE PRECAMBRIAN ERA

Crystalline **metamorphic schists** and **gneisses** that were originally layers of shale, sandstone, and limestone are at least 1.75 billion years old. Some very dark-colored layers in these old metamorphic rocks originally were volcanic rocks. Of course the original rocks actually are older than 1.75 billion years—that's merely the time they were changed into schists and gneisses by intense heat and pressure. They probably were formed about 2 billion years ago. We know what kinds of rocks these old metamorphics originally were by the metamorphic minerals they contain. For example, some that were derived from sedimentary shales contain a **mineral** called **sillimanite** which contains much aluminum, as does **clay**, the most common mineral in shales.

BENDING AND BREAKING DURING THE PRECAMBRIAN

The layered metamorphic rocks in the Rocky Mountain National Park area were folded at least three times. Shortly after the original metamorphism, the old rocks were bent into large folds trending nearly northwest. During a second folding they were bent into east-west folds as the 1.7-billion-year-old granites were emplaced. A third folding accompanied shearing along northeast-trending zones after the 1.4-billion-year-old granites crystallized.

During the Precambrian Era rocks in Colorado were broken by numerous faults and joint planes. Although most faults of Precambrian age trend northwest, others that trend north-northwest cut the east side of the Front Range. Nearly all these faults resumed moving many times during their histories. Dark-colored volcanic dikes that are slightly older than the 1.4-billion-year-old granites fill several of the faults. Segments of the so-called "Iron Dike" fill some of these north-northwest faults in a narrow belt crossing the Front Range from south of Boulder to near the Wyoming border. A few east-northeast-trending fault zones cut all the Precambrian rocks in the northern part of the Front Range.

DON'T TAKE GRANITE FOR GRANTED

About 1.7 billion years ago the old metamorphic rocks were invaded by fluids that crystallized into large masses of granite. In most places these fluids merely flowed between the layers of the metamorphics. At a few places however, the granites filled old

Tightly folded 1.75-billion-year-old schist along the Fall River Road near Marker 14. The complete fold in the center of the picture is about 1 foot across. Schist probably was folded about 1.4 billion years ago.

Uniformly medium-grained granite at Rainbow Curve on Trail Ridge Road.

Granitic pegmatite dikes (white) filling fractures in metamorphic rocks near the Fawn Valley Inn, just east of the Fall River Entrance Station that are about 1.75 billion years old. Dikes probably are about 1.4 billion years old. Large dike is about 3 1/2 feet wide.

cracks that cut across the layering. More granites invaded the metamorphic rocks about 1.4 billion years ago. These later granites cut across the metamorphic layering in some places and bent it aside elsewhere.

DURING THE PALEOZOIC

The first major subdivision of geologic time after the Precambrian, the Paleozoic Era, began about 570 million years ago. During that time most of the northern Front Range was above sea level. Slowly-flowing, meandering streams wore the land down to a nearly featureless plain underlain by Precambrian rocks. In some places the streams deposited mud and sand on the bottom of an ancient ocean. In most places erosion later removed these sediments. Sandstones were deposited along the Gore Range southwest of the National Park; later they were bent and faulted. Erosion later removed nearly all of the sandstones except for remnants along a belt from Pikes Peak northwestward to Arapaho Pass just south of the Park. These remnants fill cracks in the old Precambrian rocks, indicating that the cracks were open beneath the sea, creating so-called "sandstone dikes".

The only Ordovician, Silurian and Devonian rocks known in north-central Colorado are fragments contained in volcanic **pipes**. Pipes containing many pieces of sedimentary rocks embedded in volcanic matrices were intruded explosively into Precambrian rocks of the Front Range between 400 and 360 million years age, mostly during the Devonian Period. One very small pipe is in the Fish Creek Valley southeast of the town of Estes Park.

Near the end of the Mississippian Period the Front Range rose and was again eroded. An old mountain range called the Front Range Highland arose in north-central Colorado about 325 million years ago. A major fault bounded this old range on the southwest, but the northeast side was merely bent up like the hinge of a huge trapdoor. The fault apparently continued to move intermittently during the Mesozoic and Cenozoic Eras. Younger faults later cut the northeastern side of this ancient Front Range Highland during the Mesozoic and Cenozoic Eras. Thin layers of Pennsylvanian and Permian sedimentary rocks were laid down in an ocean east of the Highland.

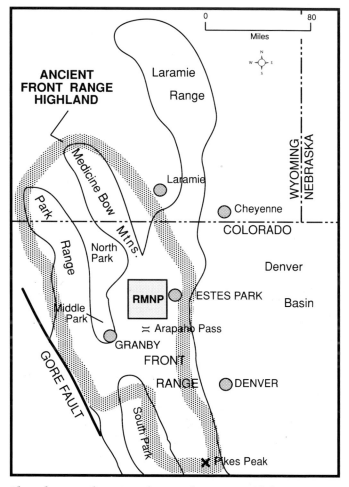

Sketch map showing the northern part of the ancient Front Range Highland.

DURING THE MESOZOIC

The Mesozoic Era began about 245 million years ago. The old Front Range Highland stopped rising early in the Mesozoic except for some faulting that continued intermittently until Late Jurassic time or later. Streams flowing across the Highland laid down the Morrison Formation consisting mostly of sandstones, mudstones and shales which contain many dinosaur fossils and uranium deposits. The Morrison was deposited on an old land surface directly overlying Precambrian rocks. Thick shales were laid down over much of Colorado when the ocean returned between 90 and 100 million years ago during the Cretaceous Period. Near the close of the Cretaceous, the seacoast vacillated back and forth many times, leaving thick sandstones near the shorelines that alternated with thick shales deposited in the ocean. The sea finally made up its mind about 71 million years ago and withdrew eastward from Colorado for the last time, leaving the Foxhills Sandstone as a final memento of its visits.

A TIME OF VIOLENCE

Strong mountain building resumed in the ancient Front Range Highland, including Rocky Mountain National Park, near the end of the Cretaceous Period about 72 million years ago. It continued until about 50 million years ago during the Eocene Epoch of the Tertiary Period.

This time of strong mountain-building, called the Laramide **orogeny**, produced a series of generally northwest-trending mountain ranges. The borders of these ranges followed faults that first moved during the Precambrian. Part of the ancient Front Range Highland became sites of the Front Range, the Medicine Bow Mountains and the Park Range.

The eastern flank of this new Front Range extended northwestward from Colorado Springs, Colo. to the east side of the Medicine Bow Mountains. Mountains within the Front Range reached their present boundaries, however, between 66 and 58 million years ago during the Paleocene Epoch.

Volcanism was rampant during this time of violence. About 55 to 54 million years ago a belt of igneous intrusive bodies and volcanos was emplaced across Colorado from the San Juan Mountains to near Rocky Mountain National Park; some volcanos also erupted outside it. The oldest volcanic rocks in the Never Summer Mountains belong to this volcanism.

The eastern side of the Front Range is very close to the deepest part of the Denver Basin, a huge down warp beneath the Great Plains of eastern Colorado. Within a distance of only a few miles, the east flank of the Front Range rose at least 16,000 feet above the floor of the basin. The deepest part of the basin is almost beneath the city of Denver. The summits of the mountains at this time probably were only 4,000 to 6,000 feet above sea level. As the Front Range rose, erosion removed nearly all of the covering sedimentary rocks. Using the debris from this covering, streams built up a sheet of new sediments called the Laramie Formation along the eastern base of the mountains. This sheet was the last rock unit to be deposited entirely during the Cretaceous Period. It was covered by still younger **sandstones** and **conglomerates** that contain fragments of Precambrian rocks, in addition to more pieces of Paleozoic and Mesozoic rocks. These chunks of Precambrian rocks indicate that although the Front Range rose abruptly, erosion rapidly wore it

down to the once buried, very old Precambrian rocks.

MORE UPS AND DOWNS

After the time of violence, streams wore down the mountains until about 40 million years ago, late in the Eocene Epoch until they had cut broad, nearly planar land surfaces across the Precambrian rocks. Within the National Park only scattered remnants of those deeply weathered surfaces still exist. At that time the mountain summits along the present Front Range were worn down until they stood only a few hundred feet above their nearby valleys.

The northern part of the Front Range, including the National Park, rose again after the Eocene erosion until the mountain tops were about 5,000 to 6,000 feet above sea level. The old Eocene erosion surface was tilted so that it sloped more steeply away from the mountains. During this renewed uplifting, rivers cut deep canyons in the mountains and deeply dissected the Eocene erosion surface. The ancestral North Fork of the Colorado River wore a canyon at least 1,000 feet deep at La Poudre Pass, and Beaver Creek cut a similarly deep canyon at Milner Pass. This extensive erosion also produced spectacular hogbacks along the east flank of the Front Range by washing away the soft layers from the tilted sedimentary rocks, leaving strikingly prominent ridges of the hard layers. One can see some of these hogbacks at Lyons, Colo. on the highway to Estes Park, and others at the mouth of the Big Thompson Canyon just west of Loveland, Colo.

EVERYTHING BLEW UP!

About 37 million years ago, as the Oligocene Epoch began, everything changed. New volcanoes west and southwest of the Front Range erupted for about 3 million years, filling the Eocene canyons with volcanic ash and nearly filling the basins on both sides of the range. Mountain tops in the Park, however, weren't completely submerged in ash. This explosive vulcanism was an economic event as well as a geologic one because many important mineral deposits in the Colorado Mineral Belt south of Rocky Mountain National Park formed either at this time or slightly after it (see p. 229).

Northwest of the Park, volcanoes in the Never Summer Mountains, including one at Lulu Mountain, began erupting about 28 million years ago. These eruptions included at least one **nuée ardente**, a glowing cloud of hot gas and molten rock like the one that destroyed the city of St. Pierre on the island of Martinique in 1902. The eruptive cloud from Lulu Mountain deposited thick, welded ash-flow tuffs –not lava– that cap older Oligocene volcanic rocks on Specimen Mountain. This cloud, or another one like it, continued eastward at least as far as Lava Cliffs where it filled a shallow valley in the old Precambrian rocks. During this eruptive episode volcanoes in the Never Summer Mountains spewed out enough material to refill all the canyons in the western part of the National Park. Volcanic debris also overlapped some 54-million-year-old flows from a volcano at Mount Richthofen.

The **nuée ardente** erupted at the same time that the west side of the Front Range was being strongly uplifted.

Welded ash-flow tuff along Trail Ridge road, just west of Lava Cliffs parking area. Elongated, lens-like, light-colored fragments are "squashed" pumice.

IF IT'S FULL OF DIRT IT HAS TO BE CLEANED OUT AGAIN!

Beginning about 24 million years ago, during Early Miocene time, block faulting and general land subsidence began in the Rio Grande **rift** that extends northward through the mountains from Mexico to southern Wyoming. The faults along the sides of the Kawuneeche Valley belong to this rift which is still very slowly subsiding today.

Also at the start of the Miocene Epoch volcanism in the western part of the National Park began to die down and erosion took over again. Streams washed nearly all the piles of volcanic debris out of the canyons and off the mountains. So much of this material was cleaned out that it clogged the downstream ends of the valleys and covered the lowlands where it was mixed with new volcanic ash from still-active volcanoes west of the Park. These sediments were redeposited (reworked) as tan to gray layers of sand and silt, with a few layers of white volcanic ash. Some of these sediments (the Troublesome Formation) crop out in highway cuts along U.S. 34 (Trail Ridge Road) just south of the entrance road into Grand Lake Village.

At some time in the Miocene Epoch, perhaps about 18 million years ago, the Front Range began rising intermittently. Streams began washing away nearly all the old volcanic debris, such as the Troublesome Formation, that they had recently laid down. Many streams resumed their old pre-volcanic courses and re-excavated their former valleys that had been filled with soft volcanic rocks because these were the easiest places in which to dig. New erosion surfaces were cut across the old, hard rocks at high levels in the mountains. Probably near the end of the Miocene, many mountain ranges, including the Front Range, collapsed slightly along new faults that even cut the Miocene sediments and erosion surfaces. A few faults offset remnants of these Miocene erosion surfaces along Trail Ridge.

JUST BEFORE THE ICE AGES

So much of the old volcanic debris was washed farther down and even out of the canyons during the Pliocene Epoch that the streams couldn't carry all of it. The water slowed after it left the steep mountains. Streams began refilling some valleys they had just cleaned out. The oldest of these new stream deposits contain many boulders and cobbles but younger ones are mainly sand and silt mixed with volcanic ash. This renewed valley-filling ended about 7 to 5 million years ago but not before the water-borne debris had almost buried some mountain ranges. Streams reached the Great Plains from the Park Range by flowing completely across both the Medicine Bow Mountains and the Laramie Range on the newly-laid debris.

Troublesome Formation (sedimentary) in highway cut n Grand Lake village. Beds of eroded and redeposited volca debris are interlayered with slightly harder layers of volca ash that protrude slightly from the face of the cut.

During the Pliocene Epoch the Continental Divide was far to the west of its modern location. Great canyons were cut throughout the Front Range at this time with floors only about 450 feet above modern stream levels. Many of the canyons were cut entirely across the modern Front Range. Although they are now cut off from their original Pliocene headwaters, many parts of these old canyons still exist. They have been considerably modified, however, by glaciers at high elevations, by newer streams that captured and isolated their headward parts and by crustal movements, including faults, that changed the slopes of the valleys.

The climate became drier during this final episode

of canyon-cutting. Although it was still more humid than our modern climate, this drier climate probably signalled the approach of the Great Ice Ages. Large amounts of water near the poles began to freeze, leaving less water for the rest of the earth. The mountains of the Front Range were broadly uplifted at about the same time, mostly as fault-bounded blocks of Precambrian rocks. Some blocks went up, some went down. Mountain summits in the National Park rose as much as 4,000 to 5,000 feet, reaching almost to their present elevations above 12,000 feet. They attained their present elevations by continual slow uplift during the Pleistocene and Holocene Epochs.

THAR AIN'T MUCH GOLD IN THEM THAR HILLS!

During Colorado's 19th-century mining boom, prospectors crawled over nearly every inch of Rocky Mountain National Park but little gold or silver was found. Along the western edge of the Park a few small mineral-bearing veins filled minor faults along the Kawuneeche Valley.

Few reports were written about these mineral deposits. Apparently one of the vein minerals was native lead, because some old fur trappers told Abner Sprague that they picked up lead "nuggets" which they simply beat into shape for bullets. Stream gravels along the North Fork of the Colorado River contained a little placer gold derived from the veins, especially near Lulu City. Lead carbonate veins near Lulu City bore a little silver and other veins west of Gaskil contained carbonates and sulfides of lead, copper and silver. Veins in Mount Shipler locally were rich in silver, but most ores from the North Fork area were described as being of poor quality. This probably meant they were hard to smelt and expensive to ship because they were very heavy with high lead contents.

A few other mining prospects were staked within the National Park. The best known of these were the Eugenia Mine on Battle Mountain, the workings at Prospect Canyon on the Bear Lake Road and "Miner Bill" Currrance's holes in Mount Chapin along the Fall River Road. All of these apparently were gold prospects, but nothing is known of the mineralogy or modes of occurrence of the gold-bearing minerals (if any). Miner Bill probably followed small gold-bearing quartz veins filling fractures in the Iron Dike.

Near Allenspark, close to the southeastern corner of the Park, 900 claims for gold were filed in the early days, but no mineral production was reported, even though Allenspark is on the edge of the Colorado Mineral Belt. Small quantities of gold probably accompanied small quartz-pyrite veins in faults and small fracture zones.

GLACIERS OF THE ICE AGES[1]

The Great Ice Ages! Even the name brings up mental images of landscapes covered by ice and snow, and of large, hairy, elephant-like animals (mammoths) searching for food in an Arctic desert. Our minds also conjure up visions of skin-clad "cave-men" carrying clubs and spears, hunting those mammoths for dinner.

The Ice Ages caused many fantastic events that surpassed even our wildest mental images. Cold climates completely changed many plant and animal communities of the world. So much of the earth's water was frozen that not enough was left to fill the oceans. A dry-land bridge appeared between Russia and Alaska. Ancestors of the American Indians walked to North America across this bridge about 40 to 30 thousand years ago. By quickly freezing mammoths in the glacial ice and tundra of Siberia, the last Great Ice Age provided 12-thousand-year-old mammoth steaks that were served at a formal dinner in Moscow during the early 1900s. Some Siberian mammoths were frozen so quickly that they still had Arctic buttercups in their mouths.

During the Great Ice Ages long, thick, **alpine glaciers** chiseled out the scenery of Rocky Mountain National Park as we see it today. The scenery along the Continental Divide in the Front Range resulted from three active glacial processes: (1) Glaciers quarried rock from the heads of their valleys; (2) by gouging out their valleys they steepened and deepened them, and also ground away, smoothed and polished all the rock ledges along the way; and (3) they built characteristically-shaped ridges and mounds of rock debris (moraines) in the valleys. These great scenic changes are emphasized by spectacularly steep, scoop-shaped amphitheatres (**cirques**) along the highest parts of the Front Range from which the ice flowed. Westward views of some of these amphitheatres from Glacier Basin and from Sprague Lake are magnificent.

Perhaps the first known human Colorado residents actually watched the last Great Ice Age glaciers in the mountains melt as they butchered camels on the Great Plains between 17 and 16 thousand years ago (Cassels, 1983, p. 40-43). The Clovis people, who may have seen the last remnants of the Late Pinedale age glaciers while they hunted mammoths in the mountains between 11,500 and 11,000 years ago (Haynes, 1985, p. 1199), left some of their distinctively fluted weapon points in and near Rocky Mountain National Park.

The Great Ice Ages were followed by other less intense ice ages, including the Little Ice Age which continues to the present (Leet and Judson, 1965, p. 200; Allison and Palmer, 1980, p. 322). We live during a time in which modern glaciers temporarily have retreated toward their sources but have not departed.

[1] Because glacial features are so varied and complex, specific bibliographic works used in compiling this section are identified. Complete titles are in the list of references at the end of this chapter.

WHY DID THE GLACIERS FORM?

The earth's climate began cooling about 10 to 7 million years ago (Wick, 1981, p. 12-14; Barry and others, 1985, p. 637, 639). By 5 to 3 million years ago it was so cold that very large, thick fields of snow began to pile up around both poles of the earth and near the heads of high mountain valleys. These snow fields gradually changed into ice, starting the first of the Great Ice Ages. Although Ice Ages were long thought by geologists to have started only about 10,000 years ago, they are now known to have begun much earlier. One glacial episode in northwestern North America perhaps began as much as 5 million years ago. Much recently acquired, world-wide evidence now indicates that intense widespread glaciation began about 2.4 million years ago. As cooling continued, thick and very extensive i**ce sheets**, also known as **continental glaciers**, covered the land surfaces for long distances from both poles. These ice sheets were much larger than the modern ones covering Antarctica, the Arctic Ocean, and Greenland. They covered nearly all of northern and eastern Canada, as well as most of the United States north of the Ohio and Missouri Rivers but they did not cover the high mountains. Instead, many high Rocky Mountain valleys were filled by slowly flowing rivers of ice that are called **alpine glaciers**. Some mountain ranges were covered by i**ce caps** because so much ice flowed into mainstream glaciers from tributary valleys that the glaciers merged, burying all but the tops of the mountains.

Many theories have been proposed to explain why the climate cooled so much and for such a long time, but so far as is now known, no single factor of the earth's environment seems solely to have been responsible. Among the possible causes are variations in the sun's heat and shading of the earth's surface by huge clouds of dust blown into the atmosphere from volcanos or kicked up by infalls of huge meteors. Another possibility is increasing amounts of water and carbon dioxide leading to more luxuriant plant life. This in turn could have caused huge forest fires that filled the atmosphere with smoke (the well-known greenhouse effect). However, increased cloud cover paradoxically could either raise temperatures near the the earth's surface by preventing infra-red radiation outward into space, or cool it by shading the surface from the sun (Obermiller, 1989). Burning wood, coal and oil for fuels increases the amount of carbon dioxide in the atmosphere, stimulating increased cloud cover. This modern effect may not be greater than that produced by huge forest fires which ignited large coal beds at their outcrops early in the Great Ice Ages (Osterwald and others, 1981, p. 41). Finally, climates may have been effected as the earth's orbit shifted slightly because of gravitational variations due to re-alignments of planets and stars, and to comets that intruded the solar system. Several of these slight environmental changes may have combined to cause the Great Ice Ages (Mitchell, 1965), but even that is speculation. We simply do not know. Either a drop of a few degrees in average temperatures or a little more winter-time snow might bring back the big glaciers (Allison and Palmer, 1980, p. 322).

MODERN GLACIERS

Within Rocky Mountain National Park, 15 small glaciers and fields of stagnant ice still remain as tiny relics of glaciers that grew during the Audubon and Arapaho Peak Glaciations (Richmond, 1960, p. 1381). At least six are still active glaciers because at times their ice moves slowly down their valleys. Although they are tiny, these glaciers have many attributes of large glaciers. They contain blue glacial ice, some start flowing from headwall cracks (bergschrunds), form crevasses at their surfaces, contain ice caves, calve icebergs into their **tarns** and deposit **moraines** at their ends and sides.

All of these tiny glaciers are named for early settlers in the Estes Park region or other well-known early people. Some were named and later renamed, which confuses early historical accounts of them.

The National Park Service measured changes in Tyndall and Andrews Glaciers annually for many years so that their recent histories are well known. Although the stagnant ice fields are stationary most of the time, the ice in them may move following winters of high snowfall. Geologist W. T. Lee probably was correct when he stated that some Rocky Mountain National Park glaciers are intermittent (1917, p. 30).

Most of the snow carried by winter storms is dropped on the west side of the mountains because the storms are blocked by the mountain crests. Much of the snow that builds the glaciers and ice fields in the Park is picked up from the western slopes of the Front Range by strong westerly winter winds blowing across the mountains. As these winds cross the mountain crests they suddenly lose velocity and can no longer carry the snow; most of it collects along the lee sides of the mountains. Westerly winds can drop heavy snow along the eastern side of the Front Range in the Park at the same time that the sun shines at the lower elevations in Estes Park. Glaciers that are fed mainly by snow blown over mountains are called "Ural-type glaciers" because they are common in the Soviet Union (Outcalt, 1965a; 1965b).

Although their sizes vary almost yearly, the glaciers in the Park seem to be almost in balance with the supply of snow, when studied over periods of several years (Outcalt, 1965b). Their larger cousins in Switzerland also are generally balanced between accumulated snowfall and reduction by evaporation and melting (Swiss Nat'l. Tourist Office, 1984, p. 1). Modern Swiss glaciers advance and retreat only with variations of weather and climate.

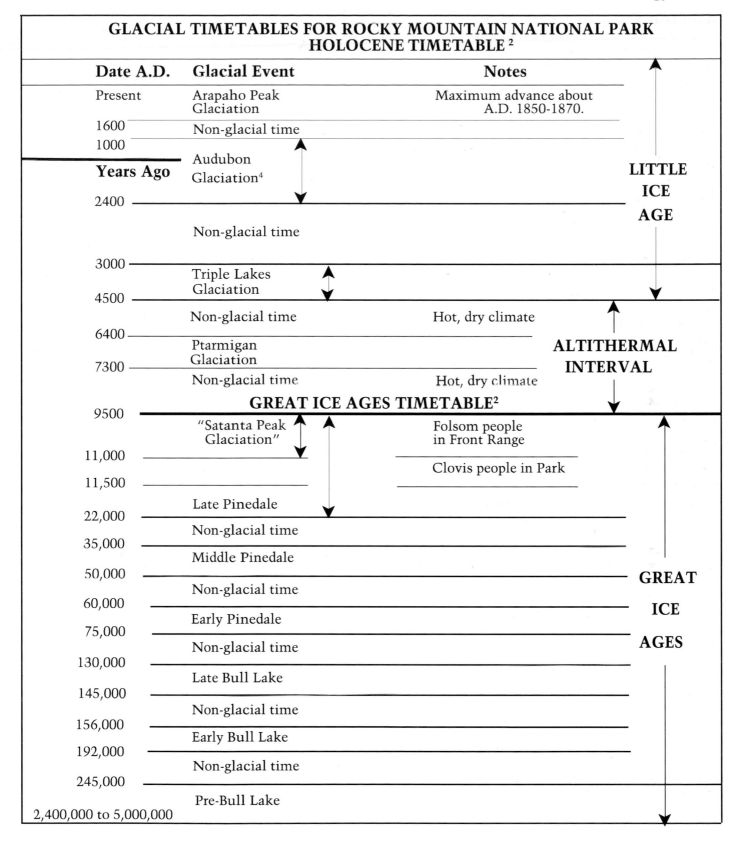

GLACIAL TIMETABLES FOR ROCKY MOUNTAIN NATIONAL PARK
HOLOCENE TIMETABLE [2]

Date A.D.	Glacial Event	Notes	
Present	Arapaho Peak Glaciation	Maximum advance about A.D. 1850-1870.	LITTLE ICE AGE
1600	Non-glacial time		
1000			
Years Ago	Audubon Glaciation[4]		
2400			
	Non-glacial time		
3000	Triple Lakes Glaciation		
4500			
	Non-glacial time	Hot, dry climate	ALTITHERMAL INTERVAL
6400	Ptarmigan Glaciation		
7300	Non-glacial time	Hot, dry climate	

GREAT ICE AGES TIMETABLE [2]

9500	"Satanta Peak Glaciation"	Folsom people in Front Range	GREAT ICE AGES
11,000		Clovis people in Park	
11,500			
22,000	Late Pinedale		
35,000	Non-glacial time		
50,000	Middle Pinedale		
60,000	Non-glacial time		
75,000	Early Pinedale		
130,000	Non-glacial time		
145,000	Late Bull Lake		
156,000	Non-glacial time		
192,000	Early Bull Lake		
245,000	Non-glacial time		
2,400,000 to 5,000,000	Pre-Bull Lake		

[2] Modified from Carrara, 1986; Beget, 1983.
[3] After Madole, 1976a, b; 1980: Colman and Pierce, 1981; Pierce and others, 1975.
[4] Mahaney, W. C., 1972.

Andrews Glacier

Andrews Glacier is at the head of Andrews Gorge at about 11,050 feet elevation. The glacier is in one of the cirques carved by the ancient Bartholf Glacier during the Great Ice Ages (p. 240). Although it is only about $1/4$ mile long and $1/10$ mile wide, Andrews was measured nearly every year between 1932 and 1957 (unpublished reports in the Rocky Mountain National Park library) because one can easily hike to it. When measured after the hard winter of 1934-35 Andrews Glacier had re-advanced 73 feet. Meltwater from Andrews Glacier drains into a small tarn and flows eastward into Loch Vale and Glacier Creek. Abner Sprague, a pioneer resident of Moraine Park, named the glacier for his brother-in-law, E. B. Andrews, who was a well-known amateur naturalist (Rocky Mtn. Nature Assoc., 1959, p. 6). As shown in the photographs, Andrews Glacier changed considerably between 1909 and 1954.

Andrews Glacier, August 1909.
(R. G. Coffin, NPS collection)

By August 30, 1939, Andrews glacier had shrunk considerably, but had built a lateral moraine on its right side. (J. H. Heger, NPS)

Snout of Andrews Glacier in September 1937, showing layers of rock debris in the ice and a small lateral moraine (bottom center). Beyond the glacier Andrews Tarn fills a small bedrock basin gouged out by the ice. Past the tarn the steep drop-off is a giant stairstep into the glacially-carved U-shaped valley below.
(H. R. Gregg, NPS)

Andrews Glacier from the northeast corner of the tarn, September 6, 1946. (NPS)

Andrews Glacier September 6, 1949 showing crevasses at south edge. Figure shows scale.
(H.R.Gregg, NPS)

Crevasse at edge of Andrews Glacier on August 30,
1954. Man in center of crevasse indicates scale. (NPS)

Crevasse at edge of Andrews Glacier, open to bedrock
at bottom, August 30, 1954.   (NPS)

Tyndall Glacier

Tyndall Glacier, in the headwall of Tyndall Gorge at about 12,380 feet elevation, is about $\frac{1}{2}$ mile long and $\frac{1}{3}$ mile wide but its size and shape vary considerably with changes in the annual amounts of snow. During the hard winter of 1934-35, Tyndall re-advanced 34 feet. This glacier has many features characteristic of much larger ones. In most years a prominent large crack (bergschrund), just below the rock cliff at the cirque headwall marks the active head of the glacier. Normally the ice cracks as it flows around a rock ledge at the south edge of the glacier, creating crevasses at the bend. In some years these crevasses are very prominent. Because this glacier sticks to a steep mountain-side it really is a hanging glacier.

Tyndall Glacier may be the most-photographed one in the Park because it is easily seen from several places on the Bear Lake Road. It is just below the skyline between Hallett Peak and Flattop Mountain. If you want to see it at closer range, hike westward for about five miles on the Flattop Mountain Trail from Hallowell Park to the rim of Tyndall Gorge. The glacier was named for Dr. John Tyndall, a well-known 19th-century English scientist who worked in the western U.S. (Rocky Mtn. Nature Assoc., 1959, p. 7-8).

Tyndall Glacier had a steep face during the drought of the 1930s. The bergschrund is very near the top of the glacier. Transverse lines in the ice are boundaries of flow layers marked by thin zones of rock debris.

(NPS)

Hallett Peak (left) and Tyndall Glacier (arrow) from the Late Pinedale age moraine at the north edge of Bear Lake parking lot.

Tyndall Glacier without a bergschrund taken from Flattop Mtn. on September 23, 1938.

(H.R.Gregg, NPS)

Inside the ice cave in Tyndall Glacier on August 26, 1955.   (J.H.Heger, NPS)

Sprague Glacier

This glacier is at about 12,360 feet elevation at the head of Spruce Canyon. It is about $^4/_{10}$ mile long and about $^3/_{10}$ mile wide. Meltwater from Sprague Glacier drains into the Big Thompson River in Forest Canyon. Enos Mills measured its movement at 0.08 inches per day in 1906 (Lee, 1917, p. 30). It was named for Abner Sprague who settled in Moraine Park in 1875 (Rocky Mtn. Nature Assoc., 1959, p. 9). Sprague Glacier is difficult to reach—please ask a Park Ranger before attempting to visit it.

Bergschrund on Tyndall Glacier, probably during the 1930s.   (NPS)

Tarn at snout of Sprague Glacier in 1956. Tiny icebergs break away from the snout and float in the tarn.   (Herkenham, NPS)

Icebergs in the Sprague Glacier tarn, 1956.   (Herkenham, NPS)

Bergschrund at head of Sprague Glacier on September 15, 1954.   (Joan Seear, NPS)

Sprague Glacier, September 15, 1954. Headwall crack (bergschrund) is in upper right of the glacier. (NPS)

Rowe Glacier

Rowe Glacier (pronounced "row", as in "rowdy"), the northern-most glacier in the National Park, is in the Mummy Range on the northeastern slope of Hagues' Peak at about 12,920 feet elevation. This glacier was only about $^1/_4$ mile long and $^4/_{10}$ mile wide in 1956 but when F. H. Chapin photogaphed it in 1889, it was much larger. Its meltwater drains into the North Fork of the Thompson River. Enos Mills determined that Rowe Glacier moved 1.01 inch per day in 1896; in 1907 it had slowed to 0.06 inch per day (Lee, 1917, p. 30). In 1884 W. L. Hallett found a crevasse in the glacier which first indicated that it truly was a moving glacier (Stone, 1887, p. 153-154). Rowe was first named Mummy Glacier but mountaineer Chapin re-named it Hallett's Glacier in 1887 after Hallett, his climbing companion. Because that name caused confusion with the name Hallett's Peak, the National Park Service renamed it in 1932 for early settler Israel Rowe who discovered it in 1880 (Rocky Mtn. Nature Assoc., 1959, p. 10).

Rowe Glacier is also difficult to reach—please ask a Ranger before attempting to visit it.

Rowe Glacier in 1956.   *(Herkenham, NPS)*

Rowe Glacier on September 9, 1930.   *(McLaughlin, NPS)*

Seracs *(ice hummocks) on the surface of Rowe Glacier in 1888 or 1889.*
(F. H. Chapin, NPS collection)

Taylor Glacier

Taylor Glacier is an extremely steep mass of ice at about 12,800 feet on the north wall of Loch Vale Gorge. Like Tyndall, it is a hanging glacier. In 1956, it was about $^6/_{10}$ mile long and $^3/_{10}$ mile wide. Taylor Glacier is clearly visible from Moraine Park as a mass of white ice and snow with two snow-filled avalanche tracks leading down onto it which give it an inverted swallow-tail shape. Its white surface commonly has dark-colored scars resulting from recent avalanches and rockfalls. Instead of an end moraine, rockfalls build up **talus** at its snout which has become a **rock glacier** (White, 1971, p. 50-53).

Abner Sprague named this glacier for A. A. Taylor, a Kansas schoolmaster, who spent a summer in Estes Park in the early 1890s (Rocky Mtn. Nature Assoc, 1959, p. 11). The trails leading to it are obscure and difficult to follow—again, please ask a Ranger.

Taylor Glacier in 1956. A crevasse extends about half way across the glacier near the middle. The rock glacier is in the lower left corner of the picture. (Herkenham, NPS)

Taylor Glacier in 1956. Sky Pond is in the right foreground. Below the snout is the rough surface of the rock glacier. Just below the rock glacier is the riser of a giant stairstep. (Herkenham, NPS)

Mills Glacier

Mills Glacier has been a subject of lively arguments among geologists for many years because they don't agree whether or not it should be called a glacier (Trimble, Stephen, 1984, p. 24)—does it or does it not move? The glacier is at about 13,100 feet elevation, on the east face of Longs Peak high above Chasm Lake. The ice mass was about $^2/_{10}$ mile long and $^3/_{10}$ mile wide in 1960 but its actual width is hard to determine on a map because of its unusual inverted L-shape. F. H. Chapin detected no movement of Mills Glacier in 1888 nor did Enos Mills find any movement of the glacier in 1907. Mills, however, measured about 0.04 inches per day in 1908, and about 0.07 inches per day in 1909 (Lee, 1917, p. 30).

Mills Glacier and Chasm Lake on Longs Peak in 1889.
(F. H. Chapin, NPS collection)

Aerial view west-southwest showing the east face of Longs Peak, el. 14,255 feet, in 1966. The cirque containing Chasm Lake and The Diamond are in the deep shadow. The Mills Moraine is the large ridge in the lower right quarter of the picture and another cirque on the north side of Mt. Meeker is in the left center. Mills Glacier is in the shadow on the left side of the Chasm Lake cirque. The Kawuneeche Valley and Colorado's western slope are behind Longs Peak. The Gore Range is on the distant skyline.
(Phillips, USFS, in NPS collection)

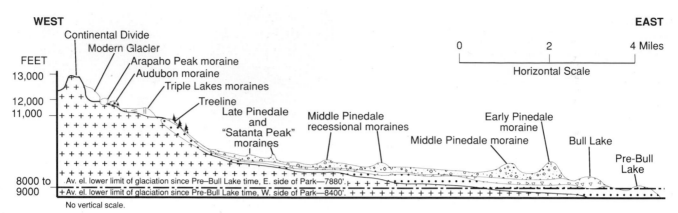

Idealized diagram showing relationships of the major glacial moraines in Rocky Mountain National Park. Modified from Madole (1976b, p. 300).

ANCIENT GLACIERS

Most high valleys in Rocky Mountain National Park contained alpine glaciers several times during the Great Ice Ages. Some glaciers even flowed beyond the Park boundaries but not far enough to reach the Great Plains (Trimble, D. E., 1980; Trimble, Stephen, 1984; Madole, 1976b, 1980; Richmond, 1960).

Great Ice Age **glaciations** in the Rocky Mountains were named for places in the Wind River Mountains of west-central Wyoming where moraines of equivalent ages were first studied (Blackwelder, 1915; Moss. 1951; Richmond, 1962; 1964). Names applied to glacial debris dating from the last two glaciations of the Great Ice Age in the Wind Rivers, the Bull Lake and Pinedale, still are used in Rocky Mountain National Park (Birkeland and others, 1971; Richmond, 1974, p. 42-50; Meierding and Birkeland, 1980, Fig. 10).

Debris left during the oldest glaciations in the Front Range cannot be directly correlated with any classic localities, however, so they are simply lumped together and called "Pre-Bull Lake" glaciations. Debris from these very old glaciations is widespread in the Rocky Mountains but is still poorly understood (Mears, undated, p. 25, 27).

Glaciers of the Great Ice Ages in the Park were named by pioneer geologists who first studied their moraines and cirques. Although modern names have been substituted for some of the early ones, the old ones are used in this book because of their historical importance. Equivalent modern names are italicized.

Thompson Glacier *(Forest Canyon Glacier)*

The Thompson Glacier, on the eastern side of the Front Range, flowed about 13 miles down the Big Thompson River from cirques as high as 12,700 feet near Forest Canyon Pass and along the southwest side of Forest Canyon, where the ice probably was as much as 1,500 feet thick. During the Bull Lake and Early and Middle Pinedale advances it extended about $2/_3$ miles east of the National Park boundary near the Beaver Meadows Entrance Station where its snout elevation was 7,760 feet. It was only $2\,^9/_{10}$ miles long during the Late Pinedale advance.

Bartholf Glacier *(Glacier Gorge Glacier)*

The Bartholf Glacier originated from cirques south, west, and northwest of Bear Lake at elevations between 12,000 and 12,280 feet. It extended northeastward down Glacier Creek for about 11 miles to the Big Thompson River where its Bull Lake age end moraines are at elevations of about 7800 ft., $2\,^1/_2$ miles east of the National Park boundary. During the Late Pinedale advance this glacier also was only about $2\,^9/_{10}$ miles long, extending only to Bear Lake at about 9475 feet. During the "Satanta Peak Glaciation," ice of the Bartholf Glacier did not extend below about 10,800 feet above sea level. The modern Tyndall, Andrews, and Taylor Glaciers and a number of dormant ice fields occupy cirques excavated by the Bartholf Glacier during the Pre-Bull Lake Glaciations.

Fall River Glacier

The Fall River Glacier originated at about 12,240 feet elevation near Fall River Pass. During the Bull Lake Glaciation it flowed eastward nearly 8 miles down the valley of Fall River through Horseshoe Park, stopping just east of the Fall River Entrance Station. Its Early Bull Lake–age **terminal moraines** at this point are about 8,050 feet above sea level. During the Pre-Bull Lake Glaciation it extended <u>at least</u> $^3/_4$ mile farther east but the low parts of the Pre-Bull Lake age moraine are gone, so that its exact length and elevation can't be measured. The Pre-Bull Lake age glacier may have been as much as 6 miles longer than the Bull Lake age glacier (Fuller, 1923; 1925).

The Fall River Glacier received much ice from a major tributary glacier along Roaring River and from the cirque on the east end of Sundance Mtn. During the Pre-Bull Lake or possibly Early Bull Lake Glaciations the Fall River Glacier may have overflowed Deer Ridge into Beaver Meadows, contributing ice to the lower end of the Thompson Glacier. During the Pre-Bull Lake Glaciation it also may have overflowed into the Tahosa Valley via Beaver Brook. During the Late Pinedale advance the Fall River Glacier was restricted to the upper parts of Fall River Canyon.

Mills Glacier

The Mills Glacier in Pinedale time flowed for about 4 1/4 miles from cirques on the east face of Longs Peak and on the north face of Mt. Meeker to about 8,940 feet elevation in the Tahosa Valley, outside the National Park boundary. It flowed southeastward across Tahosa Creek and Colorado Highway 7 (the Peak-to-Peak Highway) to follow Cabin Creek and the Little Thompson River eastward to near Mirror Lake at about 7,800 feet. Apparently this glacier flowed from a cirque elevation of about 13,400 feet.

During the Bull Lake Glaciation the glacier was about 2,000 feet thick. It may have been thicker during the Pinedale Glaciation, because the Early Pinedale age ice certainly flowed farther, breaching the end moraines left by both Bull Lake age advances (Trimble, Stephen, 1984, p. 20-24). During the Pre-Bull Glaciations it may have extended far down the Tahosa Valley following the Cabin Creek and Little Thompson River drainages to about 6,400 feet elevation, roughly 4 miles southeast of Pinewood Springs and 14 miles from the cirque headwalls. Perhaps the glacier also extended much farther down the South St. Vrain drainage during the Pre-Bull Lake. It was very small during the Late Pinedale because the end moraine of that age is only about 2 1/2 miles from the Chasm Lake cirque.

The large and prominent Mills Moraine is the north lateral moraine of this glacier. The subdued south lateral moraine has not been formally named. Mills Glacier quarried out The Diamond on Longs Peak piece-by-piece; because the structure of the rock was nearly vertical and almost at right angles to the direction of ice flow, a huge, nearly smooth rock face resulted.

Wild Basin Glacier

In the southeastern corner of the National Park the Wild Basin Glacier flowed eastward from a group of cirques in a huge fan-shaped basin along the Front Range. Some of the cirques were at elevations of as much as 12,600 feet. During the Bull Lake Glaciation ice of this glacier flowed eastward for about 8 miles to an elevation of at most 8,000 feet along Rock Creek, just east of Allenspark. Ice of Pre-Bull Lake age reached down the valley of North St. Vrain Creek beyond Allenspark, and possibly to near Coffintop Mountain about 8 miles east of Allenspark at an elevation of about 6,200 feet. Near Allenspark, moraines from the Pre-Bull Lake, Bull Lake, and Pinedale Glaciations all are crossed by Colorado Highway 7. Roadcuts near Allenspark are the best places in or near the National Park to see Pre-Bull Lake age moraines.

Colorado River Glacier

On the western side of the Park the Colorado River Glacier stretched southward almost 20 miles from an elevation of about 12,000 feet along the Continental Divide north of Lulu City to about 8,400 feet at the south end of Shadow Mountain Lake (Richmond. 1974, p. 50; Meierding, 1977). The Colorado River Glacier was unique. So much tributary ice was added to it from cirques along the west flank of the Front Range and the east side of the Never Summer Mountains, that it became an **ice cap** that was over 2,000 feet thick in some places. It nearly buried all but the highest summits of both ranges during the Bull Lake and Pinedale Glaciations and probably did so during the Pre-Bull Lake Glaciations. The ice was so thick that some turned northeastward, crossed the Continental Divide at Milner Pass, and flowed down the Cache la Poudre River to about 9000 feet elevation forming the Cache la Poudre Glacier (Richmond, 1974, p. 50). During the Pinedale Glaciation the Cache la Poudre Glacier extended down the Poudre valley for about 10 miles and during the Bull Lake Glaciation it extended even further.

North Inlet Glacier

The North Inlet Glacier was a major tributary to the Colorado River Glacier. It flowed from ten cirques along the western side of the Front Range at about 13,000 feet for about 8 miles down to 8,400 feet at Grand Lake. The main street of Grand Lake was cut through one of its end moraines. The North Inlet Glacier received its snow from direct precipitation during winter storms, so it was not an Ural-type glacier.

East Inlet Glacier

The East Inlet Glacier, another important tributary to the Colorado River Glacier, flowed from cirques along the west side of the Continental Divide opposite Wild Basin that were as high as 12,400 feet and from other cirques at the head of Paradise Valley at about 12,000 feet elevation. The ice flowed down to 8,400 feet elevation to enter Grand Lake near the West Portal of the Alva B. Adams water diversion tunnel. The East Inlet Glacier also received its snowfall from direct precipitation, and like the North Inlet Glacier, was not an Ural-type glacier.

North Fork Big Thompson River Glacier

The North Fork Thompson River glacier flowed from cirques along the east and northeast sides of Hagues Peak, Rowe Peak and Skull Point (Icefield Pass) at elevations of 12,000 to 13,000 feet. It flowed into the valley of the North Fork Big Thompson eastward for about 4 7/10 miles to a point just outside the Park boundary. Until one is far enough upstream to see the **cirques, tarns** and **morainal lakes**, evidence of this glacier is hard to find because of the dense forest cover.

South Fork Cache la Poudre Glacier

During the Pinedale Glaciation a small glacier, here termed the South Fork Cache la Poudre Glacier, flowed from cirques on the north side of Sugarloaf Mountain, the west side of Stormy Peaks and from Icefield and Mummy Passes northeastward down the South Fork and an unnamed tributary for about 5 miles, passing outside the Park boundary. The maximum elevation of its cirques was about 12,000 feet on Sugarloaf Mountain; its snout elevation was about 8,800 feet just upstream from the mouth of Fall Creek. During the Bull Lake Glaciation it extended about 1 mile farther down the South Fork (Richmond, 1974, p. 50). The thickness of the ice is not known.

AFTER THE GREAT ICE AGES—THE HOLOCENE EPOCH

About 18 thousand years ago, world-wide climates warmed and by about 14 to 13 thousand years ago the Late Pinedale–age glaciers began melting (Madole, 1976b, p. 308-311). Their disappearance took about 2,000 to 4,000 year and ushered in the geologists' Holocene Epoch (See Chart, p. 231). Since then all glaciers in Rocky Mountain National Park have been small with obscure moraines. Most moraines from Holocene glaciers are close to the lower ends of old Great Ice Age cirques. As a last gasp of the Great Ice Ages, Front Range climates cooled slightly producing what some geologists have termed the "Satanta Peak Glaciation." Although deposits from this cooling cannot be dated accurately, they seem to overlap in time some moraines of Late Pinedale age. The "Satanta Peak Glaciation" may have been a waning phase of the Late Pinedale as suggested by Madole (1976b., p. 311).

THE ALTITHERMAL INTERVAL

After the Late Pinedale-age glaciers melted between 11,000 and 9,000 years ago (Carrara, 1986; Beget, 1983, p. 392), the climate became hot and dry beginning the Altithermal Interval that lasted until 4,900 years ago. The Great Ice Ages, which closed at the conclusion of the Late Pinedale glaciation, did not end abruptly and at the same time everywhere; transitions to Holocene climatic conditions varied geographically. For example, the transition was completed about 11,000 years ago in southeastern Montana, 10,000 years ago in Yellowstone National Park and 9,500 years ago in the southern Black Hills (Albanese, 1988). In the Colorado Front Range this transition was completed 11,000 to 10,000 years ago at elevations between 8,500 ft. and 9,500 ft. (Madole, 1976b, p. 311).

During the droughts of the Altithermal, glaciers disappeared entirely, perhaps twice, from the Front Range (Richmond. 1960, p. 1374), and the Front Range was isolated by deserts on the Great Plains to the east (Trimble, Stephen, 1984), in the Wyoming Basins to the north, and on the Colorado Plateau to the west.

The mountains became a refuge for big-game animals seeking cooler temperatures and better forage (Benedict, 1968; 1973; 1978). Early people followed the animal herds (their food supplies) into the Park and also crossed the passes over the Continental Divide (Husted, 1965, p. 497). During the Altithermal Interval even the continental glaciers on Greenland and Antarctica retreated toward the poles. Between the two major droughts of the Altithermal a minor glacial advance, the Ptarmigan Glaciation, slightly cooled the Front Range between 7,300 and 6,400 years ago.

MORE ICE AFTER THE ALTITHERMAL

Following the hot and dry interval the climate in the Rocky Mountains cooled again, and small glaciers of the Triple Lakes Glaciation re-occupied the cirques of the Great Ice Ages (Richmond, 1960; Meierding and Birkeland, 1980; Richmond, 1965). The Triple Lakes ushered in a time of modest glacial re-advances that is called the Little Ice Age or Neoglaciation. The Little Ice Age also includes the Audubon and Arapaho Peak Glaciations. The Arapaho Peak continues to the present.

Little Ice Age glaciations in north-central Colorado were unique because both ice glaciers and rock glaciers formed (White, 1971, p. 43-44). Rock glaciers are moving masses of quarried-out rocks cemented by ice, but the mixed rock and ice flow very much like true ice glaciers. Northward from Rocky Mountain National Park there were mostly ice glaciers but to the south only rock glaciers grew in response to the cooler weather. The present end moraine of Tyndall Glacier contains so much ice that it is becoming a rock glacier.

Within each glaciation after the Altithermal, ice advanced and retreated several times (Richmond, 1974; Birkeland and others, 1980). During the Audubon and Arapaho Peak Glaciations the ice also retreated and re-advanced several times within the last 2,000 years; the maximum extent of one such advance was between A.D. 100 and A.D. 1000 (Richmond, 1974, p. 68-69; Benedict, 1968, p. 82). In general, alpine glaciers in the Rocky Mountains also re-advanced several times since A.D. 1000 but some in the Front Range may have disappeared during the 11th- and 12th-centuries (Richmond, 1974, p. 69-72). During the first advance of the Audubon Glaciation, glacial ice in the Front Range reached its maximum extent about A.D. 1650 (Benedict, 1968, p. 79). During the Arapaho Peak advances glaciers in the Park reached their maximum lengths during a cycle of very cold, snowy winters between A.D. 1850 and A.D. 1870. Glacial moraines dating from the Arapaho Peak are the largest of those from the Little Ice Age in the Rocky Mountains and may have buried or destroyed older moraines left during the 16th-, 17th- and 18th-centuries (Richmond, 1965, p. 226).

Longs Peak from Toll Pass on Trail Ridge Road, June 1987. Just beyond the snowbank in the foreground is a large solifluction terrace with several ponds. Another terrace is just beyond the small snowbanks near the left edge of the picture. To the right of Longs Peak is the large U–shaped valley of Glacier Gorge. The Keyboard of the Winds (a saw-toothed divide) is on the skyline to the right of the summit of Longs Peak.
(F. W. Osterwald)

TO THE ARCTIC IN COLORADO!

In addition to all that glaciers do directly to modify the scenery, other fascinating landscape changes related to glaciation result from Arctic-like climates in tundra-covered high mountain terrains near glaciers or the sites of former glaciers. These changes result from special effects called **periglacial** processes. They are unique to Alpine and Arctic regions.

Tundra is treeless land on which mosses, lichens, many low shrubs and perennial flowering plants grow. Most active tundra is marshy, and is underlain by dark, mucky soil. Much tundra covers perennially frozen ground or **permafrost**. Many periglacial processes combine to produce tundra. In fact, the chief differences between the Alpine tundra in Rocky Mountain National Park and lands above the Arctic circle are the much steeper angles at which sunlight strikes the ground in Colorado so that it warms the ground surface more efficiently.

Periglacial processes were very active on tundra areas in the National Park during the Ice Ages; many results of their action can be seen along Trail Ridge and Fall River Roads. Most periglacial features in the National Park bear individual and distinctive plant communities, and many are veritable gardens in summer (Willard, 1979). Periglacial features in the Park are relics of the Ice Ages, but most are now dormant. Where water is abundant some are still active, however (Richmond, 1974, p. 59-65). During the cold climates of the Great Ice Ages periglacial processes actually were at work on the Great Plains east of the National Park, on the Laramie Plains in southern Wyoming (Mears, 1987) and in North Park, Colorado at elevations much lower than our present mountain summits. Tundra probably existed in many places where these low–elevation periglacial processes worked.

Bouldery solifluction terraces on the southwest side of Sundance Mtn. from Forest Canyon Overlook in September 1987. Some of the boulders have moved downhill in ill-defined streams. The foregound is covered with solifluction mantle. (F. W. Osterwald)

Solifluction mantle on gently sloping ground along the Tundra World Nature Trail, July 1987.
(F. W. Osterwald)

The ground in tundra regions freezes perennially where snow or thick vegetation mats do not insulate it from the very cold air to create permafrost. Where the ground is insulated or if the uppermost layers of frozen ground thaw however, water saturates the thin soil covers. This saturated soil initiates one of the most important periglacial processes called **solifluction**. The wet ground is boggy and many specialized plants grow, so it stays green all summer.

If water from the upper melted layer of permafrost trickles downward into cracks in bedrock, millions of rocks are broken loose. When water freezes it expands about 9 percent, breaking the bedrock under the tundra in exactly the same way that glaciers quarry rocks from their cirques. These loosened rocks, together with the saturated soils, make up large fields of mixed rock and soil that characterize tundra. When soil around loose rocks thaws in the spring and summer, it mixes with water eventually becoming completely saturated. These soil-water mixtures flow downhill like slurries (solifluction) removing soil from around the rocks. Such mixtures of soil and loose rocks at and near the ground surfaces make up **solifluction mantle**. The rocks weather where they stick up above the ground; further freezing and thawing breaks off the sharp corners so they gradually become rounded boulders. Very old rocks become even more rounded as well as being broken into smaller and smaller pieces.

Separating soils from rocks by heaving and frost-sorting and removing the soil by solifluction produces new land forms that characterize Alpine tundra. When solifluction moves both rocks and soil downhill, many linear, wavy and lobate forms made up of soil and rock debris appear across the tundra slopes. If several "waves" of mostly fine grained solifluction debris flow downslope, the results are irregular mounds or long, narrow flats oriented across the tundra slopes. These mounds accumulate soil debris and water behind them, becoming **solifluction terraces**. If the debris lobes flow far enough and carry enough rocks from which the soils have been separated, they become rock glaciers which are end results of moving **block streams** and steeply sloping **felsenmeers**. When enough soil accumulates for tundra plants to grow, the actively growing turf generates force enough to shove rocks in the terrace slightly outward from the slope, producing **turf-banked terraces**. Turf-banked terraces are narrow, low ledges of turf trending diagonally across the slopes that are easily mistaken for animal trails. Excellent ones can be seen in the cirque just south of the Alpine Visitor Center on Fall River Pass. Locations of many periglacial features are in the individual road-guides.

Frost-sorting

Repeated episodes of freezing and thawing set up complicated vertical forces in the ground that lift loose rocks out of the soil, piling them on each other

Large solifluction terrace with pond, upper part of Ol Fall River Road. Alpine Visitor Center is on the skylin at the end of the road. August 1985.

at the surface, and tilting them at odd and unnatural angles. These processes are called **frost-heaving** or **up-freezing** (Anderson, 1988). The forces that lift them up, however, are very complex (Anderson, 1988; Washburn, 1956; Embleton and King, 1968, p. 485-567). Rocks actually are lifted out of the ground because the fine-grained soil around them expands when it freezes in winter, thus raising the blocks bodily along with masses of frozen soil. When the frozen soil thaws in the spring and summer it collapses about 9 percent in volume, leaving the rocks sticking up above the ground.

Up-freezing completely covers some level or gently sloping tundra ground with jumbled and tilted rocks forming **felsenmeers** (a very descriptive German word meaning "rock seas") that are also called rockfields. They are known as fellfields by botanists. An extensive felsenmeer covers much of the Tertiary age **welded ashflow tuff** (see p. 48, 107, 108) above Lava Cliffs. A good, though small, felsenmeer is just north of the Toll Memorial on Trail Ridge (Willard, 1979, p. 20). Another one is easily seen on the rather steep slope just below the Forest Canyon Overlook on Trail Ridge Road.

Patterned Ground

At sites where enough rocks are ejected from the ground onto surface slopes they may be channelled into stream-like lines trending downhill. These are called **block streams**, **rock slopes**, **rubble streams** or **rubble sheets** (Washburn, 1973). Some prominent narrow block streams line the steep mountainside north of Iceberg Lake, beside Lava Cliffs. Where rocks are segregated into broader roughly ribbon-like bands on slopes gentler than those on which block streams form, they comprise rock stripes.

Where loose rocks remain mixed with soil on gently sloping tundra, they may not be channelled into streams at all, but are re-arranged by up-freezing into sorted net-like, polygonal or roughly circular patterns on the surface that are called **rock nets**, **rock polygons**, **rock circles** or **rock garlands**. The rocks are shoved sideways by horizontal forces at the ground surface because they get colder much faster than the soil around them does. The cold at the bases of the rocks sets up these horizontal forces because the ground freezes and expands near the rocks pushing unfrozen soil away from the rocks (Embleton and King, 1968, p. 491-502). This process concentrates rock slabs with their long sides nearly vertical. Eventually the slabs fill shallow troughs that outline mounds covered by tundra plants (see photo p, 246).

If this confuses you, it should. Types of patterned ground are not sharply divided but instead make up a continuous series of forms ranging from solifluction mantle to rock stripes to rock streams to felsenmeers. One persons rock net may be someone else's rock garland. Even experts don't agree on the names of patterned ground features. Patterned ground is easy to see beside the parking lot at Rock Cut and along the Tundra World Nature Trail to the Toll Memorial, just north of Rock Cut (Richmond, 1974, p. 62), and on the slopes north and west of Lava Cliffs.

It Works Differently In Permafrost!

Different periglacial processes operate where the surface is underlain by permafrost. Masses of soil and rocks contract as they cool. When they contract at the start of winter they break, at first along very tiny cracks, because rock is easy to pull apart, but hard to crush. Rocks also contain natural cracks such as **joints** and layering planes. When water fills all these cracks and freezes, it expands in them, making the cracks longer and deeper by wedging the walls apart. More water from melted ice and snow trickles downward into the enlarged cracks in spring and summer. During winter the ice expands again. Thus ice gradually shoves the walls of the cracks farther and farther apart. With the passage of years the cracks connect, dividing both the soil and rock into large polygon-shaped blocks. This process is called i**ce wedging** and the blocks it produces are called i**ce-wedge polygons**. Some ice-wedge polygons in the Front Range are as much as 75 feet across (Benedict, 1979, p. 173), but elsewhere in the world some are as broad as 300 feet.

How To Make a Cirque

Deep snowdrifts pile up wherever shallow depressions or small gullies in the tundra are favorably oriented with respect to prevailing winter wind directions. If these drifts are so deep that some snow stays on the ground all summer, soils and rocks beneath them are slowly sorted by **nivation** (Mathes, 1900, p. 181) a periglacial process somewhat similar to solifluction.

When some of the snow melts around the edges of large drifts during spring and summer, the soil becomes so water-soaked that mixtures of water and tiny soil particles begin flowing away from the edges of the snowdrifts, leaving behind the rocks. As in the creation of felsenmeers these rocks at first are surrounded by water-soaked soil that freezes and expands during winters and in cold summer nights but because the snow partially insulates the rocks from cold air, they are gradually shoved downhill from beneath the perennial snowbanks. The rocks pile up at the downhill edges of the drifts and the soil flows away, gradually leaving small **nivation depressions** under the drifts. As the depressions deepen because so many rocks and so much soil are removed from them, even more snow collects in the hollows. The soil-water mixtures flow away from the snowdrifts to form solifluction terraces downhill from the depressions.

Nivation depressions may be the birthplaces of some cirques, but many don't become cirques. However, when the snowdrifts are deep enough and the process continues long enough, the rock piles become so high that they resemble small moraines. If enough snow accumulates in nivation depressions so that it does not melt during the summers, the snow eventually becomes ice and the drifts may become first ice fields and then small glaciers. The rocks in the piles, now moraines, then become tools for the glaciers, and the nivation depressions are on their way to becoming cirques.

A large nivation depression is on the north side of Trail Ridge Road at Little Rock Cut. In another depression along the north side of Trail Ridge Road at Toll Pass (Willard, 1979, p. 42) active nivation creates **frost boils** and small pools of water in the summertime.

Frost boils are places where mixtures of excess water and soil, liberated during spring thawing, soften the ground, creating a local quagmire. Freezing and thawing of soil-water mixtures in the boils causes a slow churning action that builds mounds and initiates frost-sorting. Where the ground surface is not insulated by mats of plants frost-boils build low mounds. Where there is a mat of insulating plants, frost boils are flat, bare spots surrounded by rings of rocks that are separated from the soil by frost-sorting. Inactive frost boils become patches of bare ground called frost scars.

This large solifluction terrace on the north side of Iceberg Pass on Trail Ridge Road contains a pond through most summers and the grass is green until early fall. The hump along the downhill side of the terrace contains a few small frost scars. Clumps of arctic willows in the middle distance grow on other terraces. Two curving lines of green willows in the left center of the picture mark possible faults with Miocene or post-Miocene movement. View northward into Fall River valley. Mummy Range is on the right skyline. June 1987.

Rock nets formed from granite bedrock beside the Tundra World Nature Trail at the Rock Cut parking area on Trail Ridge Road, June 1987. (F. W. Osterwald)

Block stream formed from welded ash-flow tuff bedrock on the north slope of the summit above Lava Cliffs, June 1987.

(F. W. Osterwald)

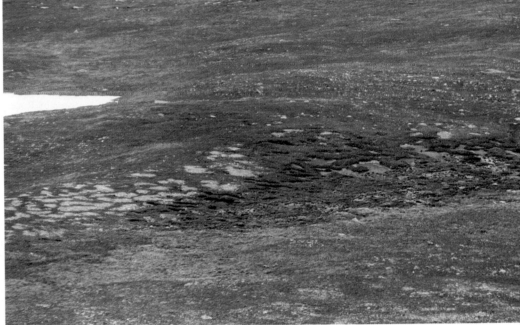

Rock streams, rock garlands, and a solifluction lobe formed on welded ash-flow tuff bedrock near the top of the north slope of the summit above Lava Cliffs. The contact of the tuff with Precambrian granite bedrock is just beyond the light-colored block stream in the middle ground which is made up of granite blocks. Active frost boils (bare reddish-spots) are in the foreground. June 1987.

(F. W. Osterwald)

View eastward from Toll Memorial Overlook on the Tundra World Nature Trail, showing a large solifluction terrace with numerous small ponds and frost boils (patches of bare ground). The snowbank is melting in a small nivation depression. June 1987.

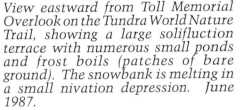

An active frost boil about 1 foot in its longest dimension, near the summit above Lava Cliffs. The small pieces of rock are being slowly ejected from the interior of the boil. June 1987.

(F. W. Osterwald)

A trip over Trail Ridge Road introduces one to nearly the entire span of geologic time as it is now known in Rocky Mountain National Park. The hard rocks underlying nearly all of Trail Ridge are ancient Precambrian granites, gneisses and schists. Precambrian faults offset these rocks in Forest Canyon and cut the "Iron Dike" at several places on Trail Ridge. Tertiary volcanic rocks cap Lava Ciffs, Specimen Mountain and the hills around Milner Pass. Miocene faults cut the Precambrian rocks near Forest Canyon Overlook. Glacial and periglacial features abound in all directions. As a late act in the play, periglacial features (solifluction terraces) eithcr found some of these Miocene faults good places in which to work or were offset by renewed fault movements during the Pleistocene Epoch. Landslides on Jackstraw Mountain probably are still active, and the alluvial fan in Horseshoe Park was formed in 1982. Only Paleozoic and Mesozoic rocks are missing.

248

GEOLOGY REFERENCES

Albanese, J. P., 1988, Overview: Geologic factors related to PaleoIndian site distribution in the northwestern plains [abs.]: Geol. Soc. America Abstracts With Programs, v. 20, n. 7, 1988 Annual Meeting, p. A136.

Allison, I. S., and Palmer, D. F., 1980, Geology: 7th Ed., McGraw Hill Book Co., New York, 579 p.

Anderson, Suzanne P., 1988, The upfreezing process: Experiments with a single clast, Geol. Soc. America, Bull. v. 100, p. 609-621.

Anonymous, 1986, News notes, in Geotimes, v. 31, p. 22-27.

Atkins, D. Ferrel, unpublished files in Rocky Mountain National Park library.

Barry, J. C., Johnson, N. M., Raza, S. M., and Jacobs, L.L., 1985, Neogene mammalian faunal change in southern Arizona: Correlations with climatic, tectonic, and eustatic events: Geology, v. 13, p. 637-640.

Beget, J. E., 1983, Radiocarbon-dated evidence of world-wide early Holocene climate change: Geology, v. 11, p. 389-393.

Benedict, J. B., 1968, Recent glacial history of an alpine area in the Colorado Front Range, U.S.A., pt. II, Dating the glacial deposits: Jour. of Glaciology: v. 7, p. 77-87.

_____, 1973, Chronology of cirque glaciation, Colorado Front Range: Quaternary Research, v. 3, p. 584-599.

_____, 1978, Getting away from it all: A study of man, mountains, and the two-drought Altithermal: Symposium on Colorado archaeology, Plains Archaeol. Assoc., 36th Ann. Mtg, Denver, Colo.

_____, 1979, Fossil ice-wedge polygons in the Colorado Front Range: Origin and significance: Geol. Soc. America Bull., Pt. 1, v. 90, p. 173-180.

_____, 1985, Old Man Mountain: Center for Mountain Archaeology, Res. Rept. No. 4, Ward, Colo., 39 p.

Birkeland, P. W., Crandell, D. R., and Richmond, G. M., 1971, Status of correlation of Quaternary stratigraphic units in the western conterminous United States: Quaternary Res., v. 1, p. 298-227.

Blackwelder, Eliot, 1915, Post-Cretaceous history of the mountains of central western Wyoming: Jour. Geology, v. 23, p. 97-117, 193-217.

_____, 1934, The building of the Colorado Rockies: Geol. Soc America Bull., v. 45.

Braddock, W. A., 1970, The origin of slaty cleavage: Evidence from Precambrian rocks in Colorado: Geol. Soc. America Bull., v. 90, pt. 1, p. 739-752.

Buchhholtz, C. W., 1983, Rocky Mountain National Park, a history: Colo. Associated Univ. Press, Boulder, Colo., 256 p.

Cairns, M. L., 1971, Grand Lake in the olden days: The World Press, Denver, 308 p.

Cargo, D. N., 1978, Exploring Rocky Mountain National Park: David N. Cargo, printed by Johnson Publishing Co., Boulder, Colo., 80 p.

Carrara, Paul E., l986, written communication.

Cassels, E. S., 1983, The archaeology of Colorado: Johnson Books, Boulder, Colo., 325 p.

Chamberlin, R. T., 1919, The building of the Colorado Rockies: Jour. Geology, v. 27, p. 145-164, 225-251.

Colman, S. E., and Pierce, K. L., 1981, Weathering rinds on andesitic and basaltic stones as a Quaternary age indicator, western United States: U.S. Geol. Survey Prof. Paper 1210, 56 p.

Corbett, M. K., 1966, The Tertiary volcanism of the Specimen–Lulu–Iron Mountain area, north-central Colorado, in Cenozoic volcanism in the southern Rocky Mountains, Epis, R. C., ed.: Colo. School of Mines Quart., v. 63, no.3, p. 51-85.

Custer, G. A., 1874, My life on the Plains: Univ. of Neb. Press, Lincoln, Neb. (repr. 1962), 626 p.

Dennis, Andy, and Potton, Craig, 1984, The alpine world of Mount Cook National Park: Cobb/Howard Pubs, Auckland, New Zealand, 96 p.

De Voto, R. H., 1980, Mississippian stratigraphy and history of Colorado, in Colorado Geology: Rocky Mtn. Assoc. Geologists, Denver, p. 71-101.

Eckel, E. B., 1961, Minerals of Colorado a 100-year record: U.S. Geol. Survey Bull.1114, 399 p.

Epis, R. C., Scott, G. R., Taylor, R. B., and Chapin, C. E., 1980, Summary of Cenozoic geomorphic, volcanic, and tectonic features of central Colorado and adjoining areas, in Kent, H. C., and Porter K. W., eds., Colorado geology: Rocky Mtn. Assoc. of Geologists, Denver, Colo., p. 135-156.

Elias, S. A., 1983, Paleoenvironmental interpretations of Holocene insect fossil assemblages from the La Poudre Pass site, northern Colorado Front Range: Paleogeography, Paleoclimatology, Paleoecology, v. 41, p. 87-102.

Embleton, Clifford, and King, C. A. M., 1968, Glacial and periglacial geomorphology: Edward Arnold (Publishers), Ltd,, printed by Robert Cunningham and Sons, Ltd., Alva, Scotland, 607 p.

Fell, Barry, 1982, Bronze age America: Little, Brown and Co., Boston, Mass., 304 p.

Fenneman, N. H., 1931, Physiography of western United States: McGraw–Hill Book C., Inc., New York, 534 p.

Fuller, M. B., 1923, The physiographic development of the Big Thompson River valley in Colorado: Jour. Geology, v. 31, p. 126-137.

_____, 1925, Early Quaternic drainage diversions around Mount Olympus, Colorado: Pan-American Geologist, v. 43, p. 51-54.

Haynes, C. V., Jr., 1985, Response to presentation of the Archaeological Geology Award to C. Vance Haynes, Jr.: Geol. Soc. America Bull., v. 96, p. 1199-1200.

Holland, F. R., Jr., 1971, Rocky Mountain National Park, historical background data: Unpub. Report in Rocky Mtn., Natl. Park files, 87 p.

Husted, W. M., 1965, Early occupation of the Colorado Front Range: American Antiquities, v. 30, n. 4, p. 494-498.

Jones, W. D., and Quam, L. O., 1944, Glacial land forms in Rocky Mountain National Park, Colorado: Jour. Geology, v. 52, p. 217-234.

Lee, W. T.,1917, The geologic story of the Rocky Mountain National Park: Natl. Park Service, Washington, D. C., 89 p.

_____, 1922, Peneplains of the Front Range and Rocky Mountain National Park, Colorado: U. S. Geol. Survey Bull. 730A, 17 p.

Leet, L. D., and Judson, Sheldon, 1965, Physical geology: 3rd Ed., Prentice-Hall, Inc., Englewood Cliffs, New Jersey, 406 p.

Little, H. P., 1925, Erosional cycles in the Front Range of Colorado and their correlation: Geol. Soc. America Bull., v. 36, p. 495-512.

Lovering, T. S., 1929, Geologic history of the Front Range, Colorado: Colo. Sci. Soc. Proc., v. 12. p. 59-111.

Lovering, T. S., and Goddard, E. N., Geology and ore deposits of the Front Range, Colorado: U. S. Geol. Survey Prof. Paper 223, 319 p.

Madole, R. F., 1976a, Bog stratigraphy, radiocarbon dates, and Pinedale to Holocene glacial history in the Front Range, Colorado: U. S. Geol. Survey, Jour. Research, v. 4, p. 163-169.

_____, 1976b, Glacial geology of the Front Range, Colorado: in Mahaney, W. C., ed., Quaternary stratigraphy of North America: Dowden, Ross and Co., Stroudsburg, Pa.

_____, 1980, Time of Pinedale deglaciation in north-central Colorado: Further considerations: Geology, v. 8, p. 118-122.

_____, 1982, Possible origins of till-like deposits near the summit of the Front Range in north-central Colorado: U.S. Geol. Survey Prof. Paper 1243, 31 p.

Mahaney, W. C., 1972, Audubon: New name for Colorado Front Range Neoglacial deposits formerly called "Arikaree": Arctic and Alpine Research, v. 4, p. 355-357.

Mathes, F. E., 1900, Glacial sculpture of the Bighorn Mountains, Wyoming: U.S. Geol. Survey, 21st Ann. Rept,, p. 173-190.

Maughan, E. K., 1980, Permian and Lower Triassic geology of Colorado, in Colorado Geology: Rocky Mtn. Assoc. Geologists, Denver, p. 103-110.

Mears, Brainerd, Jr., undated, Evolution of the Rocky Mountain glacial model, in Coates, D. R., ed., Glacial Geomorphology: Geomorphic Symposia Series at Binghampton Proc., Pubs. in Geomorphology, State Univ. of New York, Binghampton, N. Y.

_____, 1987, Late Pleistocene periglacial wedge sites in Wyoming: Geol. Survey of Wyo., Mem. 8, 77 p.

Meierding, T. C., 1977, Age differentiation of till and gravel deposits in the upper Colorado River basin: Univ. of Colorado, Ph. D. thesis, 353 p.

_____, and Birkeland, P. W., 1980, Quaternary glaciation of Colorado, in Kent, H. C.,and Porter, K. W., 1980, Colorado geology: Rocky Mountain Association of Geologists, Denver, Colo., p. 165-177.

Mitchell, J. M., 1965, Theoretical paleoclimatology, in Wright, H. E., and Frey, D. G., eds., The Quaternary of the United States: Princeton Univ. Press, Princeton, N.J., p. 881-901.

Moss, J. A., 1951, Late glacial advances in the southern Wind River Mountains, Wyoming: American Journal of Science, v. 249, p. 865-883.

Musselman, L. K., 1971, Rocky Mountain National Park administrative history, 1915-1965: Natl. Park Service, Open-file Rept., 235 p.

Obermiller, Tim, 1989, A delicate balance, Univ. of Chicago Mag., v. 81, n. 3, p. 14-19.

Osterwald, F. W., Maberry, J. O, and Dunrud, C. R., 1981, Bedrock, surficial, and economic geology of the Sunnyside coal-mining district, Carbon and Emery counties, Utah: U.S. Geol Survey Prof. Paper 1166, 68 p.

Outcalt, S. L., 1965, The regimen of the Andrews Glacier in Rocky Mountain National Park, Colorado, 1957-1963: Water Resources Research, v. 1, p. 273-282.

_____, 1965, A survey of Neo-glaciation in the Front Range of Colorado: Colo. Univ. Studies, Ser. in Earth Sci., n. 2, 123 p.

Pearson, R. C., 1980, Mineral resources of the Indian Peaks study area, Boulder and Grand Counties, Colorado: U. S. Geol. Survey, Bull. 1463, 109 p.

Pettijohn, F. J., 1949, Sedimentary rocks: Harper & Brothers, New York, 596 p.

Richmond, G. M., 1960, Glaciation of the east slope of Rocky Mountain National Park, Colorado: Geol. Soc. America Bull., v. 71, p. 1371-1383.

_____, 1962, Three Pre-Bull Lake tills in the Wind River Mountains, Wyoming, in Geol. Survey Research, 1962, U.S. Geol. Survey Prof. Paper 450D, p. 132-135.

_____, 1964 Three Pre-Bull Lake tills in the Wind River Mountains, Wyoming—a reinterpretation, in Geol. Survey Research, 1964, U.S. Geol. Survey Prof. Paper 501D, p. D104-D109.

_____, 1965, Glaciation of the Rocky Mountains, in Wright, H. E., Jr., and Frey, D. G., The Quaternary of the United States: Princeton Univ. Press, Princeton, N. J., p. 217- 230.

_____, 1972, Appraisal of the future climate of the Holocene in the Rocky Mountains: Quaternary Research, v. 2, p. 315-322.

_____, 1974, Raising the roof of the Rockies: Rocky Mountain Nature Assoc., Estes Park, Colo., 81 p.

Ritter, D. F., 1978, Process geomorphology: W. C. Brown Co., Dubuque, Iowa, 603 p.

Rocky Mountain Nature Association, 1959, Glaciers in Rocky Mountain National Park: Rocky Mtn. Nature Assoc., Estes Park, Colo., 15 p.

Ross, R. J., and Tweto, Ogden, 1980, Lower Paleozoic sediments and tectonics in Colorado, in Colorado Geology: Rocky Mtn. Assoc. Geologists, Denver, p. 47-56.

Sara, W. A., 1973, The glaciers, in McCaskill, L. W., ed., West-land National Park (3rd Ed.), Pegasus Press, Christchurch, New Zealand, 71 p.

_____, 1979, Glaciers of Westland National Park, 2nd Ed: E. C. Keating, Government Printer, Wellington, New Zealand, 52 p.

Stone, G. H., 1887, A live glacier on Hagues Peak, Colo.: Science, v. 10, p. 153, 154.

Stupovsky, Michel, and Gravenor, C. P., 1974, Water release from the base of active glaciers: Geol. Soc. America Bull., v. 85, p. 433-436.

Swiss National Tourist Office, 1984, Switzerland's glaciers: magnificent masses of ice: written communication 3 p.

Taylor, R. B., Theobald, P. K., and Izett, G. A., 1968, Mid-Tertiary volcanism in the central Front Range, Colorado, in Cenozoic volcanism in the southern Rocky Mountains, Epis, R.C, ed: Colo. School of Mines Quart., v. 63, no. 3 p. 39-50.

Trimble, D. E., 1980, The geologic story of the Great Plains: U.S. Geol. Survey Bull. 1493, 55 p.

Trimble, Stephen, 1984, Longs Peak, a Rocky Mountain chronicle: Rocky Mtn. Nature Assoc., Estes Park, Colo., 112 p.

Tweto, Ogden (Comp.), 1979, Geologic Map of Colorado: U.S. Geol. Survey Map, Scale 1:500,000.

_____, 1980, The tectonic history of Colorado, in Colorado Geology: Rocky Mtn. Assoc. Geologists, Denver, p. 5-9.

_____, 1980, Precambrian geology of Colorado, in Colorado Geology: Rocky Mtn. Assoc. Geologists, Denver, p. 37-46.

_____, 1980, Summary of Laramide orogeny in Colorado, in Colorado Geology: Rocky Mtn. Assoc. Geologists, Denver, p. 129-134.

U.S. Geological Survey, 1974, Permafrost: Information Leaflet, Washington, 8 p.

Van Tuyl, F. M., and Lovering, T. S., 1935, Physiographic development of the Front Range: Geol. Soc. America Bull., v. 46, p. 96-108.

Wahlstrom, E. E.,, 1947, Cenozoic physiographic history of the Front Range, Colorado: Geol. Soc. America Bull., v. 58, p. 551-572.

_____, 1956, Petrology and weathering of the Iron Dike, Boulder and Larimer Counties, Colorado: Geol. Soc. America Bull., v. 67, p. 147-163.

Warner, L. A., 1980, The Colorado lineament, *in* Colorado Geology: Rocky Mtn. Assoc. Geologists, Denver, p. 11-21.

Washburn, A. L., 1956, Classification of patterned ground and review of suggested origins: Geol. Soc. America Bull., v. 67, p. 823-866.

_____, 1973, Periglacial processes and environments: St. Martin's Press, New York, N. Y., 320 p.

Walder, Joseph, and Hallett, Bernard, 1985, A theoretical model of the fracture of rock during freezing: Geol. Soc. America Bull. v. 96, p. 336-346.

Wegemann, C. H., 1944, A guide to the geology of Rocky Mountain National Park: Natl. Park Service, Washington, D.C., 32 p.

Weimer, R. J., 1980, Recurrent movement on basement faults, a tectonic style for Colorado and adjacent areas, *in* Colorado Geology: Rocky Mtn. Assoc. Geologists, Denver, p. 23-35.

White, S. E., 1971, Rock glacier studies in the Colorado Front Range, 1961 to 1968: Arctic and Alpine Research, v. 3, n. 1, p. 43-64.

Wick, Peter, 1981, Traces of the Ice Ages, *in* Kassev, Peter, and Haeberli, Wilfried, eds., Switzerland and her glaciers: Kummerly and Frey, Geographical Publishers, Berne, Switzerland, p. 10-25.

Willard, B. E., 1979, Plant sociology of alpine tundra, Trail Ridge, Rocky Mountain National Park, Colorado: Colorado School of Mines Quarterly, v. 74, n. 4, 119 p.

Zumbuhl, Heinz, Budmiger, Georg, and Haeberli, Wilfried, 1981, Historical documents, *in* Kasser, Peter, and Haeberli, Wilfried, eds., Switzerland and her glaciers: Kummerly and Frey, Geog. Publishers, Berne, Switzerland, p. 48-69.

NATURE

"I never see a little tree bursting forth from the earth, peeping confidently up among the withered leaves, without wondering how long it will live, what trials and triumphs it will have. I always hope that it will be a home for birds. I always hope that it will find life worth living, and that it will live long to better and beautify the earth."

——Enos A, Mills, <u>Your National Parks</u>, 1917.

LIFE ZONES

In addition to its magnificent scenery, spectacular geology and fascinating history, Rocky Mountain National Park is also blessed with abundant plants, mammals and birds that live in distinct communities termed **life zones**. These zones are distinctive assemblages of plants and animals that have achieved a balance between local climate and elevation. The Park contains three of the six life zones in Colorado. The **montane life zone** extends from about 6000 ft. to 9000 ft. in elevation. The **subalpine life zone** extends from about 9000 ft. to upper **treeline** (the elevation above which no trees grow regardless of their size or shape), which at this latitude is between 11,400 ft. and 11,500 ft. The **alpine tundra life zone** is above upper treeline. In this part of Colorado, the elevation of upper treeline is about 11,400 ft. and lower treeline is about 5600 ft. The commonly used term **timberline** refers to the upper elevational limit of continuous subalpine forests with upright trees (Mutel and Emerick, 1984, p. 229).

Major species of trees delineate zonal boundaries; these boundaries are not sharp, so the zones merge and overlap each other. Many plants and animals live in more than one zone but the critical features of each zone are the assemblages.

Many factors, in addition to climate and elevation, affect the growth of plant and animal communities. Soil type, slope conditions, topography, moisture, humidity, wind and temperature also change the balance between climate and elevation. Some plants and animals thrive in wet, moist areas; others prefer dry, sunny slopes. Wind direction and velocity affect plant growth in many ways. Near treeline (commonly called "timberline") the spruces and firs are dwarfed and mis-shapened by fierce winds and short growing seasons. Changes from one zone to another are easier to observe in the mountains than they are on the Plains because one can quickly go from one zone into another by going up or down in elevation.

Within each life zone, various **ecosystems** comprise specific biological differences. Thus we find ponderosa pine, Douglas fir, aspen and lodgepole pine forest ecosystems within the montane zone. Also within the montane zone are mountain meadows, grasslands and streambank (riparian) ecosystems. Each ecosystem attracts and supports a wide, but distinct, variety of plants, birds, insects and mammals. Commonly, the north-facing slope of a valley supports a different ecosystem from that found on an opposite south-facing slope.

Engelmann spruce and subalpine fir forests dominate the subalpine zone, but limber and lodgepole pines also grow there. These forests are very important because they accumulate much snow. Mountain meadow and streambank ecosystems in the subalpine zone provide ample food and nesting material and thus help sustain large and diverse animal communities.

Between the **subalpine** and **alpine tundra zones** is a narrow, discontinuous zone of stunted, gnarled and windswept trees that make up what is called the **forest-tundra transition life zone**. This zone of **krummholz** trees has a wide variety of plants because the two zones overlap and species are intermixed.

The **alpine tundra life zone** is a very special part of Rocky Mountain National Park. The drive across Trail Ridge offers one a chance to experience Arctic-like vistas and climate without traveling northward thousands of miles. Within this mountaintop zone are ecosystems of alpine meadows, areas of open treeless rock-strewn ground (**fellfields**), depressions and hollows where heavy snows accumulate forming boggy areas around **solifluction terraces** and small ponds. Each of these distinctive ecosystems attracts plants that are specially adapted for survival in the extreme alpine climatic conditions. Each ecosystem offers unique discoveries for its visitors.

The flora and fauna in the Park have been extensively studied. Many excellent books describe in detail the plants, mammals and birds. Suggested references are on p. 255; each is highly recommended. Those marked with an asterisk are particularly useful in identifying wildflowers, trees, birds and mammals in the field.

IDENTIFYING CONIFERS

Conifers are quite easy to identify because the leaves (needles) and cones of one genus are quite different from other genera. **Pines** have needles gathered together at the base (in clusters of two to five) bound into little sheaths that commonly wear off after the first year's growth. The cones contain seeds in their thick, overlapping woody scales.

Spruce needles are scattered over the twigs singly, are sharp-pointed and four-sided. When the needles fall from the twigs, they leave roughened surfaces like small vegetable graters. Cones hang downward like pendents and have parchment-like scales.

Firs have flat, blunt needles that leave smooth round scars on the twigs when they fall off. Cones in Douglas firs are numerous and hang like pendents. Subalpine firs have fewer cones that grow erect and cluster near the tops of the trees.

Junipers have needles that are subdivided into tiny segments resembling scales. These are from 1/2 to 1 inch long and attached closely to twigs. Cones look like small bluish berries.

IDENTIFICATION KEY FOR CONIFERS

To use the key, start with 1A and follow the numbers as directed.

1A. If the needles are 1 inch long or longer, and the seeds are in cones, go to — — — — — — — — — — — — —2

  B. If the needles look like scales less than 1 inch long, and the seeds are in berries go to— — — — — **11**

2A. If the needles are in bundles of two to five, go to — — — — — — — — — — — — — — — — — — — - **3**

  B. If the needles are single, go to —7

3A. If the needles are in bundles of two or three, go to — — — — — — — — — — — — — — — — **4**

  B. If the needles are in bundles of five, go to — — — — — — — — — — — — — — — — **6**

4A. If the needles are 3 to 6 inches long, mostly in bundles of three or two; cones are 3 to 5 inches long; and the bark is reddish-brown on mature trees, the tree is a — — — — — — — — — — — **PONDEROSA PINE**

(Pinus ponderosa)
Up to 150 ft. tall.

  B. If the needles are 3/4 to 3 inches long, mostly in bundles of two, go to — — — — — — — — — —5

5. If the needles are yellow-green, in bundles of two, 1 1/2 to 3 inches long; the tree is tall and slender with thin bark; cones are 1 1/2 to 3 inches long that remain on the branches for years without opening or dropping their seeds, the tree is a — — — — — — — — — — — — — — — — **LODGEPOLE PINE**

(Pinus contorta var. *latifolia)*
Up to 100 ft. tall.

6. If the needles are in bundles of five, from 1 1/2 to 3 inches long, slender, long-pointed, not toothed; the cones are from 4 to 10 inches long and do not have bristles; the bark is smooth and silvery gray on young trees, grayish black on mature trees, the tree is a — — — — — — — — — — — — — — — — **LIMBER PINE**

(Pinus flexilis)
Up to 80 ft. tall.

7A. If the needles are stiff, four-sided, (not rounded) and sharp pointed, go to— — — — — — — — — — — **8.**

   B. If the needles are not stiff, flat, nor sharp-pointed, go to – — — — — — — — — — — — — **9.**

8A. If the needles are very stiff, sharp and green to silvery gray-green; the cones are 2 1/2 to 4 inches long; and the tree has dark gray bark, it is a– — — — — — — — — — — — — **COLORADO BLUE SPRUCE**

(Picea pungens)
Up to 100 ft. tall.

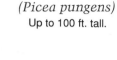

   B. If the needles are dark green but not as stiff and sharp as **8A**; the cones are 1 to 3 inches long; and the main trunk is smooth and a clean, cinnamon-brown color, the tree is an — — — — — — — —

ENGELMANN SPRUCE
(Picea engelmannii)
Up to 125 ft. tall.

9. If the needles are dark green; the 1-1/2 to 3-inch cones hang down and three-pointed bracts stick out be tween the cone scales, the tree is a — — — — — — — — — — — — — — — — — — **DOUGLAS FIR**

(Pseudotsuga menziesii)
Up tp 100 ft. tall

10. If the needles are about 1 inch long and tend to turn upward so the foliage appears flattened on branches; the 3- to 4-inch purplish-brown cones stand up; the grayish-white bark is smooth, the tree is a — — — — — —

SUBALPINE FIR
(Abies lasiocarpa)
From 60 to 100 ft. tall.

11A. If the conifer is a shrub less than 3 ft. high, has sharp, prickly needles at the ends of the branches and the branches have white lines down them, it is a —————————— **DWARF JUNIPER**
(Juniperus communis)

B. If the tree is as much as 20 ft. tall, and most of the needles are divided into tiny segments (like scales) and are flattened against the branchlets, it is a ——— **ROCKY MOUNTAIN JUNIPER**
(Juniperus scopulorum)

SELECTED NATURE REFERENCES
* indicates excellent field references

Alberts, E. C., 1963, Rocky Mountain National Park, Colorado: U.S. Dept. of Interior, Washington, D.C., 66 p.

* Armstrong, D. M., 1987, Rocky Mountain mammals, a handbook of mammals of Rocky Mountain National Park and vicinity, Rocky Mtn. Nature Assoc., Estes Park, Colo., 224 p.

Baerg, H. J., 1955, How to know the western trees: Wm. C. Brown Co., Dubuque, Iowa, 170 p.

Beidleman, R. G., 1979, Rocky Mountain National Park: Rocky Mtn. Nature Assoc., Estes Park, Colo., 12 p.

* Collister, Allegra, 1970, Birds of Rocky Mountain National Park, Mus. Pictorial no. 18, Denver Mus. of Nat. Hist., Denver, Colo., 68 p.

Kalmbach, Kathryn and others, 1988, The search for our botanical legacy in Rocky Mountain National Park: The Green Thumb, v. 45, no. 1, Denver Botanic Gardens, p. 16-23.

* Marinos, Nic, and Marinos, Helen, 1981, Plants of the alpine tundra: Rocky Mtn. Nature Assoc., Estes Park, Colo., 65 p.

* Mutel, C. F., and Emerick, J. C., 1984, From grassland to glacier: Johnson Books, Boulder, Colo., 238 p.

Nelson, R. A., 1969, Handbook of Rocky Mountain plants: Dale Stuart, Tucson, Ariz., 134 p.

* _____, 1970, Plants of Rocky Mountain National Park: Rocky Mtn. Nature Assoc., Estes Park, Colo., 168 p.

* Pesman, M. W., 1967, Meet the natives: 7th rev. Ed., Denver Botanic Garden, Denver, Colo., 219 p.

* _____, 1988, Meet the natives: 8th Ed., Denver Botanic Gardens, Denver, Colo., 237 p.

* Russo, Ron, and Olhausen, Pam, 1987, Mammal finder: Nature Study Guild, Berkeley, Calif., 93 p.

Shattil, Wendy, Rozinske, Bob, and Titlow, Budd, 1986, Rocky Mountain National Park beyond Trail Ridge: Westcliffe Publishing Inc., Englewood, Colo., 80 p.

Smithson, Michael, 1986, Rocky Mountain, the story behind the scenery: Kc Publications, Las Vegas, Nev, 48 p.

Torbit, S. C., 1987, Large mammals of the central Rockies: Bennet Creek Publications, Monte Vista, Colo., 71 p.

Trimble, Stephen, 1984, Longs Peak, a Rocky Mountain chronicle: Rocky Mtn. Nature Assoc., Estes Park, Colo., 112 p.

U.S. Department of Agriculture, undated, Trees native to the forests of Colorado and Wyoming: Washington, D.C., 24 p.

* Weber, W. A., 1976, Rocky Mountain flora: Colo. Associated Univ. Press, Boulder, Colo., 484 p.

* Whitney, Stephen, 1985, Western forests: Adoph Knopf, New York, N. Y., 672 p.

* Willard B. E., and Smithson, Michael, 1988, Alpine wildflowers of the Rocky Mountains: Rocky Mtn. Nature Assoc., Estes Park Colo., 40 p.

* Zwinger, A. H., and Willard, B. E., 1972, Land above the trees: Harper & Row, New York, N. Y., 489 P.

GLOSSARY

Definitions are from Stokes, L. L., and Varnes, D. J., 1955, Glossary of selected geologic terms: Colo. Sci. Soc., Proc. v.16, 165 p.; from Gary, Margaret, McAfee, Robert, Jr., and Wolf, C. L., eds., 1971,Glossary of Geology: Amer. Geol. Inst., Washington, D.C., 857 p.; and from Mutel, C. R., and Emerick, J. C., 1984, From grassland to glacier: Johnson Books, Boulder, Colo., 238 p.

adit, n. A horizontal entrance into a mine.

albite, n. A mineral that is essentially a silicate of aluminum and sodium.

alluvial fan, n. A sloping fan-shaped mass of loose rock debris deposited by a stream or flood where it issues from a narrow mountain valley onto a plain or broad valley.

alpine, adj. Characteristic of or resembling the European Alps or any high mountainous region, especially mountainous regions above timberline (treeline).

alpine glacier, n. Any glacier in a mountain range originating in a cirque and flowing down a valley, except those that are **ice caps** or **ice sheets.**

alpine tundra life zone n. A community of plants and animals living above treeline. In the Park this averages between 11,400 ft. and 11,500 ft.

augite, n. A common rock-forming mineral regarded as a mixture of complex calcium, iron, magnesium and aluminum silicates. It is black or greenish-black in color.

bedrock, n. Solid, undisturbed rock uncovered by erosion or which is beneath only surficial gravel, sand or soil.

block stream, n. An accumulation of large rock fragments in a valley bottom or on a slope along which it moves or has moved slowly under its own weight or aided by frost action.

boulder, n. A detached piece of rock larger than a volleyball.

cirque, n. A steep-walled, scoop-shaped depression high on the side of a mountain caused by headward erosion by a mountain (alpine) glacier.

clay, n. (1) "Clay" as a rock is a fine-grained aggregate consisting wholly or dominantly of microscopic and submicroscopic mineral particles derived from the decomposition of rocks. It is plastic when wet and hard when dry, largely because it contains **clay minerals.** (2) "Clay" as a size term refers to rock or mineral particles less than $1/_{256}$ mm in their longest dimension.

clay minerals, n. A large group of naturally occurring hydrous aluminum silicates that break down into colloidal, extremely minute shreds or flaky particles.

climax ecosystem, n. A final, self-perpetuating community of plants and animals that live in a specific climate under specific soil and water conditions that will persist as long as the same living conditions prevail.

cobble, n. A detached piece of rock between a tennis ball and a volleyball in size.

conglomerate, n. Consolidated gravel. The contained rock and mineral pieces may be of varied types, and are rounded and smoothed by transportation by water or from wave action.

contact, n. The surface between two different kinds or ages of rock. When shown on maps, contacts are the lines bounding rock units.

continental glacier, n. A huge, thick mass of ice that covers a large part of a continent. Syn. *continental ice sheet.*

diabase, n. A dark-colored igneous rock whose essential minerals are plagioclase and augite. The plagioclase crystals are long, narrow and lath-like, and are oriented in all directions; **augite** fills the spaces between the plagioclase laths.

dike, n. A sheet-like body of igneous rock filling a fissure in older rocks which it entered as a molten fluid. The fissure cuts across the structure of the older rock.

ecosystem, n. A system made up of a plant and animal community and the physical–chemical environment with which it is interrelated.

end moraine, n. A moraine produced at the lower or outer end of an actively flowing glacier.

erratic, n. A rock fragment, usually of large size, that was transported from a distant source by glacial ice.

esker, n. A long, narrow, sinuous ridge of mixed sand and gravel, considered to have been deposited by a stream of water flowing through crevasses and tunnels in a stagnant glacier.

exfoliation, n. The breaking off or spalling off of thin nearly concentric shells from rock surfaces as a result of changing temperature, of freezing and thawing, of chemical and physical reaction, or of the release of forces stored in the rock.

fault (zone), n. A break or breaks in rock along which movement has taken place.

fault gouge, n. Finely ground, mud-like material that fills or partly fills a fault or fault zone.

fellfield, n. Open, treeless, rock-strewn ground that is above treeline with sparce vegetation. Also called "stone field" or "boulder field."

felsenmeer, n. A German word meaning "rock sea," referring to a land surface covered with a continous veneer of large, angular and subangular blocks of rock that were derived from underlying bedrock by intensive periglacial frost action. Usually formed on tundra at high elevations or high latitudes, on gently sloping or flat surfaces, but may also form on moderately steep slopes under favorable conditions. Also called "block field."

floodplain, n. The surface or strip of smooth land adjacent to a river channel, constructed by the present river and covered by water in times of high water.

fold, n. A bend or flexure in a layer or layers of rock.

forest–tundra transition life zone, n. A narrow, discontiuous community of subalpine and alpine plant and animal species intermingled in a distinctive zone. In Rocky Mountain National Park this zone is between 11,000 ft. and 11,500 ft. in elevation.

frost boil, n. An accumulation of water from melted underground ice resulting from spring thawing and mixed with soil. A low mound forms on the land surface by frost heaving.

frost–heaving, n. The uneven lifting, upward movement and general distortion of soil, rocks and vegetation at the land surface because of freezing beneath the ground surface which causes the soil to expand (see also **upfreezing**).

giant's stairway or staircase, n. A glacial valley whose floor is shaped like a broad staircase composed of a series of irregular step-like benches (the treads) separated by steep cliffs (the risers).

glacial scratches or striations, n. Long, delicate, finely-cut nearly straight and parallel furrows or lines engraved into a bedrock surface by rubbing and grinding of rock fragments embedded in the ice at the base of a moving glacier. They are usually oriented in the direction of ice flow. The rock fragments within the ice also are scratched and furrowed.

glaciation, n. (a) The formation, movement and recession of glaciers or ice sheets. (b) A minor part of geologic time during which glaciers become extensive.

glacier, n. A large mass of ice formed on land by the compaction and recrystallization of snow. The mass moves slowly downslope amd spreads outward by plastic flow or creep because of the force resulting from its own weight. The ice survives from year to year without melting away during the summers.

glacier outburst flood, n. A sudden, often annual, release of meltwater either from within a glacier or from a glacier-dammed lake. Some such outbursts result in catastrophic floods either from melting of drainage channels or from enough water accumulating beneath a glacier to cause it to float.

gneiss, n. A layered metamorphic rock with grains large enough to see with the naked eye. The layers have differing mineral compositions, causing outcrops of gneiss to appear banded.

granite, n. A visibly granular igneous rock in which the minerals grains are arranged in an interlocking manner. Granite is mostly feldspar with some quartz, and with lesser amounts of mica and horblende.

granite gneiss, n. A gneiss with the mineral composition of granite.

ground moraine, n. Rock debris dragged along in and beneath glacial ice and laid down as an irregular sheet when the ice melts.

hanging valley, n. A glacial valley whose mouth is at a higher elevation than the floor of a larger valley to which it is a tributary.

hematite, n. A common ore mineral of iron whose composition is 30% oxygen and 70% iron. It commonly occurs as a red to reddish-brown mass or as shiny steel-gray crystals. Its cherry-red color when ground to a fine powder (its streak) is characteristic.

horn, n. A sharply pyramidal peak in a mountainous region. Horns are cut as three or more glaciers originating on the same mountain quarry out their headwalls until only a sharp pinnacle remains of the mountain.

hummock [frost], n. A mound of earth raised up by frost action in an area underlain by permafrost.

ice cap, n. The perennial covering of ice and snow on mountain ranges resulting from the coalescing of a number of alpine glaciers into a massive ice body that covers nearly all the mountain tops.

ice sheet, n. A large body of glacial ice that spreads in several or all directions from a center, having considerable thickness and covering the entire land surface in an area of more than 50,000 square kilometers [syn. *continental glacier*].

igneous rock, n. A rock or mineral that cooled and solidified from molten or partly molten rock material (magma). One of the three main classes of rocks.

intrusive, adj. Said of an igneous rock that has ascended from the depths of the earth in a hot mobile state, has been slowed or stopped in its ascent so that it cooled and solidified before reaching the earth's surface.

joint, n. A fracture or parting plane in rock along which there has been little if any movement parallel with the walls.

kame, n. A long, low, steep-sided mound, knob, hummock, or short irregular ridge composed of poorly sorted but stratified sand and gravel deposited by a stream within or under a melting glacier near its margin.

kettle, n. A steep-sided, normally basin- or bowl-shaped depression in glacial deposits and without surface drainage. Kames probably form as large detached blocks of stagnant ice, buried or partially buried in the glacial debris, melt and permit the ground surface to sag.

krummholz, n. A German word for "crooked wood" that refers to stunted gnarled and windswept trees at treeline.

lateral moraine n. A ridge-like deposit of glacial debris along the side of a glacier or glaciated valley.

lichen, n. A specialized plant-like organism composed of a fungus and an alga, living so closely together that they appear to be one.

life zone, n. Communities of plants and animals that live together having achieved a balance between local climate and elevation.

Little Ice Age, n. A time of limited but pulsating expansion of alpine glaciers in many parts of the world that marked a return to cool climates and the end of post-glacial warming during the Altithermal Interval.

meander, n. One of a series of loop-like bends or curves in a stream channel.

meander, v. Said of a stream flowing in a series of broad looping curves.

medial moraine, n. An elongate mass of morainal debris carried in or upon the middle of a glacier, usually formed by the merging of two coalescing glaciers.

metamorphic rock, n. One of the three main classes of rocks. They are changed deep within the earth from rocks that were originally igneous or sedimentary by intense heat and pressure or by other materials that infiltrate them.

mica, n. A group of natural rock-forming minerals having nearly perfect cleavage (splitting) in one direction producing thin, tough, elastic plates or laminae. Micas are silicates of aluminum, potassium, magnesium and iron that contain water.

mica schist, n. A foliated, crystalline metamorpic rock composed essentially of quartz and mica.

microcline, n. Potassium feldspar (potassium aluminum silicate) with minor amounts of sodium. It is the common feldspar of granitic pegmatites.

midden or midden pile, n. A pile of conifer cones and parts of cones deposited by squirrels as they break the scales from cones to get the seeds. Other mammals, such as woodrats, also build up middens.

mineral, n. A naturally occurring, inorganic substance.

montane life zone, n. In Rocky Mountain National Park, a community of plants and animals found between 6000 ft. and 9000 ft. elevation.

moraine n. A mound or ridge of unsorted, unstratified glacial debris deposited by the direct action of glacial ice.
See also **lateral, medial, recessional, terminal, ground moraine.**

nivation, n. Erosion of rock or soil beneath a snowbank and around its fluctuating margin, caused by freezing and thawing, but also involving chemical weathering, solifluction, and meltwater transport of weathering products. The rock fragments beneath the snow are piled around its downslope margin; the soil is mixed with water in a slurry and flow away down the slope. In general, the "digging in" and "hollowing out" effected by a snowbank.

nivation depression, n. A small, shallow recess, depression or cirque-like basin formed and occupied during part of the year by a snowbank that, through nivation, may be one of the factors localizing and initializing glaciers in mountainous regions.

nueé ardente, n. A French term meaning "glowing cloud" referring to a swiftly flowing, turbulent, incandescent, gaseous cloud erupted from an exploding volcano. It also contains ash and other fragmental volcanic debris in its lower part.

orogeny, n. The process by which great elongate chains and ranges of mountains are formed. Through usage the word has come to also imply the <u>event</u> of such mountain-building as well as the process.

outcrop, n. That part of a rock mass that appears at the surface of the ground and is bare and exposed.

outwash, n. Rock debris removed from a glacier by meltwater and laid down by streams downstream beyond the glacier itself.

outwash plain, n. A plain composed of rock debris derived from a glacier and spread out by streams beyond the terminal moraine.

outwash terrace, n. A bench-like deposit extending along a valley downstream from an outwash plain or a terminal moraine.

park, n. An open, grassy area surrounded by tree-covered mountains. The sizes of parks vary greatly.

patterned ground, n. Land covered by well-defined, more or less symmetrical forms outlined by piled up rocks or other debris. The forms include circles, polygons, nets, steps, garlands, stripes and streams formed by intensive frost action in periglacial slope mantle.

peat, n. Partly decayed, moisture-absorbing plant matter found in stagnant shallow ponds and swamps. Peat is dark brown to yellowish, matted, semicarbonized plant material in which remains of leaves, twigs, stems and roots are discernible. It represents the first stage in the formation of coal, has a high carbon content and is used for fuel when dried.

peat bog, n. A marshy place where peat forms or has formed.

perched erratic (block), n. A large, detached rock fragment, generally boulder-sized, probably transported and deposited by a glacier and left in a mechanically unstable position on a hillside.

periglacial, adj. Pertaining to processes, conditions, areas, climates and topographic features in regions near glaciers or former glaciers and influenced by the cold temperatures.

pegmatite, n. A coarse-grained igneous rock, resembling granite in composition, with interlocking crystals of quartz, feldspar and mica. Pegmatite may also contain other economicaly important minerals or rare minerals not found in other kinds of rocks.

permafrost, n. Soil, subsoil, other surficial material or even bedrock that remains perenially frozen.

pipe, n. A nearly vertical, volcanic conduit through the earth's crust, filled with broken up volcanic rock and fragments of older rocks through which the conduit passes.

(rock) polygon, n. A form of patterned ground whose arangement of surficial stones is roughly tetragonal, pentagonal or hexagonal and formed by intense freezing and thawing (**up-freezing**).

pothole, n. A smooth, roughly circular, bowl-shaped or cylindrical hollow in bedrock in a stream bed, formed by the grinding action of a stone or stones that are whirled around and kept in motion nearly at one spot by eddies or by the force of the stream current. On rock surfaces that are exposed to the air, similar holes may be formed by chemical and physical reactions which loosen grains of the rock so that they can be removed by the wind.

Precambrian, adj., n. The earliest major subdivision of geologic time, being the elapsed time from the formation of the earth to the beginning of the Cambrian Period about 570 million years ago. The first era of the earth's history.

Precambrian rock, n. A rock formed during the Precambrian Era.

quartz, n. The most common mineral, occurring in igneous, sedimentary and metamorphic rocks. It is anhydrous silicon dioxide, being 46.7% silicon and 53.3% oxygen. It can be of many colors, but is mostly clear or white and has a characteristic greasy look.

recessional moraine, n. A terminal moraine of a melting glacier, built during a temporary halt in the glacier's retreat.

ribbon forest, n. A grove of trees (a tree island) near treeline that is subjected to extreme interaction of snow and wind. Where snow is deep the leeward branches are killed by weight of the snow while the windward branches are killed by wind. Only branches and seedlings that are on the sides of the grove can survive, resulting in a long, narrow strip of stunted trees.

rift, n. A major flaw in the earth's crust, caused by large forces that thin and slowly pull a strip of it apart, allowing the strip to sag. Rifts contain many faults caused by local forces that break the rocks, dropping many blocks downward into the sagging strip.

riparian, adj. Adjacent to or on the banks of a stream.

roche moutonnée, n. French words meaning "fleecy rock." Used to describe glaciated rock outcrops that look like huge fleecy-backed sheep when seen from a distance. The upstream side of the outcrop is smoothed and striated by the ice; the downhill side of the outcrop is rough and jagged where the ice plucked out parts of the rock.

rock, n. An aggregate of **minerals**.

rock circle, n. An arrangement of stones (bedrock fragments) in patterned ground that resembles a circle. It is not truly a circle.

rock glacier, n. A mass or poorly sorted angular boulders and fine rock debris cemented by interstitial ice, occurring in high mountains or in a permafrost area and derived from a steep cliff by frost action. It has the same general appearance and slow movement as a small alpine glacier and has rounded, transverse and arc-shaped ridges at its lower end.

rockslide, n. Downward and usually rapid movement of newly detached fragments of bedrock sliding on bedding planes, joints, faults or any other plane of separation.

sand, n. Rock or mineral particles that are less than 2 mm and more than $1/16$ mm in diameter.

sandstone, n. A medium-grained sedimentary rock made up of sand grains cemented together.

schist, n. A crystalline metamorphic rock with closely spaced foliation (layering) which tends to split easily into thin slabs or flakes. With thicker foliation the rock grades into **gneiss**.

sediment, n. Loose, unconsolidated fragmental debris from the weathering and erosion of rocks and which has been carried to another location by water or wind.

sedimentary rock, n. One of the three main kinds of rocks, consisting of sediment that has accumulated in layers and been consolidated.

shale, n. A general term for sedimentary rocks that consist of consolidated muds, clays and silts.

sheet flood, n. A broad, moving expanse of storm water that spreads as a thin, continuous, relatively uniform sheet over a large area.

silt, n. Muddy, fine-grained sediment carried or laid down by rivers or oceans. The word generally applies to unconsolidated material that is smaller in size than sand and larger than clay.

sillimanite, n. A brown, grayish pale-green or white metamorphic mineral that occurs in long, slender, needle-like crystals. It is crystalline aluminum silicate.

soil, n. All fine-grained, unconsolidated material that overlies bedrock. Geologically, soil should be capable of supporting plant life.

solifluction, n. Slow, viscous, downhill flow or creep of soil and other loose material that is saturated with water. Although it can occur in tropical regions, it is especially active at high elevations and in Arctic regions where the surface is underlain by frozen ground (not necessarily permafrost). The frozen ground acts as a barrier to downward percolation of water. The process is started by frost action and is accelerated by meltwater from alternate freezing and thawing of snow and ground ice.

solifluction terrace, n. A low ridge or bench formed by solifluction across or at the foot of a slope. It may form curved lobes, because of uneven motion of the moving material.

stone-banked terrace, n. A sorted step in a tundra slope whose steep front is bordered by stones. The term should be used for a terrace-like feature that lacks a regular pattern. Stone-banked terraces are not well-defined forms of patterned ground.

stone garland, n. A sorted step consisting of a tongue-shaped mass of fine material enclosed on the downslope side by a crescent-shaped rock embankment, similar to but smaller than a stone-banked terrace.

stone net, n. A type of sorted periglacial polygon.

stone stripe, n. A sorted stripe consisting of coarse rock debris between wider stripes of fine-grained material.

subalpine life zone n. In Rocky Mountain National Park, the zone of forested mountains between 9000 ft. and 11,400 ft. to 11,500 ft.

talus, n. An accumulated heap of rock fragments derived from and lying at the base of a cliff or very steep slope.

talus slope, n. A slope covered mostly by talus.

tarn, n. A small, deep, steep-banked lake filling a bedrock basin carved by a glacier in high mountains.

terminal moraine, n. An end moraine extending across a glacial valley as an arcuate or crescent-shaped ridge of rock debris that marks the farthest advance of a glacier. The outermost end moraine of a glacier.

Tertiary period, n. The first period of geologic time during the Cenozoic era. The Tertiary period was preceded by the Cretaceous period of the Mesozoic era and was succeeded by the Quaternary period.

Tertiary rocks, n. Rocks formed during the Tertiary period.

timberline, n. The upper elevational limit of continuous subalpine forests of upright trees.

tree islands, n. Group of coniferous trees bunched closely together by strong winds and snow. Branches on the windward sides are killed and those on the lee side become misshapen into "flag trees." Over long periods of time tree islands slowly migrate and form long narrow strips aligned directly up or across the slopes.

treeline, n. The elevation above or below which trees grow, regardless of their size or shape. In the Park, upper treeline is about 11,400 ft. and lower treeline elsewhere in Colorado is about 5,600 ft.

tundra, n. A Lapp word referring to a treeless ecosystem at high latitudes or above upper treeline in the mountains.

turf-banked terrace, n. A nonsorted, irregular, terrace-like step in a slope that is not a clearly defined form of patterned ground, but which catches soil and water so that turf can grow on the tread of the step. The growing turf expands, exerting an outward force on loose rock in the step so they become the riser of the step.

upfreezing, n. Any frost-induced movement of an object relative to the soil surrounding it (Anderson, 1988, cited in geology references, p. 248).

U–shaped valley, n. A stream valley whose original V–shaped cross-section has been ground and gouged out by a glacier so that it acquires a flattened U–shape in cross section.

V-shaped valley, n. A valley, usually cut by a stream, which has a cross-section that looks like a flattened V.

welded ash-flow tuff, n. A rock formed of hot material blown from a volcano. Rock fragments are so hot that they are plastic and become flattened by the weight of the overlying material. Because all the material is hot it sticks tightly (becomes welded) together .

wetland, n. An area in which water is at or near the land surface.

USEFUL INFORMATION

ENTRANCE STATIONS

On the eastern side of the Park, **BEAVER MEAD-OWS ENTRANCE STATION** is on US 36 about 3 miles west of Estes Park. The **FALL RIVER ENTRANCE STATION** is along Fall River on US 34 about 5 miles west of Estes Park. On the western side of the Park, **GRAND LAKE ENTRANCE STATION** is 1.5 miles north of Grand Lake.

The Park is open 24 hours a day year round. Entrance fees are charged. US 34 across Trail Ridge and Milner Pass normally is open from Memorial Day until mid–October. All other paved roads in the Park are kept open year-round. During the ski season, Trail Ridge Road is open to Many Parks Curve.

VISITOR CENTERS
ESTES PARK AREA

The main Visitor Center is at the **PARK HEAD-QUARTERS BUILDING**, 3 mi. west of Estes Park along US 36. An orientation film about the Park is shown frequently in the summer. Books, film and maps are for sale and schedules on guided walks, campfire and other programs by Park Naturalists are available. Evening programs are held in the auditorium during summer months and on weekends during winter. Back-country hiking permits are required and can be obtained at the Back-country office adjacent to the headquarters building.

The **ESTES PARK TOURIST INFORMATION CEN-TER**, operated by the Estes Park Chamber of Commerce, is on the south side of US 34 just east of the triple highway junction of US 34, US 36 and US 34 BY-PASS. Information is available on accommodations, restaurants and shopping in the Estes Park area, as well as on the many other activities for visitors.

GRAND LAKE AREA

KAWUNEECHE VISITOR CENTER is about 1.5 mi. north of Grand Lake near the west entrance of the National Park. Books and maps are for sale. Naturalists at the Center will help plan your visit to the Park and will issue back-country overnight hiking permits. Evening programs are held at the Timber Creek Campground Am-

phitheater during the summer months.

The **GRAND LAKE CHAMBER OF COMMERCE OFFICE** is at the junction of US 34 and Colo. 278 at the western edge of the village of Grand Lake. The Chamber supplies information on lodging, restaurants, shopping and other facilities and activities in the Grand Lake area.

NATIONAL PARK

ALPINE VISITOR CENTER, at Fall River Pass on Trail Ridge Road, is open from June through September. A small museum devoted to the alpine tundra and a book shop are in the Park Service building. Park Naturalists will answer questions and help you plan your visit. **FALL RIVER STORE**, adjacent to the Visitor Center, has a snack bar, gift shop and book store. Emergency medical services are available here.

MUSEUMS
ESTES PARK AREA

MORAINE PARK MUSEUM is in the old Moraine Park Lodge overlooking Moraine Park, the beautiful glaciated valley of the Big Thompson River. It is open from May through September. The museum has exhibits of birds and mammals that live in the Park and an excellent display and taped program on the glacial history of the Park. Books and maps are for sale. The building is on the National Register of Historic Places.

ESTES PARK AREA HISTORICAL MUSEUM, at the intersection of US 36 and 4th Street in Estes Park, is open daily from May through September. There are many interesting exhibits about Estes Park, an extensive collection of historic photographs, an unusual collection of old tools and even a Stanley Steamer automobile. Donations are accepted.

MACGREGOR RANCH MUSEUM is less than 2 miles north of Estes Park on the Devils Gulch Road to Glen Haven (see map page 194). The MacGregor home is open from Memorial Day to Labor Day from 11 AM to 5 PM, Tuesdays through Saturdays. Visitors can see what life was like on a working mountain cattle ranch about 100 years ago, and learn something of the history of an early family who settled in Estes Park. Donations are accepted.

ENOS A. MILLS' HOMESTEAD CABIN is 8 miles south of Estes Park on COLO 7. Mills' daughter, Enda, and her husband Robert Kiley still live on the property. They have a wide-ranging display of Mills' books, photographs and belongings in his first cabin, built in 1885. They also delight in taking visitors on guided nature trips. The path to the homestead cabin is lined with many nature exhibits. The cabin is on the National Register of Historic Places. The Kileys also lead nature seminars for Metropolitan State College (Denver). Visitors are welcome year-round. Donations are accepted.

LULA W. DORSEY MUSEUM at the **YMCA of the ROCKIES**, dedicated in 1979, is the west wing of the the old Wind River Lodge, built in 1923. The Dorsey Museum has an extensive collection of historic photographs, artifacts and period room settings. These settings reflect lodge accomodations from 1910 to the 1940s. YMCA corporate archives also are housed in the museum which is dedicated to preserving the history of the YMCA since its inception in 1907. Open daily from Memorial day to Labor Day.

GRAND LAKE AREA

On the west side of the Park, the **NEVER SUMMER RANCH** was a guest ranch and working cattle ranch owned by the Holzwarth family from 1918 until 1973. It was then sold to the Nature Conservancy with the understanding that the land be preserved as open space. In 1974 the land was re-sold to the National Park Service. A half-mile walk across the North Fork of the Colorado River leads to the Holzwarth home and to old tourist cabins complete with their original furnishings.

KAUFFMAN HOUSE, one of the early hotels in Grand Lake, was restored by the Grand Lake Area Historical Society and is open for tours from 1 PM to 5 PM, June through August. It overlooks the lake on Pitkin Street, about one block south of Grand Avenue. This museum gives the visitor a rare opportunity to see what hotel accommodations were like around the turn of the century. The log building, built in 1892, is now on the National Register of Historic Places. Donations are accepted.

CAMPGROUNDS

Camping is permitted only in designated campgrounds. **ASPENGLEN C.G.** is near the Fall River Entrance. **MORAINE PARK C.G.** and **GLACIER BASIN C.G.** are on the Bear Lake Road. Reservations are required in the summer. **LONGS PEAK C.G.** and **U.S. Forest Service OLIVE RIDGE C.G.** are west of COLO. 7 along the eastern edge of the Park, south of Estes Park. **TIMBER CREEK C.G.**, beside the Colorado River, is about 10 miles north of Grand Lake.

Camping limits vary. Except for Moraine Park and Glacier Basin, sites are first come, first served. Wood gathering is not permitted except at certain backcountry campsites, but firewood is sold in Estes Park and Grand Lake. Fires are permitted only in grates at the campgrounds and picnic areas. Aspenglen, Longs Peak and Timber Creek campgrounds are open all year.

Outside the National Park a number of campgrounds for tents, trailers and RV's are operated privately.

PICNIC AREAS

Numerous picnic areas are found throughout the Park. Larger ones, with restroom facilities, are near trailheads and along the major roads.

FACILITIES FOR THE HANDICAPPED

A back-country camping area for handicapped persons is available. Call (303) 586-4459 for details, location and reservations.

A trail designed for people in wheelchairs encircles a portion of Sprague Lake. Along the beaver ponds on Hidden Valley Creek 6 miles from the Park Headquarters Building (at mile 1.9 on the TRAIL RIDGE ROAD—WESTBOUND MILE BY MILE GUIDE®) is a boardwalk with wheelchair access. This is a fine place to see beaver, actually observe waterfowl and to fish for greenback cutthroat trout on a catch-and-return basis only.

Several parking areas along the floor of the Kawuneeche Valley have wheelchair access for fishing in beaver ponds.

Restrooms for the handicapped are located on Trail Ridge Road at ROCK CUT, at the ALPINE VISITOR CENTER and at several picnic areas along the Colorado River. Campground restrooms also are accessible to handicapped people. Braille and captioned audio-visual materials are available at Visitor Centers.

HIKING

More than 355 miles of hiking trails are within the Park. Some trails are slow easy walks along mountain streams and meadows; others are much more difficult. Details on length and difficulty are briefly summarized in the guides. If you plan to hike any distance from a trailhead, carry the appropriate USGS 1/24,000 scale topographic map or maps that cover your route.

Ask for additional information at Park Headquarters. Many books are available that describe all these trails. Register with a Park Ranger for overnight backpacking, fire permits and campsite assignments. Overnight vehicle parking at trailheads requires advance permission.

HORSEBACK RIDING

Horses and guides can be hired at livery stables at Sprague Lake and in Moraine Park. Outside the Park, horses can be rented at a number of liveries for day trips or longer periods. Because horses are not permitted on some hiking trails, check with Park personnel for trails that are open for horse-back riding.

SKIING

Ski Estes Park is in Hidden Valley, along the eastern slope of Trail Ridge Road at elevations between 9200 ft. and 11,500 ft. This ski area has both T-bar and poma lifts. Cross-country skiing and snowshoeing are possible on some of the trails in the Park, especially around Bear Lake, in upper Moraine Park and on the western side of the Park in the Kawuneeche Valley.

TOURS

A shuttle bus runs from a parking area opposite Glacier Basin Campground to Bear Lake during the summer months. It stops at several places along the road and is a convenient way to reach Bear Lake.

Tours are available for those who do not wish to drive their own cars into the mountains. Ask at the Tourist Information Centers in Estes Park and Grand Lake.

PARK REGULATIONS

No off-road vehicular travel is permitted; vehicles must remain on roads and in parking areas.

Pets are permitted on leashes along the roads, but are not allowed on trails or in the back country.

A permit is required for any specimen collecting. Except for fish, all wildlife is protected from hunting and harassment. Use a camera for lasting souvenirs of your trip.

Fishing is permitted in designated areas. Artificial fly lures must be used, but children, aged 12 years or younger, may use bait. A Colorado fishing license is required. Park waters are not stocked for recreational fishing.

DO NOT feed or attempt to touch the birds, chipmunks or ground squirrels that beg for food at parking areas, and in picnic and camping grounds. Feeding makes them depend upon humans for food, and increases their populations to unsustainable levels. Chipmunks and squirrels can carry bubonic plague.

DRIVING HINTS

There are **no** service stations within the Park, so check your fuel gauge in either Estes Park or Grand Lake before leaving on a drive.

Do not keep your foot on the brake pedal when descending steep grades—use the compression of your engine to slow the car by driving in a lower gear. Also drive in a lower gear when climbing steep grades. An old "rule-of-thumb" is: go down the hill in the same gear you used to go up. It is easier on the engine, transmission, clutch and brakes, and reduces the chance of the car overheating because the fan turns faster. Do not depend on an automatic transmission to know what to do—downshift it manually.

Be sure to set the parking brake when stopped.

If your vehicle stalls or acts like it is not getting gas, don't panic. It is probably just a vapor lock in the fuel line, which is apt to happen on warm days at high elevations, especially if the carburetor is adjusted for a low elevation. Stop and wait for the engine to cool. Put a wet cloth around the outside of the carburetor—evaporation of the water will cool the line and condense the fuel vapor. Turn off the air conditioner until the engine returns to normal temperature.

Please obey all speed limit signs and don't be in a rush to see the Park. Traffic over Trail Ridge in the summer can reach more than 700 vehicles per hour, so stop at the numerous parking areas to view the scenery and read ahead in the MILE BY MILE GUIDE®. Be sure to lock the car when leaving it unattended.

PRECAUTIONS

CLOTHING

Take plenty of warm clothing. Sudden summer storms—with rain, thunder, lightning, hail, high winds and even snow can appear very quickly in the alpine climate.

ELECTRICAL STORMS

If the base of your neck or your scalp tingles or your hair rises, get inside your car immediately. These are sure signals that a charge of static electricity is building up on you. Lightning can strike even on a clear day. If you are caught outside in a thunderstorm, avoid standing beside large isolated trees or rocks, power lines or telephone poles. Make sure that you are not the highest object in the vicinity. Squat with your hands clasped around your knees, so that your only contact with the ground is your feet; this will reduce your profile and also maximize the electrical resistance between you and the ground. Rubber-soled shoes will aid in increasing this resistance by partly insulating your body from the ground.

WOOD TICKS

Pesky wood ticks appear at low elevations in the mountains between February and May. They may appear at higher elevations later in the summer, although the tick season usually ends by the middle of July. They can carry both Colorado Tick Fever, and the much more serious Rocky Mountain Spotted Fever.

Before hiking, even in grass and shrubs, spray repellents on clothing, especially on boots, pants and jackets. Don't forget the insides of the pant legs. Ticks do not like smooth or light-colored clothing. Check your clothing and body as often as possible. If a tick attaches itself to your skin, gently remove it with tweezers, pulling it out in a straight line. If the head remains embedded, see a doctor.

HIGH-ALTITUDE SICKNESS

The change from elevations below 5500 ft. to the high elevations in the Park can cause breathing problems. Because of less oxygen in the air, you instinctively breathe more deeply, which may make you feel dizzy, light-headed, or even nauseated. If this happens, don't panic, but sit or lie down for a short time or get to a lower elevation.

Take it easy for the first day or two and don't over-exert yourself. Small walk-around oxygen bottles can be rented or purchased for those with respiratory problems. The practice of breathing into a paper bag to inhale more carbon dioxide is sometime recommended. While this practice may alleviate the nausea and headache of high altitude sickness, it also worsens the far more serious condition of fluid in the lungs. When out of your car or hiking above treeline, walk more slowly than normal. Avoid alcohol.

SUNBURNS

Remember that at high-altitude air the air is thin and does not filter out as much of the harmful ultra-violet radiation from the sun as the air at sea level, thus the skin burns quickly. Use a good sunscreen lotion, wear a hat <u>with a brim, and have good eye protection</u>.

PRECAUTIONS ALONG STREAMS

Be careful when fishing or playing along the streams and rivers. During spring run-off, the force of the water is much stronger than it appears. Sudden thunderstorms upstream can raise water levels rapidly, even if the sun is shining downstream. Do not stay in low areas during these storms. If you suspect such a storm is imminent move to high ground immediately.

DRINKING WATER

When hiking carry your own drinking water. Do not assume that stream or lake waters are safe to drink. Giardia, a parasite which causes severe stomach and intestinal disorders, is found in the waters of the Park.

FIRES

Be extremely careful with fire when camping or picnicking. DO NOT throw cigarette butts or matches out the car windows—anywhere. Fire is a major threat to the beautiful forests and to the animals that live in them.

LITTER

Deposit all trash and litter in the trash cans along the roads or carry it out of the National Park.

INDEX
Bold-Face Numbers Are Illustrations

NOTES

NOTES